Institutions of Reading

Studies in Print Culture and the History of the Book

Institutions of Reading

The Social Life of Libraries
in the United States

Edited by
THOMAS AUGST AND
KENNETH CARPENTER

University of Massachusetts Press
Amherst and Boston

Copyright © 2007 by University of Massachusetts Press
Printed in the United States of America

LC 2007004226
ISBN 978-1-55849-591-3 (paper); 590-6 (library cloth)

Designed by Dennis Anderson
Set in Adobe Garamond Pro by Dix Digital Prepress
Printed and bound by The Maple-Vail Book Manufacturing Group

Library of Congress Cataloging-in-Publication Data

Institutions of reading : the social life of libraries in the United States /
edited by Thomas Augst and Kenneth Carpenter.
    p. cm.
  Includes bibliographical references and index.
  ISBN 978-1-55849-590-6 (cloth : alk. paper)
  ISBN 978-1-55849-591-3 (paperback : alk. paper)
1. Libraries and society—United States—History.
2. Books and reading—United States—History.
3. Books and reading—Social aspects—United States.
4. United States—Intellectual life.
I. Augst, Thomas. II. Carpenter, Kenneth E., 1936–
  Z716.4.I57 2007
  021.2—dc22
                          2007004226

British Library Cataloguing in Publication data are available.

This book has been published with the assistance of a grant from
the Davies Project at Princeton University.

Contents

Illustrations

Acknowledgments

THIS VOLUME has its origin in a conference, "The History of Libraries in the United States," held April 11–13, 2002, in Philadelphia and hosted by the Library Company of Philadelphia, America's first lending library. The conference, as well as this volume, stemmed from an initiative taken by the Center for the Book at the Library of Congress, under the direction of John Y. Cole, to examine the place of library history in the social and cultural history of the United States.

The book in hand, *Institutions of Reading,* is not, however, simply an edition of the conference proceedings. Although early versions of a few of the essays published in this volume were first presented at the meeting, more than half are entirely new. They extend the chronological coverage to the twenty-first century and develop in new directions the central questions that emerged from the conference about the nature and purposes of the library. Although it may be a truism to many readers of these essays that "library" is only an umbrella term that encompasses—and to the public can even conceal—a variety of institutions and experiences, we are pleased to have assembled a volume that so clearly demonstrates the diversity of American libraries.

A three-day conference* that includes speakers from abroad is a time-consuming and expensive undertaking. We thank James Green and his colleagues of the Library Company of Philadelphia, who handled the vital work involved in making local arrangements. We also thank the institutions whose financial support made the conference possible: the Bibliographical Society of America; The Center for the Book, Library of Congress; The Council on

---

*For a report on the conference, see Kenneth Carpenter and Thomas Augst, "'The History of Libraries in the United States': A Conference Report," *Libraries & Culture* 38 (2003): 61–66. Stephen Ferguson and the staff of the Davies Project prepared a more complete record of the conference, which includes papers supplied by speakers as well as transcriptions of presentations by speakers, panel discussions, and question sessions. Reference copies of these materials have been deposited at the Library Company of Philadelphia, the American Antiquarian Society, and the Princeton University Library.

Library and Information Resources; The Gladys Krieble Delmas Foundation; and the Davies Project, Princeton University. Because the conference was a crucial part of the genealogy of this volume, those institutions also share in its publication. We especially thank the Davies Project for significantly defraying publishing costs.

T. E. A.
K. E. C.

Institutions of Reading

Introduction

Thomas Augst

In october 2004 a new library that exists everywhere and nowhere opened its doors to the public. The materials circulated by Google Book Search are available on the Internet anywhere on the World Wide Web, but through digital imaging technology they exist as electronic data rather than physical objects stored on a shelf. By November 2005, the Authors' Guild and a group of publishers had filed suit against Google, arguing that the new library infringed on copyright protections of intellectual property, stealing the labor of creating and publishing texts under the pretext of promoting "fair use" of knowledge. In challenging the long-standing legal and economic status of publication and authorship, this new library also challenges basic categories that have, for hundreds of years, associated libraries with the storage, preservation, and circulation of the print medium. When accessed through Google's search engines, the many books in this library become one book, as one newspaper commentary noted: "continuous, omni-conversant, cross-referencible down to line, word, and letter." [1] In this context, authorship and publication cease to belong to the inviolable integrity of a printed volume as a whole. In the interactive multimedia environment of the online library, reading becomes less a discrete activity than an interactive, often collaborative processing of information: collecting, posting, mailing, editing, reviewing, commentating, and republishing. As they compose ideas from many sources and create ever-larger collections of documents, images, music, and videos on personal computers, flash memory cards, iPods, and other devices, readers in the twenty-first century become, more than ever, librarians.

In transforming some of our most basic forms and concepts of knowledge, the advent of the digital library invites us to think in new ways about the history of the book. As an institution, the library lends itself both to empirical

---

1. Mathew Battles, "Library of Babel: Google Goes in Search of the Never-Ending Book," *Boston Globe,* 26 December 2004, D4. Also see Kevin Kelly, "Scan This Book!" *New York Times Magazine,* 14 May 2006, 43–71.

study of change over time and to qualitative histories of individual readers. For this reason, it furnishes common ground to scholars whose methods and theories have often left them working at cross-purposes in the history of the book.[2]

With the growth of book production and the rise of literacy rates in the eighteenth and nineteenth centuries, libraries helped to expand the size of the reading public. Pioneering scholarship such as Jesse Shera's *Foundations of the Public Library* (1949) told this history as a linear story that culminated with the tax-supported public libraries. Emerging from a larger "consensus history" that thrived during the Cold War, this story took as self-evident the importance of libraries, collapsing the expansion of public access to books and education with the onward march of democracy in the United States. To the extent that libraries had become tax-supported public agencies, they offered a potentially tidy case study of the progress of liberal ideals and institutions, freely distributing public goods in ways that supported individual freedom and equal opportunity. Self-confident and optimistic, the histories of libraries and other cultural institutions were essentially company histories, which overlooked the fact that access to cultural resources remained unequal, conditional on one's race, gender, and class. By the 1960s and 1970s, a new historiography concerned with social and popular phenomena and fed by European critical theories found supposedly beneficent and progressive institutions to be essentially conservative agents of economic rationalization and social control. In turning from official centers of American culture to its contested margins, however, scholars often flirted with what Neil Harris has called "a new Manichaeism" that, no less than the liberal story of progress, simplified the "complex relationship between the founding of our cultural institutions and the ongoing efforts to modernize national societies." As Harris argues, institutions have their own cultures, characterized by both resistance and accommodation to dominant social values. Like universities and museums, libraries were both temples of tradition and engines of progress: they represented contradictory choices and divided loyalties in a

---

2. For a comprehensive survey of scholarship in the history of reading, see Leah Price, "Reading: The State of the Discipline," *Book History* 7 (2004): 303–20. For a comprehensive guide to scholarship in library history, see Andrew Wertheimer and Donald G. Davis, Jr., *Library History Research in America* (Washington, DC: Library of Congress, 2000). For recent collections that reconsider the history of the library from multidisciplinary perspectives, see R. Howard Bloch and Carla Hesse, eds., *Future Libraries* (Berkeley: University of California Press, 1993); and Thomas Augst and Wayne Wiegand, eds., *Libraries as Agencies of Culture* (Madison: University of Wisconsin Press, 2001). For an invaluable analysis of the number and kind of libraries in early America, see Haynes McMullen, *American Libraries before 1876* (Westport, CT: Greenwood, 2000).

"struggle to govern the course of modernization and the organizational logic of the modern world."[3]

In widening access to books, libraries also fostered new kinds of individual and collective experience that would become central to modern print culture. What we now call the library evolved from a dynamic relationship between the expansion of the reading public and changing definitions of intellectual and cultural achievement. Throughout most of the twentieth century, literary critics indebted to the methods of New Criticism concerned themselves with interpreting the aesthetic value of a small canon of texts, remaining relatively indifferent to the physical formats, social contexts, and institutional networks in which actual reading takes place. More recently, as literary studies explored more historical perspectives on the meaning and uses of texts, scholars came to theorize the value of reading in proto-psychological terms, as an abstract, cognitive process binding strangers in virtual kinship: the "imagined community" of the modern nation state, for example, the anonymous intimacy of "the public sphere," the discipline of subjects, the "interpellation" into "hegemony." While seeking to analyze the social implications of print culture, these perspectives often subordinated the material experience of reading to arguments about the implication of textual content, the values imparted to "ideal" or "implied" readers by discourse. As a result, the proliferation of print itself became a symptom of a disenchanted modernity, a medium of mass communication supplanting traditional, local forms of social membership—among family, friends, and neighbors—with impersonal and symbolic forms of identity. While dismissing an older generation's quasi-spiritual, aesthetic, or technical regard for the autonomy of the literary text, critics and historians of the book have nevertheless accomplished an analogous alienation of reading from the spaces and practices of everyday life—the city streets, book groups, parlors, lecture halls, schoolrooms, and especially libraries in which individuals came to practice and value their experience of the printed word.[4]

In opening up the history of print culture to the institutional collection,

---

3. Neil Harris, *Cultural Excursions: Marketing Appetites and Cultural Tastes in Modern America* (Chicago: University of Chicago Press, 1990), 98, 110, 107, 105. On the "consensus history" of the mid-twentieth century more generally, see Peter Novick, *That Noble Dream: The "Objectivity Question" and the American Historical Profession* (Cambridge: Cambridge University Press, 1988).

4. Recent scholarship that analyzes reading within such spaces and practices of everyday life includes: Thomas Augst, *The Clerk's Tale: Young Men and Moral Life in Nineteenth-Century America* (Chicago: University of Chicago Press, 2003); David Henkin, *City Reading: Written Words and Public Spaces in Antebellum New York* (New York: Columbia University Press, 1998); Elizabeth Long, *Book Clubs: Women and the Uses of Reading in Everyday Life* (Chicago: University of Chicago Press, 2003); and Ronald Zboray and Mary Sarecino Zboray, "Books, Reading, and the World of Goods in Antebellum New England," *American Quarterly* 48 (1996): 587–622.

preservation, and diffusion of knowledge, we can situate reading more fully within its many physical and historical contexts, and better understand its place at the crossroads of collective behavior and individual experience. Libraries occupy a middle ground between social artifacts and linguistic effects. Whether built in physical or virtual space, libraries are places where otherwise abstract theories and historical generalizations about changes in what or why people read become entangled in the particular, immediate facts of where and how they do so. In libraries, the seemingly private and solitary nature of reading itself becomes a feature of social life. They are the kind of places where, as David Henkin puts it, "even when people use books to create a barrier between themselves and the people around them, they do so in public view."[5] In this volume, the institutional history of reading is in part chronological, moving from exclusive eighteenth-century spaces for the private consumption of otherwise scarce cultural goods, to state and philanthropic investments in the collection and circulation of information as a public good. Illuminating how the institution became a battleground over the purpose and form of reading in modern life, the essays in this volume also invite us to think about the methods with which scholars in different disciplines have made culture an object of inquiry. Libraries helped to build a modern audience for print by building the social life of reading: physical and virtual spaces in which to meet other readers, symbolic meanings and practical uses for reading, new technologies for remembering the past and embracing the future.

Social Spaces of Reading and Forms of Community

In a builder's manual that was reprinted throughout the later eighteenth century, the term "library" refers to a bookcase (see figure I.1). With its measurements and its elaborate crown molding, the manual's do-it-yourself diagram identifies the cultural power of the library in a physical form that is at once exalted and mundane: the display of books in a gentlemen's study. With the diffusion of printed books in the early modern era, a library gave form to a newly intimate experience of reading characterized by silence and solitude. At a moment when printed books remained luxury goods, the opportunity to read in a library expressed larger privileges and power that came with owning property.[6] In the grandiose mansions that colonial merchants built in

---

5. Henkin, *City Reading,* 7.

6. The English educator and philosopher John Locke, for instance, signed each book in his painstakingly catalogued personal collection, usually marking the price he had paid for a given vol-

the eighteenth century, a library afforded gentlemen a retreat, free from the obligations of profession and of domesticity. It was, as a historian has recently noted, the "most private part of the house for him," but also the "place where he entered the widest of all publics, the international scientific and literary community—the 'republic of letters.' "[7] Within its walls, amongst its shelves of carefully selected and organized volumes, the library created the physical and psychological space for privacy, where an elite few gained the liberty to retire, to study, to reflect, to cultivate learning and taste. Embodying individual autonomy in the possession of books read in silence and solitude, the gentleman's private library epitomized ideals about the purpose of books that would become central to the modern ideology of private reading. Especially as it has taken root in modern systems of secondary and higher education, that ideology argued that reading was something best done apart from the social contexts and practices in which books obtain value and use in the everyday world.[8]

The essays in this volume survey the various shapes and sizes that libraries have assumed in the United States, analyzing some of the social settings in which reading came to be located beyond the private collections of ministers and gentlemen. As James Raven points out, early American libraries were missionary projects that justified the exercise of colonial power as the advancement of learning. As such, books were emblems of a complex performance of social authority which, both inside and outside of institutions such as the Charleston Library Society, helped to define the boundaries of "civilization" in the colonial hinterlands. The pleasures of homosocial conviviality—the cultivation of "fellow feeling," "brotherhood," and friendship with one's peers—were a primary benefit of membership in these private societies. As they indulged formal and informal opportunities for sociability, meetings

---

ume on its eleventh page. Inscribing his intimacy with his collection, Locke's signature also expressed his possession of learning, "knowledge accumulated in the books that the eye takes in a glance," as Roger Chartier has noted. Roger Chartier, "The Practical Impact of Writing," in *A History of Private Life: The Passions of the Renaissance,* ed. Chartier, trans. Arthur Goldhammer (Cambridge : Harvard University Press, 1989), 140, 135.

7. Jessica Kross, "Mansions, Men, Women, and the Creation of Multiple Publics in Eighteenth-Century British North America," *Journal of Social History* 33 (1999): 393. As Kross notes, "Studies had long been available to ministers and larger merchants, professions which required undisturbed space—for books, ledgers, and writing paraphernalia—and undisturbed time. During the eighteenth century merchants and lawyers might have offices away from their dwelling. But the mansion opened up a male space untied to or contaminated by profession. Here, away from clients, women, children, servants, and visitors, elite men came as close as any in the eighteenth century could come to the *vita contemplativa,* life devoted to thought and the intellect."

8. On the ideology of private reading, see chap. 5 in Augst, *The Clerk's Tale,* and Long, *Book Clubs.*

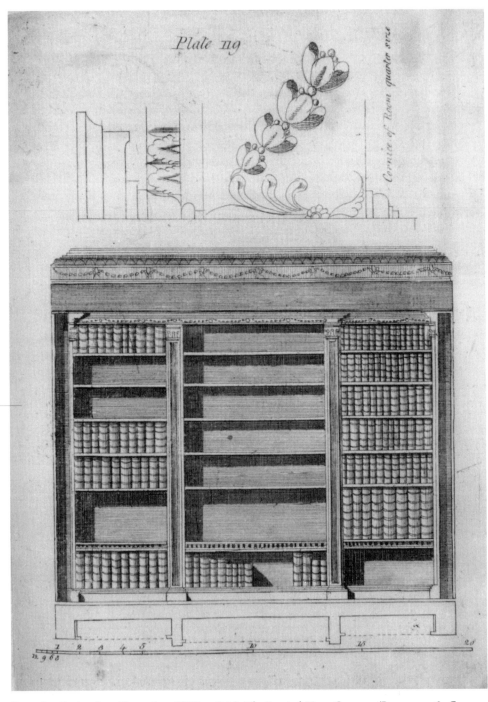

Figure I.1. Design for a library, from William Pain's *The Practical House Carpenter* (Boston, 1796). Courtesy American Antiquarian Society.

might tend to drunken debauchery rather than the polite erudition members sought to project to outsiders. So too, library societies bound pleasures and prerogatives of colonial power with moral purpose. While many of these men were killing native Americans or trafficking in slaves, after all, they were expanding the reach of learning. Including works of ancient and modern classics, philosophy and natural science, while steering clear of religious controversy and "polemical divinity," the collections built by these libraries linked scattered and isolated provincial elites to "an abstraction of community," as Raven notes, "that reached back and forth across the English countryside, the Irish Channel, *and* the Atlantic." Conduits of refined cosmopolitanism, eighteenth-century social libraries fostered political and cultural unity, affording members a structured pursuit of leisure in which "liberality" — license of conduct and thought — became rational exercises in rule-bound order.

The men who formed these societies were seeking not only to solidify their own aspirations and status, but to convert the personally anxious, socially fragile colonial enterprise into the permanent structure and impersonal offices of "culture." Even before the American Revolution, however, these membership libraries were competing with another institution — the commercial circulating library — that offered different sorts of books and new ways of organizing the meaning and uses of reading in their local communities. As James Green demonstrates, in dense seaboard cities such as New York and Philadelphia, membership libraries faced competition from commercial libraries within a rapidly expanding marketplace of both readers and books. With the more timely availability of imported books, colonial booksellers "for the first time became purveyors of fashion." While selling these books directly to the public, bookstores also operated circulating libraries that, like video rental stores of the late twentieth century, rented their wares to a wide public. By the 1760s, these circulating libraries helped to satisfy a widening demand for current novels and, by offering incentives for rapid exchange of books, fostered extensive reading practices. Although rental libraries were typically short-lived, their specialization in popular genres of entertainment, and their appeal to readers of modest means and especially women, pushed the more enduring social and subscription libraries to become more accessible and popular. In effect, they helped to commercialize reading as a form of leisure and entertainment, and lent seemingly ephemeral pleasures of the novel new social authority as objects of fashion and taste.

The large majority of libraries in early nineteenth-century America did not have separate buildings of their own, but rather operated informally out of peoples' homes or in other spaces such as schoolhouses or churches. In some cities and towns, however, private membership or proprietary libraries came to house their collections and activities in impressive buildings, that, as Michael Baenen argues in his essay on the Portsmouth Athenæum, straddled the categories of public and private by which scholars typically interpret both the act of reading and nineteenth-century social history more generally. The Athenæum, for example, seems to have been valued less for the opportunity to borrow books than for the chance to read newspapers and journals in a communal space. Although the library provided a clubby retreat for Portsmouth's mercantile and banking elites, its mission, rules of membership, and the content of its collection became objects of vigorous debate in the local press. In and around spaces such as the Athenæum, the public sphere in Portsmouth was not abstract and distant, but a highly personalized arena of partisan attack, which was more likely to generate vandalism and character assassination than any rational debate about central matters of civic concern. As they became a touchstone for larger class conflicts and political debates in the antebellum years, social libraries and other fraternal societies enlisted newly enfranchised white men into what de Tocqueville described as the "art of association," helping to transform American politics from an elite duty to a more egalitarian, sometimes dangerous sport of contestation.

In helping to expand the audience for print culture to new populations, library societies often challenged boundaries of class, gender, and race that had largely kept books as the expensive possession of learned elites. Excluded from other educational spaces and institutions, African Americans in the antebellum North used libraries to pursue classical ideals and objects of liberal education. As Elizabeth McHenry points out, the Phoenix Society of New York in the 1830s and similar institutions offered opportunities to acquire "a literary character," through which black Americans might combat widespread belief in their racial inferiority. As either an adjunct or the guiding purpose of these societies, libraries were primarily literary institutions, sponsoring classes and lectures as well as access to books and periodicals. There African Americans developed skills and values that derived from "exposure to texts and the rigorous critical analysis and discussions that they prompt." Rather than the solitary activities we now assume them to be, their literary practices had sociability as a primary motive and community building as its primary end. Reading in this context was a collaborative process, where people who were technically illiterate could listen and, as in the reading rooms of Portsmouth, engage in social and intellectual exchanges that, well into the nineteenth century, continued to define civic duty as a peculiarly literary enterprise. What literary societies created in space, newspapers sought to create over time: presenting miscellaneous "collections" of poetry and fiction, which would not only shepherd and elevate the tastes of the African American community, but foster literary productions and cultural preservation by which black people might institutionalize a history of their own.

With the commercial expansion and consolidation of the print medium, social and membership libraries gave social form to the otherwise anonymous circulation of texts. "Any text creates a public by moving through multiple hands," as Michael Warner points out, and in developing spaces and strategies to facilitate and manage this movement of texts, libraries created physical communities of readers, bound not only by shared texts but by common practices of sociability, education, and amusement.[9] Because their fortunes rose and quickly fell on their ability to attract and retain patrons and members, circulating and propriety libraries of all sorts sought to understand not only what books readers wanted, but what readers wanted from reading more generally within an expanding market for leisure and entertainment. In this sense, the social life of libraries in the United States is also the history of how new styles and motives for reading came to be institutionalized within the mass market of print. There is, after all, only so much room on the bookshelf. Whether the cosmopolitan fraternities of eighteenth-century letters, or circulating and public outfits devoted to tracking the popular taste, libraries institutionalized judgments about the value of reading by developing systems of selection and preservation: sorting the "improving" literature from "lumber," high from low, the scholarly from the popular. Balancing traditional associations of printed texts with scholarly erudition and genteel propriety with more modern uses for entertainment and status display, libraries were among the first institutions to confront the social effects of mass media.

Values of Reading and the Cultural Politics of Taste

As it created expansive, heterogeneous communities of readers, the development of a mass market for print entailed new contests over the form and value of reading. As private and commercial circulating libraries sold their services to women, for example, they came to be identified as female institutions that—by focusing on the provision of popular novels in particular—undermined the traditional moral and intellectual functions of reading itself.[10] In an engraving by Endicott and Swett published in 1831, "The Circulating Library" is a woman, outfitted head to toe in books (see figure I.2). The image attests to the

---

9. Michael Warner, *Publics and Counterpublics* (Cambridge: MIT Press, 2001).

10. As Jesse Shera observed some time ago, "The widespread criticism that arose in response to the circulating library was identical, both in origin and motive, with that brought to bear against the popularity of the novel." Jesse Shera, *Foundations of the Public Library: The Origins of the Public Library Movement in New England, 1629–1855* (Chicago: University of Chicago Press, 1949), 152.

power of industrial production to make goods—duodecimo-sized novels no less than the calicoes and broadcloths that poured out of Manchester factories in the later eighteenth century—abundant and cheap. It also argues that, by expanding the audience for books, circulating libraries would displace the value of books from what they contained to where they moved within the changing tides of consumer fashion. The book, in short, would become just another commodity, whose promiscuous circulation among the lower or less learned classes would further unleash the irrational, feminine norms of envy and self-indulgence that moralists associated with the commercial revolution

THE CIRCULATING LIBRARY.

Figure I.2. "The Circulating Library," by Endicott and Swett (1831). Courtesy American Antiquarian Society.

in general. Undoing the manly virtues of thrift, prudence, and self-restraint on which the health of society depends, reading here becomes mainly another exercise in vanity, guided not by practical need but the merely ornamental, if amusing, wants of popular fashion. The reader's gaze is not raised to heaven, or lost in abstract, higher-order values of truth and wisdom, after all, but frankly and openly engaged with its anonymous audience, inviting the viewer's appraisal. Significantly, the figure depicted in the image is not actually reading, confirming a misogynist prejudice that women's mental inferiority made them unfit for intellectual exertion. A woman, in other words, would more likely wear a book than read it. Like choosing clothes and cultivating manners, reading is literally a habit one wears in public—meanings and pleasures cultivated not in the solitude of the gentleman's library, but within the mass market of goods and leisure.

As this image suggests, the history of libraries is also a history of taste: how Americans learned to navigate the material universe of mass production, to make judgments about the new practices, spaces, and communities that the widening availability of ever-cheaper printed objects brought in its wake. In my own chapter I consider the evolving symbolic meanings of public libraries, situating a Russian Jewish immigrant's experience of the Boston Public Library within larger contests for moral authority that emerged with a mass culture of print. Throughout the nineteenth century, municipal leaders embraced a variety of public spaces and institutions as instruments of social reform that would rescue Western civilization from the inequalities and materialism bred by industrial capitalism. The massive building campaigns underwritten by tax revenues and private philanthropy led to an unprecedented enlargement of social and symbolic functions of the library in American life. Centrally located in downtown business districts and new civic centers that were built as part of the City Beautiful movement, public libraries would provide convenient access for what was invariably referred to as "the masses," seeking to attract patrons to reading as an improving leisure activity, when they might otherwise go to theaters or saloons. At the same time, they sought to standardize and personalize the meaning of reading as a practice of citizenship, valuing books not as *goods*—private property that enforced educational and social distinctions—but a public good, whose benefit to community required popular circulation and use. Like the museums, concert halls, and parks built throughout the Progressive Era, public libraries became spaces of civic devotion, places where even poor immigrants might pursue the self-transformation and social mobility that continue to define the ethos of liberal individualism.

The huge buildings erected for both public and private libraries gave physical and bureaucratic permanence to elitist ideals of cultural achievement, housing collections of books and art in ostentatious monuments encrusted with tons of marble, fine glass, and mosaics. Private philanthropists provided three-quarters of the money used to construct major library buildings before 1894, wishing to be remembered for the American inheritance of Western civilization instead of their rapacious, sometimes violent pursuit of private gain.[11] Elizabeth Amann considers the imperial legacies and personal motives that guided the tastes of one philanthropist and collector, Archer Huntington, in founding the Hispanic Society of America—an institution without precedent, "devoted entirely to the study of a cultural other." As Amann suggests, the Spanish manuscripts, rare books, and artifacts of folk life that Huntington acquired were in a sense spoils of the Spanish American war, which left the Spanish government too broke to prevent American plunder of its cultural patrimony. Like the collections of European arts and antiquities where J. P. Morgan, Isabella Stewart Gardner, and other plutocrats took refuge from the immigrant hordes transforming American cities, the Hispanic Society represented a trophy room for the global expansion of American empire that, following the 1898 defeat of Spain, would be military as well as financial. Unaccountable to taxpayers, or the pressure of ethnic constituencies that urban political machines brought to bear on public libraries, private research libraries like the Hispanic Society remained a sleepy, genteel preserve for students and dilettantes, "a select resort of bibliomaniacs," as the *New York Herald* described the Lenox library in 1882, "conducted on the principle of doing the least good to the least number."[12] Such institutions would become invaluable resources for students and scholars, but also mausoleums for Romantic ideals of culture, casting their imposing but anachronistic shadows over urban communities that were being continuously transformed by new immigrant populations.

While private philanthropists borrowed from European models of connoisseurship, antiquarianism, and scholarship in amassing their collections, public libraries in the twentieth century would develop standards of literary taste that were shaped by the commercial marketplace. They would institutionalize new criteria for choosing and valuing books in ways that mirrored the agencies of what the German émigrés Max Horkheimer and Theodor Adorno would call the modern "culture industry." Indeed, as Janice Radway points out, we might think of Harry Scherman's Book-of-the-Month Club as a kind of library, but one adapted to the particular exigencies of the mass

---

11. Donald Oehlerts, *Books and Blueprints: Building America's Public Libraries* (Westport, CT:, Greenwood, 1991), 17.

12. Cited in Phyllis Dain, *The New York Public Library* (New York Public Library, 1972), 12.

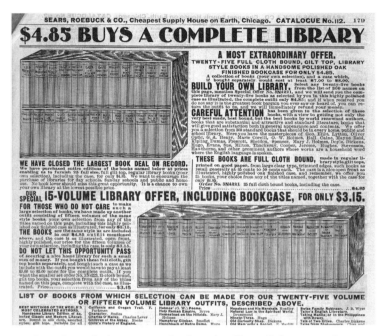

Figure I.3. One of several advertisements for "complete libraries" that appeared in a stationery catalogue of Sears, Roebuck, and Company (ca. 1903). Courtesy of Wilson Library, University of Minnesota.

production and distribution of consumer goods. Unlike the ready-made, off-the-shelf "libraries" marketed by publishers in the late nineteenth century and retailed on a national scale in the pages of the Sears, Roebuck Catalogue (see figure I.3), however, the Book-of-the-Month Club sought to *produce* a readership through mail-order subscription in much the same way twentieth-century public libraries aimed to do by other means. Whether dispensed by the Club's advertising of its recommendations and its judges' personalities, or by female librarians installed at circulation desks at Carnegie libraries across the nation, personalized advice matched the offerings of the mass market of print to the personal needs and tastes of individual readers. Shaped by modern networks of professional expertise, both institutions qualified and differentiated diverse uses of reading in ways that conceived "the literary universe *not* as an organic, uniform, hierarchically ordered space but rather as a series of discontinuous, discrete, and noncongruent worlds." Even in the separate white and black libraries of Durham, North Carolina, librarians increasingly turned to standards of "middlebrow" taste, creating communities of readers through institutional distribution of culture.

As they sought to develop and dignify a professional mission, modern librarians would prescribe values for popular reading that reflected their own image of "the reader." In Door County, Wisconsin, no less than Durham, North Carolina, however, official narratives about the proper contents and purposes of reading would be negotiated at the local level. As Christine Pawley demonstrates, the introduction of bookmobiles in the 1920s had its genealogy in an ideology of public outreach that, as with selection criteria, children's reading rooms, and closed stack policies, sought to control the content of reading while popularizing its practice. But by carrying library service beyond the confines of physical space, bookmobiles also extended reading practices beyond the reach of professional ideology, where they would be shaped by the practical imperatives and personal relationships that bound otherwise anonymous, dispersed members of the "public" in actual communities. From the oral history of a driver named Bob, Pawley recovers the social networks and informal values that continue to shape the use and management of public libraries. Like more recent professional campaigns to "save librarianship" by getting rid of the library as a physical space, the provision of curbside service may have undercut the rationale for tax support of libraries as public goods.[13] If the automobile fed suburban growth and white flight from urban centers more generally, the bookmobile made physical visits to city and town libraries unnecessary. In this sense, they contributed to larger patterns of decentralization endemic to the development of cultural institutions in the twentieth century, where cosmopolitan pleasures of leisure and entertainment that previously had been identified with the excitement of urban life came to be distributed through national systems and commercial networks of radio, movies, and television.[14]

---

13. Abigail Van Slyck, "The Librarian and the Library: Why Place Matters," *Libraries and Culture* 36 (2001): 519. On political contests waged over taxation for library service in post–World War II Wisconsin, see Christine Pawley, "Reading vs. the Red Bull: Cultural Constructions of Democracy and the Public Library in Cold War Wisconsin," *American Studies* 42 (2001): 87–103. On the private sponsorship of culture in a planned community in Celebration, Florida, see Juris Dilevko and Lisa Gottlieb, "The Celebration of Health in the Celebration Library," ibid., 105–34.

14. As Neil Harris notes, new media allowed "Americans everywhere to duplicate the possibilities that only physical concentration had previously permitted." Art and culture which had once belonged exclusively to communities that could physically afford to house theaters, libraries, museums, and opera houses could, in the twentieth century, "be expended over the microphone or through the camera and sent anywhere electricity and receivers existed." As Harris notes, "One might speculate whether or not the middle classes would have fled in such numbers to suburbia without the protection of the media, the knowledge that physical removal did not mean empty leisure hours or abandonment of traditional amusements." Harris, *Cultural Excursions*, 26.

In twentieth-century America, popular images of the library as an institution would continue to be dominated by women. Where "the Circulating Library" cast the common reader as a woman, dramatizing the surrender of scholarly rectitude to the caprice of fashion, later critics ranging from Thorstein Veblen to Ann Douglass would, in similar ways, describe a feminization of culture, interpreting the styles and practices of mass consumption as a weakening of aesthetic and intellectual standards. But the image of women turning to circulating libraries for the latest novels speaks as well to the more specific gendering of the library as a modern institution. By 1933, some three-quarters of the nation's public libraries owed their origins to the fundraising and organizational work of women's clubs.[15] As several essays in this volume demonstrate, women would fill the underpaid, lower ranks of the profession as reading room attendants and cataloguers. In the Progressive Era, as they catered to the needs of children and immigrants, women librarians would extend the separate sphere of nineteenth-century womanhood into public service, making domestic middle-class norms of spiritual nurture and maternal protection the lingua franca of community welfare. As a result, the library's feminine cultural image would come to represent the threat of tradition, rather than change, to a modern cultural order oriented to the values of technological innovation and marketplace opportunism. Throughout the mid-twentieth century, musicals such as *The Music Man,* films such as *It's a Wonderful Life* and *Desk Set,* and novels such as *Main Street* would popularize a stereotype of spinsters enforcing silence in musty and quaint libraries, as though the printed book were itself vaguely old-fashioned—a vestige of small-town nostalgia and Victorian morality (see figure I.4).

New Media and the Organization of Knowledge

As we have seen, "library" is an amorphous term, a concept that describes a range of phenomena in the social history of reading. In its many institutional forms, the library itself is an artifact of the history of classification—both the outcome of and the engine for technological and social changes in the organization, preservation, and dissemination of knowledge. The invention

---

15. Ann Ruggles Gere, *Intimate Practices: Literacy and Cultural Work in U.S. Women's Clubs, 1880–1920* (Urbana: University of Illinois Press, 1997), 122. On the role of women and the development of children's reading rooms in Carnegie libraries, see Abigail Van Slyck, *Free to All: Carnegie Libraries and American Culture, 1890–1920* (Chicago: University of Chicago Press, 1995). On the rhetoric of feminization in professional discourse, see Jaclyn Eddy, " 'We Have Become Too Tender-Hearted': The Language of Gender in the Public Library, 1880–1920," *American Studies* 42 (2001): 135–54.

Figure I.4. Donna Reed plays a modern stereotype of the librarian in Frank Capra's 1946 movie *It's a Wonderful Life*. Because George Bailey was never born, his future wife Mary cowers before the gin joints and gambling dens of Pottersville after closing up the public library. "You're not going to like it," George's guardian angel warns. "She's a spinster!" Courtesy of Republic Pictures.

of movable type was, of course, the technical innovation for which the concept and functions of the modern library were designed. The densely "wired" quality of the digital age perhaps makes it easier to recognize the printed book as "MAJOR TECHNOLOGICAL BREAKTHROUGH," as a spoof press release that circulated on the Internet a few years ago suggested: a "Bio-optic organized knowledge device" that requires "no wires, no electric circuits, no batteries, nothing to be connected or switched on. It's so easy to use, even a child can operate it." [16] In its compact size, portability, and durability the printed book made it easier to move and store large quantities of knowledge, while its regular type, high contrast legibility, and sequentially uniform pages eased reading and discontinuous sampling. Making the form of knowledge as indelible as ink on paper, as tangible as a volume one could move, manipulate, and mutilate, modern printing technologies made possible both the wide disper-

16. "Headline: MAJOR TECHNOLOGICAL BREAKTHROUGH," courtesy of Matthew Kirshenbaum.

sal of books and their accumulation and storage in central locations. If only in theory, printing and its allied technologies of distribution and collection made it feasible to gather all human knowledge in one place.

The advent of the printed book stoked fantasies of universal libraries that are as ancient as the Tower of Babel and the library at Alexandria. Throughout the early modern period, scholars and publishers compiled anthologies, catalogues, bibliographies, compendiums, and encyclopedias, both as practical tools of scholarly communication and erudition, and as thought experiments, utopian campaigns to conquer a universe of knowledge that with time only grew more unwieldy in scale and esoteric in scope. As they sought to balance Enlightenment ideals of the comprehensive unity of knowledge with practical limitations on acquiring, storing, and circulating books, American librarians would seek to design technologies for mass distribution of culture that were intellectual as well as material. In 1793, in the first American guide to collecting, the Harvard librarian Thaddeus Harris declared, "books have become so exceedingly numerous as to require uninterrupted attention, through more than the longevity of an antediluvian, to peruse them all." For anyone who was not a professional scholar, scarce leisure time was "interrupted by the necessary avocations," and contracted by the "unavoidable duties and cares of life. Since but *few* books can be perused by the generality of people, they should be those only which are *most excellent.*" Harris specifically directed his advice on building a "small and cheap library" not to the learned, but "common readers," "at a distance in the country," with "few opportunities for knowing the characters even of books which have been long in use." [17] Through such guides to reading, he and the librarians who followed him would seek to institutionalize literary taste for mass audiences: to transform reading from a special expertise, founded on ownership and proximity of books, to a *productive* and efficient form of leisure within what F. B. Perkins in 1876 called the "trackless, if not a howling wilderness" of the "printed records of past and present human knowledge and mental activity." [18]

The revolution in print unfolded with the development of modern infrastructures of knowledge: new technologies for the organization, preservation, and management of library collections. Following the example of Henri Labrouste's construction of the Sainte Geneviève (1843) and the Bibliothèque

---

17. Thaddeus M. Harris, "Introduction," *A Seleced* [sic] *Catalogue of some of the most esteemed publications in the English Language. Proper to form a social library: with an Introduction upon the Choice of Books* (Boston, 1793).

18. F. B. Perkins, "On Professorships of Books and Reading," in *Public Libraries in the United States of America. Part 1* (1876; rpt. Champaign: University of Illinois, Graduate School of Library Science, 1965), 235.

Nationale (1850s) in France, American libraries were among the first public buildings to use self-supporting iron skeletons, which made it possible to build huge reading rooms and multiple-level bookshelves in one fireproof location.[19] Modern libraries depended on new mechanical designs for the storage of books, but also on the creation of uniform standards and processes for managing and retrieving their expanding collections: a complex infrastructure of work practices and organizational routines that would become part of the behind-the-scenes operations of bureaucratic institutions. [20] The card catalogue, for instance, was an innovation in information technology that, as Barbara Mitchell reminds us, was integral to the growth of library collections and their new mission of public access. In place of bound catalogues that were out of date as soon as they were printed, these new catalogues offered librarians a flexible but permanent record of acquisitions that would eventually be entrusted to the unsupervised searches of individual patrons. As Mitchell shows, the creation of the first public card catalogues in the Boston area was subsidized by the labor of educated middle-class women. Bringing their skills in writing and foreign languages to the time-intensive gathering and scripting of catalogue cards, these women enabled Harvard and other major libraries to maintain an atmosphere of genteel propriety in what had become the mass production of bibliographic information. Their low wages and confinement to largely manual skills of copying and filing helped to pave the way for the emergence of the pink-collar sector, the women secretaries and typists who by the early twentieth century would staff the lower ranks of business and government offices.

The space books occupy is cognitive as well as physical, those technologies we design to organize and manage the diversity and reach of knowledge, in both its present and future states. By the 1920s, women were finding wider opportunities for library work that went beyond the scripting of catalogue cards. Nella Larsen and Marianne Moore, who were both trained as librarians and employed in branches of the New York Public Library, also found an alternative education in the institutional aesthetics and gender politics of classification. As Karin Roffman asks, what would American modernism look like if it were identified not with the university training of male writers such as T. S. Eliot, but with the formation of female authors by public libraries? For critics like George Santayana and Van Wyck Brooks, the aggressive public

---

19. Oehlerts, *Books and Blueprints,* 22, 23.

20. The technology of classification is constituted by "work practices, beliefs, narratives, and organizational routines." Susan Leigh Star and Geoffrey Bowker, *Sorting Things Out: Classification and Its Consequences* (Cambridge: MIT Press, 1999), 319.

outreach and middlebrow values of public libraries made them emblematic of the anti-intellectual, feminizing drift of American culture more generally. As they encountered Melvil Dewey's library methods and acquired experience in the practical work of library services, however, Larsen and Moore came to see how cultural authority is produced through systems of rationality. Throughout her career, Moore would use lists, categories, and indexes to generate experiments in poetic form, while Larsen would make the resistance to status categories of race, class, and gender a primary theme in novels such as *Quicksand* and *Passing*. For both, literary art itself was a self-conscious system of knowledge, involving intellectual patterns of coherence and selection. Like their peers in New York's avant-garde, they also saw art as a form of social experimentation that could challenge the systems of knowledge that shape human institutions of education, marriage, and individualism. In making spaces for themselves and their work outside an emerging system of cultural capital, Moore and Larsen helped to develop a tradition of bohemian skepticism that remains a major legacy of literary modernism.

As it crowded the stacks in library buildings throughout the nineteenth and twentieth centuries, knowledge turned out to have a limited shelf life—or rather, with the evolution of media technology, to have outgrown the capacity of the print medium to store and disseminate information with the speed and efficiency demanded by modern service economies and what Manuel Castells terms "the network society." New technologies enabled the transfer of printed texts to new formats, and made the once-primary function of the library, *to collect,* itself obsolete. In telling the story of Robert Binkley and the Joint Committee on Materials for Research, Ken Carpenter suggests how photographic technology sparked new efforts in the 1930s to design and sponsor new institutions and forms of scholarship. The advent of microfilm helped to speed a transformation already under way of academic institutions into centers for the advancement of learning, bound by specialized standards of training and inquiry, disciplinary associations and professional organizations, and the dissemination of a common research archive. Microfilm would preserve and make accessible newspapers, periodicals, card catalogues, and scholarly publications, but also manuscript materials, images, and imprints that had been preserved by libraries because of their uniqueness or rarity. Especially with the growing threat of totalitarianism, however, it also promised, if only for Binkley, to promote democratic freedom by fostering new systems of inquiry—to create a national design for culture as a community enterprise. By freeing research from what Binkley called "the tyranny of print"—a paper tyranny that, following the use of wood pulp in the later nineteenth century, was already proving highly perishable—microfilm could decentralize the control of communication on which fascism depended. It might also blur the classification of expertise on which modern institutions of authority depended by making, as Carpenter observes, the writing of literature and the family or local history "as common throughout America as local art shows or amateur theatricals."

Until the twentieth century, one of the library's primary functions — to collect and preserve materials about the past — remained safely linked to the apparent stability of the print medium. As publication processes, research collections, and catalogue systems were adapted to microfilm as well as electronic and digital formats for the Internet, however, the very presence and shape of the historical archive have become newly protean. As a result, Roy Rosenzweig argues, the future of the past — the methods, concepts, and objects with which we practice historical inquiry across the humanities and social sciences — has become uncertain. The rapid obsolescence of computer and software technology that brought information into the electronic era has left us with countless records that literally cannot be saved or read. Given the volatility and fragility of technological innovation, where will scholars one hundred years from now turn for evidence about our present moment, and what standards will they use to navigate the sheer quantity of data and to evaluate its authenticity? The collections libraries assembled and stored throughout the nineteenth and twentieth centuries were themselves highly selective, unrepresentative of ephemeral materials and experiences that, for reasons of convenience or ideology, never became a part of the public patrimony. As the virtual library ushers in what Rosenzweig describes as "a fundamental paradigm shift from a culture of scarcity to a culture of abundance," scholars have the opportunity to reexamine the boundaries between experts and amateurs, objective facts and subjective tastes, study and leisure, by which the reading of textual documents itself was institutionalized as a practice of history.

ADAPTING NEW technologies to its evolving forms and functions, the modern library embraced a more general faith in progress — that the library, as an institution, can be an engine of social and scientific modernization. In Edward Bellamy's novel *Looking Backward* (1881), for instance, set in the year 2000, the protagonist makes a visit to the Boston Public Library. There is, however, no description of a building, circulation or reference desks, or reading rooms: the library offers only "the temptation of the luxurious leather chairs with which it was furnished," "book-lined alcoves" in which to "rest and chat awhile." The narrator then compares the "glorious liberty that reigns in the public libraries of the twentieth century" to "the intolerable management of those of the nineteenth century, in which the books were jealously railed away from the people," to be obtained with "time and red tape calculated to discourage any ordinary taste for literature."[21] As Bellamy suggests, the library of the future would be built on faith that technological progress would reduce the cumbersome and unreliable factors of human labor in the timely delivery of books.

Now that we have passed the year 2000, Bellamy's oblique image of the library of the future offers a remarkably prescient image of the domestication of knowledge. Following the development of integrated circuitry and the invention of the now ever-shrinking microchip in 1968 by Robert Noyce, the very presence of the library as a physical and social space, with all its antiquated and cumbersome processing of people and paper, has become peripheral to the storage and distribution of information. As with the Library of Congress's American Memory Project or Google's virtual library, entire archives of books, periodicals, and documents are becoming available to readers, to be searched and read over the Internet from the ease and comfort of one's home. "The library of the future is inscribed where all texts can be summoned, assembled, and read — on a screen," as Roger Chartier notes. As a library without walls, electronic access to texts has made the Enlightenment dream of the library truly virtual, connecting "the closed world of any finite collection and the infinite universe of all the texts ever written."[22]

And yet, as all of the essays in this volume demonstrate, libraries in the United States have served needs and aspirations that go beyond the physical problems of where and how to store information. Despite the advent of the Internet and the opening of Google's online archive, libraries continue to occupy physical space in thousands of communities across the United States, and to furnish the primary infrastructure for our individual and collective experience of culture.[23] (See figure I.5.) So what, then, is a library? How have libraries fostered communities of readers, and shaped the experience of reading in particular communities? How did the development of modern libraries alter the boundaries of private and public life? *Institutions of Reading* offers at once a social history of literacy and leisure, an intellectual history of librarians' innovations in mass distribution of printed books and periodicals, and a cultural history of the organization of knowledge in an increasingly diverse urban society.

---

21. See chap. 15 of Edward Bellamy, *Looking Backward: From 2000 to 1887,* at http://xroads .virginia.edu/~hyper/BELLAMY/ch15.html.

22. Roger Chartier, "Libraries without Walls," in *Future Libraries,* ed. Block and Hess, 48.

23. As Wayne Wiegand points out, more people visit libraries than public parks, movie theaters, and other popular venues for recreation. See Wayne Wiegand, "To Reposition a Research Agenda: What American Studies Can Teach the LIS Community about the Library in the Life of the User," *Library Quarterly* 73 (2003): 369–82.

Figure I.5. The new downtown Minneapolis Public Library, designed by Cesar Pelli, opened on May 20, 2006. Much of the building's $138 million cost was paid for by a 2000 tax referendum. Traditional features of public library architecture such as a children's room, open-stack bookshelves, and reference services are incorporated with the soaring atrium of a "library commons," working fireplaces, and over 300 computers for free Internet access. Photos by Thomas Augst.

Chapter 1

Social Libraries and Library Societies in Eighteenth-Century North America

James Raven

On January 8, 1760, Daniel Crawford, prosperous Carolina merchant, scholarly book collector, and vice-president of the Charleston Library Society, presided at the society's annual general meeting. He stood in for the president, William Henry Lyttelton, governor of South Carolina for the past four years, who was reelected at this meeting as titular head of the Library Society. Crawford's first task from the chair, as custom dictated, was to read out the society's rules. At this "anniversary" meeting, the twelfth since the library's foundation in June 1748, the reading of the rules was followed by "a very handsome and elegant speech from the chair" to thank the outgoing vice-president (and former president) Gabriel Manigault, by far the richest merchant and plantation owner of South Carolina.[1] Various members then informed the society that on that very day, Governor Lyttelton had returned to Charleston from war with the Cherokee. In consequence, the anniversary meeting resolved to establish a committee of seven senior library members to compose an address to Lyttelton to inform him that he had been reappointed as library president and to congratulate him on the slaughter of the brute Indian and the protection of the colony. Extraordinarily, the Library Society then reconvened the next morning to hear the draft address, revise it (it would be interesting to know in what ways), and then send it to the governor, together with an enquiry as to "when he would be waited upon by the Society." Members did not have to tarry long. On the next day, January 10, Lyttelton received the delegation, thanked the society for its loyal address, and pledged continued support for its endeavors.[2]

---

1. Charleston Library Society (hereafter CLS), Journal-Book, 1759–80 (hereafter J.), fol. 15 with copy and Lyttelton's response fols. 16–17. I am most grateful to Carol Jones, Assistant Librarian, CLS, for further transcription of this entry.

2. CLS, J., fols. 16–17. This account of the address to Lyttelton corrects that given in James Raven, *London Booksellers and American Customers: Transatlantic Literary Community and the Charleston Library Society, 1748–1811* (Columbia: University of South Carolina Press, 2002), 75.

In fact, entries in the Library Society's Journal-Book, recording attendance and decisions made at its meetings, offer a public transcript that often masks a more complex narrative. The truth was that in January 1760 Lyttelton had returned in some disarray from a continuing Indian war that he had done much to precipitate and that was not settled until late 1761 (more than a year after he had left Charleston for the plum appointment of governor of Jamaica).[3] The Library Society's address to its president further confirmed the ideals and aspirations of the membership in phrases that echoed the preamble to the society's rules read out by Crawford. As the preamble declared:

> As the gross ignorance of the naked Indian must raise our pity, and his savage disposition our horrour and detestation, it is our duty as men, our interest as members of a *community*, to prevent our descendants from sinking into a similar situation. To obviate this possible evil, and to obtain the desirable end of handing down the European arts and manners to the latest times is the great aim of the members of this Society, who are ambitious of approving them-selves worthy of their mother country, by imitating her humanity, as well as her industry, and by transporting from her the improvements in the finer as well as the inferiour arts.[4]

Those who listened to Crawford's reiteration of the aims of the Charleston Library Society and its ambition to promote civility and learning included most of the leading merchants, slave traders, lawyers, clerics, and physicians of the town (population about 5,000 whites and 6,000 blacks by 1770).[5] The Library Society had been swiftly acknowledged as central to the intellectual life of the town. Founded by 19 young merchants and professionals, the society boasted 129 shareholding members by its second anniversary. Its early presidents included the physician and scholar John Lining and the self-made merchant and founder of the great planter and South Carolinian political dynasty, Charles Pinckney. The first librarian, John Sinclair, traded in food and imported dry goods. Samuel Brailsford, first secretary of the library, was a merchant and slave trader together with his brother and fellow library founder, Morton.

The Charleston Library Society founders were all young men (most below the age of twenty-four) and of religious and ethnic origins that reflected the diverse white population of the town, including Huguenots, Quakers, Scots, Londoners, Irish, and East Anglians. Of the society members recorded in

---

3. John Oliphant, *Peace and War on the Anglo-Cherokee Frontier, 1756–63* (Baton Rouge: Louisiana State University Press, 2001).

4. CLS, *Rules and By-Laws*, 1762, iv.

5. Raven, *London Booksellers and American Customers*, 20.

1750, 38 were styled "esquire" (with 7 suffixed as "honourable"), 16 "doctor," 2 "captain," 3 "reverend," and 68 "messr." Unsurprisingly, many members were related to each other. At each anniversary meeting the members elected (or reelected) a president, vice-president, treasurer, librarian, steward, and a secretary and correspondent. Within a decade of the society's foundation, members also elected a London bookseller.[6] The fabulously wealthy Gabriel Manigault was the first of the Library Society presidents to serve more than one year but also the last before the Revolution to be drawn from the membership. For the twenty years after 1758, the society decided to advertise its increased grandeur and consequence by electing either the colonial governor (like Lyttelton) or the lieutenant governor as its titular head. By contrast, the librarian was, by at least 1770, a salaried position. The day-to-day executive power effectively resided with the secretary, a role usually combined with that of correspondent and one also accorded a stipend.

The rules read out by Crawford (and sent as a printed pamphlet to every new member) specified conditions of shareholding, borrowing, fines, and election and service on the Library Society committee. The accumulation of capital stock from members' initial subscriptions and then from five shilling weekly contributions and fines, was designed to endow a learned academy (not even partially achieved until 1785), but the stock also enabled the society to act as a bank, lending money to successful applicants at advantageous rates. Library Society membership and share ownership was confined to one person in each household. Under the foundation rules four general meetings of the society were convened each year. The first, deemed the anniversary meeting, took place on the second Tuesday of every January, followed by quarterly meetings on the first Wednesday in April, June, and October. Under the third rule of the society, as reformulated in 1762, the president (or in his absence, the vice-president) chaired all meetings to "keep regularity and decency, sum up all debates and put questions, call for all reports of committees, and accounts from the Treasurer and others." Additional extraordinary meetings were permitted, and all meetings were advertised publicly by the secretary-correspondent.

Under the Library Society rules, only a single pamphlet or book could be borrowed on each occasion, although multivolume works were counted as single books. Members were expected to read promptly. Loans were limited to four days for pamphlets, twelve days for duodecimos and octavos, sixteen days for quartos, and twenty-four days for folios. Under the rules,

---

6. CLS, *Rules and By-Laws,* 1750, rules 2 and 3, after a rule declaring the title of the Society (1762, rules 1 and 2).

a five-shilling fine was imposed for every twelve hours overdue. Borrowers living outside Charleston were granted time extensions engagingly calculated at twelve hours for every six miles' distance.[7] Members were indeed increasingly dispersed as the estates accumulated. Headrights of fifty acres for each imported slave sanctioned the expansion of plantations so that settlements such as Goose Creek, eighteen miles from Charleston, became satellite communities outside the town. As they extended their plantations or acquired new ones, many library members, like the celebrated botanist and resident of Goose Creek, Alexander Garden, and the Brisbanes, magnificently established on the Ashley River, sought longer-term loans for their books. Not that this scattering of library members, which would have seemed excessive in Britain, was unusual in eighteenth-century North America. Similar lending allowances are evident elsewhere. In Baltimore, according to the 1797 library rules, "persons at the distance of five miles and upwards from town, may keep the books, which they take, one-third of time longer than others."[8] In Charleston in 1762 Dr Deas moved at the April quarterly meeting "that oyl cloth be provided for the packing up Books that Country members may send for."[9]

Concern that the Charleston Library Society might fail was evident from the outset. Members paid heavy forfeits to escape office and attendance at meetings. All society members were under the obligation of serving as an officer once in seven years, and any member refusing to comply was fined £5, although members were excused if deemed "country members" living at a distance from Charleston. This was usually allowed on application, although several high-profile requests were thrown out by general meetings.[10] The Library Society committee repeatedly punished defaulters. From 1770 the secretary was charged with reading out the names of any committee members "neglecting to attend at their stated times of meeting."[11] Further rules debarred members from voting or attending a committee meeting once they were six months in arrears with subscriptions or fines. The same rules stipulated that "the name of every member dismissed the society shall be hung up in the library, with an account of the sum due by him to the society; and also the name of every member who is indebted for six months subscription."[12]

Nervousness about the Library Society's future was evident in other ways.

---

7. Raven, *London Booksellers and American Customers,* 55.

8. By-laws, prefacing *Catalogue of the Books, &c Belonging to the Library Company of Baltimore* (1797).

9. CLS Quarterly Meeting (hereafter QM), April 1762, J. fol. 31.

10. Notably, "after some debate," CLS Quarterly Meeting, July 1775, J. fol. 169.

11. CLS, *Rules and By-Laws,* 1770, rule 13 (strengthening rule 11 of 1762).

12. CLS, *Rules and By-Laws,* 1762, rule 18; *Rules and By-Laws,* 1770, rule 20.

Although a visitor in 1763 described the society as "at present in a flourishing State,"[13] in the same year it was reported at the anniversary meeting that "the Spirit of this Society is much lessen'd & the Vigor it first set out with almost annihilated."[14] In response, members proposed meeting together every Wednesday at Dillon's tavern (at 6 p.m. in winter and 7 p.m. in summer) to "associate together . . . in order to converse freely on such matters as may ocurr & they conceive may be of utility to be offer'd to the monthly Committee."[15] In a further attempt to strengthen the institution, potential library committee members were sought from amongst the citizenry of Charleston whether or not they were already Library Society members. John Hume, for example, was admitted as a member in July 1759 and then elected to the committee at the next general meeting in October. William Mason was admitted a member in June 1764 and put on the committee and elected secretary all at the same meeting.

The Library Society as it developed at Charleston, therefore, combined intellectual and social ambition within a carefully policed structure. Meeting procedures resembled those of a debating society. The original rules of the society stipulated that any member speaking must address his remark to the president, who also determined who might speak.[16] Similar practices were later confirmed by associations such as the Medical Society of South Carolina (almost all of whose members also belonged to the Library Society). Rules here stated that "Members shall address the President standing; and no member shall be interrupted whilst he is speaking, unless he be called to order by the President."[17] Meetings adopted debating manners similar to those of the Westminster Commons and the colonial assemblies—and, like them, were probably observed more in the breach than is indicated in the minimally constructed formal records.

At Charleston, dinners followed society meetings. From the outset, the elected steward was charged with providing "a sufficient dinner" for which each member paid forty shillings one week in advance.[18] The dinners enticed the more remote members to meetings and provided all with an opportunity for discussion and affability, complementary to the formal meeting. It was a

---

13. George Milligen-Johnston, *A Short Description of the Province of South Carolina . . . in the Year 1763* (London, 1770), 37.

14. CLS, Anniversary Meeting (hereafter AM), Jan. 1763, J. fol. 34.

15. CLS, AM Jan. 1763, J. fol. 34.

16. CLS, *Rules and By-Laws* 1750, rule 22 (rule 34 by 1762, rule 3 in 1772).

17. CLS, *Rules and By-Laws* 1750, rule 7, cited in Joseph I. Waring, ed., *Excerpts from the Minutes of the Medical Society of South Carolina from 1789 to 1820* (Charleston: Nelsons' Southern Printing & Pub. Co., 1959?), 1: 2.

18. CLS, *Rules and By-Laws* 1750, rule 20 (brought forward to rule 7 in 1762).

practice common to many early colonial societies. The Charleston German Friendly Society, for example, concluded all its quarterly meetings with dinners. They were gracious and appropriately lavish affairs. A surviving bill to the treasurer for the 1778 Charleston Library Society dinner amounted to £432 for thirty-five gentlemen, or £12.6s per head.[19] These charges were for what has been called elsewhere "decorous dining,"[20] a practice confirming a centerpiece of public and political sociability, a confirmatory unity, whatever other divisions of the local elite.[21] Meetings commenced as early as 9 or 10 a.m.,[22] and the dinners were held at times varying from 11 a.m. to the early afternoon, usually in the back room of a town center tavern.[23] From the early nineteenth century, the society advertised its anniversary meetings with later dinners. In January 1804, dinner was provided at 3.30 p.m., following a meeting in the Library Room of the Court House at noon, with the quarterly meeting of June that year starting at 1 p.m.[24]

In such ways the Charleston Library Society, formally established with its elegant statement of mission that proclaimed public and beneficent intent, served as a private club, reminiscent of other civic societies, and like most of them, without a permanent dining room or even a purpose-built library room.[25] The separation of public and private was not simple or absolute, however. The colonial proprietary library was a social institution characterized by its discursive functions, a private society exerting a more formative influence in the civilizing mission than other civic associations. In Charleston, the Library Society acted as a philanthropic but exclusive institution, while adopting current notions of a "social library" as one providing a collection of materials assembled, preserved, and issued for loan under detailed rules, and maintained for members by fee, subscription, or payment into joint stock. The books and other library possessions were usually maintained in part of an existing civic building or library keeper's or other member's house, which

---

19. CLS, MSS 29 "Financial Records," Receipt Book, 1770–1789, entry 1 July 1778.

20. Richard D. Brown, *Knowledge Is Power: The Diffusion of Information in Early America, 1700–1865* (New York: Oxford University Press, 1989), 49.

21. Cf. Barbara G. Carson, *Ambitious Appetites: Dining, Behavior, and Patterns of Consumption in Federal Washington* (Washington, DC: American Institute of Architects Press, 1990).

22. The 1755 AM, which commenced at 9 a.m., had been preceded by an audience with the president, open to all members, at 3 p.m. the previous Wednesday, *South Carolina Gazette,* 2 January 1755; more typically, in 1767 William Mason advertised the quarterly meeting of October as being at 10 a.m., *South Carolina Gazette,* 28 September 1767.

23. AM 8 January 1765, J. fol. 50.

24. *Charleston Gazette and Daily Advertiser,* 18 January 1804; *City Gazette* [Charleston], 19 June 1805.

25. The building for the Redwood Library, Rhode Island, erected in 1750, was the first such in North America; the Library Company of Philadelphia opened a new building in 1791.

might also serve as a reading-room (if not yet an "athenæum") with set times of opening.[26]

The exclusivity of much Library Society activity must also refine interpretations of these sodalities as accessible communities of interest and fellow feeling.[27] Many similar societies (notably including the Masonic lodges) combined civility with exclusivity, appropriating rigid protocols in pursuit of specific ideals of polite sociability.[28] Although after the Revolution Masonic and other society memberships seem to have been less concerned with fortune, rank, and hierarchy, in the colonial period many associations espoused elitism (and were also almost entirely male formations). The *South Carolina Gazette* of January 9, 1755, described a procession of more than one hundred Charleston gentlemen to St. Philip's Church on St. John the Evangelist's Day. Those gathered included the Ubiquarians and the Freemasons, and after church all adjourned to the Corner Tavern where with "harmony and regularity" they dined and spent the rest of the day and evening together. Such events contributed to a rapidly developing civic culture, if socially narrow and open to accusations of extravagant living. The Library Society had the most obvious claim among these societies to an elevated pursuit of civilization through the stock of the printed page.

As at Charleston, the early social libraries reflected the particular character of their towns and communities and did not simply emulate developments in Britain. English book clubs of the 1710s and 1720s provided certain models for widened local book provision, but beyond basic proprietary and subscription structures, the particularities of membership and constitutional and financial arrangements were hugely diverse. As has also been pointed out in the seminal study of the early public libraries of New England, even differences between proprietary institutions (with joint-stock ownership of transferable shares based on common-law partnerships) and subscription institutions (usually as common-law corporations) were often not clear cut.[29] Distinctions between annual fee-paying members and shareholders might not, for example, be at all obvious in terms of borrowing or book recommendation rights, and

26. Cf. Donald G. Davis, Jr., and John Mark Tucker, *American Library History: A Comprehensive Guide to the Literature* (Santa Barbara, CA, and Oxford: ABC-CLIO, 1989), 56.

27. See David Shields, *Civil Tongues and Polite Letters in British America* (Chapel Hill: University of North Carolina Press, 1997), xvii–xviii, with particular emphasis upon Shaftesbury's contemporary cultural analysis.

28. See Steven C. Bullock, *Revolutionary Brotherhood: Freemasonry and the Transformation of the American Social Order, 1730–1840* (Chapel Hill: University of North Carolina, 1996), esp. 26–29.

29. Jesse H. Shera, *Foundations of the Public Library: The Origins of the Public Library Movement in New England, 1629–1855* (Chicago: University of Chicago Press, 1949), 58; catalogues are listed in Robert B. Winans, *A Descriptive Checklist of Book Catalogues Separately Printed in America, 1693–1800* (Worcester: American Antiquarian Society, 1981).

sometimes it was only according to financial stake-holding and membership transfer by inheritance or sale that distinctions within a library corporation might be discerned. A library's common fund for book and print purchase might be financed by annual fees, fines, investment, or a mixture of all three. The formal titles of the libraries, great and small, ranged from Library Company to Society Library and Library Society, but many, like the Portsmouth Society Library (to give the Portsmouth Social Library its foundation title) were more generally styled social libraries.

The most flourishing libraries were those built from mercantile wealth, and the use of the joint-stock principle provided a surer foundation for a library's continuation than did personal foundations, despite recurrent concern in many libraries about membership numbers and activities. As Alexander Hamilton reported of the Philosophical Society, an adjunct to the Newport Library: "I was surprised to find that no matters of philosophy were brought upon the carpet. They talked of privateering and building of vessels."[30] Nevertheless, many foundations owed much to personal initiative. Abraham Redwood at Newport, Rhode Island, shared with Franklin at Philadelphia a single-minded mission to encourage other educated gentlemen of the town to establish a library. Several social libraries, like those at Newport and Salem, also served to rejuvenate an existing or recently defunct literary and philosophical association.

By 1748, the founding year of the Charleston Library Society, at least eleven other social libraries, two only partially secular, had commenced in North America: the Library Company of Philadelphia (1731, with the Union Library founded in 1746), the Book-Company of Durham, Connecticut (1733), the Library of Guilford, Saybrook, Killingworth, and Lyme, Connecticut (1737), the United English Library of Woodstock and Killingly, Connecticut (1745), the Philogrammatican Library at Lebanon, Connecticut (1739), the United English Library of Pomfret, Connecticut (1739), the Library Company of Darby, Pennsylvania (1743), the Society Library of Milford, Connecticut (1745), the Germantown Library (1745), and the Redwood Library, Newport, Rhode Island (1747).[31] In East Hampton, New York, the Philogrammatican Library was founded in 1753, followed by the New York Society Library in 1754, the Albany Social Library in 1758, and the Huntington, New York,

---

30. Cited in Shera, *Foundations*, 39.

31. For a list of these and other colonial libraries, see "American Libraries before 1876," a database of the Davies Project at Princeton University (http://www.princeton.edu/~davpro/databases/index.html). More libraries no doubt existed, and records for additional libraries or for one of the libraries here listed may surface, as in fact happened during the completion of this study; documents relating to the Philogrammatican Library subscription library were offered for sale by Joseph Rubinfine, in his Catalogue 133 (West Palm Beach, FL, 1996), item 32.

Social Library in 1759. Thirty-three prominent gentlemen founded the Portsmouth Social Library, New Hampshire, in 1750, supporting it by members' subscriptions and by a lottery allied to a workhouse project, until the library's effective dissolution at the Revolution.[32] Elsewhere in New England further social libraries were founded at Newington, Connecticut, in 1752, and at Providence (the Library Company) in 1753.[33] In Boston two social libraries were established in 1758 by bequest of Thomas Prince.[34] The Salem Social Library in 1760 headed more than a dozen New England social libraries founded in that decade, with more than 50 founded in New England by 1780. The majority were in Connecticut, and many were also short-lived, unable to survive the passing of generations and gradually increasing access to books by greater importation and the establishment of more small-town book merchants.[35]

The most successful, grander social libraries like those at Newport and, later, Baltimore, were not only distinguished from the smaller community libraries by their elite membership, complexity of rules, and adjunct social occasions but were more obviously independent of British exemplars. The 1731 Library Company of Philadelphia was founded twenty-seven years before one of the earliest British proprietary libraries, the Liverpool Library of 1758 (and twenty years before the foundation of the British Museum).[36] A certain American rather than transatlantic inferiority complex is observable in the newspaper advertisement that appeared in New York in 1754 to announce the arrival of the Society Library's first shipment of books:

> New-York, now has an Opportunity [and] will show that she comes not short of the other Provinces, in Men of Excellent Genius, who, by cultivating the Talents of Nature, will take off that Reflection cast on us by the neighbouring Colonies, of being an ignorant People.[37]

As has also been readily demonstrated for the New England social libraries before 1850, many smaller establishments tended to constitute specialist

32. Jim Piecuch, "'Of Great Importance Both to Civil and Religious Welfare': The Portsmouth Social Library, 1750–1786," *Historical New Hampshire* 57 (2002): 67–84; historians claiming that a tontine assisted in the construction of the library seem to have misinterpreted what was effectively an arrangement for the sale and transfer of shares; see 69–70.

33. Included in Grace F. Leonard and W. C. Worthington, *The Providence Athenaeum, A Brief History, 1753–1939* (Providence: The Athenaeum, 1940).

34. Shera, *Foundations of the Public Library,* 51–52.

35. See ibid., 55, table 3; James Raven, "The Importation of Books to Colonial North America," *Publishing History* 42 (1997): 21–49. See also the database "American Libraries before 1876."

36. See Paul Kaufman, "The Community Library: A Chapter in English Social History," *Transactions of the American Philosophical Society,* n.s. 57, pt. 7 (Philadelphia, 1967).

37. *New-York Mercury,* 14 October 1754.

libraries either by membership or by holdings.[38] A few were based on clerical collections, such as that sent by Isaac Watts to Lebanon and that given by the rector of Portsmouth to its fledgling library. Early church social libraries included the Ecclesiastical Library of Newport (1743) and the Church Library of Yarmouth, Maine (1747). In total some 386 social libraries were founded in New England before 1800, with diverse collections and constitutions. The majority were not large. Only 19 of the New England social libraries ever held more than 5,000 books in the eighteenth century. By contrast, 305 librar-ies stocked under 1,000 books (and of these, 68 libraries held under 100).[39] As Jesse Shera concluded, "viewed collectively, the large numbers of social libraries do constitute an impressive picture; examined independently, the component libraries are revealed as being far from strong."[40]

For all such differences between social libraries, certain similarities were fundamental. The earliest depended almost entirely upon book purchases from London (with, certainly in the case of New York and Charleston library societies, surprisingly few members donating or bequeathing books).[41] The secretary-correspondent, or the library-keeper, as the Durham Book-Company, the Lebanon Philogrammatican Society, and the New York Society Library (among others) styled their elected librarian, was particularly charged with book delivery arrangements. Many of the New England libraries, most notably the Salem Social Library, ordered books from Boston booksellers, but these booksellers, of course, depended almost exclusively before the 1780s on importation from Britain. The Salem library's agent, Jeremy Condy, commanded one of the most extensive London-to-Boston book trades of the 1760s.[42] Supplies to social libraries from London booksellers and book agents continued into the first two decades of the nineteenth century despite the fast-advancing American publishing and reprint industry (whose titles begin to make a great impact in library catalogues from the Embargo period onward). When the Baltimore Library Company opened in 1797, 1,300 of its 2,000 foundation volumes had been supplied directly from London.[43]

The more elevated characteristic common to all library societies was the combination of social ambition with a resounding moral imperative. The

38. See Shera, *Foundations,* 72, table 5.

39. Ibid., 75, table 8.

40. Ibid., 75.

41. Philadelphians were notably more generous; see Edwin Wolf, *"At the Instance of Benjamin Franklin": A Brief History of the Library Company of Philadelphia,* rev. and enl. ed. (Philadelphia: Library Company, 1995), 16, 31, 32, 38, 40–46.

42. See Elizabeth Carroll Reilly, "The Wages of Piety: The Boston Book Trade of Jeremy Condy," in *Printing and Society in Early America,* ed. William L. Joyce et al. (Worcester: American Antiquarian Society, 1983), 83–131.

43. Raven, *London Booksellers and American Customers,* 99.

Boston bookseller and London book importer Henry Knox confirmed his dedication to "those Gentlemen in the Country who are actuated with the most genuine Principles of Benevolence in their Exertions to Exterminate Ignorance and Darkness, by the noble medium of Social Libraries."[44] The founders of the Portsmouth Social Library intended to establish "a good collection of books" for "the advancement of learning and increase of all useful knowledge."[45] Proprietary libraries empowered shareholders and subscribers both by the acquisition of textual and scientific knowledge and by the pursuit of particular formal and informal social practices. The library society operated as a repository of learning and instruction, but also as a social passport and a conduit for polite society. The pioneering historian of printing and the book in Salem described its library as a "veritable Social Register of Salem."[46]

In social libraries from New England to Georgia, reading and private discussion accompanied educational and social activities, which might include public lectures and demonstrations, debates, dining and civic parades, and commitment to community welfare projects. The development of these libraries underscores the importance of a literary and scientific sociability in which books, prints, and scientific instruments acted as a catalyst for social and political exchange and advancement. The demonstrations of electrical and scientific apparatus at the Library Company of Philadelphia were widely copied by other libraries. In Charleston, members of the Library Society expended much energy and endured extraordinary frustration in their attempt to buy and then have repaired in London telescopes, a solar microscope (intended for public exhibitions and lectures), and other scientific and mathematical instruments.[47] The success of the orrery constructed in 1770 by David Rittenhouse and sold to the College of New Jersey (Princeton) also encouraged other social libraries to explore the possibility of similar commissions to supplement their globes and mounted telescopes.[48]

The acquisition of books and equipment by these quasi-learned societies often contributed to ambitions to found separate academies or—again as part of the increasing social ambition of the membership—to establish other community institutions. Such projects were rarely realized, despite

---

44. *Massachusetts Gazette,* 31 March 1774.

45. Piecuch, "Of Great Importance"; Michael A. Baenen, "Books, Newspapers, and Sociability in the Making of the Portsmouth Athenaeum," *New England Quarterly* 76 (2003): 378–412, esp. 380.

46. Harriet S. Tapley, *Salem Imprints, 1768–1825: A History of the First Fifty Years of Printing in Salem, Massachusetts, with Some Account of the Bookshops, Booksellers, Bookbinders, and the Private Libraries* (Salem: Essex Institute, 1927), 245.

47. Raven, *London Booksellers and American Customers,* chap. 11 and illustrations 12–15.

48. Ibid., 177–79.

the grandly phrased and engraved library manifestos of public enlightenment. The involvement of library committees in other activities distracted
from book collection and may have contributed to recruitment difficulties.
At Portsmouth the determination of Social Library members to put the
poor of the town to work by building a workhouse preoccupied the society
during its first decade, and the eventual building of the structure seems to
have exhausted the energies of many of the library founders.[49] Elsewhere,
and notably at Philadelphia and Charleston, enthusiasm for creating a library
museum or cabinet of curiosities brought other problems. The donation of
local flora and fauna, together with more exotic objects such as Eskimo par-
kas, limbs of Egyptian mummies, turtle shells, and stuffed animals, resulted
in rotting embarrassment for various library committees by the turn of the
century. At Charleston the natural history collection and a troubled investment in scientific instruments were part of the broader strategy to endow
a college, but such projecting, as at Portsmouth, undermined rather than
boosted morale.[50]

In fact, the related but often divergent histories of early American academies and libraries suggest much about the course of the aspirations of library
societies. In his study of colonial Virginian society, Rhys Isaac identified
"liberality" as the defining characteristic of gentility. Liberality demonstrated
independence, disinterestedness, freedom from material want in return for
the acceptance of community responsibilities, and "a certain disposition in
the soul that all these freedoms made possible."[51] The visible exercise of liberality confirmed authority. In the colonial context where, as Timothy Breen
has argued, the conduct of cultural power augmented relatively weak political
structures,[52] the respected learning of the library society represented a key
determinant of exclusive social authority, transmitted by highly formalized
display and hospitality. Meetings, debates, dinners, and parades demanded
ceremonial and formal etiquette calculated to both engage with and personify
polite culture — if, in most cases, entirely masculine, and often intersecting
with other fraternities.[53] Library membership maintained social esteem. Even
the architecture of the library expressed social status, a built environment

---

49. Piecuch, "Of Great Importance," 72–77.

50. Wolf, *"At the Instance of Benjamin Franklin,"* 16–19; Raven, *London Booksellers and American Customers,* 65–66.

51. Rhys Isaac, *The Transformation of Virginia, 1740–1790* (Chapel Hill: University of North Carolina Press, 1982), 131–32 (131).

52. T. H. Breen, *Tobacco Culture: The Mentality of the Great Tidewater Planters on the Eve of Revolution* (Princeton: Princeton University Press, 2001).

53. Raven, *London Booksellers and American Customers,* 44.

described, indeed, as a broker of "tensions between individuals and communities, the public and the private, the material and the symbolic."[54]

Elsewhere I have developed three general conclusions after trawls through the surviving archives of early American society libraries from Boston to Savannah. My first claim is that the diverse social libraries of colonial North America, with their collections largely purchased after suggestions by members (and shareholders) rather than being built up by donations from outside, were established not only to emulate British examples (the most famous of which actually postdated the earliest American societies), but also to encourage reading for locally driven improvement and civility in specifically American environments. My second claim is that print-led ambitions relied upon a particular cultural dependency that we must understand more completely if we are to recover the intellectual history of colonial America. We have to guard against false assumptions about the ready availability of texts and account for "cultural lags" across the Atlantic caused by transportation, distribution, and financing difficulties. My final contention is that a rapid change in stocking policy and reading tastes set in at the end of the eighteenth century, challenging the libraries' purchasing and their members' borrowing of seriously minded literature.[55] As will be argued below, this change in reading tastes altered the character of existing overseas literary dependency. The apparent dilution of library orders for books of improvement by orders for books of entertainment reflected an *increasing* rather than diminishing European commercial influence for some twenty years after Independence in 1784. This new form of cultural dependency, continuing into the first decade of the nineteenth century, further contrasts with the founding ambitions of the American proprietary libraries. We might even argue that the new Europeanized and commercialized "useless" reading was actually more serious *reading*. Shocked reaction from library committees and the few surviving early borrowing records suggest that such books were being read, and being read more thoroughly than the earlier orders for approved erudition and instruction.

The colonial dependency of the libraries was not as straightforward as it

---

54. Thomas Augst, introduction to *Libraries as Agencies of Culture,* ed. Thomas Augst and Wayne Wiegand, special issue of *American Studies* 42 (2001) 3, 5–22 (5).

55. Raven, *London Booksellers and American Customers;* James Raven, "Commodification and Value: Interaction in Book Traffic to North America, c. 1750–1820," in *Across Boundaries: The Book in Culture & Commerce,* ed. Bill Bell, Philip Bennett, and Jonquil Bevan (Winchester and New Castle, DE: St Paul's Bibliographies and Oak Knoll Press, 2000), 73–90; James Raven, "The Export of Books from London," in *The Colonial Book in the Atlantic World,* ed. Hugh Amory and David D. Hall, vol. 1 of *A History of the Book in America* (Cambridge: Cambridge University Press and American Antiquarian Society, 2000), 183–98; and cf. James Raven, "The Representation of Philanthropy and Reading in the Eighteenth-Century Library," in *Libraries and Culture* 31 (1996): 492–510.

might seem. In Britain, the development of private, commercial, and proprietary (both subscription and shareholding) libraries was an important prop to the upsurge in publication rates and was a particular feature of the late eighteenth-century book trade.[56] In various ways modest, often short-lived, literary and scientific groups emulated the major metropolitan institutions, including the prestigious royal and national academies of sciences. Most included a library (and, often, a scientific collection and curiosity cabinet). Although British social libraries were relatively few in number by the mid-eighteenth century, one survey lists more than 3,000 such libraries established at some time between 1700 and 1799, with 923 "society libraries" and 1,005 "subscription libraries" operating in Britain at some point before 1850.[57]

The foundation of American social libraries confirmed that civilization was transportable and sustainable. Such an endeavor, evident also in the remote and isolated towns of Britain, was even more pronounced in the provinces overseas. The evidence of the mission is all around. The bookplates of the New York Society Library, for example, offered visual manifestos of the idealized process (see figures 1.1 and 1.2). In the imaginary scenario in the New York plates, an Indian brave kneels on the floor of a library, his tomahawk discarded, and he receives a book from Minerva, goddess of wisdom and knowledge. The primitive appears as the abased convert to knowledge. "Emollit mores" [it softens manners] is proclaimed above and then across the shelves.[58]

In 1792, Samuel Jennings, a Philadelphian living in London, completed a large (5½ × 7 ft.) oil painting, *Liberty Displaying the Arts and Sciences,* for the new library building (opened 1791) of the Library Company of Philadelphia. On the threshold of the temple of learning, three freed slaves kneel in obeisance to a seated, gracious, and modestly dressed Liberty, her emblematic cap beside her (see figure 1.3), her right hand gently proffering the catalogue of the Philadelphia library. The spines of other books depicted read: Milton's *Works,* Thomson's *Seasons,* Howard on Prisons, Homer, Virgil, and "Philosophy" and "Agriculture." The foreground is strewn with the paraphernalia of liberal and polite learning, counterpointed in the background, beyond another group of would-be beneficiaries, by incoming ships in full sail.

---

56. See James Raven, "From Promotion to Proscription: Arrangements for Reading and Eighteenth-Century Libraries," in *The Practice and Representation of Reading in England,* ed. James Raven, Helen Small, and Naomi Tadmor (Cambridge: Cambridge University Press, 1996): 175–201.

57. As of December 1998, Robin Alston's "Library History Database" website (www.r-alston. co.uk/contents.htm) listed 3,071 libraries operating at some time between 1700 and 1799.

58. The plates are discussed in more detail in Raven, "The Representation of Philanthropy and Reading."

Figure 1.1. The second bookplate of the New York Society Library, 1789, designed by Peter R. Maverick. Reproduced by permission of the New York Society Library.

The quest for imported learning brought special tensions. In Philadelphia, local booksellers increasingly supplied the library, but twice-annual shipments arranged by London Quaker merchants Woods and Dillwyn and then Samuel Woods (from 1783) continued to at least 1823, despite mounting difficulties. Even within a few years of the foundation of the Library Company, its

Figure 1.2. The third bookplate of the New York Society Library, 1797, designed by Peter R. Maverick. Reproduced by permission of the New York Society Library.

Figure 1.3. Samuel Jennings, *Liberty Displaying the Arts and Sciences,* oil on canvas, London, 1792. Reproduced by permission of the Library Company of Philadelphia.

directors accused its London booksellers of overcharging.[59] Secretary Joseph Breintnall wrote to the bookseller William Meadows in 1736: "I could wish the Prices you set upon them may be moderate, and that it would sute you to serve us according to your Letter of Septr last, wherein you write you will venture to say no man in London shall be more reasonable in Prices than you. The Directors are assured that some of your Books are overcharged, which has inclined them to think of trying another Bookseller."[60] As suggested else-

---

59. Library Company of Philadelphia, "Book of Minutes, Containing an Account of the Proceedings of the Director," vol. 1, fols. 44–45, 47, 60, 63, entries and copies of letters, 12 August 1734, November 1734, 5 November 1735, 12 and 13 July 1736. The complaints are still continuing in June 1789: vol. 3, fol. 165.

60. Library Company of Philadelphia, "Book of Minutes," vol. 1, fol. 63, 13 July 1736. The Company eventually replaced Meadows by William Innys in July 1739 (vol. 1, fol. 189).

where, the history of the Charleston Library Society could easily be called "reprimanding the bookseller," as the members, desperate to acquire the best and latest publications, but also the grandest antiquarian books (incidentally suggesting important considerations about how the currency of literature was perceived), appointed and then successively and cursorily dismissed many of the leading booksellers of London.[61] Many early colonial library members insisted they be treated by London suppliers as ordinary English provincial customers. This was despite the twofold problems of distance and money transfer arrangements that usually made booksellers' expectations of up to six months' credit an impossibility. By 1757, the New York Society Library's £28.10s debt to Moses Franks of London had been outstanding for three years—and was only discharged by conceding 82 percent interest and a total payment of £52. Additional demands from colonial library committees for the acquisition of expensive and antiquarian books, for special binding and packing requirements, and for titles and editions sometimes inadequately described, placed many booksellers in impossible quandaries. Those with successful English provincial custom might well have been glad to be relieved of colonial service, despite its lucrative rewards when orders, payment, and interest charges could be accomplished.[62]

What did this supply of literature and improving reading bring about? The answer—at least for the larger and longer-lasting social libraries—seems to be the consolidation of an elite unity and a conservatism that attempted to construct deliberate bridges between ideological and religious difference. Some libraries—notably several in New England—were founded in the belief that greater religious learning served to consolidate and improve community life, but at many of the larger (and, in fact, more successful) institutions, book acquisition entailed more cautious literary selection, policed either by a library committee or by vote of the membership. Before considering late-century changes, therefore, we should acknowledge two further features of the idea of the social or "society" library as expressed by contemporaries.

The first of these considerations is that the representation of the library as an outstation of civilization in the wilderness offered members an acute sense of purpose but also demanded unity, however independently minded the shareholders and subscribers. In the participatory culture of their library, members claimed different British and religious affiliations and demonstrated

61. James Raven, "Gentlemen, Pirates, and Really Respectable Booksellers: Some Charleston Customers for Lackington, Allen & Co.," in *The Book Trade & Its Customers, 1450–1900: Historical Essays for Robin Myers,* ed. Arnold Hunt, Giles Mandelbrote, and Alison Shell (Winchester and Newcastle, DE: St Paul's Bibliographies and Oak Knoll Press, 1997), 247–64.

62. Raven, *London Booksellers and American Customers,* 102–32, 160–62.

marked political differences; library members' concerns about free-ranging reading underpinned attempts to impose a harmony conducive to the broader aims of polite learning. The dissemination of literature to counter new Dissent might have been prominent at many early social libraries across New England including at Pomfret, the Ecclesiastical Library of Newport, and (based at least on the conspicuous contribution of Rev. Arthur Browne) Portsmouth, but sectarian proselytizing was pointedly reproved elsewhere.

In the larger libraries, early literary policing included filters against what the New York Society Library called "thorough religion" and what the Charleston library called "polemical divinity." At Philadelphia, members in need of funding might have written to John Penn hoping that "virtue, learning and religion" might "increase and flourish" in his house, but under one tenth of the titles listed in the earliest Library Company catalogue were theological (compared to the third of titles that were historical). Even in many New England libraries, by-laws guarded against sectarianism: in 1787 members of the Royalston (Massachusetts) Social Library agreed upon a subject-specific schedule for book purchase in which divinity was restricted to 30 percent of the total budget; the Meredith Bridge Social Library at Laconia, New Hampshire, prohibited the use of proprietors' funds for the acquisition of "professional books in law, physic, or divinity"; the "Committee on Purchase and Inspection" of the Library Society of Arlington, Vermont, restricted books on divinity to below "one-thirtieth part of the value of the Library"; and, aside from donations, the United Society of Union, Rhode Island, excluded "religious and political dissertations favoring any one party or sect more than another." [63]

The various eighteenth-century library catalogues of the Library Company of Philadelphia and the libraries at Newport, Providence, New York, and Charleston (themselves offering an important review of taxonomy [64]) reflect serious shelves. Moral and political philosophy, classical literature, legal and historical works were well represented, although Charleston had so relatively little theology that many orders of the first two decades of the nineteenth century concentrated on a re-stocking, catch-up operation in religious controversy. Even this might be interpreted as an exercise designed to understand and contain particular convictions. For those members concerned by the increased acquisition of novels and belles-lettres, the purchase of distinguished, if previously neglected, theological and philosophical titles pointed to an ambition to offer opportunities for scholarly as well as general reading.

---

63. Shera, *Foundations*, 108–9.
64. Catalogues listed in Winans, *Descriptive Checklist.*

This also suggests the significance of thorough provenance research—it is important not to confuse eighteenth-century accessions (and the often limited purchase of controversial tracts) with early nineteenth-century retrospective collecting.

The second observation is that the social library project contributed to a progressive distancing of refinement from commodification in the eighteenth century. The library was inescapably bound to the intricacies of elite social consolidation. This was true of modestly sized enterprises as well as the grandest: at Portsmouth the library founders included the five wealthiest men of the town.[65] At all times aware of their vulnerable position, members of a privileged and wealthy elite employed library societies to reinforce political and cultural unity.[66] In this respect, social libraries stood out (at least until the early nineteenth century) against certain commercialization trends—and most particularly because members proposed the purchase of their own books.

British newspapers noticed the ambitions of these American libraries, although often in supercilious tone. A *London Chronicle* front-page essay on the state of Rhode Island in 1775 declared:

> Arts and sciences are almost unknown; except to some few individuals; and there are no public seminaries of learning; nor do the Rhode Islanders in general seem to regret the want of them. The institution of a library society, which has lately taken place [in fact 28 years earlier], may *possibly* in time produce a change in these matters.[67]

By 1800, however, reports from London reflected change. The *General Evening Post,* for example, reported:

> the Philo-historic Society in Pennsylvania have opened a communication with similar Societies in the other provinces of the Western World, for the diffusion of Useful Knowledge. . . . The choicest Collections of Books have been purchased in different languages . . . and the Fine Arts and Belles Lettres are making the greatest progress on the other side of the Atlantic.[68]

This is more positive and encouraging. Useful knowledge was still the priority, but belles-lettres now also had their place.

---

65. Piecuch, "Of Great Importance," 67.

66. Cf. Rebecca Starr, *A School for Politics: Commercial Lobbying and Political Culture in Early South Carolina* (Baltimore: Johns Hopkins University Press, 1998).

67. *London Chronicle,* 12 October 1775. I am grateful to Antonia Forster for drawing my attention to this essay.

68. *General Evening Post,* 22 May 1798.

An even more obvious marker of change is revealed in transatlantic correspondence. Accompanied by shame-faced apologetics from the various presidents and committees, orders from the late 1790s sent to London for the classics (both ancient and modern) and the philosophical and natural science texts began to be diluted by requests for fashionable novels, plays, and other works of entertainment. There is a striking unanimity of view from the august committees of the American society libraries at the turn of the nineteenth century. The match across geographically disparate archives is the more remarkable because there could not have been any collusion between the various correspondents. Charles Cotesworth Pinckney, president of the Charleston library, conceded of his order to Bird, Savage and Bird, the library's then London suppliers: "the bulk of the Catalogue [the Society's requirements] innumerates Books of much lighter reading than our last, but in a Society such as ours, we are obliged to consult all tastes and to have many books of mere amusement as well as books of instruction and science." When in September 1801, the same president opened the library's business correspondence with Lackington, Allen & Co., he again confessed to the change, "apprizing you that as our Society is numerous & of course variant in the taste, that we trust you will adapt your selection to suit as well those who are fond of serious & erudite subjects as those who love to amuse themselves with light & trivial reading."[69] In the same year the secretary of the New York Society Library declared to his British agent that "the Taste of several of the Members of the Library is so much turned to the reading of novels that it will be absolutely necessary to have a supply of this kind of Books."[70] In Baltimore, the Library Company's founding committee decreed that acquisitions were to "consist chiefly of books in general demand" and "of general utility."[71] The largest class in the 1809 Baltimore catalogue was theology, followed by history, then politics, and only then fiction, but even so, the library directors decreed that "they were not unmindful of employing a competent share of [the funds] for gratifying the taste of genius and providing for the entertainment of those readers who seek amusement and instruction in works of a lighter and less durable kind."[72] From its foundation in 1809, the Savannah Library Society

---

69. CLS, Copy Book of Letters, texts given in full in Raven, *London Booksellers and American Customers*, 292, 310–11.

70. New York Society Library archives, Keep papers, J[ohn] Forbes, draft of a letter for the Purchasing Committee, to Rev. John M. Mason, Glasgow, 1 October. 1801. I am indebted to Sharon Brown, NYSL, for her assistance in locating this.

71. Stuart C. Sherman, "The Library Company of Baltimore, 1795–1854," *Maryland Historical Magazine* 39 (1944): 9.

72. Directors' report, 26 April 1802, cited in Sherman, "Library Company of Baltimore," 16.

bought large quantities of fiction, and novels comprised the main category in its first printed catalogue of 1839 — 16 percent of the total (20 percent including novels and belles-lettres), compared to just 3 percent theology.[73]

Why was this? In one respect library membership seemed different. Women, lest we forget, featured very little in the early history of the social and proprietary library. The recognition of men and women in the Liverpool Library slogan was a rarity (the Liverpool Library advertised assistance to "Gentlemen *and Ladies* who wish to promote the Advantage of Knowledge"). The library institutions constructed a largely masculine space in which women were publicly marginalized. Even when some women were admitted as shareholders, as at New York, Philadelphia, and then Baltimore, most women were associated with the libraries as borrowers of books under their husband's or father's authority. They acted as adjuncts to male leadership, observing or conforming to male behavior in an overwhelmingly male social institution.

What might be called the "feminization" of the library in the early nineteenth century did reflect, it seems, pressure from women readers of library society books and periodicals, even though their demands were represented only indirectly, through the requests made by an often exclusively male membership. Greater female borrowing and participation were conducted under the guise of the usually male head of household in whose name the library subscription was maintained. As confirmed by the apologetic letters of the library committees, new orders for novels and the like also reflected a broadened, more relaxed attitude by many of the gentlemen members themselves toward the sorts of books they considered their library might properly stock.

Many fashionable novels continued to be supplied directly from London (with Lackington and Allen a common supplier), but American novels and the reprints of London novels and other popular literature from New York, Philadelphia, and Boston proved irresistible and much-demanded. Both library stock and membership diversification also represented an encroachment on what we might deem the early library society's promotion of male homosociability. In the case of some libraries, such as the Library Company of Philadelphia, the New York Society Library, and the Baltimore Library Company (where nonmembers were allowed access under the general assembly's act of incorporation), male hegemony was diluted. In Philadelphia, women shareholders numbered 29 in 1800, from a known total membership of about

---

73. *Savannah Library Catalogue* (1839) and ms. original, Georgia Historical Society, Savannah Library Society papers, collection no. 695; I am grateful for the assistance of Jewell Anderson, archivist, GHS.

800 by 1820;[74] in other libraries, such as the Charleston Library Society and the Savannah Library Society, the site of exclusively male activity shifted more visibly to the committees, the dinners, and the public ceremonials, now in some contrast to advancing female influence in book selection and borrowing.

A further important consideration is the increase in both private and circulating libraries. As research continues to chart the development of colonial domestic libraries,[75] we can begin to evaluate the ways in which private acquisition worked in concert with the literary supplies offered by the early social libraries. In addition, the advance of circulating libraries from the 1750s also has to be taken into account. In the next essay in this volume, James Green discusses the development of American circulating libraries, emphasizing the extent to which the circulating library obviated the expensive purchase of books, including read-once-only novels, and even the costly membership of a library society. Certainly, in the inventories of Carolina domestic libraries surveyed by Walter Edgar very few women's titles appear. Hannah Glasse's *Art of Cookery* and Smith's *Complete Housewife* were rare exceptions.[76] It was only by the beginning of the new century that the wives and daughters of the propertied began to acquire substantial collections of modern literature for themselves.[77]

Another cause of the change has to do with modes of supply. The isolation that lent the library society enterprise both its vigor and its urgency was a very real challenge that had to be overcome by methods not confronted by similar institutions in Europe. The Philadelphia, New York, Charleston, and later Baltimore libraries all maintained direct London connections, all employing London book-buying agents and booksellers right into the 1820s and beyond, even when from the 1770s (at least) colonial booksellers also offered their services to supply large quantities of European books. They were assisted by new relationships with the London wholesalers. In London by 1800, as in other major European cities, large bookselling firms now offered a range of services formerly conducted at different sites and by different personnel.

In part, also, requests for novels by social libraries might indeed indicate a

---

74. Wolf, *"At the Instance of Benjamin Franklin,"* 20, 38.

75. Recent examples include Piecuch, "Of Great Importance," and Baenen, "Books, Newspapers, and Sociability."

76. Walter B. Edgar, "The Libraries of Colonial South Carolina" (Diss., University of South Carolina, 1969), 46.

77. Emma Philadelphia Middleton, for example, daughter-in-law of the CLS president, Ralph Izard, owned at least twenty-five books of her own (as confirmed by book plates in the Izard Library), and these included popular novels by Bage, Burney, Brooke, and Edgeworth, travel books, and two magazines, *The Lady's Magazine* and *The Literary Magazine and British Review;* see Robert F. Neville and Katherine H. Bielsky, "The Izard Library," *South Carolina Historical and Genealogical Magazine* 91 (1990): 149–70 (162).

certain despairing and indiscriminate ordering policy, as well as a willingness to go along with the more cavalier suggestions of their supplying bookseller or agent. Hundreds of novels did arrive from London in the early nineteenth century, but many were clearly the detritus of London bookshops. This disposal of spares and poor sellers might well have been more significant than the much-discussed consignments of unsalable titles or "rum books" sent out from London first by the likes of Robert Boulter and Richard Chiswell in the late seventeenth century, and then later, in much larger quantities, by Thomas Osborne, William Strahan, and, most notoriously, James Rivington (among others).[78] The American venturing by some early nineteenth-century booksellers seems to have resulted in a repeat of the dumping of "rum books."

There is one final issue. *Reading* now left more of a mark in the society library records, and the surviving borrowing records of the period also suggest the advancing demand for fiction. In the register for the Baltimore Library Company, covering the years 1800 to 1803, for example, the popularity of fiction is clear. In 1800, the borrowing of modern novels far exceeded that of any other literature in the library. In that year almost exactly a quarter of all books borrowed (24.9 percent) were novels, with "literature and criticism" accounting for a further 16 percent. Biography, the next most popular category, comprised 16.4 percent of all borrowings, voyages and travel 14.8 percent, and history 13.7 percent. An 1822 borrowing register from the Savannah Library also charts the extraordinary popularity of fifty-year-old novels of Frances Burney, Henry Brooke's *Fool of Quality,* and much other seasoned fiction besides. At Philadelphia, the novels of Charlotte Smith and Walter Scott were proudly displayed, and, as another example, the earliest extant borrowing records of the Charleston Library Society, dating from 1811, also amply demonstrate the increase in fiction lending. They certainly contrast to the earlier ordering records and the recorded literary discussions of members. The earlier and later holdings of imaginative literature provide the surest and most obvious contrasts. "Literature" comprised 10 percent of the total by title at Charleston in 1770 but 23 percent in 1811, confirming the new enthusiasm of library members in the early nineteenth century for novels and romances. By comparison, the stock of classical literature diminished slightly over these forty years, law and politics remained roughly constant, but the proportion of travel writing doubled (from 4 to 9 percent). Biography and history declined slightly as a proportion of the total Library Society collection.[79]

---

78. See Stephen Botein, "The Anglo-American Book Trade before 1776: Personnel and Strategies," in *Printing and Society in Early America,* ed. William Joyce et al. (Worcester: American Antiquarian Society, 1983), 74–79; and Raven, *London Booksellers and American Customers,* 7, 92.

79. For more detail, see Raven, *London Booksellers and American Customers,* 184–203.

All these registers offer an important cautionary record to compare with the stock lists of the social libraries. Of course, the breadth of the holdings was important to a few members, many of whom browsed and read in the library room as well as borrowing books, and the compass of the holdings was important also to the stature and esteem of the library. However, in terms of popular borrowing tallies (which we can only assume echoed reading experiences) fiction and belles-lettres were well out in front. The actual *number* of such volumes also increased very markedly. The two printed Charleston *Catalogues* of 1806 and 1811, offering a fascinating profile of the expansion in the library's holdings in the early nineteenth century, confirm that total holdings, by volume, increased by an extraordinary 40 percent between 1806 and 1811.

The significance of this transformation can be best summarized in terms of the changing idea of the library and of its social and cultural resonance. In the first place, the foundation of the various social libraries was grounded in considerations that were more ambitious (or, one might argue, more purposefully linked to status and civic enhancement) than simple shelf-stocking policy or reading expectations. Second, the desire to advance sociability and civilization in colonial North America was rooted both in the colonial situation and in effective, if necessarily selective, cosmopolitanism. As Richard Bushman has put it, "America enjoyed bits and pieces of London."[80] Early American library development hinged upon the social, political, and business worlds constructed by the different trades across the Atlantic—relationships perhaps most effectively studied to date by economic historians.[81] Third, the social and political engagement of the Library Society was by no means passive. Power in the colonies was exerted by cultural forces quite in addition to the systems and hierarchies resulting from the grounding economic conditions of empire. In situations where local political authority might be weakened by the absence or lack of confidence in a traditional, familiar structure, this fashioning of symbolic power was largely enabled by forms of material consumption (and hence energetic importation) that forged new knowledge, differences, and values.[82] To borrow the observation of Anthony P. Cohen:

---

80. Richard L. Bushman, "American High-Style and Vernacular Culture," in *Colonial British America: Essays in the New History of the Early Modern Era,* ed. Jack P. Greene and J. R. Pole (Baltimore: Johns Hopkins University Press, 1984), 368.

81. Notably, David Hancock, *Citizens of the World: London Merchants and the Integration of the British Atlantic Community, 1735–1785* (Cambridge: Cambridge University Press, 1995).

82. See, for example, T. H. Breen, "Baubles of Britain: The American and Consumer Revolutions of the Eighteenth Century," *Past and Present* 119 (1988): 73–104; T. H. Breen, "An Empire of Goods: The Anglicization of Colonial America, 1690–1976," *Journal of British Studies* 25 (1986): 467–99; and Cary Carson, Ronald Hoffman, and Peter J. Albert, eds., *Of Consuming Interests: The*

"people construct community symbolically, making it a resource and repository of meaning, and a referent of their identity."[83]

In such ways histories of library institutions, their members, their material collection, and their usage can help in investigating the relationship between print and the different appearances, understandings, and expressions of such politically charged "community." Gabriel Manigault in South Carolina described his Library Society as a "private community,"[84] his terminology conceptualizing a unified group acting within a broader local society, that did significant cultural work by cultivating a sense of literary and social belonging. Here, moreover, was an abstraction of community that reached back and forth across the English countryside, the Irish Channel, *and* the Atlantic, supplying texts to foster argument, but also a sociability that countermanded colonial political divisions among members.

The final point has broader implications. In recent cultural histories of the eighteenth century, various concepts of sociability have been proposed in refinement of or in contrast to the idea of stringently politicized communities. A sociability commonly based on taverns, salons, coffeehouses, and the like has been considered in its wider, discursive effects as unbounded or at least only informally contained. David Shields, for example, has modified the influential and general evaluations of Habermas, rightly emphasizing Habermas's uninterest in the nonpolitical and, at least superficially, nonideological inducement to the formation of private societies. Agreed, the American social libraries were not simply communities of conscience, and many (to adapt Shields's words) "confessed wit, affection, or appetite as the grounds of community, not conscience."[85] But questions of access and of the construction of class identities should not be downgraded. The development of the library societies and library companies suggests socially instrumental institutions, formally organized. The quest for unity did not proscribe hierarchical division.

By contrast, the ideal of learned reading, as has often been pointed out, offered in the Revolutionary and early national period the allure not just of social advancement but of a purported democracy of understanding and

Style of Life in the Eighteenth Century (Charlottesville: Published for the United States Capitol Historical Society by the University Press of Virginia, 1994). Underlying theories are discussed in Robert Bocock, *Consumption* (London: Routledge, 1993); and Martyn J. Lee, *Consumer Culture Reborn: The Cultural Politics of Consumption* (London: Routledge, 1993).

83. Anthony P. Cohen, *The Symbolic Construction of Community* (London: Ellis Horwood and Tavistock Publications, 1985), 118.

84. CLS, QM 3 October 1764, CLS, "Journal," fols. 45–46.

85. Shields, *Civil Tongues and Polite Letters in British America,* xvi.

egalitarian improvement. This reasoning famously characterized Franklin's eulogy to libraries in his *Autobiography,* but it fit uneasily with the founding declarations made by Franklin's fellow library founders across the colonies. As noted above, most manifestos emphasized the nobility of learning that supported the "liberality" of gentility. Many of the young men establishing proprietary libraries at midcentury were aspirant rather than established political or economic worthies, but within a generation or so their library presidents and committees comprised some of the most elite names available. Although regarded and indeed described by their members as "public" librar-ies, such shareholding, subscription societies clearly formed elite institutions, promoting a liberality that also represented freedom from material need. This mission, moreover, was enabled by the entrepreneurial understanding and dexterity of many of the founding members and their merchant and profes-sional successors.

The degree to which library institutions invited wider public participation became much more variable in the early national period. Many new founda-tions (notably Baltimore) explicitly aimed at inclusivity, but we should not underestimate geographical differences and residual loyalties. Large paintings of George III and Queen Charlotte remained over the doors of the Charleston Library Society at least until the 1820s, something hardly to be countenanced in Philadelphia, Boston, or New York. The relationship between national and state identity was similarly variable, at least according to basic comparisons of library correspondence and holdings. The further consequence of the attempts of many smaller social libraries to increase membership was to confuse further the boundaries between proprietary and subscription libraries by demoting or circumventing share-ownership requirements in return for new categories of paying membership. The untidiness of many rearrangements was the greater when measured against the advance of town circulating libraries from the late eighteenth century.[86]

It was, above all, the general cast of literary interests that changed so dra-matically in the early nineteenth century. Decline and fragmentation have headlined the post-Revolution story of the social library, most conspicuously in New England,[87] but the closure and reformation of the dozens of small town libraries is counterpointed by the survival and reorientation of many of the larger libraries. Times were troubled—not just because of the fires that destroyed foundation collections at Providence in 1758 and at Charles-

---

86. Shera, *Foundations,* 71, 73–75, 127–55.

87. Ibid., 123–29; see also discussion of the Portsmouth dissolutions and refoundings in Baenen, "Books, Newspapers, and Sociability."

ton twenty years later (as well as the destruction of the New York collections in the Revolution in 1776), but because of post-Revolutionary social turbulence that undermined existing elites and the status-enhancement projects of many library societies. In the survival of the major social libraries, we observe the evolution of different membership profiles and different reading practices (despite the frequent protests from unchanging governing committees and personnel).

Reading had at first been conceptualized in programmatic language. As late as 1783 and the resumption of London trade after the war, the correspondent of the Library Company of Philadelphia assured Woods and Dillwyn that "tho we would wish to mix the *Utile* with the *Dulce,* we should not think it expedient to add to our present stock, anything in the *novel* way."[88] The founding "moral, useful, reading" was intended to be communal and consensual, not ideological, an exercise in the promotion of civility but also of intellectual containment. Four or so generations later, the breakdown in concepts of this function was, paradoxically, fueled by a continuing (and even strengthening) dependency of supply from London—the new imperialism was grounded in what, borrowing from concerns of the time, we might term "useless reading" and in commodified literature (by a new vociferousness among an enlarged membership and by new efficiencies in London marketing and wholesaling). The conceits of a 1794 letter from Woods and Dillwyn to the Philadelphia library cannot disguise the tensions over new supplies and the latitude given to the firm to send over additional books:

> In making provision for a number of minds we allow there may be as much Difficulty as in catering for the Bodies that belong to them. In both cases the truth of the old Adage may be perceived "De Gustibus non disputandum est." A vitiated Taste is not to be gratified, nor what would injure the Constitution to be admitted. Our aim is to assist you in setting before your Company some wholesome and well-dressed Dishes among which every one may consult his own taste, and indulge his appetite with Moderation and Profit.[89]

For members determined to extend the intellectual resources of their library, the widening of book acquisition challenged the values established by American library society founders in emulation of particular notions of civility. The civic image of the proprietary libraries was clearly sustained (eventually by grandiose new buildings, which allowed library collections to

---

88. Cited in Wolf, *"At the Instance of Benjamin Franklin,"* 24–25.
89. Library Company of Philadelphia, Letter files, letter from Woods and Dillwyn, 31 March 1794.

migrate from the custody of court- and state-houses), but many more library members were now enthusiastic readers, less burdened than their predecessors by wider social obligations and the pursuit of self-promotion. The transformation and adaptation of many social libraries enabled both the development of special associations determined by reader interests and by occupational, gender, or age profiles, and the diversification of established "library societies" to embrace wider-ranging collections and services.

Chapter 2

Subscription Libraries and Commercial Circulating Libraries in Colonial Philadelphia and New York

James Green

From the 1730s to the 1760s, all American libraries that circulated books to the public were subscription libraries. They were owned and supported by private individual shareholders, who could borrow books so long as they paid their annual subscription dues. Some were also open to the general public for reference, and some, like the Library Company of Philadelphia, even had provisions for non-shareholders to borrow books upon payment of a cash deposit. Then in the 1760s a new type of library suddenly appeared, commercial circulating libraries. These were individually owned — generally by booksellers — and patrons could borrow books for a modest fee. Because their owners were entrepreneurs who hoped to turn a profit, they tended to reach out to the public by advertising, by making their premises inviting especially to women, and by stocking the most current and popular books. In towns where there was already a well-established subscription library, these new libraries appealed to readers who for any number of reasons could not or did not want to join a subscription library. They offered a different type of reading material and a different type of reading experience. There is no direct evidence of outright competition for readers between these two types of library, but indirect evidence can be found in changes that occurred in subscription libraries at the exact times and places where commercial circulating libraries began to flourish. These changes included more liberal acccss policies and a more popular choice of books, both of which made the subscription libraries more like the new commercial ones. This kind of competition can only be inferred in cities with a complex library environment, including both numerous circulating libraries and multiple subscription libraries with a strong public presence. There were only two such cities in the colonies, New York, and Philadelphia. This essay will focus mainly on Philadelphia, where documentation is plentiful in the archives of the Library Company of

Philadelphia and in the circulation register of a 1770 commercial library, but evidence suggests a similar competitive environment in New York.

At the end of the first part of his *Autobiography*, written in 1771, Franklin described the founding of the Library Company in 1731.

> And now I set on foot my first Project of a public Nature, that for a Subscription Library. I drew up the Proposals . . . and by the help of my Friends in the Junto, procur'd Fifty Subscribers of 40/ each to begin with & 10/ a Year. . . . This was the Mother of all the N American Subscription Libraries now so numerous.[1]

Following his terminology, these libraries are still called "subscription librar- ies," as if the apparatus of subscribing, buying shares, and paying annual dues was their defining characteristic. When Franklin resumed writing his *Autobi- ography* in 1784, he told the same story again, but this time emphasizing other aspects of the Library Company: it was also a public library—and one from which books could be borrowed.

> Not having any Copy here [in Passy] of what is already written, I know not whether an Account is given of the means I used to establish the Philadelphia publick Library. . . . I will therefore begin there. . . . The Members of the Junto [Franklin's discussion group for mutual improvement] had . . . hired a Room to hold our Club in. I propos'd that we should all of us bring our Books to that Room, where they would not only be ready to consult in our Conferences, but become a common Benefit, each of us being at Liberty to borrow such as he wish'd to read at home. . . . Finding the Advantage of this little Collection, I propos'd to render the Benefit from Books more common by commencing a Public Subscription Library.[2]

His object was to build a permanent reference collection, "ready to consult," but also a collection that would circulate to those who "wish'd to read at home." He also wished it to be open not only to shareholders, but also to the public. According to the "Short Account of the Library" appended to its first extant catalogue (1741; see figure 2.1),

> Those who are not Subscribers may notwithstanding borrow Books, Leaving in the Hands of the Librarian, as a Pledge, a Sum of Money proportion'd to the Value of the Book borrow'd, and paying a small Acknowledgment for the Reading.[3]

---

1. J. A. Leo Lemay, ed., *Benjamin Franklin. Writings* (New York: The Library of America, 1987), 1372.

2. Ibid., 1379–80.

3. *A Catalogue of Books belonging to the Library Company of Philadelphia* (Philadelphia: Printed by B. Franklin, 1741), 56.

A
CATALOGUE
OF
BOOKS
BELONGING TO THE
LIBRARY COMPANY
OF
PHILADELPHIA.

Communiter bona profundere Deûm eſt.

PHILADELPHIA: Printed by *B. Franklin,* 1741.

Figure 2.1. Title page of *A Catalogue of Books Belonging to the Library Company of Philadelphia* (Philadelphia: Printed by B. Franklin, 1741). Courtesy of the Library Company of Philadelphia.

In practice, nonmembers were required to pay from four to eight pence per week depending on the size of the book, and to leave a cash deposit of twice the book's value with the librarian.

Thus the Library Company was by no means free, but it placed a substantial library within the reach of most middle-class Philadelphians. Nor was it ever publicly funded, though it was formally chartered in 1742 by the Proprietors of Pennsylvania as a company, what we would call a nonprofit organization operated for public benefit. Nor do we know exactly how "the public" was defined. The first shareholders spanned a fairly wide social spectrum from mechanics and tradesmen like Franklin to gentlemen of means, but they were all free white men. We know members of a shareholder's family could borrow books. But would a woman not related to a shareholder have been able to borrow a book on the terms stated for non-subscribers? How about an indentured servant or a free African? Would they even be permitted to read in the library without borrowing? The library's records offer no clues. The Library Company was certainly not what we would call a public library today, but it was as close to being a public library as any in colonial America.

Before 1731, circulating libraries in the colonies were rare. Of the three known seventeenth-century New England town libraries, in Boston, New Haven, and Concord, Massachusetts, only Concord had regular provisions for borrowing books, and there is no indication that it continued to exist after 1672, the year it was founded.[4] Thomas Prince imagined a circulating collection adjunct to his New England Library in 1726, but that part of his scheme was deemed impractical and apparently not implemented.[5] Not until the Revolutionary era did students regularly borrow books from Harvard's library.[6]

The only circulating libraries known to be functioning in the colonies

4. Jesse H. Shera, *Foundations of the Public Library: The Origins of the Public Library Movement in New England, 1629–1855* (Chicago: University of Chicago Press, 1949), 25. ALB1876 (American libraries before 1876), a database hosted by Princeton, confirms that these were the only public libraries in colonial America. Cf. http://www.princeton.edu/~davpro/databases/index.html

5. Hugh Amory, "A Boston Society Library: The Old South Church and Thomas Prince," in *Bibliography and the Book Trades, Studies in the Print Culture of Early New England*, ed. David Hall (Philadelphia: University of Pennsylvania Press, 2004). Amory notes that Prince "also left his Church 'all my Books that are in Latin, Greek, & in the Oriental Languages, to be kept, and remain in the Public Library for ever.' This second 'Public' or 'South Church Library,' according to its separate bookplate, goes back to 1718, when Prince began to serve as the Church's pastor with his classmate Joseph Sewall. It is next attested in 1726, when he approached Judge Sewall, Joseph's father, with a 'Schem for a Lending Library.' The Judge deemed it 'inconvenient' — i.e. an inappropriate project for a church."

6. Mark Olsen and Louis-Georges Harvey, "Reading in Revolutionary Times: Book Borrowing from the Harvard College Library, 1773–1782," *Harvard Library Bulletin*, n.s. 4 (1993): 57–72, describes the first surviving records of books charged to Harvard students. There was sporadic bor-

when Franklin was a young man were adjuncts to the libraries established by the English philanthropist Thomas Bray around 1700. Bray set up Provincial Libraries in Boston, New York, Philadelphia, and Charleston, and smaller Parochial Libraries in a number of towns and villages throughout the colonies. He intended the Provincial and Parochial Libraries to be permanent reference libraries, but he saw a need for circulating collections as well, so he added a "Layman's Library" to each of them. These consisted of a selection of popular devotional works that the ministers could loan to parishioners and discuss with them when they were returned. He included multiple titles of some books so they could be given away, especially where they might help lure sinners into the fold. Bray established forty-two Layman's Libraries and sent over 34,000 additional books and tracts to be given away, but no trace of them has survived. It is doubtful that any of these libraries lasted very long. Nor were they expected to; Bray intended their holdings to be dispersed gradually among the people.[7]

In at least one instance, however, local authorities modified Bray's scheme and made his whole library into a circulating collection. In 1700 the South Carolina Assembly passed a law allowing any inhabitant of the colony to borrow from the Provincial Library just established in Charleston. Twelve years later, noting heavy losses of books from the collection, the Assembly passed a new statute with provisions intended to mitigate the "unrestrained Liberty" of the 1700 law. It appointed eminent trustees and erected elaborate checks and sanctions to prevent the loss of books, but these efforts were in vain, and books continued to be reported lost or stolen. Another cause of the library's neglect was the disapproval of some parts of the community who thought its Anglican bias was too marked. Whatever the reasons, the library melted away some time before 1724, when a local schoolmaster noted that there was no library in the town.[8] The problem with circulating libraries was that they tended to self-destruct gradually as borrowers read the books to pieces or simply failed to return them. A permanent reference collection was seemingly different from and incompatible with a circulating library.

The Library Company was the first public circulating library in the colo-

---

rowing by students before that date. Cf. Thomas Hollis's admonishing letter of 1735: "You let your books be taken at pleasure to Mens houses, and many are lost. Your (boyish) Students take them to their chambers, and teare out pictures and Maps to adorne the Walls; such things are not good." Quoted in Peter J. Gomes, "Thomas Hollis of London and His Gifts," *Harvard Library Bulletin*, n.s. 13 (2002): 11.

7. Charles T. Laugher, *Thomas Bray's Grand Design: Libraries of the Church of England in America, 1695–1785* (Chicago: American Library Association, 1973), 34, 52–54.

8. *The Laws of the Province of South Carolina* (Charleston: L. Timothy, 1736), 77, 207; James R. Raven, *London Booksellers and American Customers: Transatlantic Literary Community and the Charleston Library Society, 1758–1811* (Columbia: University of South Carolina Press, 2002), 34.

nies that succeeded in maintaining a permanent collection. The subscription scheme was the means used to achieve permanence and sustainability. It worked because borrowers had a strong financial incentive to return books; otherwise shareholders forfeited their share and non-shareholders their cash deposit. (It also helped that the librarian was held financially accountable for damage and losses.) The library was a hybrid of public and private, supported by private subscription but was also a chartered nonprofit institution open to the public.[9] This hybrid was peculiarly suited to the American colonies, and it flourished. Libraries on the same principle soon appeared in other large towns: the Charleston Library Society; the New York Society Library; and three emulators in Philadelphia itself, the Association, Amicable, and Union Library Companies. They also appeared in 16 smaller towns in New England by 1760, rising to 51 towns by 1780.[10]

There is no clear English model for Franklin's subscription library scheme, though it bears similarity to private book clubs like the 1710 Spalding Gentlemen's Society. The earliest so-called subscription library in England was Fancourt's in Salisbury, established some time in the 1730s; he moved it to London in 1742, where it was called a circulating library. It is not clear whether it was privately owned, but at least it was open to the paying public. When chartered subscription libraries more along American lines were introduced in England later in the eighteenth century, they were not nearly so successful or widespread as commercial circulating libraries.[11]

Perhaps just because subscription libraries were so widespread in the colonies, commercial circulating libraries were slow to appear. In fact they were unknown until 1763, when more or less simultaneously they appeared in Annapolis, Charleston, and New York. The idea spread to Boston in 1765, Philadelphia in 1767, and Baltimore in 1773.[12] This sudden proliferation reflects the general expansion of reading and print production that was taking place throughout the Atlantic world, and nowhere more rapidly than in America. Literacy rates were increasing steadily in the northern colonies, rising from 70 percent among white men in 1710 to 90 percent by 1790. Literacy rates among white women were lower when measured by the ability to

---

9. Edwin Wolf et al., *"At the Instance of Benjamin Franklin": A Brief History of the Library Company of Philadelphia,* rev. and enl. ed. (Philadelphia: The Library Company of Philadelphia, 1995), 5–11.

10. Shera, *Foundations,* 55, 68.

11. Paul Kaufman, *The Community Library: A Chapter in English Social History* (Philadelphia: American Philosophical Society, 1967), 25, estimates the ratio of commercial to subscription libraries in eighteenth-century England at ten to one. Amory speculates that Franklin would have known about the circulating library Prince projected in 1726 ("A Boston Society Library," 3).

12. David Kaser, *A Book for a Sixpence: The Circulating Library in America* (Pittsburgh: Beta Phi Mu, 1980), 19–43, noting several earlier instances of informal lending of books by booksellers.

write, but reading ability may have been much higher, especially in the cities. This meant not only more readers, but also a widening circle of readers, more women and more of middling economic status. The number of printers and printing centers was also increasing, and the quantity of print they produced more than doubled between 1740 and 1770. Imported books always made up the larger part of what colonial Americans read, however, and during that same period from 1740 to 1770 book imports increased more than tenfold in the middle colonies, with the rate of change accelerating in the 1760s.[13]

These changes may not have had much effect on the bulk of the population, but in Philadelphia and New York, the local book culture was becoming more and more like that of York or Bristol, or even of Dublin or Edinburgh. Booksellers for the first time became purveyors of fashion, as their contacts with British exporters became closer and the time lag between publication and reception in America dwindled to a matter of months. This is just another aspect of the rise of consumerism and the quest for refinement that historians see in all aspects of late colonial culture. It is also perhaps an aspect of the accelerating convergence of English and American culture and society that according to some historians preceded and to some extent brought on the Revolution. What it meant for the widening circle of urban readers was not only new kinds of reading material but new reading practices and experiences; and circulating libraries were an important part of that. Circulating libraries made it possible for readers of middling economic status to read a great many more books than ever before. Even the borrowing terms and fees encouraged them to read quickly and exchange their books often. Novels were perfectly suited to this type of reading, and thus the novel emerged in the 1760s as a type of book that was more often borrowed than owned, like videos today. The same can be said of plays. A few novels or plays in a circulating library's stock could quickly reach hundreds of readers, and create a fashion that could sweep like wildfire through a small city such as Philadelphia, with a mere 5,000 households in 1765.[14]

---

13. James Raven, "The Importation of Books in the Eighteenth Century," James N. Green, "English Books and Printing in the Age of Franklin," and Ross W. Beales and E. Jennifer Monaghan, "Literacy and Schoolbooks," in *The Colonial Book in the Atlantic World*, ed. Hugh Amory and David D. Hall, vol. 1 of *A History of the Book in America* (Cambridge: Cambridge University Press and the American Antiquarian Society, 2000), 183–93, 276–95, 380.

14. Richard L. Bushman, *The Refinement of America: Persons, Houses, Cities* (New York: Knopf, 1992); Jack Greene, *Pursuits of Happiness: The Social Development of Early Modern British Colonies and the Formation of American Culture* (Chapel Hill: University of North Carolina Press, 1988); T. H. Breen, "'Baubles of Britain': The American and Consumer Revolutions of the Eighteenth Century," *Past and Present* 119 (1998): 73–104. Green, "English Books," in *The Colonial Book*, ed. Amory and Hall, 261ff. For Philadelphia's population in the late colonial period, see Russell F. Weigley, ed., *Philadelphia: A 300-Year History* (New York: W. W. Norton, 1982), 79.

Even in the largest colonial cities there was a limit to how many libraries could thrive. When a new library came into existence, it had to carve out a niche, either by taking patrons away from the libraries already established or by somehow attracting new patrons; and often the old libraries changed to adapt to the new environment. This dynamic was all the more complex when different types of libraries with different financing offering different services to different clienteles tried to coexist. For example, the first circulating library in New York was established at just the moment when the city's subscription library was temporarily closed for business. In August 1763, New York's City Hall closed for repairs, necessitating the closure of the subscription library housed there, the New York Society Library (established 1754). Days later bookseller Garrat Noel announced the opening of a circulating library. He saw the City Hall renovation as a business opportunity, an opening in the market, and he leapt into it. By August 1765, the City Hall repairs were complete and the library reopened, and on September 19 Noel placed his last newspaper advertisement, after which no more is heard of his library.[15]

In 1771, another attempt was made to launch a new library in New York, but this time it was a second subscription library, the Union Library Society. Its competitive advantage was that its shares were considerably cheaper. The day after the new library was announced to the public, the Society Library applied for a charter from the governor, an action that strongly suggests that it felt a threat of competition. The new library soon surpassed the old in number of subscribers, and so the old one found it prudent to reduce the price of its shares in 1772. In 1774, bookseller Samuel Loudon, sensing an expanding market for books and readers, opened a circulating library, the first since Garret Noel's closed nine years before. Three months later the Union Library Society moved into City Hall to share quarters with its erstwhile competitor. Apparently there was room for two libraries in the marketplace of readers, but not yet three.[16]

The library environment in Philadelphia was even more complex. In the years before the Revolution there were four subscription libraries (the Library Company, 1731, the Union Library Company, 1746, the Association Library Company, 1757, and the Amicable Library, 1758) and three commercial circulating libraries (Lewis Nicola's, 1767, Thomas Bradford's, 1769, and Robert Bell's, 1774). Franklin's Library Company for many years was seemingly

---

15. Austin Baxter Keep, *History of the New York Society Library* (New York: De Vinne Press, 1908), 78–106.

16. Ibid., 115–16, and 108–10. By 1772, a share in the Society Library cost about 14 pounds (see note 20 below). The 1773 *Charter, and Bye-Laws* stated that new shares could be had for just 5 pounds if purchased before May 1774 (p.14). This remained the price until 1791 (ibid., 216).

unaffected by the three rival subscription libraries in the city, but in 1763 the death of its long-serving librarian Robert Greenway ushered in a period of instability and change. The librarian was personally responsible for the collection, and upon stepping down from his post he was obliged to take inventory and replace any missing books at his own expense. This rule was supposed to be an incentive for him to enforce the rules about returning books. Before Greenway the librarianship had turned over every year or two, so this was not a serious burden, but he had held the office for seventeen years, during which time no inventory had been taken. Now the required inventory revealed that Greenway had been lax and "Books to a considerable value were missing." The deeply disturbed directors attempted to seek restitution from Greenway's estate, apparently in vain.[17] Thus began a period of instability and change. For years to come librarians rash enough to take the job quit after their first annual inventory, despite ever increasing salary offers, rising from £6 annually to £60 by 1773.[18]

So disturbed were the directors by their losses that they decided that henceforth only the librarian would be allowed access to the shelves, and that books would be brought to members in a space known as "outside the rails." (The Library was then in a room or rooms on the second floor of the east wing of Independence Hall.) When some members objected, a counterproposal was made that those who wished to have access to the shelves should sign a bond making them liable, along with the librarian, for a share of any lost books. This sparked a formal members' protest. At a special meeting, the members made yet another proposal: drop the rule holding the librarian accountable for the books, and exclude nonmembers from the Library altogether. All of these proposed changes were too radical for the directors, and they stood their ground, decreeing that nonmembers and members alike were to be served outside the rails, and "No person except the Librarian is to be admitted into the Library."[19]

By this time the Library Company was no longer the only library in Philadelphia. Three new subscription libraries had arisen since 1746, and within a few years circulating libraries would begin to appear as well. By demanding better library services, its shareholders were beginning to act like consumers with a choice. It took a few years for the library's directors to realize that they needed to change their practices in order to retain their shareholders and attract new ones in this more competitive environment.

---

17. Library Company of Philadelphia Directors' Minutes (hereafter LCP Minutes) I:219, 21 November 1763; I:225, 13 February 1764.

18. Ibid., I:86, 10 May 1773.

19. Ibid., I:226, 12 March 1764; I:230, 27 August 1764; I:233, 14 January 1765.

The Library Company's greatest competitive disadvantage was the steadily rising cost of its shares, from two pounds in 1731 to over fifteen in the mid-1760s. The rise in library share prices has sometimes been considered by historians as an appreciation of their value or the result of some kind of speculation, but in fact it was a consequence of a little-understood practice of all the early subscription libraries in Philadelphia and New York: no new member could have a share for less than other members had already invested. Thus someone who bought a Library Company share in 1732 had to pay the original forty shillings plus the ten shillings annual dues the first sharehold-ers had paid in 1731, and so forth year by year. In effect the cost of a share rose automatically ten shillings per year. Each of the three new subscription libraries that arose in Philadelphia after 1746 had initially priced its shares at forty shillings, but all the new libraries had the same annual dues of ten shil-lings and the same rule about equal investment, so shares of all four libraries became more expensive to buy with each passing year. The older the library (and the larger the collection), the more expensive it was to join. Presumably most people looking to buy a share in a library chose one of the newer ones.[20] As a result, only ten new shares had been issued in Greenway's seventeen years, leading both to an overall decline of revenue at just the moment when the librarian's salary had to be raised and to a sharp reduction in the rate of growth of the collection.[21]

When Lewis Nicola opened a circulating library in Philadelphia in 1767, it cost £21 to join the Library Company, plus the 10 shillings annual dues. By contrast, a year's subscription to Nicola's library cost $3, or about 22 shillings, later reduced to $2. Readers could also subscribe for shorter periods, and undoubtedly most chose the lowest rate, six pence a week. (See figure 2.2.) Readers were allowed to take out only one book at a time, but the library was open six days a week, compared to one day a week at the Library Company, so an avid user of Nicola's library could exchange books daily and spend as little as a penny a book.[22]

Nicola expected to attract a broad demographic to his establishment.

20. Keep, *New York Society Library*, 173, quotes the *New York Gazette*, 19 September 1765, with reference to the New York Society Library: "A share in the Library is now worth 10 l. 10 s." and goes on to note, "which quotation indicates increased market valuation." But that is simply the total of the original share cost (5 pounds in 1754) plus eleven years of dues at 10s. per year. The Association Library Company made this practice into a formal rule by setting the price of a new share at "such a sum of money as . . . will at the time of each subscription, render the subscriber's share of equal value with any of the rest." *A Catalogue of Books, belonging to the Association Library of Philadelphia* (Philadelphia, Printed by William Bradford, 1765), 4.

21. Library Company of Philadelphia, Register of Shares, Ms., ca. 1800, 17.

22. Advertisements in *Pennsylvania Journal*, 10 September 1767, *Pennsylvania Gazette*, 12 January 1769, *Pennsylvania Packet*, 23 December 1771. Lewis Nicola (1717–1807) emigrated to Philadelphia

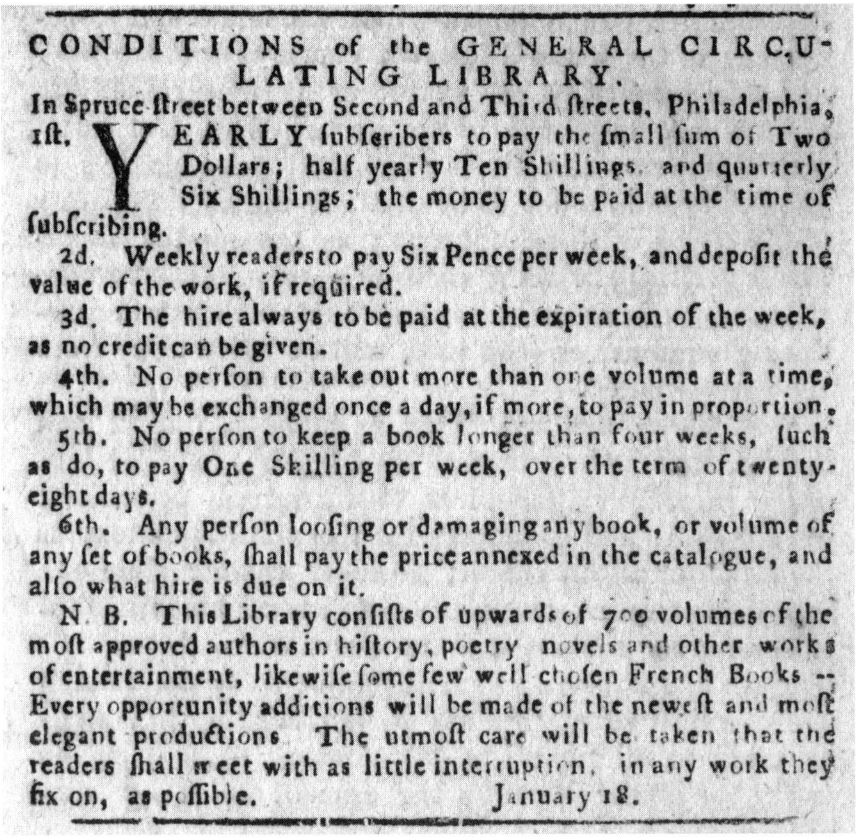

CONDITIONS of the GENERAL CIRCU-
LATING LIBRARY.
In Spruce-ſtreet between Second and Third ſtreets, Philadelphia,

1ſt.   YEARLY ſubſcribers to pay the ſmall ſum of Two
Dollars; half yearly Ten Shillings, and quarterly
Six Shillings; the money to be paid at the time of
ſubſcribing.

2d.   Weekly readers to pay Six Pence per week, and depoſit the
value of the work, if required.

3d.   The hire always to be paid at the expiration of the week,
as no credit can be given.

4th.   No perſon to take out more than one volume at a time,
which may be exchanged once a day, if more, to pay in proportion.

5th.   No perſon to keep a book longer than four weeks, ſuch
as do, to pay One Shilling per week, over the term of twenty-
eight days.

6th.   Any perſon looſing or damaging any book, or volume of
any ſet of books, ſhall pay the price annexed in the catalogue, and
alſo what hire is due on it.

N. B.   This Library conſiſts of upwards of 700 volumes of the
moſt approved authors in hiſtory, poetry novels and other works
of entertainment, likewiſe ſome few well choſen French Books --
Every opportunity additions will be made of the neweſt and moſt
elegant productions The utmoſt care will be taken that the
readers ſhall meet with as little interruption, in any work they
fix on, as poſſible.   January 18.

Figure 2.2.   Advertisement for Nicola's General Circulating Library, *Pennsylvania Journal*, 18 January 1770. Courtesy of the Library Company of Philadelphia.

Women and young people were welcome, and they could choose their own books without the supervision of husband or father. For a year or two Nicola's library even shared space with a bonnet shop, a place women and girls felt comfortable entering, and a place devoted to their pleasure. By contrast, all the Library Company's shareholders were men at that point.[23]

---

from Ireland in 1766 and first operated a dry goods store, which may at first have shared quarters with his circulating library. For nine months in 1769 he published *The American Magazine, or General Repository*, in which he included several papers presented at the American Philosophical Society, of which he was a curator. As an officer in the Revolutionary army he wrote a *Treatise of Military Exercise* (Philadelphia, 1776); see Robert F. Haggard, "The Nicola Affair: Lewis Nicola, George Washington, and American Military Discontent during the Revolutionary War," *Proceedings of the American Philosophical Society* 146 (2002): 139–69.

23. Wolf, *"At the Instance of Benjamin Franklin,"* 19–20.

Another competitive advantage of Nicola's library was in the choice of books. The Library Company was a collection of worthy and approved titles, already aging as any permanent collection does. No catalogue of Nicola's library survives, but his advertisements mention a collection of 500 volumes, rising to over 1,000 by 1771, and many new novels are mentioned by title. A taste for novel reading was developing belatedly but rapidly in the 1760s in the colonial seaport towns, and Nicola catered to it, while the Library Company ignored this and other new kinds of light reading. Its 1764 catalogue listed over 1,000 books but only one English novel, *Tom Jones.*

In 1768, perhaps in response to the challenge posed by Nicola's library, the Library Company stopped the annual escalation of share prices and froze the price at ten pounds. The minutes record the reasons for this decision:

> The Directors then took into consideration the high price of a share in the Library Company which now amounts to £21 and the inconveniences attending its continually encreasing. After mature deliberation, they unanimously agreed that it would be expedient to lower the Price of a Share to Ten Pounds and to fix it at that sum, by which means it was supposed many People would be induced to purchase in, and the annual income of the Company be considerably augmented.

Almost immediately seventeen new members were enrolled, and in November an order for fifty-five new books was sent off to England, the first in a long time.[24]

This change made Library Company shares much cheaper and also nearly the same price as those of the younger and smaller subscription libraries. This removed their competitive advantage and set the stage for a series of rapid mergers. By the middle of 1769, the Library Company had absorbed all the shareholders, books, and property of the other three subscription libraries. As a result of this merger, the library doubled in size to over 2,000 titles, and the number of novels rose to a respectable sixty-four. The number of shareholders tripled. One of the other libraries had a few women members, who by this merger automatically became members of the Library Company. No notice of this change was taken in the minutes, but from then on a small but growing number of shareholders were women.

The consolidation of the subscription libraries reduced the number of libraries in town to two, one much larger and more affordable subscription library and Nicola's circulating library. Thomas Bradford, the youngest scion

---

24. LCP Minutes, I:254, 11 January 1768; I:262, 1 November 1768. As noted above, the New York Society Library reduced its share prices in 1773.

of an old printing and bookselling family, now perceived a niche for a second commercial circulating library, and he proceeded to open one in September 1769, just a few weeks after the consolidation of the subscription libraries was finalized. It was not located in the family printing office, bookstore, and coffeehouse at Front and Market Streets, but rather in his house in a more residential neighborhood near Fourth and Arch Streets. Nicola's library was at Third and Spruce Streets, in a different residential quarter, and the Library Company was near Fifth and Chestnut Streets, close to the State House but still near the western edge of the thickly settled part of the city. These locations were only a few blocks apart; nevertheless it is striking how nearly equidistant the three libraries were from one another, and from Bradford's coffeehouse, which was in the commercial center of the city. This choice of location is one more suggestion that the circulating libraries saw themselves competing with one another as well as with the Library Company. It is especially striking because ordinary commercial establishments tended to compete by clustering together. The location of the three libraries suggests that readers wanted libraries close to their homes and their domestic life, rather than in a central location where the whole city came to work or shop.

We know more about Bradford's library than any other colonial circulating library, thanks to the survival of a ledger of circulation records for one year (1771–72; see figure 2.3). From this I have been able to reconstruct a catalogue and some facts about the clientele. The contents of Bradford's library were dramatically different from those of the Library Company, and that apparently was his competitive strategy. The stock of 300 titles was 63 percent fiction, compared with less than 4 percent at the Library Company, even after the mergers of 1769. Moreover the novels were for the most part new; three-quarters of them first appeared in the preceding decade.[25] Bradford was putting all his money on one type of book, betting that this new genre would take the city by storm, and it did: some 7,000 volumes circulated that year, fully 86 percent of them novels.

In clientele, too, there was little overlap with the Library Company, since almost half of Bradford's borrowers were women.[26] The Bradford library was probably in his front parlor, and the actual manager appears to have been his

---

25. This was a much higher proportion of fiction than can be found even in other commercial libraries where catalogues are extant. Kaser, *Book for a Sixpence,* 173, analyzes those catalogues by subject and finds fiction accounting for 14 percent in John Mein's Boston catalogue of 1765 and 24 percent in Aikman's 1773 Annapolis catalogue. Note, however, than the total number of novels in Aikman's library, 205, actually exceeded Bradford's (195).

26. Thomas Bradford, Library Register, 1771–1772, Historical Society of Pennsylvania, collection no. 70.

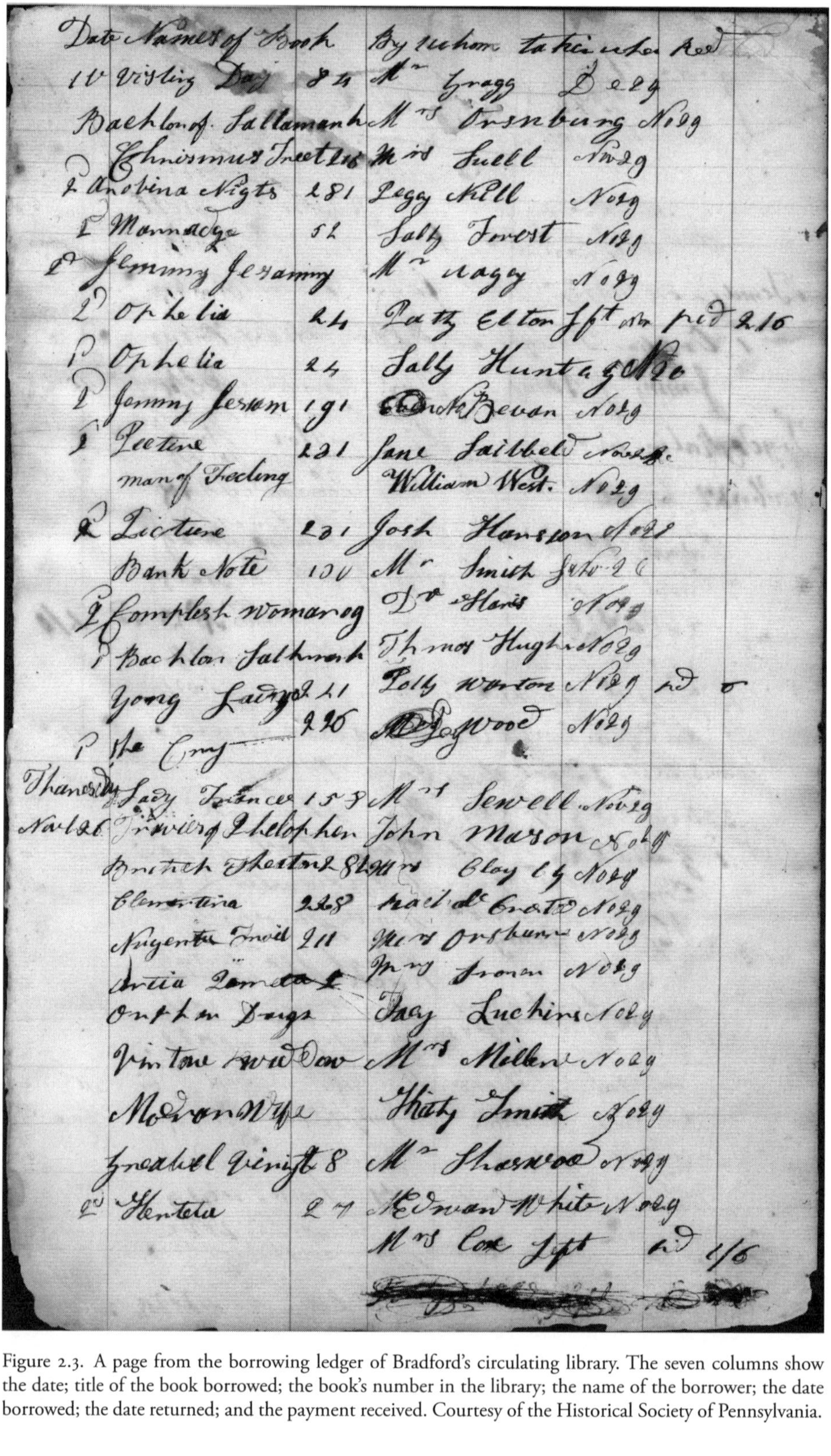

Figure 2.3. A page from the borrowing ledger of Bradford's circulating library. The seven columns show the date; title of the book borrowed; the book's number in the library; the name of the borrower; the date borrowed; the date returned; and the payment received. Courtesy of the Historical Society of Pennsylvania.

wife Polly. In effect it was a shop, where you chose your book and took it away, but it was also part of a domestic space, and Mrs. Bradford may have welcomed customers and friends through the same door if not in the same room. The ledger shows that regular readers visited almost daily in the same groups; they were probably sociable with each other and with Mrs. Bradford. There was no public room at the Bradford library where you could read comfortably and consult a variety of reference books, as there was at the Library Company. That difference accords with the different types of books in the two libraries and the different reading practices they involved. Bradford's library had only a few nonfiction books, and those were small and portable. The novels, plays, and light verse that made up almost the entire collection were meant to be read in domestic spaces and for pleasure.

In September 1769, just four days after Bradford opened his circulating library, the directors of the newly consolidated Library Company adopted a new set of rules, which made the subscription library more effective as a circulating library than ever. Nine of the twelve directors were new to the board, having just been elected by the newly expanded membership, whose wishes were no doubt reflected in these new rules.[27] Opening hours were extended from one to three days a week (Tuesday, Thursday, and Saturdays, four hours each afternoon), and for the first time since 1764 members were permitted within the rails. (Nonmembers still had to be waited on outside.) Also the loan period was extended and the number of books members could borrow at one time was increased.[28]

The borrowing fees paid by non-shareholders were left unchanged at 4 to 8 pence per volume per week, which was competitive with Bradford's and Nicola's charge of 6 pence per week if you exchanged books just once a week. However, in a commercial library you could exchange your book every day if you wanted to, and still pay just 6 pence; and the Bradford ledger shows that many people did just that. Now that the Library Company was open three days a week, books could potentially be exchanged more often, and the question naturally arose, should the charges be lower if the book was kept

---

27. The Library Company's board of directors was elected by the shareholders at the annual meeting each May. In the relatively stable times from 1731 to 1760, all twelve board members were usually reelected each year, as long as they lived. In 1761 three of the original 1731 directors were still in office, including Franklin, and the combined years of service of the twelve members was 177. Between 1761 and 1767, nine of the twelve seats turned over, and the combined years of service fell to 97 in 1767. That younger board was the group that "after mature deliberation" decided to freeze the price of a share. After the merger of 1769, two-thirds of the members were new, and not coincidentally two-thirds of the directors they elected that May were new as well. The combined years of service of the 1769 board members totaled 22. Cf. Library Company, Register of Shares, 275–82.

28. LCP Minutes, II:22, 25 September 1769.

out a shorter period of time. The directors' answer was no, and to the table of charges they added for the first time this qualification: "no smaller sums, altho' the book or books should be return'd within the week."[29] The addition of this clause shows how aware the Library Company directors were of the terms offered by the commercial libraries, even if they hesitated to emulate them.

Another indication that readers were asking for the same privileges they enjoyed at the commercial libraries is recorded in the minutes. Evidently the librarian had begun in some cases to waive the requirement that borrowers who were not members leave a cash deposit of double the book's value. This came to the directors' attention in 1772, and they noted, "It being represented to the Board that a practice hath been introduced of letting out Books on Hire without Deposits, notwithstanding the Rule to the contrary; the Librarian is enjoined to observe the said Rule strictly for the future."[30]

In 1770, another change in the rules extended borrowing privileges to members of shareholders' families. The minutes record that "Some Complaints having been made that the Rules of the Library, with Respect to preventing Members sons & others from having access to the Books, are too strict: It is agreed that any Person approved of by the Directors & having an Order from a Member shall be admitted within the Rails in the same Manner as a Member."[31] Presumably any family member or servant could still take out books specifically requested in writing by a shareholder, but now "sons & others" could browse the shelves and choose their own books. It is not clear whether wives and daughters might be included as "others."

In 1772, the Library Company moved to much larger quarters in Carpenter's Hall and once again extended its hours: now it was open daily two to seven. New bookshelves were ordered with locked hinged doors covered with wire mesh, so that nonmembers could be admitted into the library proper and could browse the spine titles of the books, and the librarian could open or close each bay of shelves at his discretion. A visitor from Massachusetts described the room:

> Soon after dinner, the bell of the Church near Carpenter's Hall rang, which informed us that the Library of the Hall was open, for the purpose of receiving and delivering books. We immediately repaired to it. . . . Every modern author of any note, I am told, is to be met with here, and large additions are annually made. The books appeared to be well arranged and in good order. But the

---

29. Ibid.
30. Ibid., II:78, 28 December 1772.
31. Ibid., II:31, 5 February 1770.

number of books, and the arrangement, are not so large nor so ornamental as the library at Cambridge, but approaches nearer to it than any other on the continent. I was pleased with a kind of net-work doors to the book-shelves, which is made of a large wire sufficiently open to read the labels, but no book can be taken out unless the librarian unlocks the door. This is a necessary security from any persons taking books without the knowledge of the librarian. Here were a large number of gentlemen. I was introduced to a number of the members of the Philosophical Society. . . .[32]

The Library Company had changed enormously since Greenway's death, but with its imposing architecture and illustrious clientele, it was still quite different from Tom and Polly Bradford's living room.

Not long after the Library Company moved in 1772, both Nicola's and Bradford's libraries closed.[33] Apparently the older library's responses to the challenges posed by commercial libraries were effective, but there are signs that the Bradford library was past its peak even before then. The circulation ledger for 1771–72 shows that hardly any new books were added in the course of that year, thereby destroying the main advantage Bradford had over the Library Company, risking the loss of his most faithful customers, and generally undercutting his basic business strategy.

At least one entrepreneur, however, thought there was room in Philadelphia for a commercial library if conducted with panache. In 1774 a new circulating library was opened by Robert Bell, a recent immigrant with long experience as a bookseller in Scotland and Ireland and already famous as a flamboyant auctioneer. Bell occupied the building that had housed the old Union Library Company before it merged with the Library Company; thus he was literally filling a vacant niche in the local library system. Bell brought the sophistication of the British Isles to his establishment, and it became a gathering place for all kinds of writers and public figures.[34] Bell's library, however, turned out to be vulnerable precisely because it was so popular. It became the haunt of British officers during their occupation of Philadelphia in 1777 and 1778; after their evacuation it fell out of favor and was moribund when he died in 1784.

---

32. William Parker Cutler, *Life, Journals and Correspondence of Rev. Manasseh Cutler* (Cincinnati: R. Clarke, 1888), I:281–83. Cutler made his visit during the Constitutional Convention of 1787, when the Library Company opened its doors to all the delegates, so his description may reflect a state occasion.

33. The precise dates of their closure can not be determined. Bradford's last advertisement appeared in the *Pennsylvania Journal*, 23 June 1773 ("All persons who have any Books belonging to the Circulating Library in Second-street, are desired to return them immediately.") and according to Haggard, "The Nicola Affair," Nicola moved with his family to Allentown, Pennsylvania, "in the early 1770s."

34. Green, "English Books," 283–91.

We will never know whether subscription libraries in Philadelphia and New York would have succeeded in luring readers away from circulating libraries or preventing their members from defecting, because the Revolution killed off the colonial commercial libraries, in those two cities and everywhere else. Purely commercial libraries turned out to be highly vulnerable to the economic instability of the 1780s and early 1790s. Thus the subscription libraries were left in possession of the field after the war, stronger and more popular than ever. The changes that had been made to the Library Company in the 1760s continued to erase many of the advantages of the commercial libraries. In 1783, as soon as the smoke of war had cleared, William Prichard opened a circulating library in Philadelphia, but the postwar depression killed it off in 1788. Not until well into the 1790s did other libraries arise to compete with the Library Company. Now commonly known as the City Library or the Public Library, it was more of a public institution than ever.

The New York Society Library survived revolution and occupation more or less intact, and in the postwar years only one significant circulating library arose to compete with it. John Fellows's Circulating Library started business in 1793 and was taken over and greatly expanded by Hocquet Caritat in 1797.[35] By 1800, Caritat had a library of over 3,000 volumes and a stock of books for sale or rent of over 30,000 volumes. His 1804 catalogue included almost 2,000 novels. That was certainly competition for the New York Society Library, which owned only a bit more than 2,500 titles in all. This rapid expansion, however, left the Caritat library vulnerable to the usual business risks. In 1804, Caritat returned to his native France and sold the business to publisher Isaac Riley, whose bankruptcy shortly thereafter put an end to the largest American library of its time.[36]

In both Philadelphia and New York, the two cities where commercial and subscription libraries were in dynamic relationship, the advantages enjoyed by the commercial libraries were many. They offered more new books, more light reading, longer opening hours, lower costs to borrowers, convenient location, and access for women and young people. Subscription libraries tried to emulate commercial libraries in each of those areas, but because of the obligation to their shareholders to maintain and preserve permanent refer-

---

35. Cf. the list of libraries in Kaser, *Book for a Sixpence,* 127–63. The only other New York library of the 1790s listed there is Aarondt Van Hook's Reading Room, which advertised a small "standing library."

36. George Gates Raddin, Jr., *Hocquet Caritat and the Early New York Literary Scene* (Dover, NJ: Dover Advance Press, 1953), 30–34. For the holdings of the New York Society Library, see Robert Winans, *Descriptive Checklist of Book Catalogues Separately Printed in America, 1693–1800* (Worcester: American Antiquarian Society, 1981), items 179 and 281.

ence collections, they could not go nearly as far in making their collections accessible to all. On the other hand, the weakness of commercial libraries was their very impermanence. Maintaining their heavily used collections and satisfying the ever-increasing demand for new books were costly, so most commercial libraries were unable to sustain themselves for more than a few years or to compete with a new venture with all new stock. But the ease with which a new venture could be launched was itself a kind of strength. Thus in both cities, no commercial library lasted more than a few years, but new ones kept popping up. Meanwhile the subscription libraries had to consolidate and become more like commercial libraries, but they endured. Moreover, in both cases they were able to function effectively as their cities' de facto public libraries until the mid-nineteenth century or later, precisely because the competition with commercial libraries had made them more accessible to people of moderate income, to women and children, and to the growing number of readers who read not only to become learned, virtuous, or polite, but also to have fun.

Chapter 3

A Great and Natural Enemy of Democracy?

Politics and Culture in the
Antebellum Portsmouth Athenæum

Michael A. Baenen

From the manner in which the loafers in and about the Athenæum catch at anything uttered against it, a person would think it was high treason to mention it in any other terms than those of praise and approval. That it has an influence, upon this community, I will readily admit, but that influence out of its own sphere of action, is of the most blighting and withering cast. It is the great, and, I was about to say, the natural enemy of the democracy of numbers in this town. There is scarcely a year since its incorporation that it has not been found in opposition to the popular will. Considered simply as a literary institution it is well enough, but its ostensible object has been and is still perverted. Though like the Venetian Inquisition its movements and powers are unseen, its officials and mutes are always ready to fulfil its commands and requirements. For myself Mr Editor, no professional intimations or threats from it or its members, shall ever deter me from speaking of it as I think, and I trust there is still enough of the old fashioned independence of character remaining with the citizens of this town to neutralize its prodigious efforts to bring this community like a willing sacrifice, to the feet of Nicholas Biddle and his British allies.

T<small>HUS</small> D<small>ID</small> one newspaper correspondent, signing himself "Stark," in tribute to a great Revolutionary hero, describe the leading library and reading room of Portsmouth, New Hampshire. By presenting it, in classic Jacksonian

Research for this essay has been greatly facilitated by the assistance and enthusiasm of the Athenæum staff, and the development of a database of Athenæum proprietors benefited enormously from biographical information compiled by former librarian Carolyn Eastman and former archivist Kevin Shupe. Richard M. Candee has provided encouragement, leads to sources, and thoughtful criticism; Thomas Hardiman commented on an earlier version of this essay. Invaluable comments came from the organizers and participants of the April 2002 conference on the History of Libraries in the United States — particularly Thomas Augst, Matthew Battles, and most of all the ever generous and thoughtful Kenneth E. Carpenter.

language, as not the arsenal of democracy but its sworn opponent, he sought to make the Portsmouth Athenæum a campaign issue in the 1838 state election. It is surprising to hear a library compared to the Bank of the United States, but perhaps the Athenæum really was to Portsmouth what the Bank was to the country—in Tocqueville's words, "a great establishment," with "an independent existence; the people, who destroy or raise all powers, can do nothing about it, which astonishes them. In the midst of the universal movement of society, the sight of this unmovable point shocks them, and they want to see if they cannot get it to shake like the rest." [1]

STARK ADMITTED that "considered simply as a literary institution" the Athenæum was "well enough," but it was more than a collection of books. It also had a newspaper reading room, previously operated by the New-Hampshire Fire and Marine Insurance Company and acquired by the Athenæum in 1823, along with the elegant three-story building that housed it. To "many of the proprietors" the first-floor reading room was "the most interesting" part of the building, and a "large portion" of the membership gathered "daily" in this "place of general resort," where "the interchange of opinions and good feelings" might "be enjoyed without let or hindrance." (See figures 3.1 and 3.2.) Memoirs and newspaper references testify to a lively social scene. During the 1830s about 25 subscribers a year to the reading room joined the Athenæum's 100 stockholders. Its popularity as a rendezvous attracted a range of other activities—auctions, petitions for signature, a promising invention on display—and affected the rest of the Athenæum. The quieter and more private library upstairs came to host a wide range of meetings that would have been out of place downstairs, both regular meetings of such groups as the Portsmouth Savings Bank and special events like a lecture by Noah Webster to the town's "literati." [2]

---

1. *New-Hampshire Gazette,* 20 February 1838; Alexis de Tocqueville, *Democracy in America,* trans. and ed. Harvey C. Mansfield and Delba Winthrop (Chicago: University of Chicago Press, 2000), 170.

2. Portsmouth Athenæum Proprietors' Meeting Minutes, 7 January 1835 and 6 January 1836, Portsmouth Athenæum Records (hereafter PA Records), Ms. 1, Portsmouth Athenæum (hereafter PA); *Portsmouth Journal,* 23 July 1831. The proprietors' first two minute books cover the periods from the initial organizing efforts through 7 January 1857 and from 6 January 1858 through 5 January 1887 (PA Records, box 2, folders 12 and 13, respectively); the first three volumes of the surviving directors' minutes cover the periods 6 January 1823–1 January 1827, 8 January 1827–7 January 1846, and 12 January 1846–18 February 1884 (box 7, folders 16, 17, and 18, respectively). Subsequent references will be in the form Proprietors' (or Directors') Minutes, followed by date. Information on subscribers for the period 1825–45 is in Account Book ("Ledger B"), 1823–93, box 12, folder 1, PA Records, fols. 55–76, which can be supplemented by subscription lists for individual years in box 10, folders 20, 21, 22, 25, 26, and 27 and, for the years 1837–46, by an assessment book in box 13, folder 17. Quota-

Figure 3.1. The Adamesque building of the Portsmouth Athenæum, shown here in a late nineteenth-century photograph, has been a commanding presence at the heart of the city's commercial district since its construction in 1805. Before the Athenæum took it over, the building housed, besides a newspaper reading room, St. John's Masonic Lodge, another organization central to the associational life of the local elite. Photo: Davis Brothers, Portsmouth. Courtesy Portsmouth Athenæum.

Figure 3.2. This 1891 view of a group of Portsmouth Athenæum patrons shows the Italianate decorative scheme adopted for the ground-floor reading room in 1855. The year after this photograph was taken, under the influence of the Colonial Revival, a group of proprietors undertook renovations that aimed to return the room to its Federal origins; in the process, they turned it into a shrine to the city's past glory. Photo: L. V. Newell, Portsmouth. Courtesy Whalley Library and Museum, St. John's Masonic Lodge No. 1, Portsmouth, N.H.

The shared experience of the reading room, plus the availability of other privileged social space, resulted in the formation of a community, and in this respect the Athenæum is part of the historical continuum of male sociability that runs from the coffeehouses of Restoration London and the polite literary circles of the eighteenth-century American colonies to Freemasonry and other fraternal orders. Like the elite urban men's clubs that were just beginning to emerge in Boston, New York, and Philadelphia, it offered long hours, a shared social space, and a limited but not excessively small membership. Before the Civil War, Portsmouth supported more than half a dozen different newspaper reading rooms, each with a distinctive clientele—some explicitly partisan, others oriented toward a specific social group. But no other reading room in Portsmouth survived as long as the Athenæum, or had a civic presence to

_____

tions from the Portsmouth Athenæum records appear, with modernized spelling and capitalization, by permission from the Athenæum. The early development of the Athenæum, its transformation following the acquisition of the insurance company building, and the social life of the reading room are discussed in detail in my "Books, Newspapers, and Sociability in the Making of the Portsmouth Athenæum," *New England Quarterly* 77 (2003): 378–412.

match its handsome building in "the most public place in town." And none evoked such antagonism.[3]

STARK'S LETTER of 1838 was one salvo in an ongoing skirmish over the civic role of the Athenæum. In 1836, the *Portsmouth Journal* asked its readers, "Why is it that Portsmouth is so far behind the spirit of the age?" The seaports of neighboring Massachusetts and Maine and the interior towns of New Hampshire were prospering—why not Portsmouth? The Whig editor found his answer in a local political culture that attacked both "wealth and education—this as useless, and that as aristocratical." Men of liberal education had been removed from the School Committee, and the town taxed the Athenæum—"an institution which is an honor to our town, established by much persevering labor, and sustained by heavy individual assessments." Instead of extending its "fostering care" over the Athenæum, under Democratic leadership the town compelled it "to pay a tax, or have its books thrown upon the parade, and disposed of under the auctioneer's hammer for the benefit of the town!" The assessment on the Athenæum was "a small matter in amount," but, just as the Stamp Act had, it "involved principles . . . at variance with the prosperity and interests of the town." Compelling the Athenæum, "from the benefit of which no class, sect or party is excluded," to "pay the town for its existence" would chill "every spirit of enterprise" and check "the introduction of any kindred institutions for the general good among us."[4]

In response, the Democratic *Gazette* argued that Portsmouth suffered economically because her leading merchants had stifled the spirit of industry within the town while investing their own capital elsewhere. The municipal tax levied on the Athenæum hardly constituted "a barbarous movement": the books were not taxed, while the building itself, "situated in the centre of the town" and worth as much as $8,000, no more deserved exemption from taxa-

---

3. *New-Hampshire Gazette*, 4 October 1831. The members of the Athenæum were affluent white men, well established in business, but a common experience of print and shared literary endeavors—what Anne Ruggles Gere, in *Intimate Practices: Literacy and Cultural Work in U.S. Women's Clubs, 1880–1920* (Urbana: University of Illinois Press, 1997), has broadly called "literacy practices"—fostered the development of community for other groups in antebellum America as well: see especially Thomas Augst, "The Business of Reading in Nineteenth-Century America: The New York Mercantile Library," *American Quarterly* 50 (1998): 267–305 (on merchants' clerks); Mary Kelley, " 'A More Glorious Revolution': Women's Antebellum Reading Circles and the Pursuit of Public Influence," *New England Quarterly* 76 (2003): 163–96; and Elizabeth McHenry, *Forgotten Readers: Recovering the Lost History of African American Literary Societies* (Durham: Duke University Press, 2002), 23–140. On the emergence of elite men's clubs in the largest antebellum cities, see Edward Pessen, *Riches, Class, and Power before the Civil War* (Lexington, MA: D. C. Heath, 1973), 222–30.

4. *Portsmouth Journal*, 4 July 1836.

tion than did the buildings housing the Democratic or Mechanics' reading rooms. In the past the *Journal's* own party had taxed the Athenæum, although now it was serving as "the rallying point of the aristocracy." The library on the second floor and the small museum on the third might be "creditable" to Portsmouth, but the reading room was the seat of an "Athenæum junto" that was "infinitely worse" for Portsmouth than the Federalists' Essex junto had been for the country. The "middling interests" of Portsmouth suffered the "pernicious effects" of this "down stairs cabinet," since no one could safely undertake "enterprises of moment without becoming in some degree attached to it." Many of its members had "souls more circumscribed than that of a holy inquisitor of the 14th Century—with notions of political right and wrong that would do honor to the sublime conceptions of the Autocrat of all the Russias."[5]

Partisan division intensified in New Hampshire in the years after 1836. The state had long been a Democratic stronghold, but the Whigs gained strength in the wake of the Panic of 1837, and the state election in March 1838 "restored the two-party system" across the state. The expectation that the election would be unusually close led to bitter newspaper coverage: Whig editors congratulated one another on conducting the campaign "with unusual dexterity" and making the Democrats sweat "most fervently"; their opponents replied in kind.[6] In Portsmouth, the largest town in the state, the two parties were almost evenly balanced, and their campaigns were correspondingly aggressive. Arguing that the Whigs used their control over local business and civic institutions to overawe the electorate, Stark and other writers in the *Gazette* claimed that the Athenæum was the headquarters of a plot to seize power from the people.

One series of articles satirized the inept attempts of the "the federal managers" inside the Athenæum and "their out door coworkers" to generate popular support. Other Democratic critiques of the Athenæum were more severe. One *Gazette* correspondent complained that the members of the town's elite were

---

5. *New-Hampshire Gazette,* 7 July 1836. The *Gazette* also complained that the signature of a prominent Democrat had been defaced in the visitors' register; on the defacement of the visitors' register, see Proprietors' Minutes, 7 January 1829. The earliest surviving visitors' register covers the dates 22 February 1827–7 June 1829; pages have been removed at both front and back: PA Records, box 5, folder 9. The dispute over municipal taxation was still remembered some years later: *Gazette,* 4 May 1841.

6. Donald B. Cole, *Jacksonian Democracy in New Hampshire, 1800–1851* (Cambridge: Harvard University Press, 1970), 195; Asa McFarland to Charles W. Brewster, Concord, 26 February 1838, Charles W. Brewster Papers, box 1, folder 1, New Hampshire Historical Society, Concord (hereafter, NHHS). McFarland was editor of the *New Hampshire Statesman* in Concord, Brewster of the *Portsmouth Journal.*

so "clannish and exclusive" that no one who did not share their politics dared to enter the Athenæum "even upon urgent business . . . without danger of being insulted and assaulted by some of their bullies." The alleged victims of such abuse included the former Naval Store Keeper in town, and it was hinted that Democratic Congressman Samuel Cushman (1783–1851), an Athenæum proprietor, had also been assaulted on the premises. Not even the image of a Democrat was safe: a bust of Secretary of the Treasury Levi Woodbury in the library room had been "purposely covered with tobacco spittle by some mean, dirty scoundrel" and then, "after it had been ordered to be cle[a]nsed of the filth, . . . grossly bruised and disfigured." One Democratic writer, claiming that the reading room had been the scene of elite political operations long before the Athenæum took over its operation, asked the former Federalists of Portsmouth if they remembered "when poor men who, through want, were held in abeyance to your will, stood trembling in front of the old Insurance Office . . . waiting to receive at the hands of your party a ticket which in their hearts they hated?"[7]

It is difficult to judge some of these charges, but the Whig *Journal* did not dispute the claim that the former Naval Store Keeper had been assaulted inside the Athenæum. The political affiliation of the members lends some credence to Democratic claims: in 1834, three-fifths of the proprietors signed a petition opposing the withdrawal of federal deposits from the Bank of the United States, and in 1838 the Whigs nominated proprietors for state senator, for five of six seats in the lower house, and for four of five seats on the Portsmouth board of selectmen. But the picture was more complicated, for many leading Democrats likewise belonged to the Athenæum. In all, fifteen shareholders ran for major state or municipal office in 1838, ten as Whigs and five as Democrats.[8]

The Athenæum membership was more heavily Whig than Portsmouth as a whole, where the two parties were almost evenly matched, but its directors assured the membership that "political opinions . . . are never suffered to have any influence in the management of the affairs of this institution." While the *Gazette* claimed that Democrats were not safe in the building, the

---

7. *New-Hampshire Gazette*, 13 February, 27 February, 3 April, and 10 April 1838. The satire of the *Gazette* articles is labored at best, and some of the allusions remain obscure, but the repeated references to the Athenæum as the seat of Whig organizing are clear: see also the issues of 20 February and 6 and 12 March 1838, and replies in the *Portsmouth Journal*, 17 February and 3 March 1838. The unnamed Naval Store Keeper would have been Richard H. Ayer, who held the position from May 1829 through April 1837; the *Gazette* had aired this charge before, on 7 July 1836.

8. *Memorial of Merchants and Others, of Portsmouth, N.H. In relation to the Public Deposites*, 23d Congress, 1st Session, HR Doc. No. 102: The signers included 58 shareholders and at least 5 former and 19 future proprietors. On the memorial, see Cole, *Jacksonian Democracy*, 132–33.

Journal countered that leading Democrats patronized the Athenæum "every day, without molestation." Nor were they marginalized. In fact, only two months earlier one of the Democratic candidates for selectman, Isaac Waldron (1773–1843), had been reelected to the seat he had held on the Athenæum's board of directors since 1827, and he remained a director until his death in 1843. Waldron served the Athenæum while also exemplifying Portsmouth's Democratic business interests: he was president of the Commercial Bank, one of the "pet banks" that received federal deposits withdrawn from the Bank of the United States, and he held a Democratic commission as federal pension agent.[9]

Waldron's election and his long tenure were, in fact, political necessities. Portsmouth was too heavily Democratic for the Athenæum to fulfill its role as an elite gathering-place effectively if it excluded Jacksonians or too obviously sidelined them. Portsmouth business partners usually shared political as well as religious affiliations, but the town was too small and closely divided for either Whigs or Democrats to succeed in business without an ability to work across party lines. It seems that Whig shareholders understood that there should always be at least one Democrat among the Athenæum directors: after Waldron's death in 1843, his seat on the board went to Richard Jenness (1801–72), the leading local Democrat of the next generation.

The most prominent Democrat among the proprietors was Levi Woodbury (1789–1851), who served as a director for six years at the beginning of the 1820s and retained his share in the Athenæum for the rest of his life. The bust of the treasury secretary that was vandalized had been a gift from Richard Ela, a New Hampshire lawyer on Woodbury's staff in Washington; its mutilation must have been intensely embarrassing to the directors. In accusing the Athenæum of complicity in the vandalism, the *Gazette* for obvious partisan reasons neglected to report that the institution had offered a $50 reward for information leading to the detection of the perpetrator (see figure 3.3), and had bought a new bust of Woodbury as a replacement. The Whigs on the board might not agree with Woodbury's politics, but they could hardly condone vandalizing the image of a distinguished proprietor and officer of the United States government. There was never any official acknowledgment

---

9. Proprietors' Minutes, 2 January 1833; *Portsmouth Journal,* 7 April 1838 and 5 August 1843. Although the Whigs, in a stunning upset, took Portsmouth in both the state and municipal elections of 1838, their margin of victory was razor-thin: they won the crucial bellwether vote, for moderator of the town meeting on the morning of the state election, by only 9 out of 1,247 votes cast: *Journal,* 17 March 1834. On the assignment of deposits to pet banks in Portsmouth, see Cole, *Jacksonian Democracy,* 130–31, and Frank Otto Gatell, "Spoils of the Bank War: Political Bias in the Selection of Pet Banks," *American Historical Review* 70 (1964): 53.

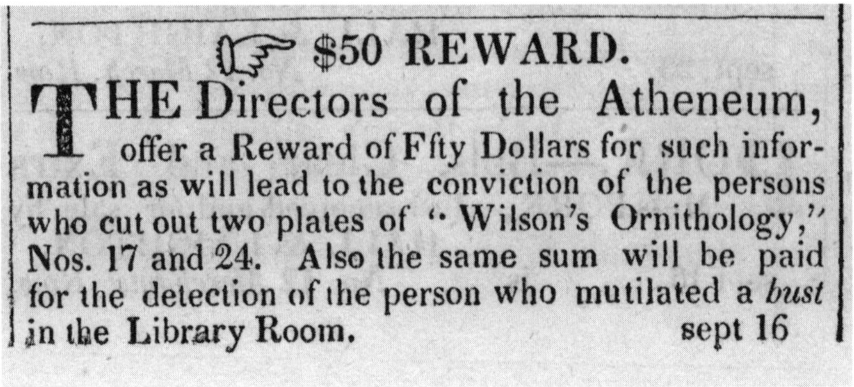

☞ $50 REWARD.

THE Directors of the Atheneum, offer a Reward of Ffty Dollars for such information as will lead to the conviction of the persons who cut out two plates of "Wilson's Ornithology," Nos. 17 and 24. Also the same sum will be paid for the detection of the person who mutilated a *bust* in the Library Room. sept 16

Figure 3.3. September 1837 advertisement in the *Portsmouth Journal.* Courtesy Portsmouth Athenæum.

that politics might have been involved, and in fact the Athenæum carefully avoided mentioning whose bust had been defaced. In the Whig *Journal,* "A Proprietor" suggested that the vandalism must have been juvenile mischief, since such "a mode of venting political spleen . . . would be contemptible even in a savage." [10]

The political situation inside the Athenæum, then, was more complicated than Stark claimed. Whigs were overrepresented in comparison with the electorate as a whole, and during periods of partisan tension Jacksonians apparently suffered some ugly incidents. The directors, however, consciously attempted to run a nonpartisan institution, to coopt Democrats into visible positions of leadership, and to ensure that they received a due measure of respect. This should not surprise us, because Athenæum members who disagreed over politics were still likely to have much else in common. Stark cast his attack on the aristocracy of Portsmouth in terms of party, but the real fault lines that separated Athenæum members from the rest of Portsmouth were social and economic, for its affluent proprietors were hardly representative of the town's population.

A SHARE in the Athenæum cost $100, as much as at any social library in New England aside from the Boston Athenæum, and no resident of Ports-

10. *Portsmouth Journal,* 30 September 1837. On the history of the bust, see Directors' Minutes, 6 February, 11 September, and 12 December 1837. The proprietors discussed measures to enhance library security at three meetings in January 1838. There appear to be no references to the incident in the Levi Woodbury Papers at the Library of Congress, consulted in the microfilm edition.

mouth paying more than $20 in municipal taxes was allowed to become an annual subscriber rather than a proprietor. Those who could afford to buy a share had to. At the same time, membership was almost obligatory for the town's wealthiest men. In the mid-1830s, nine of Portsmouth's ten most highly assessed individual taxpayers owned shares, and 33 of the top 50. Just over half of the proprietors were merchants; the few mechanics among the shareholders—a blacksmith, a tanner—were successful and eminently respectable. Almost all the attorneys in town belonged. The typical proprietor owned taxable property assessed at a bit more than $10,300, and nine-tenths of the shareholders owned more than $1,000 in property. (Only one, the local agent of the Portland Stage Company, paid just a poll tax; joining him among the least propertied members were some of the shipmasters and lawyers and the town's treasurer and tax collector.) As the 1830s came to an end, the median age of the proprietors was between 49 and 50.[11]

The proprietors themselves were overwhelmingly Unitarian and Episcopalian, and the ministers of Portsmouth's leading Protestant congregations were influential members, although their unique status may have precluded their frequenting the reading room on a regular basis. Charles Burroughs (1787–1868; see figure 3.4), minister of St. John's Church (Episcopal), who had been active in establishing the Athenæum, served as its president from 1829 to 1868. His Congregational, Unitarian, and Universalist colleagues had the benefit of shares held by their congregations for their use.[12] The ministers of Portsmouth's Baptist, Free Will Baptist, and Methodist congregations, on the other hand, did not have such entrée into the library or reading room.

In his attack on the Athenæum, Stark called attention to its connections with the Bank of the United States, and indeed, six out of seven directors of the Bank's local branch, including its president, were proprietors, as were the cashier and the clerk of its loan office. But Biddle's Bank was not uniquely represented, for Athenæum stockholders dominated Portsmouth banking. At the end of the 1830s, every bank president in Portsmouth was a proprietor, as were four-fifths of all bank directors and the cashiers of five of the six commercial banks; the sixth bank cashier was a subscriber to the reading room. Only two of Portsmouth's commercial banks had more than one director who was *not*

---

11. A list of the 110 individuals assessed for more than $50 in municipal taxes appeared in the *Portsmouth Journal*, 27 June 1835. For comparative share prices, see Jesse H. Shera, *Foundations of the Public Library: The Origins of the Public Library Movement in New England, 1629–1855* (Chicago: University of Chicago Press, 1949), 77.

12. South Church (Unitarian) purchased a share in 1833, and North Church (Congregational) in 1839. Thomas F. King (d. 1839), who served as Portsmouth's Universalist minister between 1828 and 1835, gave his share to the congregation in 1836.

an Athenæum shareholder. (Both were among the banks that received federal deposits pulled from the Bank of the United States.) In Portsmouth, access to capital depended on the decisions of Athenæum proprietors. As the *Gazette* put it, "These men are the controllers of our banking institutions, and in a great measure the directors of our trade. They can smile up, or frown down whom they please. . . . Every man's business is more or less subject to their control." The role of Athenæum members in credit decisions was nationalized in the late 1840s, when reading room regular W. H. Y. Hackett (1800–1878)

Figure 3.4. The Reverend Charles C. Burroughs, whom a contemporary remembered as "for a long period *the* foremost" citizen of Portsmouth." Courtesy Portsmouth Historical Society (on deposit, Portsmouth Athenæum)

became the Portsmouth agent for Lewis Tappan's Mercantile Agency, predecessor of R. G. Dun & Company.[13]

In Portsmouth, Athenæum membership did not consolidate an emerging upper class, as Ronald Story has suggested it did in Boston.[14] Portsmouth had no new class of industrial capitalists. And there were limits to the barriers that could be raised between the elite and the rest of the citizens in a small, face-to-face community: in 1840, more than one out of every 20 adult white males in town was a proprietor. Still, there is little doubt that the Athenæum was the central social institution of a tight-knit elite that continued to dominate civic life. Stark framed his indictment of elite leadership in partisan terms, but the prominent Jacksonians who belonged to the Athenæum were unlikely to share his resentment of the continuing power of the gentry.

By the time of the 1828 presidential campaign, Portsmouth's Jacksonians were operating their own explicitly partisan Democratic Republican (later, simply "Democratic") Reading Room, offering members an opportunity to catch up on the news, to socialize, and to organize. Having suspended operations after 1833, that reading room was reorganized in time for the state elections in March 1835. The *Gazette* hoped that in this new incarnation the reading room might "meet with sufficient patronage so as to make it a *permanent* and *saving* concern," and the organizers urged "every democrat" to subscribe. Although most visible during the annual campaign season in late winter and early spring, the room appears to have operated year-round. Throughout its decade-long existence, the Democrats' reading room was peripatetic, moving every year or two. One constant was its connection to the *New Hampshire Gazette,* and in 1837 the *Gazette* finally began to operate the reading room directly, boasting that the papers it received by exchange allowed the room to offer "probably . . . the largest collection of papers in the place," for the small annual subscription of $1. After this last effort, the Democrats gave up hope of making their reading room pay, and by 1838 the

---

13. *New-Hampshire Gazette,* 7 July 1836. These figures include the Portsmouth Savings Bank as well as the commercial banks; almost all of the trustees of the Savings Bank also sat on the board of one of the commercial banks. The proportion of bank directors who were Athenæum proprietors actually increased slightly after the closure of the Portsmouth branch of the Bank of the United States, from 44 of 59 in 1834 to 39 of 49 in 1839. For names of directors: *Edmonds' Portsmouth Register and Directory* (Portsmouth: Joseph M. Edmonds, 1834), 80–83, and *Edmonds' Town Directory . . .* (Portsmouth: Joseph M. Edmonds, 1839), 137–39. Kevin Lafond has identified Hackett as the Portsmouth agent in the course of research in the R. G. Dun & Company records at Baker Library, Harvard Business School, Boston.

14. Ronald Story, "Class and Culture in Boston: The Athenæum, 1807–1860," *American Quarterly* 27 (1975): 178–99.

Gazette was simply making its exchange papers available to subscribers free of charge in its counting room, during business hours.[15] The Democrats presented their reading room as a legitimate, above-board political association, in contrast to the covertly politicized Athenæum.

In the late summer of 1840, the Whigs opened their own Free Whig Reading Room—located, rather remarkably, in the same building as the *Gazette,* which complained of this "unlawful and arbitrary encroachment." As a Whig character remarked in a satirical scene printed in the *Gazette,* "We can hear all the Democrats have to say." Evidently the Democrats did not think that the establishment of the new, explicitly partisan reading room would deprive the Athenæum of its Whig patronage: at one point in the same scene, the stage directions call for "the leading Whigs" to enter from the Athenæum, among them the "Late President of the Branch Bank"—Athenæum proprietor Alexander Ladd (1785–1855)—and the "Earl of Jeffrey," a hit at the notorious social pretensions of longtime Athenæum director and librarian George Jaffrey (1789–1856).[16]

If Democrats still distrusted the Athenæum, the rowdies of Portsmouth continued to find it a tempting target. The Fourth of July "passed off very quietly" in 1840, with a "splendid display" of fireworks in the evening. The municipal authorities were not in control, however, and the celebration degenerated, with "blazing fire-balls . . . thrown indiscriminately among the multitudes collected around Market Square." When the mob met with opposition, fire-balls were thrown into the windows of the Portsmouth and New Hampshire banks. The Athenæum appears to have been the only building that was assaulted not only with the fire-balls but also with "stones of considerable size," which broke "seven panes of large glass" in the reading room.[17] As on occasions in the past—when the visitors' register was defaced, when plates were razored out of expensive books, and when the bust of Levi Woodbury was mutilated—the elite stronghold seemed to invite transgression.

A verbal attack on the Athenæum later in 1840 provides a clue to the likely

---

15. *New-Hampshire Gazette,* 6 January (italics in original) and 13 January 1835 and 17 October 1837. In 1831, the reading room was under the *Gazette* office: *Gazette,* 1 March 1831; on 23 February 1836, the *Gazette* announced that subscriptions to the reading room could be paid at the paper's office. The role of partisan reading rooms in antebellum politics would repay further study: see Jeffrey L. Pasley, *"The Tyranny of Printers": Newspaper Politics in the Early American Republic* (Charlottesville: University Press of Virginia, 2001), 8. On access to exchange papers free of charge: *Gazette,* 3 July 1838. On the importance of exchange papers during this period, see Pasley, *"The Tyranny of Printers,"* 48–49, and Richard R. John, *Spreading the News: The American Postal System from Franklin to Morse* (Cambridge: Harvard University Press, 1995), 37.

16. *New-Hampshire Gazette,* 22 September and 25 August 1840.

17. *Portsmouth Journal,* 6 July 1840.

identity of the *Gazette* correspondent who signed himself Stark two years before. At a Democratic meeting in Jefferson Hall that September, after "denouncing the U.S. Bank as a monster, causing nearly all the evils our country has been afflicted with," one of the speakers went on to arraign "the rich as the enemies of the poor, and the frequenters of the Atheneum [*sic*] as peculiarly detestable." The orator was Thomas B. Laighton, a prominent Democrat who held a patronage appointment as keeper of the White Island lighthouse, ten miles out of Portsmouth harbor. A slashing political controversialist, Laighton had a vivid style and a taste for invective. From July 1835 to his election to the state legislature in March 1837 he had been one of the two editors of the *New Hampshire Gazette,* and he probably wrote the editorial attack on the Athenæum in 1836. The one Democrat to whom any of the attacks on the Athenæum can be attributed with certainty, he may well have written all of them. The circumstances of the 1840 meeting at which Laighton condemned the proprietors of the Athenæum as "peculiarly detestable" revealed the tensions between his rhetoric and the more complex realities of political affiliation and leadership in antebellum Portsmouth. The *Journal's* correspondent thought that the president of the Democratic meeting, the rising young lawyer John Lord Hayes (1812–87), "looked a little out of countenance when 'Tom' was bawling loudest against the Athenæum and the Banks, as if he could not help it that he had been once librarian of the Athenæum, and that both his father and father-in-law are or have been Bank Presidents!" [18]

Although it was the political role of the Athenæum reading room that Laighton challenged, resentment of the exclusiveness of its library may also have fueled his anger. Laighton had grown up in a family eager for learning and self-improvement. His father, Mark Laighton, a block and mast maker, was among the twenty-one members of the Portsmouth Encyclopedia Society, founded in 1812 "for the laudable purpose of promoting useful knowledge among ourselves, and especially for the early instruction of our children and those in our care in a general knowledge of the sciences." Both Thomas and his younger brother William were eager for books and debate. They had no access to the Athenæum, but William supplemented his own collection by

---

18. *Portsmouth Journal,* 3 October 1840. There is no satisfactory published account of Thomas B. Laighton's life; the accounts of his political career in the various biographical studies of his daughter, the poet Celia Laighton Thaxter, are not reliable. I am grateful to Jane Molloy Porter for letting me read the sections on Laighton in her work in progress on the lighthouses and lighthouse keepers of the Portsmouth region, now published as *Friendly Edifices: Piscataqua Lighthouses and Other Aids to Navigation, 1771–1939* (Portsmouth, NH: Peter E. Randall Publisher LLC for the Portsmouth Marine Society, 2006).

borrowing from the Apprentices' Library; Thomas, though not an apprentice, may have done the same. Thomas went on to become the secretary of the Democratic Republican Reading Room and a director of its successor, the Democratic Reading Room. Not all of his literary activities were explicitly partisan: he served as librarian of both the Franklin Encyclopedia Society, to which William also belonged, and the Portsmouth Workingmen's Reading Club, "designed to be a debating as well as a reading club" (see figure 3.5).[19]

The *Journal* argued that "no class" was "excluded" from the benefits of the Athenæum, but in fact it gave little encouragement to an educationally ambitious workingman like Laighton. Mechanics were as little likely to patronize the library as the reading room. The library, like the newsroom, was open to subscribers as well as proprietors, but with a crucial difference. In the reading room, proprietors and subscribers were on a relatively equal footing, but only proprietors could borrow books from the library. Not surprisingly, the number of subscribers to the library, restricted to reading on the premises, stayed small. In 1839, more than three-quarters of the Athenæum's subscribers (21 of 27) subscribed to the reading room only; four paid for access to both the reading room and the library, and just two subscribed to the library alone. The subscribers to the two rooms represented different occupational groups. The subscribers to the reading room were heavily involved in shipping and naval affairs and included five shipmasters, two Navy employees, and one mariner, in addition to seven merchants, two lawyers, one bank cashier, and one teacher. The library, on the other hand, attracted professional men: the two men who subscribed to the library alone were a clergyman and a physician, and those subscribers to both rooms whose occupations are identifiable were a lawyer, a minister, and a medical student. [20]

In 1840, the proprietors of the Athenæum were asked to consider whether

---

19. Records of the Portsmouth Encyclopedia Society, 1812–18, item 1996–086, NHHS; 1839 *Directory,* 156. On the brothers' youthful reading, Journal of William Laighton, 1829–1835, Barbara Durant Isles of Shoals Collection, Ms. 58.1, box 1, PA. On the Portsmouth Apprentices' Library, see Baenen, "Books, Newspapers, and Sociability," 400; Laighton's political mentor, coppersmith and postmaster Abner Greenleaf, Sr., was the first librarian of the Apprentices' Library. On the Franklin Encyclopedia Society, established 1832, see 1834 *Directory,* 94, and, for William's membership, entry for 11 June 1834, Journal of Thomas B. Laighton, 1832–37, Isles of Shoals Collection, Ms. 58, box 2A, folder 15, PA. The library of the Workingmen's Reading Club, established 1834, was kept in the *Gazette* counting room during Laighton's editorship; the books were disposed of in 1840: *New-Hampshire Gazette,* 12 April 1836 and 8 September 1840.

20. *Portsmouth Journal,* 4 July 1836. In 1839, Horace Mann found that only one-tenth of the population of Boston had a right to use any of its social libraries: *Third Annual Report of the Board of Education, Together with the Third Annual Report of the Secretary of the Board* (Boston: Dutton & Wentworth, 1840), 51 and 56. Mann estimated that each authorized user might represent on average four readers with access; by this calculation, the 100 shares in the Portsmouth Athenæum would have reached about 5 percent of the town's 1840 population of 7,887.

A course of interesting and instructive weekly lectures are delivered during five months in the year. Tickets for the course are $2,00, admitting a gentleman and two ladies.

Annual meeting, 1st. Tuesday in May.

Mechanics' Reading Room.

No. 4 Pleasant st.

Directors.—Peter Wilson, John H. Seaward, Benj Carter Jr.

This Reading Room was established in 1826. It was originally designed exclusively for Mechanics, by whom it is principally patronized, but it is open to persons of all professions. The principal Newspapers of the Union are here taken, which affords a fine opportunity to obtain the news at a small expense. Subscription $2,00 per annum.

N. B. Clergymen are admitted to the room free of charge. Subscribers have the privilege of admitting strangers of their acquaintance free.

Annual meeting in January.

Portsmo. Working Men's Reading Club.

Formed in 1834.

Directors. Brackett Hutchings, John Christie.

Librarian. Abner Greenleaf Jr.

Selecting Committee. Tho's. B. Laighton, Tho's. P. Treadwell, John J. Lane.

This Society owns a valuable library, composed of Dobson's Encyclopedia of 21 vols., Harpers Family Library, and several other valuable works. It is designed to be a debating as well as a reading club.

No. of members about 40. Funds raised by assessment on the members, not to exceed five dollars a year for each member.

Soc. for Mutual Improvement.

(Connected with the South Parish.)

President. Rev. Andrew P. Peabody.

Secretary. John M. Lord.

Treasurer. Joseph B. Upham.

Figure 3.5. Entry in the 1839 Portsmouth directory for the Portsmouth Workingmen's Reading Club. Courtesy Portsmouth Athenæum.

their library could do more for the public good. At the annual meeting held on New Year's Day, director Andrew Preston Peabody (1811–93) offered a resolution to permit annual subscribers to the library to borrow books needed "for special consultation in the investigation of any subject of literature or science, or preparing any discourse, article, or work for the press." In such cases, an order from a member of the board would authorize the librarian to lend a subscriber specified titles. Although Peabody (see figure 3.6) was young, in the years since his ordination as minister of the South Church (Unitarian) he had already become "the great light of the town," and no one would have had a better chance of arguing successfully for more liberal access to the library. After a flurry of parliamentary maneuvering, and having reaffirmed that "no book or books [should] be lent contrary to the printed regulations of the Athenæum," the proprietors appointed a committee of six—five of them lawyers—to review Peabody's proposal and report back to the membership the following month. The usually laconic secretary noted in the minutes that there had been "much debate." [21]

The responses to Peabody's proposal illuminate the ways in which Athenæum proprietors attempted to resolve the issues between private property and public good. The preservation of the library's property had been of particular concern since the fall of 1837, when the bust of Woodbury had been mutilated and a number of books defaced. "A Proprietor" laid the blame for those "outrages" on interlopers with no vested interest in the Athenæum: "Let the room be exclusively confined to the use of those who are interested in the property and prosperity of the institution, and who have a right or properly authorised permission to use it. . . . ." Too many people frequented the library who had "no right to be there, and who never make any compensation for its use." (Suspecting that the vandalism was a juvenile prank, he decried the policy "of allowing boys to go to the Library Room, to take out books for proprietors." The practice was "fraught with much evil," for the boys were entirely unsupervised—"they stay as long as they please, and they do whatever they wish.") In much the same spirit, the committee appointed by the proprietors to review Peabody's proposal recommended against taking any action, for its members had been unable "to agree on any plan for extending the use of the library consistently as they think with its preservation and most beneficial use for the proprietors beyond what is provided for by existing regulations." [22]

Two members of the committee dissented. John W. Foster (1789–1852), a

---

21. Proprietors' Minutes, 1 January 1840; Ferenc M. Szasz, ed., "John Lord's Portsmouth," *Historical New Hampshire* 44 (1989): 148.

22. *Portsmouth Journal*, 30 September 1837; Report of Committee on Lending Books to Subscribers, 5 February 1840, PA Records, box 9, folder 15. The language of the committee report is garbled in the proprietors' meeting minutes.

bookseller and South Church deacon who had chaired the committee, and Charles W. Cutter (1799–1856), a lawyer, argued for even more liberal library privileges than Peabody had proposed. Their effort to redefine the social role of the institution drew on the long-standing claim that the Athenæum library was a public, not a purely private, trust. In 1837, the same "Proprietor" who decried unauthorized access to the books had also commented that "the public good" demanded the safe preservation of the library's property, and "the public honor . . . that it never should be injured with impunity."

Figure 3.6. The Reverend Andrew P. Peabody, unquestionably the city's leading intellectual figure at mid-century. A prolific lecturer and reviewer, he edited the *North American Review* from 1854 to 1863. He served as a director of the Athenæum from 1837 to 1860, when he left Portsmouth to become Preacher to the University and Plummer Professor of Christian Morals at Harvard. Private collection.

Only someone "base and malicious, and a detestable foe to knowledge and letters," would damage the property of a library "founded in benevolence, and designed for the general good."

Given the Athenæum's restrictive policies, these claims may seem disingenuous, but we ought not read back into the antebellum period our own definition of a "public" library, expecting that it should be open to all, and without charge. The claim of a public trust was doubtless sincere, for the social libraries of Jacksonian America inherited an Enlightened tradition. "Privately owned and sponsored," the first American social libraries had nonetheless been " 'public' in the distinctively eighteenth-century sense of being a space where civic, religious, and commercial values converged and overlapped." If access was restricted to shareholders, and limited by economic realities, it was still open, in the sense that it did not depend on prior membership in a closed society or institution, such as a college.[23]

The paradox, of course, was that the social library could become its own closed society. By 1840, the role of the Athenæum as a private institution had become clear enough—all too clear, Thomas Laighton would have said. Foster and Cutter attempted to clarify the ways in which the Athenæum should meet its obligations to the public as well as its members. The establishment of "an extensive library," they wrote, "reflects honor upon those by whose immediate exertions and pecuniary means it [is] collected and sustained, and upon the community which is capable of appreciating the benefits of such an institution." Its "promoters and proprietors" would naturally desire "to extend its benefits as far as possible beyond themselves." Although those whose money, time, and labor built up an institution such as the Athenæum had first claim on it, they would know that "a most important" benefit of their work was "the improvement which the free use of a good library may effect on the moral and literary taste" of their community. Moreover, the gifts and especially the bequests that came to a library were not intended to benefit "the small circle of individuals who, under the name of trustees, or proprietors, or corporators, may have the watch and control of such funds, but rather . . . in the utmost possible degree, the whole community."[24] The only question was how far the use of the library could be extended consistent

---

23. Ross W. Beales and James N. Green, "Libraries and Their Users," in *The Colonial Book in the Atlantic World,* ed. Hugh Amory and David D. Hall, vol. 1 of *A History of the Book in America* (New York: Cambridge University Press, 2000), 400. Shera (*Foundations,* 22) points out that the term "public library" had been "loosely applied to any collection of books not the exclusive property of a private individual."

24. Report of John W. Foster and Charles W. Cutter, 5 February 1840, PA Records, box 9, folder 15.

with its preservation and continued increase and the primary claims of proprietors.

Foster and Cutter recommended that annual subscribers to the library have the same borrowing privileges as proprietors, provided they deposit $6 security above their subscription fee. The extension of borrowing privileges would not check the sale of shares, since the bylaws already prohibited from becoming subscribers those whose means were "sufficiently ample" to allow them to purchase a share "with prudence." Among the beneficiaries would be "the young men of our community—students, *teachers of our schools,* and others," whose duties did not allow them the leisure time to read on the premises but "who would gladly avail themselves of the use of the library to aid in their pursuit of knowledge and in the general cultivation of their minds." It was "a duty, and if so, a pleasure" to aid the rising generation, "soon to exert an influence for good or ill" on the community. (The only one of Portsmouth's ten male teachers who currently had access to the Athenæum was a subscriber to the reading room.) Moreover, the Athenæum should make sure that its valuable works were available for public purposes—if, for example, "the judges of a court in session may require some book to refer to in a case before them." In such "cases of special importance" it should be possible for the directors to authorize short-term loans "to persons connected or not connected with the institution," provided adequate security were deposited.[25]

Unfortunately, it is impossible to reconstruct the ensuing debate in detail. The February meeting was not reported in either the *Gazette* or the *Journal,* and the minutes record only a series of votes, not the arguments that swayed those present. After the minority report was read, the proprietors accepted the majority's recommendation. But the minority (and perhaps Peabody as well) must have been persuasive: Foster and Cutter's report was immediately taken up for reconsideration and, in a reversal, approved. The forces of established order then rallied and on a third and final ballot succeeded in ensuring that no action would be taken on either of the two proposals to liberalize access to the library.[26]

Although the extension of borrowing privileges to subscribers would have benefited only a small number of people immediately, Foster and Cutter anticipated that liberalizing the rules would attract new subscribers to the library. Some proprietors may have feared they would be swamped by subscribers eager to avail themselves of the literary riches gathered with such difficulty during the preceding quarter-century. The Athenæum's collection was

---

25. Ibid., underlining in original.
26. Proprietors' Minutes, 5 February 1840.

by far the most extensive and valuable in town.[27] If the books circulated more freely, would they be abused and eventually destroyed? If too many new subscribers gained access—people who must not, by the terms of the bylaws, be prosperous enough to buy shares—would the institution lose its social exclusivity, perhaps its very identity? Both fears likely came into play in the final vote. The majority of the Athenæum's proprietors were not ready to open the institution fully to the younger, less affluent users Foster and Cutter would have welcomed. The library, like the reading room, would remain an elite preserve. And as the understanding of what was public changed, the Athenæum would increasingly be seen, and see itself, as an entirely private institution. At the end of the nineteenth century, President Alfred Gooding (1856–1934) seemed almost to exult that the library had "never been thrown open to the public."[28]

THE DEBATE over subscribers' privileges stayed within the family: it generated no newspaper coverage or pamphlet war, and Peabody and Foster continued to be honored members of the Athenæum. In subsequent years, some proprietors may have felt justified in making the library collections available for educational purposes, but their fellow proprietors were unwilling to turn a blind eye to such unauthorized use. They affirmed in 1848 that it was "an abuse of the purposes of the institution to use books belonging to the library in the schools of the town whether public or private" and established a fine of $1 for any shareholder who violated the regulation or helped someone else to violate it.[29]

The library collection itself reflected high cultural aspirations. For most of the 1840s and 1850s, President Burroughs, Librarian Jaffrey, and the Reverend Peabody dominated book selection through their membership on the library committee, and they sought to purchase serious books of enduring worth—to ensure that "the fountains of a pure literature" remained "open for all who will drink at them." Peabody became editor of the *North American Review* in the

---

27. At midcentury, the Athenæum was the largest single library in the state of New Hampshire, although collectively the libraries of Dartmouth College and its student societies were almost three times as large: Charles Coffin Jewett, *Notices of Public Libraries in the United States of America* (Washington: Printed for the House of Representatives, 1851), 14–15.

28. Alfred Gooding, "The Athenaeum [*sic*]," in *The Portsmouth Book* (Boston: George H. Ellis, printer, [1899]), 30.

29. Proprietors' Minutes, 5 January 1848. Peabody continued to be elected a director each year until his departure from Portsmouth in 1860 to become the Plummer Professor of Christian Morals at Harvard. Foster remained the primary local source of books for the library, chaired the annual meeting in 1842 as president pro tem, and continued to be chosen for service on ad hoc committees.

mid-1850s; Burroughs spent much of his time in Boston and was a life sub-scriber to the Boston Athenæum. A preliminary assessment of their book pur-chases suggests a conscious effort to follow the literary paths marked out by the quarterlies and the Boston Athenæum. The cultural tone the library committee encouraged showed itself clearly on those rare occasions when a bequest or some other windfall enabled them to purchase most intentionally. Then, they worked hard to complete their collection of standard authors and to keep up with the progress of British scholarship. Attempting to fill in lacunae, they used a Boston agent to arrange purchases in the London market and on one occasion ordered antiquarian titles directly from Bartlett & Welford in New York.[30]

Burroughs, Jaffrey, and Peabody sought to provide Portsmouth with lit-erary resources it would not otherwise have, serious books whose audience was limited and that the market (in the form of the booksellers' commercial lending libraries) could not provide. From one point of view, their choices might be construed as anti-democratic, in their deliberate distance from the taste (as Peabody put it) "for *popular* books, for *interesting* books, that is, for such books as one can doze over and laugh over." Some proprietors, such as Jaffrey, may have adopted a posture of cultural superiority aggressively, as part of an assertion of elite status. For others, such as Peabody, the effort to supply Portsmouth with the best that had been thought was a gesture of faith. The town needed and deserved at least one copy of the complete works of Plato, or of Mill's *System of Logic*, even though the *North American Review* admitted of the latter that "not one in a hundred of our readers has, or can be induced to have, the slightest interest in the subject."[31] These were books that would

---

30. [Andrew Preston Peabody], "The District School Library," *North American Review* 50 (1840): 508. Peabody's own Portsmouth experience might have taught him that access to good books was more limited even in "our cities and larger towns" than he suggested in this article. Ample sources exist for a full study of the development of the Athenæum's book collection. The successive printed catalogues of the library (1823, 1827, 1833, 1839, 1849, and 1862) are items 2001, 2002, 2003, 2004, 2006, and 2007, respectively, in Robert Singerman, *American Library Book Catalogues, 1801–1875: A National Bibliography* (Urbana–Champaign: School of Library and Information Science, Univer-sity of Illinois at Urbana–Champaign, 1996). PA Records include a continuous series of accession records; those for the period to 1867 are in box 19, folders 12 and 13. Other relevant manuscript material for the antebellum period includes a register of books donated to 1849 (box 24, folder 4); directors' orders paid, 1818–26 (box 15, folders 18–26); bills and receipts, 1836–60 (box 16, folders 1–15); and correspondence relating to the donation of government documents (box 25, folders 1–7).

31. [Peabody], "The District School Library," 509 (italics in original); "Mill's System of Logic," *North American Review* 61 (1845): 349. The Athenæum bought the Thomas Taylor edition of the *Works* of Plato (London, 1804) in the mid-1840s, when it was still the only complete translation of his works, even though its five "bulky" volumes constituted "one continued slander on Plato's good name, both as a man of genius and a philosopher": *Edinburgh Review* 87 (1848): 169. The Plato was imported from London at a cost of $33.00; the bookseller's bill noted that it was "very scarce": Books Imported by W. D. Ticknor & Co., [1847], box 29, folder 35, PA Records.

broaden the intellectual horizons of the readers of Portsmouth — if only they could get at them.

AT THE beginning of the 1850s, the establishment of tax-supported libraries and the debate over the future of the Boston Athenæum reopened the question of the relation between the library and its public. In Boston, the Athenæum resolved to maintain its corporate independence. In New Hampshire's largest city, an alternative scenario played itself out, for the Manchester Athenæum became a public library in 1854 with none of the antagonism a similar plan had evoked in Boston. The Manchester institution, however, had been in existence only a decade, and unlike its older namesakes in Boston and Portsmouth was not the preserve of an entrenched local elite but a favored beneficiary of the mill owners' corporate philanthropy. The transition from private to public institution was seamless, having been suggested by "certain gentlemen connected with the Athenæum" and sanctioned by the corporations that had funded it.[32]

At least one correspondent to the *Journal* thought that Portsmouth should emulate the measures to place "the refining pleasure of abundant reading matter within the reach of the mass of the population" that were under way in "almost every city in New England and many of the larger towns." He saw no reason why Portsmouth should not join in this movement and expressed his hope that the municipal government might make an annual contribution that would secure "for every resident" access to the "entire treasures" of the Athenæum, "under certain easy restrictions." As a model, he pointed to Lowell, Massachusetts, where the relatively inexpensive Mechanics Association Library (share price of $12.50) was complemented by an even larger city library requiring an annual fee of only 50 cents — although he felt that even this was still too much. But the Portsmouth Athenæum, like its Boston namesake, maintained its corporate independence. It is doubtful its proprietors would have felt that Lowell and Manchester were appropriate models. The civic leaders of Portsmouth did not have to develop an institutional and social infrastructure to counteract "the public demand for demoralizing pleasures" in a new and rapidly growing city, nor did they face the need to speed the cultural assimilation of thousands of immigrants. No single employer in Portsmouth was directly responsible for the livelihood of a large portion of the population, as were the Boston capitalists and their managers in the inland mill cities. The

---

32. Chandler E. Potter, *The History of Manchester* . . . (Manchester: C. E. Potter, 1856), 752. On corporate approval of the transaction, see [Winifred Tuttle and Helen B. Sheehan], *Seventy-Five Years of the City Library, Manchester, New Hampshire* (Manchester: [City Library], 1929), 8.

Athenæum would continue to receive occasional bequests from the members of old Portsmouth families, but no corporate contributions.[33]

Transformation into a public library might have revived the Athenæum; as it was, although it continued to count the wealthiest men in Portsmouth among its members, the reading room appeared to be losing its central place in civic life. The room had always maintained a quasi-public character, and the use of the library for meetings had further opened the building to nonmembers. In 1838, however, the proprietors voted to prohibit any other "corporations or societies" from meeting there without the permission of the directors. The first floor too was increasingly restricted to members: in 1853, the directors voted to forbid its use for auctions without special permission, and to prohibit the posting of advertisements. The room was increasingly shabby, and the number of subscribers declined steadily. The newspapers began to portray the "daily gossipers" who frequented the reading room as the aging relics of a passing era. It was suggested in 1854 that the politics in this haunt of Portsmouth's "ancient and honorable gentry" were "of course conservative," and "the little democracy decidedly loud and afraid of itself." But in fact contemporary party platforms were "so new that men of such gravity cannot be over ready to mount them." Those who frequented the room embodied the " 'let alone' idea, and all who come within their influence, straightaway become imbued with the same sentiment." Feeding the correspondent's wry humor was his conviction that the reading room "must soon rank with the bygones." [34]

Advances in communication and transportation, notably the railroad and the telegraph, meant that the news itself was no longer a scarce resource. And Portsmouth lagged behind fast-growing industrial centers, its politics and business increasingly local. By the 1850s publicists were already articulating a civic self-image based on genteel historicism, and the Athenæum seemed

33. *Portsmouth Journal,* 4 June 1853; the letter was written in response to a profile of the Athenæum that appeared in *Norton's Literary Gazette and Publisher's Circular,* 15 April 1853. For an argument that the early public libraries were an attempt to tame the dangerous classes, see Michael H. Harris, "The Purpose of the American Public Library: A Revisionist Interpretation of History," *Library Journal* 98 (1973): 2509–14, and Michael H. Harris and Gerard Spiegler, "Everett, Ticknor and the Common Man: The Fear of Societal Instability as the Motivation for the Founding of the Boston Public Library," *Libri* 24 (1974): 249–75.

34. Proprietors' Minutes, 3 January 1838; *Portsmouth Journal,* 1 September 1849; *Portsmouth Morning Chronicle,* 25 October 1854. The directors prohibited auctions and the posting of advertisements at their meeting on 10 January 1853. In 1856, the shareholders included nine of Portsmouth's ten wealthiest individual taxpayers, and 34 of the top 50: *Portsmouth City Book and Directory . . .* (Portsmouth: C. W. Brewster & Son, [1856]), 237–39.

destined to become one of Portsmouth's picturesque relics. When one tourist visited in 1863, "A gentleman sat reading in the otherwise lonely reading room. We inquired the way to the library, and passed on. A still more lonely room awaited us. The silent book shelves alone greeted us with their voiceless eloquence." The Athenæum was not the only reading room in Portsmouth facing difficulties — the Mechanics' Reading Room, "regularly sustained for nearly thirty years," closed in the early 1850s — but the success of the Portsmouth Mercantile Library, established in 1852, showed, if only for a few years, that a reading room might still find an enthusiastic public. Its members were younger and less affluent, but they staked their claim to a sort of institutional parity when they offered the use of their reading room to the members of the Athenæum during its renovations in 1855. The Athenæum accepted the offer with gratitude.[35]

TOCQUEVILLE KNEW that even in a democracy citizens would always be "stealing off" to "establish, alongside the great political society, small private societies in which similarity of conditions, habits, and mores will be the bond." In a self-consciously democratizing society, however, exclusive organizations were vulnerable to attack, and the antebellum Athenæum was nothing if not exclusive. It exemplified, as Stark angrily pointed out, a fundamental contradiction in public life. Tocqueville had said flatly that in a democracy, "one cannot entrust the exercise of local powers to the principal citizens," but in Jacksonian Portsmouth the mercantile elite continued to occupy a position of commanding influence in politics as well as business: even the Democrats, whose most eloquent spokesmen took a radical line, nominated local notables for senior office. The Athenæum and its reading room offered a tempting target for those, like Thomas Laighton, who found this situation intolerable. Had its members embraced a broader role for their library, the Athenæum might have been less vulnerable to these charges, but although it described itself in the language of education and benevolence it seemed content to turn its back on the public.[36]

The experience of the Athenæum suggests how difficult it was (and remains) for an institution founded "for the general good" to articulate and carry out a mission consonant with its rhetoric. One person's public good may

---

35. *Portsmouth Morning Chronicle,* 24 October 1863; *Portsmouth Journal,* 31 March 1849. The Mechanics' Reading Room appears in *A Directory . . . of Portsmouth . . .* (Portsmouth: Charles W. Brewster, 1851), 206, but not in the 1856 directory, the next published. The record book of the Mercantile Library Association for 1856–1916 is at the Portsmouth Public Library (formerly on deposit at PA as item S–310*).

36. Tocqueville, *Democracy in America,* 577 and 494.

be another's private privilege. The proprietor wishing to preserve the intellectual treasure of the Athenæum for succeeding generations was at the same time denying the impecunious schoolteacher or ambitious workingman access to it. The question of access—to information, to political and philosophical ideas, and to the works of the imagination—has, of course, been central to historical accounts of American libraries. In the mid-twentieth century, Jesse Shera and Sidney Ditzion established a master narrative, still influential, that suggested that tax-supported public libraries had answered the question of access. In this, they were following the lead of nineteenth-century reformers themselves, figures like Horace Mann, endeavoring to calculate how many of Boston's immigrants had access to the saving power of print.[37]

We are confronted today with dilemmas analogous to those faced by Mann, Edward Everett, George Ticknor, and their contemporaries. The media in question have changed dramatically, but the underlying issues have not. Who is entitled to have access to which cultural goods, and on what terms? Digital-era debates over intellectual property have sensitized us to the ways in which the market and politics shape the transmission of culture and our knowledge of the world around us. Our own era's attention to the cultural importance of copyright informs the most exciting recent research on the dissemination of literary and political ideas in Britain during the late eighteenth and early nineteenth centuries. Whatever our personal feelings about the Association of American Publishers and the Recording Industry Association of America, or the Electronic Frontier Foundation and Napster, as historians we must thank them all for pushing us to look in more detail and greater depth at the ways economic, legal, political, and social structures shape access to culture.[38]

Access, then, looks set to remain at the heart of library history. The challenge we face is to historicize access more fully, for the era of the "public" library and the elusive golden age of the social library alike. This requires us to locate institutions of reading more firmly in their social contexts and to attend closely to their inner lives, because the large issues played themselves out on a small scale. The historian is fortunate to have unusually abundant documentation of the Portsmouth Athenæum and its members, but the richness of the evidence is itself an artifact of the institution's elite status. The various literary activities of the young Thomas Laighton suggest how intense the desire for access to the world of print could be outside elite circles. The

---

37. Shera, *Foundations,* and Sidney Ditzion, *Arsenals of a Democratic Culture: A Social History of the American Public Library Movement in New England and the Middle States from 1850 to 1900* (Chicago: American Library Association, 1947).

38. William St. Clair, *The Reading Nation in the Romantic Period* (Cambridge: Cambridge University Press, 2004).

evidence for that desire, however, is often frustratingly fragmentary, obscure, and indirect—despite the remarkable profusion of efforts to meet it—and while attempts to quantify nineteenth-century American library developments can outline trends, they doubtless understate the absolute level of activity. Our knowledge of antebellum libraries is inevitably biased toward elite institutions. As historians, we would do well to remember the voices of those who challenged the Athenæum's exclusivity, from inside and outside the institution.[39]

39. The organizers of the Davies Project at Princeton University [http://www.princeton.edu/ ~davpro/index.html], whose database of some 10,000 "American Libraries before 1876" is now the fundamental source for statistical assessments, acknowledge, "Many more [libraries] surely existed." PA, for example, has only recently acquired an MS diary (S–822), kept between September 1845 and June 1846 by a seventeen-year-old apprentice pharmacist, Albert H. Blanchard, which details the establishment in Portsmouth of a Young Men's Library Association—not previously recorded by local historians and not in the Davies Project database. Kenneth E. Carpenter has kindly shared an essay to be published in volume 2 of *A History of the Book in America* in which he tellingly situates the social library in a broader institutional context and suggests that the public library can be best understood as one among many attempts to meet the demand for access to the world of print.

Chapter 4

"An Association of Kindred Spirits"

Black Readers and Their Reading Rooms

Elizabeth McHenry

In an 1839 letter to the editor of the *Colored American,* a member of the Phoenixonian Society, a literary society formed in 1833 by African Americans in New York City, reported that another of the city's African American literary associations, the Phoenix Society, had "gone out of existence." The letter did not detail the cause of the literary society's demise, nor did it express tremendous sorrow over its disappearance. Rather, the writer's interest was practical: he wished to know what had happened to the Phoenix Society's library, which was apparently still intact and—at least in the opinion of the letter's writer—up for grabs. Reminding his readers that the bulk of the Phoenix Society's texts had been originally donated to the society "for the improvement of the colored population of this city," he lamented that "these books now are not subserving any high interest, or adding to the mental stature of that class for which they were designed." "I am connected with a Literary Society which has enrolled among its members a considerable portion of the young and active talent of our city[,] . . . a society that has done considerable . . . [good] in the cause of Literature, and the members of which are putting forth exertions to improve their minds, and prepare themselves for usefulness among our people," he wrote. "This society has no Library, and as I hear the Library of the 'Phœnix Society' is to be given to some Literary Association, I have thought our destitute state a *demand* for this Library, and an inducement for us to put in our claims. The amount of good that the possession of this Library would effect among us, I will not pretend to calculate. Our destitute state, and inability to obtain books we sorely feel. Doubtless the influence of a good Library—such a Library as the 'Phœnix Society' are about to dispose of, would be salutary in the highest extent."[1] (See figure 4.1.)

---

1. "A Phœnixonian," "To the Editors of the Colored American," *Colored American,* 16 February 1839, unpaginated.

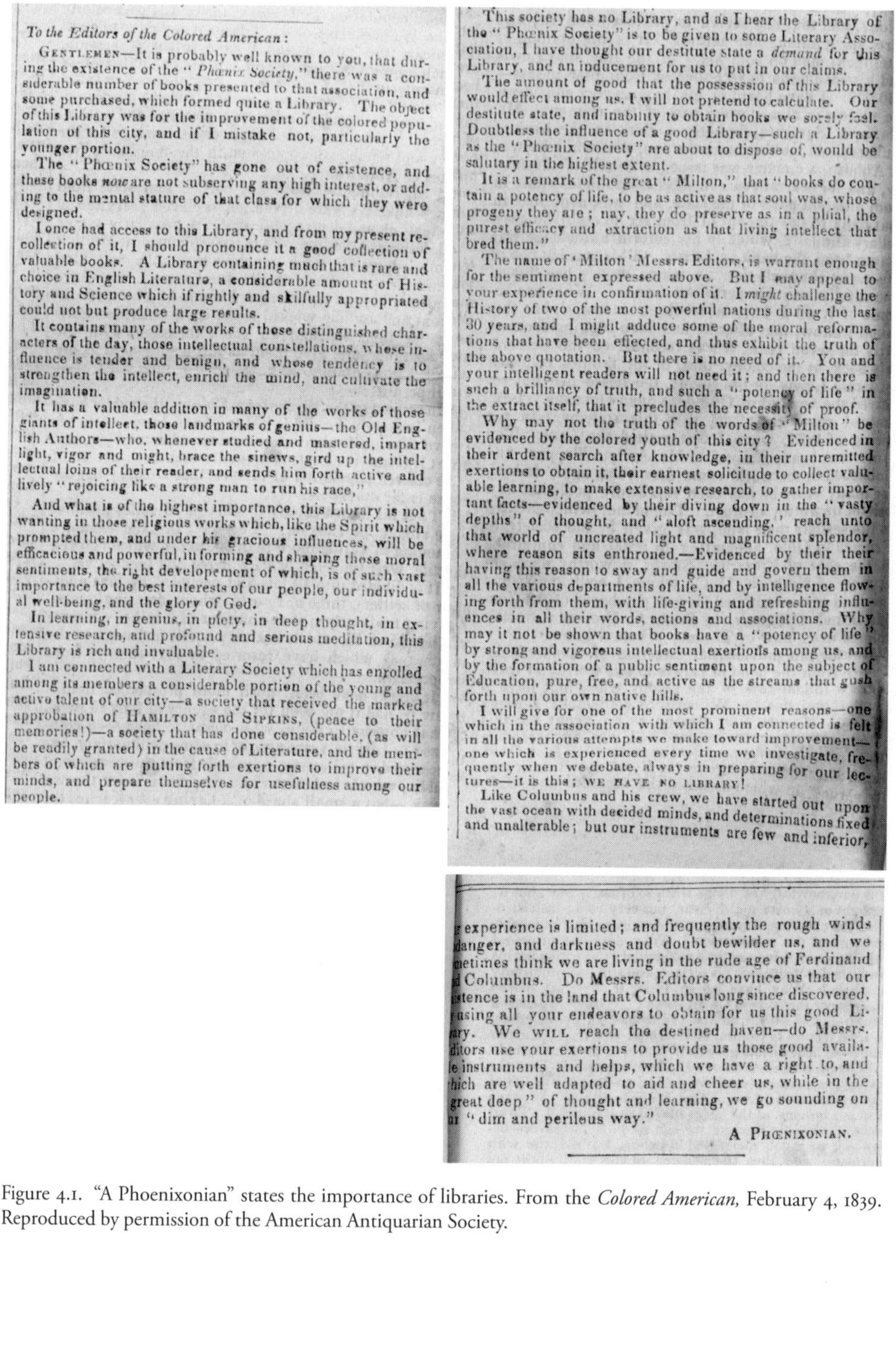

To the Editors of the Colored American:

GENTLEMEN—It is probably well known to you, that during the existence of the "Phœnix Society," there was a considerable number of books presented to that association, and some purchased, which formed quite a Library. The object of this Library was for the improvement of the colored population of this city, and if I mistake not, particularly the younger portion.

The "Phœnix Society" has gone out of existence, and these books now are not subserving any high interest, or adding to the mental stature of that class for which they were designed.

I once had access to this Library, and from my present recollection of it, I should pronounce it a good collection of valuable books. A Library containing much that is rare and choice in English Literature, a considerable amount of History and Science which if rightly and skilfully appropriated could not but produce large results.

It contains many of the works of those distinguished characters of the day, those intellectual constellations, whose influence is tender and benign, and whose tendency is to strengthen the intellect, enrich the mind, and cultivate the imagination.

It has a valuable addition in many of the works of those giants of intellect, those landmarks of genius—the Old English Authors—who, whenever studied and mastered, impart light, vigor and might, brace the sinews, gird up the intellectual loins of their reader, and sends him forth active and lively "rejoicing like a strong man to run his race,"

And what is of the highest importance, this Library is not wanting in those religious works which, like the Spirit which prompted them, and under his gracious influences, will be efficacious and powerful, in forming and shaping those moral sentiments, the right developement of which, is of such vast importance to the best interests of our people, our individual well-being, and the glory of God.

In learning, in genius, in piety, in deep thought, in extensive research, and profound and serious meditation, this Library is rich and invaluable.

I am connected with a Literary Society which has enrolled among its members a considerable portion of the young and active talent of our city—a society that received the marked approbation of HAMILTON and SIPKINS, (peace to their memories!)—a society that has done considerable, (as will be readily granted) in the cause of Literature, and the members of which are putting forth exertions to improve their minds, and prepare themselves for usefulness among our people.

This society has no Library, and as I hear the Library of the "Phœnix Society" is to be given to some Literary Association, I have thought our destitute state a *demand* for this Library, and an inducement for us to put in our claims.

The amount of good that the possession of this Library would effect among us, I will not pretend to calculate. Our destitute state, and inability to obtain books we sorely feel. Doubtless the influence of a good Library—such a Library as the "Phœnix Society" are about to dispose of, would be salutary in the highest extent.

It is a remark of the great "Milton," that "books do contain a potency of life, to be as active as that soul was, whose progeny they are; nay, they do preserve as in a phial, the purest efficacy and extraction as that living intellect that bred them."

The name of 'Milton' Messrs. Editors, is warrant enough for the sentiment expressed above. But I *may* appeal to your experience in confirmation of it. I *might* challenge the History of two of the most powerful nations during the last 30 years, and I might adduce some of the moral reformations that have been effected, and thus exhibit the truth of the above quotation. But there is no need of it. You and your intelligent readers will not need it; and then there is such a brilliancy of truth, and such a "potency of life" in the extract itself, that it precludes the necessity of proof.

Why may not the truth of the words of "Milton" be evidenced by the colored youth of this city? Evidenced in their ardent search after knowledge, in their unremitted exertions to obtain it, their earnest solicitude to collect valuable learning, to make extensive research, to gather important facts—evidenced by their diving down in the "vasty depths" of thought, and "aloft ascending," reach unto that world of uncreated light and magnificent splendor, where reason sits enthroned.—Evidenced by their their having this reason to sway and guide and govern them in all the various departments of life, and by intelligence flowing forth from them, with life-giving and refreshing influences in all their words, actions and associations. Why may it not be shown that books have a "potency of life" by strong and vigorous intellectual exertions among us, and by the formation of a public sentiment upon the subject of Education, pure, free, and active as the streams that gush forth upon our own native hills.

I will give for one of the most prominent reasons—one which in the association with which I am connected is felt in all the various attempts we make toward improvement—one which is experienced every time we investigate, frequently when we debate, always in preparing for our lectures—it is this; WE HAVE NO LIBRARY!

Like Columbus and his crew, we have started out upon the vast ocean with decided minds, and determinations fixed and unalterable; but our instruments are few and inferior,

experience is limited; and frequently the rough winds danger, and darkness and doubt bewilder us, and we metimes think we are living in the rude age of Ferdinand d Columbus. Do Messrs. Editors convince us that our stence is in the land that Columbus long since discovered, using all your endeavors to obtain for us this good Library. We WILL reach the destined haven—do Messrs. ditors use your exertions to provide us those good available instruments and helps, which we have a right to, and hich are well adapted to aid and cheer us, while in the great deep" of thought and learning, we go sounding on ur "dim and perilous way."

A PHŒNIXONIAN.

Figure 4.1. "A Phoenixonian" states the importance of libraries. From the *Colored American*, February 4, 1839. Reproduced by permission of the American Antiquarian Society.

Libraries such as the one this writer makes reference to are not commonly associated with African Americans in the antebellum United States. Indeed, our understanding of the relationships black Americans had with books, reading, and literary culture generally in the nineteenth century remains extremely limited. While we are familiar with the story of Frederick Douglass, who recounted in his 1845 *Narrative* how he contrived ways to "steal" literacy, first from poor and hungry white boys in the neighborhood in exchange for bread and then by challenging his associates in a Baltimore shipyard to write better than he, we are less familiar with stories that record the ways other African Americans from the same time period acquired and practiced their literacy. Douglass's life story is a testimony to his belief that literacy was the "pathway from slavery to freedom."[2] But what of those free blacks who, in the first decades of the nineteenth century, formed sturdy communities in the urban North? Although technically free, these individuals were subject to open hostility and discrimination, and they faced constant charges of innate black inferiority. Almost every social and educational institution and mechanism of support was closed to them except for those they founded for themselves. Of the literary practices of this population we know very little. But it is here we must look to understand the history of African American libraries. Critical attention to two institutions formed by free blacks in the antebellum North are crucial to this effort. One consisted of the reading rooms and libraries of small, independent literary societies and organizations interested in the advancement of black equality and civil rights. The other was the black press, an institution that initially replicated the function of a library by distributing reading material that would serve the needs of an increasingly literate black community.

That free blacks felt it a priority to circulate printed texts in part by forming and sustaining reading rooms and libraries suggests the extent to which they believed in the power of the written word and the importance of literary study. Like their enslaved brethren in the South, antebellum free blacks in the urban North recognized that reading was a potentially transforming activity, not only for individuals but also for society as a whole. Literary and intellectual contributions, they believed, would disprove the discourse of black intellectual inferiority, altering the standing of African Americans in American society. Taking part in educational programs and exhibiting publicly voices that were "learned," free blacks believed, would enable them to make economic gains and move into trades from which their people were largely

---

2. Frederick Douglass, *Narrative of the Life of Frederick Douglass, an American Slave* (1845; rpt. New York: Penguin, 1983), 73.

excluded. In the first decades of the nineteenth century black leaders increasingly expressed concern that "we have not produced any to excel in arts and sciences." "What station above the common employment of craftsmen and labourers would we fill," they wondered, "did we possess both learning and abilities?"[3] In the midst of a dominant society for whom knowledge of the arts, sciences, and literature was highly valued, free blacks became increasingly aware that they needed to read widely and produce documents that were sophisticated in their presentation as well as their content. At the beginning of the nineteenth century they began establishing independent societies to promote literary skills and to ensure that, as a group, they would not be excluded from the benefits associated with reading and literary study.

The literary societies they formed between 1828 and 1860 were at the heart of a political agenda for promoting opportunities and equality for the nation's free black population that was grounded in African American literary practice. Literary societies were both large and small; they planned reading lists and provided regular opportunities for black writers to publish original creations, both orally and in print. Members ensured the development of their literary skills by supporting one another while also maintaining an environment where ideas could be openly discussed and critiqued. The libraries and reading rooms established by these institutions were central to their activities and to the fulfillment of their objectives. They were locations where books and other printed texts and materials were housed; but more important, they were social locations where reading led to conversation and printed texts of all varieties could be enjoyed, discussed, and debated in the company of others.

So central was the library to the objectives of one of the earliest African American literary societies, the Colored Reading Society, formed in 1828 for "Men of Colour, who are citizens of the City and the Liberties of Philadelphia," that the rules and regulations surrounding its establishment and use dominated the society's constitution.[4] Members were to pay an initiation fee and monthly dues; "with the exception of light [and] rent," this income was to be spent entirely on books. "All monies received by this Society," reads the constitution, were "to be expended in useful books, such as the Society may from time to time appropriate." The constitution went on to specify that "all books initiated into this Society, shall be placed in the care of the Librarian belonging to said institution," whose duty it was "to deliver to said members

3. William Hamilton, *An Address to the New York African Society, for Mutual Relief, Delivered in the Universalist Church, January 2, 1809,* reprinted in *Early Negro Writing, 1760–1837,* ed. Dorothy Porter (Boston: Beacon, 1971), 36.

4. William Whipper, "Original Communications," *Freedom's Journal,* 20 June 1828, 98.

alternatively, such books as they shall demand." The librarian was also to pay "strict regard that no member shall keep said book out of the library longer than one week, without paying the fine prescribed in the constitution, unless an apology for sickness or absence." Members were reminded more than once that "those shall be the only excuses received."[5] They agreed to "meet once a week to return and receive books, to read, and express whatever sentiments they may have conceived if they think proper, and transact the necessary business relative to this institution. . . . It shall be our whole duty," they resolved, "to instruct and assist each other in the improvement of our minds, as we wish to see the flame of improvement spreading amongst our brethren and friends" (Whipper, *Address,* 108).

The guiding principle of Philadelphia's Colored Reading Society was that "the station of a scholar highly versed in classic lore . . . is indeed higher than any other occupied by man." Members looked to fill their library with texts that would allow them to cultivate both intellectual competence and artistic sensibility. They subscribed to the belief that the "acquisition of knowledge is not the only design of a liberal arts education"; in addition to amassing knowledge, a goal of their reading and their selection of texts was to "discipline the mind itself, to strengthen and enlarge its powers, to form habits of close and accurate thinking, and to acquire a facility of classifying and arranging, analyzing and comparing our ideas on different subjects" (Whipper, *Address,* 110). The "cultivation of taste" required attention to "the study of belle letters, to criticism, to composition, pronunciation, style, and to everything included in the name of eloquence" (Whipper, *Address,* 113). They believed that classical texts would facilitate the fulfillment of their ambition. From these texts, "a fund of ideas is acquired on a variety of subjects; the taste is greatly improved by conversing with the best models; the imagination is enriched by the fine scenery with which the classics abound; and an acquaintance is formed with human nature, together with the history, customs, and manners of antiquity" (Whipper, *Address,* 111). In addition to the classics and works by "our best English writers," the society filled its library with "books treating . . . the subject of Ancient Modern and Ecclesiastical History, [and] the Laws of Pennsylvania." It also subscribed to two of the most important journals of the time, the abolitionist publication the *Genius of Universal Emancipation* and the first African American newspaper, *Freedom's Journal.*[6]

---

5. William Whipper, *An Address Delivered in Wesley Church on the Evening of June 12, Before the Colored Reading Society of Philadelphia, for Mental Improvement* (1828), reprinted in *Early Negro Writing,* 108. Subsequent references to this text will be cited parenthetically as Whipper, *Address.*

6. Whipper, "Original Communications," 98. This announcement makes clear that the Reading Room Society forbade the inclusion of "every book that is chimerical or visionary" from its library.

The founders of the Colored Reading Society believed that exposure to all of these texts and the conversations they inspired would allow the society's membership to "contribut[e] something to the advancement of science [and literature] generally amongst our brethren," while also providing opportunities to "become acquainted with the transacting of public affairs" (Whipper, *Address,* 118, 110).

Like that of most early African American literary associations and their libraries, the fate of the Colored Reading Society is uncertain.[7] One of its founding members, William Whipper, was a part of a group that began the Philadelphia Library Company of Colored Persons in 1833, which suggests that the Library Company of Colored Persons may have absorbed the membership of the Colored Reading Society. Modeled after the Library Company of Philadelphia, begun by Benjamin Franklin in 1731 for "literary and scientific discussion, the reading of original essays, poems, and so forth," the membership of the Library Company of Colored Persons was composed of free black men.[8] From its first announcement, the Library Company of Colored Persons boasted that it was neither "sectarian" nor "a mere fractional effort, the design of any single society among us." Rather, the Library Company was formed in recognition of the "necessity of promoting among our rising youth, a proper cultivation for literary pursuits and improvements of the faculties and powers of their minds," and designed "to embrace the entire population of the City of Philadelphia."[9] A request for "such books and other donations as will facilitate the object of this institution" accompanied the public announcement of the organization. Books and other printed texts were to be made accessible at minimal cost. Members could read on their own or participate in a reading schedule. In addition, in order to promote research, discussion, and debate, the Library Company sponsored a weekly lecture series, which ran from October through May. The Library Company of Colored Persons was still a strong institution in 1837, when James Forten, Jr., at a meeting of the Moral Reform Society, cited it as an example of the state of learning among the colored population in Philadelphia. "Our Library Association is gaining strength every day," he reported. "We have a well supplied stock of books collected from the most useful and varied productions of

---

7. When Joseph Willson outlined the most prominent of the active literary societies of Philadelphia in 1841, the Colored Reading Society was not mentioned. See Joseph Willson, *Sketches of the Higher Classes of Colored Society* (Philadelphia: Merrihew and Thompson, 1841), 27.

8. George Maurice Abbot, *A Short History of the Library Company of Philadelphia* (Philadelphia: n.p., 1913), 3.

9. "Philadelphia Library Company of Colored Persons," *Hazard's Register of Pennsylvania,* 16 March 1833, 186 (page is numbered incorrectly in original; it should be 176).

the age."[10] By 1838 the Library Company had more than 600 volumes in its collection and at least 150 members.[11]

Although the Library Company of Colored Persons was organized by Philadelphia's black elite, the impact of its activities, like readings and lectures that were open to the public, reverberated throughout a larger segment of the black population. It shared with societies composed of less distinguished individuals the common understanding that the "condition" of African Americans could "only be meliorated by their being improved in morals, literature, and the mechanic arts."[12] The founders of New York's Phoenix Society, organized in 1833, called on "every person of color to unite himself, or herself, to [the Phoenix Society], and faithfully endeavor to promote its objects" (Phoenix 141). To facilitate this, the society had a unique policy on fees: its constitution stipulated that membership would be open to "all persons who contributed to its funds quarterly, any sum of money they may think proper." The ultimate goal of the Phoenix Society was to transform New York City's entire black population into a "useful portion of the community" (Phoenix 141). To do this they planned to "establish circulating libraries in each ward for the use of people of colour on very moderate pay—to establish mental feasts, and also lyceums for speaking and for lectures on sciences" (Phoenix 144).

It took only eight months for the Phoenix Society to begin fulfilling its goals. In a letter dated December 7, 1833, and printed in the *Colonizationist and Journal of Freedom,* Samuel Cornish, a coeditor of *Freedom's Journal,* and one of the founders of the Phoenix Society, outlined the goals and activities of the "library and Reading Room lately opened by the executive committee of the Phœnix Society." "The objects of the institution are generally improvement and the training of our youth to habits of reading and reflection," he explained.[13] Cornish's letter to the *Colonizationist and Journal of Freedom* includes an appeal for "donations from the favored people of New York, in books, maps, papers, money, etc., for the benefit of our feeble institution." The variety of printed materials Cornish lists—all considered worthy of a place in the newly formed library—offers some indication of the broad definition of what were considered valuable texts by black leaders in their attempt

---

10. *Minutes and Proceedings of the First Annual Meeting of the American Moral Reform Society, Held at Philadelphia* (1837); reprinted in *Early Negro Writing,* 238.

11. Pennsylvania Abolitionist Society, *The Present State and Condition of the Free People of Color in the City of Philadelphia* (Philadelphia, 1838), 30.

12. *Address and Constitution of the Phœnix Society of New York, and of the Auxiliary Ward Associations* (1833); reprinted in *Early Negro Writing,* 141. References will be cited as "Phoenix."

13. Samuel Cornish, "A Library for the People of Color," *Colonizationist and Journal of Freedom,* February 1834, 306–7.

to establish literary culture in antebellum black communities. The acknowl-edgment of a number of donations in a February 1834 issue of the *Emancipa-tor* indicates that his appeal was well received.[14] The Phoenix Society's library was reported to be a "good collection of valuable books" that included "much that is rare and choice in English Literature [and] a considerable amount of History and Science."[15] This was the library in which the anonymous mem-ber of the Phoenixonian Literary Society expressed interest after hearing of the Phoenix Society's demise; there is no record of any response to his query, and the fate of the Phoenix Society's library remains unknown.

It bears drawing attention to the Phoenix Society's emphasis on training African Americans in "habits of reading and reflection," for the distinction between this and more basic lessons in literacy offers important insight into the multiple purposes of the earliest African American literary societies and their libraries. In addition to "courses of lectures . . . on morals, economy, and the arts and sciences generally," the society offered three "class[es] of readers," each consisting of "25 or 30 or more." Each class was to have "selected its course of reading and appointed the readers, whose duty it shall be to read for one hour. All classes shall note prominent parts, and then retire into the adjacent room to converse on the subjects, together with occurrences of the day, calculated to cultivate the mind and improve the heart."[16] Rather than the acquisition of basic literacy, the emphasis in this description of the Phoenix Society's offerings is on the sharing of texts and the discussions that might then subsequently take place. Because the text was read aloud by an appointed "reader," it was possible to form a "class" that included those with various levels of literacy; indeed, it is likely that there were people in the Phoenix Society's "classes of readers" who were themselves technically illiterate. Because the silent reading of the text was not privileged over its oral performance, literate, semiliterate, and even illiterate members of the Phoenix Society could appreciate a text, and the discussions that followed its reading could involve those who listened to the text's performance as well as those with the ability to read it for themselves. The objectives of some of the earliest African American literary societies, libraries, and reading rooms had less to do with the development of basic literacy skills than they did with cultivating the mind by fostering basic literary skills, that is, those skills that derive from exposure to texts and the rigorous critical analysis and discussions that they prompt.

---

14. Samuel Cornish, "Phœnix Library—Donations," *The Emancipator,"* 4 February 1834. This letter was first published in the *New York Observer.*

15. "A Phœnixonian," "To the Editors of the Colored American," *Colored American,* 16 February 1839, unpaginated.

16. Cornish, "A Library for the People of Color."

Rather than a means of training individuals in basic literacy, the pursuit of literary culture that culminated in the development of African American literary societies, libraries, and reading rooms in the antebellum United States was geared toward helping their members prove, through their literary activities, the capacity of the black mind by demonstrating a propensity for developing what one early contributor to the black press called "a literary character."[17] Simply put, association with literature and literary study offered free black Americans in the urban North a way to refute widespread claims of their innate inferiority. Displays of literary character would mark black Americans as public and refined figures, giving them the positive reputation that would, in the words of one black leader, "arrest the progress of prejudice, and . . . shield [the free black community] against the consequent evils."[18] Literary study would provide free blacks with the tools needed to represent themselves more fairly and accurately and lead to the "[g]ood principles [that] will soon break down the barriers between [the black] and the white population."[19]

Additionally, reading, library use, and organized literary study were promoted as positive alternatives to the host of negative and "immoral" distractions that faced the free black community daily. Particular concern was expressed again and again for what one anonymous contributor to the *Colored American* described as "the rising generation," by which was meant those "young men whose evenings are unemployed, and who now spend their leisure hours in the theatre or porter house, (which leads to the brothel and gaming tables)." In an article titled "Literary Societies," this writer called these institutions "of more importance than any others in the present age of Societies and Associations." With more of them in the black community, susceptible young men "might be induced to make the reading room their place of resort, and thus instead of injuring their health, wasting their money, and acquiring immoral habits, they might be storing their minds with useful knowledge, and erecting a reputation which would be far superior to the ephemeral renown which pleasure confers on their votaries, and they might also establish for themselves a character which time itself could not destroy."[20] Developing literary character, the components of which included morality, self-discipline, intellectual curiosity, civic responsibility, and eloquence, was cast as both a private virtue and a civic duty; it benefited the individual, but it was essential for the common good as well. In developing literary talents,

---

17. "Examiner," "Characteristics of the People of Color—No. 3: Literary Character," *Colored American,* 16 May 1840, unpaginated.

18. "To Our Patrons," *Freedom's Journal,* 16 March 1827.

19. Samuel E. Cornish, "Original Communications," *Freedom's Journal,* 13 July 1827, 70.

20. "Literary Societies," *Colored American,* 5 October 1839, unpaginated.

individual black people contributed not only to their own improvement, but also to the advancement of their race.

Announcements of new opportunities for literary study and interaction that expressed similar concern for the many obstacles to the development of literary character in the black community appeared regularly in African American newspapers in the 1830s. Like the one placed by antislavery activist and journalist David Ruggles in the 16 June 1838 issue of the *Colored American* (see figure 4.2), most made reference both to the distractions of urban life and to the difficulties of finding access to literary texts or appropriate environments for their appreciation. Observing that "intelligence can only be acquired by observation, reading and reflection," Ruggles condemned the exclusion of African Americans "from Reading Rooms, popular lectures, and all places of literary attractions and general improvement" by those he termed "our fairer and more favored citizens." He expressed the commonly held fear that "without some centre of literary attraction for all young men whose mental appetites thirst for food, many are in danger of being led into idle and licentious habits by the allurements of vice which surround them on every side." Ruggles's effort to remedy this situation centered on the opening of a "READING ROOM, where those who wish to avail themselves of the opportunity, can have access to the principal daily and leading anti-slavery papers, and other popular periodicals of the day." The conclusion of his announcement served as an invitation to participate in the activities of the reading room: "We hope that the friends of literary improvement, among all classes of our citizens, in this part of the city, will encourage our enterprise."[21] Inherent in this and similar announcements that appeared in the newspapers of the time is the insistence that literary texts and the institutions that would provide access to them were vital to the "present and future prosperity of young men in this community."[22]

It is notable that almost every antebellum African American library or reading room for which there are extant records included in its holdings products of the African American press, and it is this source that shows precisely what free blacks were reading. Despite the apparent success of public appeals by newly formed African American literary organizations for the donation of bound books, the very fact that these were sought in this manner points to the fact that books were expensive and thus relatively difficult to procure.

---

21. "Circular," *Colored American,* 16 June 1838, 69. Charges for the use of the facilities underscore Ruggles's commitment to making it accessible to all. "Strangers" were welcomed free of charge. All others were to pay according to how long they wished to use the library: yearly rates were $2.75; monthly the charge was $0.25, and the library could be used for a week for 6 1/2 cents.

22. Ibid.

It is also notable that most of the bound books included in the library were publications by European and primarily English authors, a fact that supports the idea that one aim of African American libraries and reading rooms was to help their users enter the literary mainstream. But after 1827, when *Freedom's Journal* made its inaugural appearance, African American newspapers were in almost constant production, and the very diversity of their content made them desirable components of local libraries and reading rooms. By including productions of the African American press, libraries and reading rooms

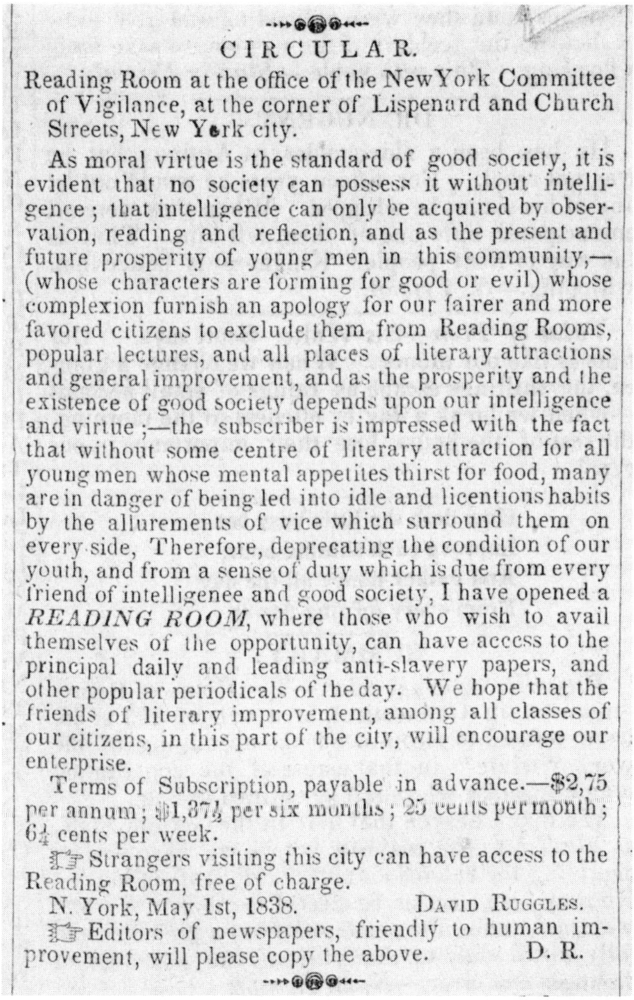

> ••••@@@@••••
> ## CIRCULAR.
> Reading Room at the office of the New York Committee of Vigilance, at the corner of Lispenard and Church Streets, New York city.
>
> As moral virtue is the standard of good society, it is evident that no society can possess it without intelligence ; that intelligence can only be acquired by observation, reading and reflection, and as the present and future prosperity of young men in this community,— (whose characters are forming for good or evil) whose complexion furnish an apology for our fairer and more favored citizens to exclude them from Reading Rooms, popular lectures, and all places of literary attractions and general improvement, and as the prosperity and the existence of good society depends upon our intelligence and virtue ;—the subscriber is impressed with the fact that without some centre of literary attraction for all young men whose mental appetites thirst for food, many are in danger of being led into idle and licentious habits by the allurements of vice which surround them on every side, Therefore, deprecating the condition of our youth, and from a sense of duty which is due from every friend of intelligence and good society, I have opened a *READING ROOM*, where those who wish to avail themselves of the opportunity, can have access to the principal daily and leading anti-slavery papers, and other popular periodicals of the day. We hope that the friends of literary improvement, among all classes of our citizens, in this part of the city, will encourage our enterprise.
>
> Terms of Subscription, payable in advance.—$2,75 per annum; $1,37½ per six months; 25 cents per month; 6¼ cents per week.
>
> ☞ Strangers visiting this city can have access to the Reading Room, free of charge.
>
> N. York, May 1st, 1838.   DAVID RUGGLES.
>
> ☞ Editors of newspapers, friendly to human improvement, will please copy the above.   D. R.
> ••••@@@@••••

Figure 4.2. David Ruggles announces the opening of his Reading Room. From the *Colored American,* 16 June 1838, 69. Reproduced by permission of the American Antiquarian Society.

affirmed their dedication to serving specifically African American interests and concerns as well as the more general needs of the community. Stories that appeared in two of the most prominent early African American newspapers, *Freedom's Journal,* which ceased publication in 1829, and the *Colored American,* published between 1837 and 1841, provided the free black community with narratives and reports that were educational tools in themselves, supplying their readers with a steady stream of interesting reading material that was consumable by a readership of various ages and literacy levels. The vignettes included in the newspaper were interesting and compelling, if often sensational. Brief enough to be consumed in short periods of time, they were also convenient to read aloud. Stories included in *Freedom's Journal* were written for sharing, in a format that lent itself to their being read aloud. In addition to their informational value, these features made the newspapers important resources for newly literate and semiliterate readers. The newspapers were perhaps most valuable for their adult readers, for whom the acquisition of education was a more independent endeavor. But they were also important tools in formal educational institutions that served free black youth. Although by 1830, New York's African Free School on Mulberry Street claimed that its library included over 450 volumes, the school also received *Freedom's Journal* and recognized it as an invaluable part of the collection.[23] When Charles C. Andrews, a teacher at the school, wrote to the editors of *Freedom's Journal* to thank them for "furnishing gratuitously, the regular weekly numbers of the 'Freedom's Journal,' for the benefit of the Library in the School" (see figure 4.3), he assured them that the newspaper was being put to use: "much good," he reported, "may be calculated to result from such a journal being perused by *such readers,* as will have access to its pages." [24]

In many ways, both *Freedom's Journal* and the *Colored American* were designed to serve as libraries unto themselves, supplying their weekly readers with the variety of texts that replicated on a smaller scale what might have been found in a well-stocked European-American reading room. Like curators or librarians, whose acquisition and control of material gives shape to a collection, the editors of the earliest African American newspapers acted

---

23. Charles C. Andrews, *The History of the New-York African Free-Schools* (1830; rpt. New York: Negro University Press, 1969), 103.

24. Charles C. Andrews, "New York African Free School," *Freedom's Journal,* 9 November 1827, 138. In his letter, Andrews calls it a "pleasing fact" that *Freedom's Journal* joined "three hundred well selected volumes" in the school's library. His pride in the collection is evident in the anecdote he relayed to readers of the newspaper: "One of our little scholars, aged about ten years, was questioned on some astronomical and other scientific subjects a few months ago, by a celebrated and learned doctor of this city; the boy answered so readily and so accurately to the queries, [and] was at last asked, how it was that he was so well acquainted with such subjects? His reply was, that he remembered to have read of them in the books of the School Library."

as stewards of literary culture, considering themselves responsible for shaping the reading choices and influencing the practices of black readers. The editors of *Freedom's Journal* promised readers that a central function of their publication would be to assist their readers in selecting "such authors as will not only enlarge their stock of useful knowledge, but such as will also serve to stimulate them to higher attainments in science." This service would help

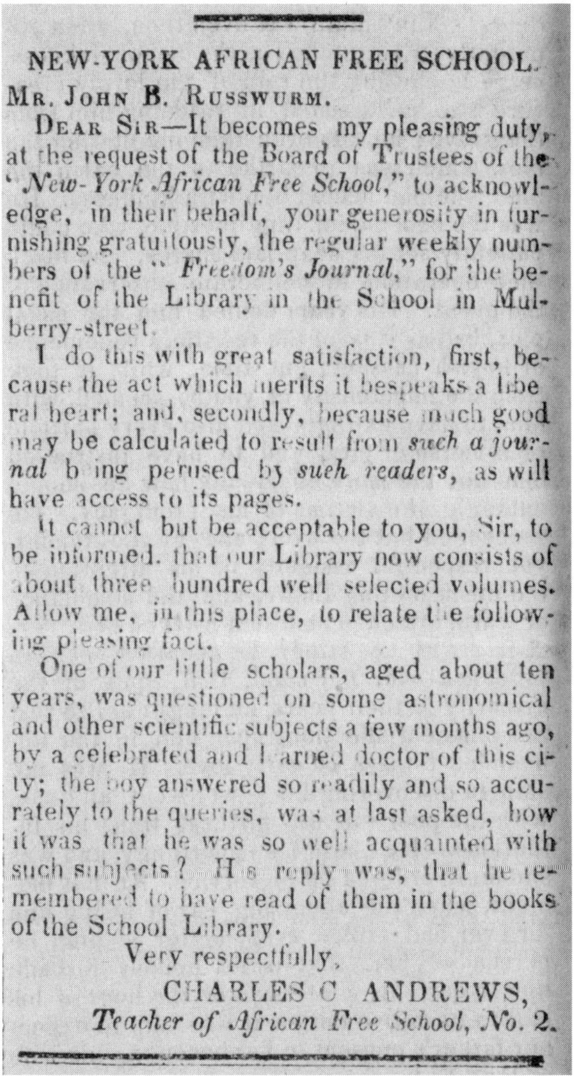

NEW-YORK AFRICAN FREE SCHOOL.

MR. JOHN B. RUSSWURM.

DEAR SIR—It becomes my pleasing duty, at the request of the Board of Trustees of the "New-York African Free School," to acknowledge, in their behalf, your generosity in furnishing gratuitously, the regular weekly numbers of the "Freedom's Journal," for the benefit of the Library in the School in Mulberry-street.

I do this with great satisfaction, first, because the act which merits it bespeaks a liberal heart; and, secondly, because much good may be calculated to result from such a journal being perused by such readers, as will have access to its pages.

It cannot but be acceptable to you, Sir, to be informed, that our Library now consists of about three hundred well selected volumes. Allow me, in this place, to relate the following pleasing fact.

One of our little scholars, aged about ten years, was questioned on some astronomical and other scientific subjects a few months ago, by a celebrated and learned doctor of this city; the boy answered so readily and so accurately to the queries, was at last asked, how it was that he was so well acquainted with such subjects? His reply was, that he remembered to have read of them in the books of the School Library.

Very respectfully,

CHARLES C ANDREWS,

Teacher of African Free School, No. 2.

Figure 4.3. A letter of thanks to John Brown Russwurm for donating copies of his newspaper to a school. *Freedom's Journal,* 9 November 1827. Reproduced by permission of the American Antiquarian Society.

readers avoid "time . . . lost, and wrong principles instilled, by the perusal of works of trivial importance." [25] Evident in this promise is the extent to which *Freedom's Journal* sought to guide its readers in their selection of texts. Articles included in the newspaper were exemplary of the ways a written text might serve as a manual to self-improvement and the standards of good character and "respectable" behavior. Titles such as "Formation of Character," "Duty of Wives," "Duties of Children," "Accurate Judgment," and "Economy" suggest that the editors of the newspaper believed they should seek to strengthen the moral condition of the individual, the race, and the nation.[26]

Freedom's Journal promoted literary study as an alternative to idleness and moral decay; the *Colored American* also did this, but was more self-conscious in its presentation of itself as a substitute for those without access to other sources of reading material. "Our people must be supplied with mental resources," insisted the writer of an introductory editorial to the newspaper. Editors of the *Colored American* agreed, offering the weekly publication to the free black population as a means of access to these needed resources. In addition to exposure to literary texts, one form of needed knowledge among the *Colored American*'s target population was perceived to be a certain level of cultural literacy, not only about their own expanding and prosperous democracy but about the distant regions increasingly within the national consciousness. The first three issues of the paper included a series of articles written for the *New York Weekly Advocate* on various historical and organizational aspects of the United States. After recounting the general history of the country from its "discovery," these articles outlined the origins and relevant statistics of each state. Included in the information communicated in this series as "useful for present and future reference" was the structure of local and federal government, anticipated population figures for the various states in 1837 based on the population in 1830, and a listing of the "Vessels of War, in the United States Navy, 1836." Subsequent issues of the *Colored American* feature an extensive article titled "Principal Features of the Various Nations on Earth," compiled specifically for the newspaper, as well as a biographical sketch of Benjamin Franklin. By offering its readers a kind of advanced course of study on national history, state statistics, and eminent American lives, the *Colored American* was implicitly demonstrating the kind of cultural literacy its editors believed necessary for creating an informed African American citizenry.[27]

25. "To Our Patrons," *Freedom's Journal,* 16 March 1827, 1.

26. See *Freedom's Journal,* 14, 21, 28 February and 21 March 1828.

27. Table: "Vessels of War, in the U.S. Navy, 1836," *Weekly Advocate,* 7 January 1837, unpaginated. For subsequent installations of the same series, "A Brief Description of the United States," see the issues of 14 and 21 January 1837.

Like the material libraries and reading rooms that existed in black communities, the *Colored American* aspired to supply its readers with lasting access to texts that would be central to their acquisition of "useful knowledge" while also providing a basis for engagement with others in productive conversation. Singlehandedly, it fulfilled the role of a reading room by distributing texts on a diverse range of subjects to an audience that could then come together to discuss and debate what they had read. In this, the *Colored American* considered itself a valuable resource that should be preserved for future rereading and later reference. Beginning with the first issue, the editors regularly published this reminder to "File Your Papers": "As the advocate will not only be devoted to the passing events of the day, but also in a great measure to useful and entertaining general matter, which may be perused at any future time with as much interest as at the present, we would suggest to our readers the importance of preserving a file of the journal. By doing this, they will, at the end of a year, have a neat little volume, and also have at hand the means of amusing and improving their minds during leisure hours."[28] This advice is telling, especially when contrasted with the anxiety expressed over the modest size of the publication by the paper's editor in its first issue: "Our paper, though somewhat small in size, will be found valuable in contents."[29] Taken together, a year's worth of individual issues of the newspaper would form a "neat little volume" — practically a book. In the same way that the *Colored American* presented reading as an imperative activity, it presented books as items to be treasured: they were promoted as the agents and, increasingly, the emblems of an appropriately cultivated intellect. Later issues of the newspaper carried advertisements for "whole libraries" containing "the most valuable Standard Religious and Scientific Works," which were available for purchase for only "twelve dollars" (see figure 4.4).[30] A library was advertised as something "every family ought to have," and the *Colored American* offered itself as an affordable collection that would, like a library of bound books, testify to the social, civic, and moral standing of its owner.[31] For the sum of $1.50 per year, it provided free blacks with both an encyclopedia of "useful information" and a source of appropriate entertainment. Even if the issues would remain unbound, possession of a full year's run of the *Colored American* was something of which to be proud.

What I have outlined here is a sort of virtual library or reading room;

28. "File Your Papers," *Weekly Advocate,* 7 January 1837, unpaginated.

29. "Our Undertaking," ibid..

30. "Cheapest Publications in the World! A Whole Library for Twelve Dollars," *Colored American,* 9 June 1838, 64.

31. "Household Libraries," *Colored American,* 7 July 1838, 80.

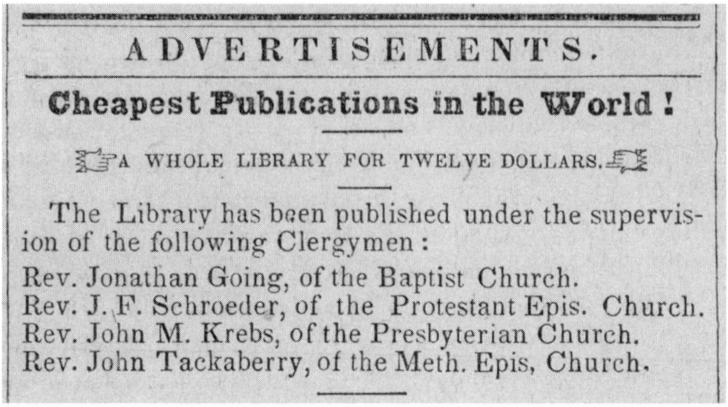
ADVERTISEMENTS.

Cheapest Publications in the World!

A WHOLE LIBRARY FOR TWELVE DOLLARS.

The Library has been published under the supervision of the following Clergymen:
Rev. Jonathan Going, of the Baptist Church.
Rev. J. F. Schroeder, of the Protestant Epis. Church.
Rev. John M. Krebs, of the Presbyterian Church.
Rev. John Tackaberry, of the Meth. Epis, Church.

Figure 4.4. Advertisement for "A whole library for twelve dollars," from the *Colored American,* 9 June 1838, 64. Reproduced by permission of the American Antiquarian Society.

throughout the antebellum period, editors of African American newspapers considered the durability of their publications a prime aspect of their appeal and distanced the publications from the ephemeral qualities of a newspaper by representing them as book-like. "People seldom preserve newspapers," these editors understood, "but almost always preserve their books."[32] Their belief that "books preserve themselves" motivated them to promote their newspapers as enduring records of African American accomplishments and cultural production.[33] Founders of the *Christian Recorder,* for instance, emphasized in the prospectus of the newspaper that it would be produced "in a form so as to be folded as a book or pamphlet, that families and individuals may have books made of it and preserved for future reference."[34] Bound or unbound, their editors insisted, issues of the *Christian Recorder* must be considered lasting texts, as good as books. This emphasis serves as a reminder that, for early black readers, printed texts were first and foremost functional. The creation of long-lasting sources of literature was considered crucial to "develop the talents of our young people, and to furnish data for future comparison."[35]

32. "Reasons why the Repository should be Continued and Patronized," *Repository of Religion and Literature, and of Science and Art.* This announcement is reprinted on the inside back cover of virtually every issue of the *Repository;* see, for instance, January 1862.

33. Ibid.

34. M. M. Clark, "Prospectus of the Christian Recorder of the African Methodist Episcopal Church," in Daniel Payne, *History of the African Methodist Episcopal Church* (Nashville: Publishing House of the A.M.E. Sunday School Union, 1891), 278–79.

35. "Reasons why the Repository should be Continued and Patronized," *Repository of Religion and Literature, and of Science and Art,* inside back cover (see, for instance, January 1862).

The support of black authors and the development of an African American literary tradition depended on the creation of lasting libraries, for literary texts would not serve to educate or inspire black people if they did not survive to reach multiple generations.

In their newspapers African Americans found what one reader of the *Weekly Anglo-African* called "a library . . . of no small value."[36] In the case of the *Weekly Anglo-African,* one particular focus of its "collection" was material that would allow its readers to appreciate and preserve the literary arts of black people. In addition to letters, essays, and extended book reviews, a regular feature of the *Weekly Anglo-African* was a "poems, Anecdotes, and Sketches" column. The content of this column was entirely explained in its title. In one issue, Frances Ellen Watkins's poem "Be Active" was followed by an anonymously authored poem called "He's None the Worse for That" and two works of short fiction, "The Negro of Brazil" by "An Old Tar" and "The Lost Diamond" by Mrs. F. D. Gage.[37] Short, moralistic vignettes appeared alongside excerpts from recently published works of fiction and nonfiction. Even the extended book reviews that were included in the *Weekly Anglo-African* offered readers significant literary texts that enhanced their critical perspective as they suggested further reading. Reviews and advertisements for Frederick Douglass's *My Bondage and My Freedom,* a biography of the Reverend Jermain W. Loguen, and William C. Nell's *The Colored Patriots of the American Revolution* shared space with recommendations for Lydia Maria Child's *The Right Way, The Safe Way.*[38] The number as well as the diversity of texts supplied on a weekly basis by the *Weekly Anglo-African* was appreciated by readers, who recognized the advantages that would accompany such literary exposure. In the words of one of the newspaper's patrons, through active interaction with the literary texts included in the *Weekly Anglo-African,* "readers are taught to think for themselves, and are stimulated to express their thoughts in appropriate language. By this means," this reader recognized, "they will make rapid advances in literature."[39] Evidently, the newspaper audience's eagerness to consume its literary offerings sometimes came at the expense of their reading another text commonly associated with African American readers: the Bible. A small item included in a February 1860 issue

---

36. Letter from Rev. Amos Gerry Beman, *Weekly Anglo-African,* 29 October 1859, 1.

37. "Poems, Anecdotes, and Sketches," *Weekly Anglo-African,* 30 July 1859, 1.

38. "A New and Exciting Book [review of *Life of Rev. J. W. Longuen*]," *Weekly Anglo-African,* 1 October 1859, 1; a review of William C. Nell's *Colored Patriots of the American Revolution* was published in the 30 July 1859 issue of the *Weekly Anglo-African,* 3; Child's work was reviewed in "New Books," *Weekly Anglo-African,* 2 June 1860, 2.

39. "Should the 'Anglo-African' Be Sustained?" *Weekly Anglo-African,* 9 June 1860, 2.

of the newspaper and titled "Popularity of the 'Anglo-African'" reported that one New York City preacher had complained to his congregation that "he knew Christians who could be found sitting up late at night reading the 'African Paper,' while their Bibles were totally neglected."[40]

In the fall of 1859, on the eve of the Civil War, the *Weekly Anglo-African* capitalized on its own successful standing as a virtual library for black readers by opening a reading room in New York City. Located at 178 Prince Street, the Anglo-African Reading Room opened with much fanfare. To publicize the existence of the reading room and ensure its immediate popularity, the committee responsible for its organization instigated "a course of popular lectures" to be held periodically at the reading room. Although they chose to promote the lectures rather than the reading room itself in their initial announcement, the text of it makes clear that the "object of the course [of lectures]" was to "aid in the establishment of a reading-room." By providing ready access to literary material and promoting attention to literary character in the black community, the reading room, this group recognized, would constitute an essential and lasting addition to the black community. Organizers hoped that the reading room would be inviting to "the masses," a space "where the barriers of complexion, sect, or party shall have no existence whatever—a place where young and old may resort to inform themselves upon the current events of the age, and enjoy the various and piquant pleasures produced by the learned review or well stored magazine." Intergenerational as well as interracial, the Anglo-American Reading Room was envisioned as a "place . . . not for the *colored man,* and not for the *white man,* but for the PEOPLE."[41]

To this end, the "list of lecturers" was to "comprehend the representatives of color and those who are not." Speakers were to encompass a wide range of subject matters and perspectives, representing "the pulpit, the bar, the bench, the editorial chair—the Presbyterian, the Congregationalist, the Methodist, the Baptist, the Universalist—learning, eloquence, and enthusiasm."[42] Reports of lectures and meetings held in the Anglo-African Reading Room suggest that these events, serious or playful, were dominated by a spirit of interaction rather than opposition. Speakers assembled could be contentious, their addresses challenging, but they were thought-provoking as well. Exposure to this sort of environment and the intellectually challenging climate it encouraged seems to have been precisely the type of exercise the reading room hoped to provide. Surely, gatherings advertised as "A little

40. "Popularity of the 'Anglo-African,'" *Weekly Anglo-African,* 4 February 1860, 3.
41. "Anglo-African Lectures," *Weekly Anglo-African,* 15 October 1859, 2.
42. Ibid.

lemonade—a few declamations and doughnuts!" were entertaining, but they were serious and academic too. As had traditionally been the case, the success of the reading room lay in its combination of intellectual exercise and society. "To sit alone and gorge one's self with venison and wine, is not our taste," wrote one correspondent for the *Weekly Anglo-African* in praise of the reading room's activities. "An association of kindred spirits can sometimes find profitable conversation over a cup of coffee, refreshing our minds as well as bodies, and sharpening the ideas by social interchange of sentiment." [43] This understanding was shared by readers of the *Weekly Anglo-African* who did not live near the Anglo-African Reading Room. Writing from Hartford, Connecticut, "Sigma" used these words to express her belief in the advantages of the social aspect of literary study afforded by reading rooms, for both men and women: "We feel glad to know that a reading room has been started in your city, and although we cannot enjoy its benefits yet we console ourselves with the idea that it will be productive of good, especially if the ladies patronize it and enter into discussions upon the merits of the different periodicals on file. Nothing calls into action and better strengthens one's judgment as this habit of conversing on what we read." [44]

That African American libraries and reading rooms were initially focused not only on housing and preserving texts but also on situating conversations around them illustrates the extent to which the literary habits of black readers were oriented toward far more than the acquisition of basic literacy skills. By reading (whether independently or as part of a group) and, most important, by participating in the conversations inspired by the texts they read in the context of a literary society library or reading room, free blacks in the urban North found ways of exposing themselves to the literary environments that would contribute to their presenting themselves as "fit for society, [and] better neighbors in any community." [45] Although African American readers would develop a taste for solitary, individual reading in the years following the Civil War, their initial understanding of reading as it developed in the antebellum period was tied to the specific context of the literary society, library, and reading room for good reason. In an atmosphere rife with political setbacks, the confusion of various antislavery efforts, and complex questions about emigration, never had there been greater need for free blacks to assert in strong, public voices their commitment to liberty and equality. These voices devel-

---

43. "Amusements," *Weekly Anglo-African,* 31 March 1860, 1.

44. Sigma, "Letter from Hartford," *Weekly Anglo-African,* 3 December 1859, 1.

45. E[lisha] W[eaver], "To Our Subscribers," *Repository of Religion and Literature, and of Science and Art* 4 (October 1859): 192.

oped and found maturity through collective reading and literary activities such as those sponsored and sustained by the texts included in the early black press as well as those collected by early African American libraries and reading rooms. These institutions' orientation toward communal reading and their focus on the discussions promoted by the various texts they included in their collections allowed free blacks to forcefully enter into public debates about the future of black Americans in the United States and to raise the voice of conscience in a society seemingly deaf to its own ideals.

Chapter 5

Boston Library Catalogues, 1850–1875

Female Labor and Technological Change

Barbara A. Mitchell

In the 1850s, Boston and Cambridge were unique among American cities in the number, size, and quality of their cultural and educational institutions, in particular their libraries. The Boston Athenæum, the Boston Public Library, the Harvard College Library, and the Massachusetts State Library burgeoned in this decade, as tens of thousands of books, pamphlets, and periodicals were acquired. This growth created a concomitant need for new, expanded catalogues to render the collections accessible to readers. To produce such catalogues, a new labor force was utilized — educated women who could write a good hand and perhaps read foreign languages. This transformation in libraries from 1850 to 1860 presaged the entrance of women more generally into the clerical work force, the emergence of modern bureaucracies, and the introduction of information technology systems in financial and other institutions after 1870.

A good deal of literature by historians of labor, business, and technology focuses on the period of 1870 onward, scholarship made possible by source materials such as more detailed census data and business archives.[1] That is also the time of focus of scholarship on women and libraries, stimulated by the readily accessible 1,200-plus-page compendium on libraries issued by the U.S. Bureau of Education and the start of publication of *Library Journal,*

---

1. See, for example, Elyce Rotella, *From Home to Office: U.S. Women at Work, 1870–1930* (Ann Arbor: UMI Research Press, 1981); Margery W. Davies, *Woman's Place Is at the Typewriter: Office Work and Office Workers, 1870–1830* (Philadelphia: Temple University Press, 1982); Alice Kessler-Harris, *Out to Work: A History of Wage-Earning Women in the United States,* 20th anniversary ed. (New York: Oxford University Press, 2003); Claudia Golden, *Understanding the Gender Gap: An Economic History of American Women* (New York: Oxford University Press, 1990); and Angel Kwolek-Folland, *Engendering Business: Men and Women in the Corporate Office, 1870–1930* (Baltimore: Johns Hopkins University Press, 1994).

both in 1876.[2] However, earlier records do exist, notably some printed annual reports and catalogues, and data is also in the archives of individual libraries. These sources shed new light on a proto-technology, the card catalogue, and its means of production, as well as on larger social, cultural, and economic forces at work in America in the third quarter of the nineteenth century.

The growth in collections, followed by new and larger catalogues and the hiring of female staff to produce them, is a pattern that repeats itself in the four Boston-area libraries. Before we examine how this occurred in each institution, however, it is important to understand the catalogue as a universal point of reference.

The Catalogue Revolution in Libraries

In his influential book *The Control Revolution,* James Beniger refers to librarians as "the first information scientists." However, he makes no specific mention of library cataloguing as an important early information management system and its implications for the organization and control of data in other environments.[3]

The first printed catalogues in book form appeared soon after the printing press was established in sixteenth-century Europe. In America, printed catalogues began with that of Harvard College Library in 1723. Printing gave a catalogue much greater utility over manuscript entries written in a blank book. Printed catalogues could be given away and sold, in this way making information to readers widely available in a very convenient form—and for a variety of purposes. Thus, the 1723 Harvard catalogue was distributed in Britain to individuals who might make gifts of books not recorded therein.[4] Since

---

2. U.S. Bureau of Education, *Public Libraries in the United States, Their History, Condition, and Management;* U.S. Department of the Interior, Bureau of Education Special Report, Part I (Washington, DC: Government Printing Office, 1876). The American Library Association, which sponsored *Library Journal,* was also founded in 1876. Elfrieda McCauley has found evidence of women serving as librarians of Sunday school, factory, and town libraries in various New England locales, especially mill towns, as early as 1834, but hers is one of the very few accounts of women in libraries prior to the 1870s: "Some Early Women Librarians in New England," *Wilson Library Bulletin* 38 (1977): 648–65. For general histories of women in libraries, see Kathleen Weibel, Kathleen M. Heim, and Dianne J. Ellsworth, *The Role of Women in Librarianship: 1876–1976: The Entry, Advancement, and Struggle for Equalization in One Profession* (Phoenix, AZ : Oryx Press, 1979); Dee Garrison, *Apostles of Culture: The Public Librarian and American Society, 1876–1920* (New York: Free Press, 1979); Kathleen M. Heim, ed., *The Status of Women in Librarianship* (New York: Neal-Schuman, 1983); and Suzanne Hildebrand, ed., *Reclaiming the American Library Past: Writing the Women In* (Norwood, NJ: Ablex, 1996).

3. James R. Beniger, *The Control Revolution: Technological and Economic Origins of the Information Society* (Cambridge: Harvard University Press, 1986), 394.

4. Hugh Amory and W. H. Bond, eds., *The Printed Catalogues of the Harvard College Library, 1723–1790* (Boston: Colonial Society of Massachusetts, 1996), xxx.

entries were often in the order in which the books were shelved, a catalogue could serve the library staff as an inventory. But most important, a catalogue was the "key" to the library for readers, wherever they might be — and not just those within the library.

Over 3,355 library catalogues were printed in America between 1801 and 1875, many of them published by the thousands of small libraries of various sorts.[5] Most catalogues had only 8, 16 or 32 pages, some low number in any case, perhaps with a few blank leaves at the end for inserting books added. For small collections, most under 5,000 volumes, intended for a limited audience, neither the compilation nor printing of a catalogue posed a significant problem.

For larger libraries, it was otherwise. Twelve thousand volumes could result in a substantial book catalogue, as was the case with the 1858 *Catalogue of the State Library of Massachusetts,* whose entries covered 338 pages.[6] Other libraries in the area were becoming much larger. The Boston Public Library grew out of nothing to 56,000 volumes in 1857, and the Boston Athenæum from 50,000 volumes in 1850 to 70,000 in 1857. As for Harvard College, its size was 84,200 in 1850, and by the end of the decade it had entered into a period of rapid growth.[7] To a later era, these sizes are small, but to many Americans of that time they were impressive. And to those responsible for these institutions, accustomed as they were to libraries staffed with only two or three people, the problem of how to provide access to the influx of books — and at what cost — was a serious challenge.

The problems of providing access to the growing quantity of books and periodicals — and to the increasing holdings of an ever-larger number of libraries — attracted some fine minds who made the second half of the nineteenth century the golden age of cataloguing. Some of the pioneers would gain distinction and renown in Boston-area libraries. Charles Coffin Jewett, while a student at Brown University, had catalogued the library of the Philermenian Society, and subsequently, as the university's librarian, he produced the landmark catalogue of its library in 1843.[8] He subsequently became librar-

5. Robert Singerman, *American Library Book Catalogues, 1801–1875: A National Bibliography* (Champaign: University of Illinois, Graduate School of Library and Information Science, 1996).

6. *Catalogue of the State Library of Massachusetts* (Boston: William White, printer, 1858).

7. For library statistics of the period, see Charles Coffin Jewett, *Notices of Public Libraries in the United States. Printed by Order of Congress, as an Appendix to the Fourth Annual Report of the Board of Regents of the Smithsonian Institution* (Washington: Printed for the House of Representatives, 1851), and William J. Rhees, *Manual of Public Libraries, Institutions, and Societies, in the United States, and British Provinces of North America* (Philadelphia: J. B. Lippincott, 1859).

8. *A Catalogue of the Library of Brown University . . . With an Index of Subjects* (Providence: Brown University, 1843). Jewett's catalogue greatly improved the use of cross-references and included an alphabetical subject index, a forerunner of the dictionary catalogue widely adopted in the twen-

ian of the Smithsonian Institution and of the Boston Public Library. William Frederick Poole, while a student librarian of one of Yale's student societies, the Brothers of Unity, published in 1848 the ambitious *An Alphabetical Index to Subjects, Treated in the Reviews and Other Periodicals, to Which No Indexes Have Been Published.* His experience led to ever more extensive indexing and to *Poole's Index to Periodical Literature.*[9] Poole, too, went on to a distinguished career, his last position being founding librarian of the Newberry Library in Chicago. Also noteworthy was Ezra Abbot's *A Classed Catalogue of the Library of the Cambridge High School with an Alphabetical Index,* prepared in 1853.[10] Charles Ammi Cutter revised the author catalogue of the Harvard Divinity School's Library while he was student librarian there from 1857 to 1859, and he later was responsible for the printed catalogue of the Boston Athenæum, one of the largest and most important catalogues of the century.[11]

Following a seminal conference of librarians and supporters of libraries in Washington in 1853, Jewett published *On the Construction of Catalogues of Libraries, and of a General Catalogue . . . With Rules and Examples* and established himself as the most prominent librarian in the country.[12] This classic treatise became the cornerstone of the debate over how best to create catalogue entries. At issue was the proper form of author and title, whether to include articles in periodicals, chapters in books, and notes on content, and the arrangement of entries in the catalogue. Much attention was paid to how subjects, or classes of knowledge, should appear, as well as the construction of a classification system, which governs the arrangement of books on the shelves. The ultimate goal was to create national standards that could be adopted by libraries nationwide. This was early information formatting of a high degree.

Compiling a catalogue was an intellectually arduous undertaking. Thus, the librarian of the American Antiquarian Society, writing in 1850 on the work involved in preparing a new library catalogue, remarked: "There are no problems in art or science that have been found more perplexing in practice, or more incapable of a satisfactory solution. . . . Men have become insane

tieth century. Jim Ranz, *The Printed Book Catalogue in American Libraries, 1723–1900* (Chicago: American Library Association, 1964), 28–38, 57–67.

9. [*Poole's Index to Periodical Literature*] (New York, G. P. Putnam, 1848).

10. *A Classed Catalogue* (Cambridge: J. Bartlett, 1853).

11. Francis L. Miksa, ed., *Charles Ammi Cutter: Library Systematizer* (Littleton, CO: Libraries Unlimited, 1977), 49. Cutter had the aid of a fellow student, Charles Noyes. The revision was due to the library's acquisition of a special collection, probably the Friedrich Lucke library, acquired in 1856.

12. Charles Coffin Jewett, *On the Construction . . .* (Washington: Smithsonian Institution, 1853).

in their efforts to reduce these labors to a system; and several instances are recorded where life has been sacrificed in consequence of the mental and physical exertion required for the completion of a catalogue in accordance with the author's view of the proper method of executing such a task." [13]

The physical aspects of catalogues were, however, somewhat straightforward — they were printed or in manuscript. The first catalogues were printed from manuscript ledgers in which librarians listed acquisitions. Once an initial printed catalogue was produced, entries could be cut out and pasted into new ledgers with blank leaves bound in for future acquisitions to be recorded; or a catalogue could be printed with interleaved blank pages for staff use. As printed catalogues grew in size, additions might be recorded in separate ledgers and printed as supplements to the last complete catalogue. In the early 1840s, the Harvard College Library adopted a "slip" catalogue of drawers holding 2 x 9 inch cards on which slips from previous catalogues were pasted and on which new acquisitions were written. [14] This catalogue was strictly for the use of library staff. In the early 1850s, the Athenæum, the State Library, and the Boston Public Library also began "working room" card catalogues, intended to be the basis for the next printed catalogues. The chief advantage of these is obvious; cards for new acquisitions could easily be interfiled.

Despite its popularity and tradition, the printed catalogue had a serious defect for growing libraries. It was out of date even as it was being prepared for publication. Ultimately it was doomed by the endless increase in collections, its intrinsic out-of-date nature, and the high costs of printing. [15] In 1862 Harvard became the first library in the Boston area [16] to create a card catalogue expressly for use by the public, that is, students, faculty, and scholars (see figure 5.1). [17] The Public Library followed suit in 1871. Although the

13. *American Antiquarian Society Proceedings . . . 1850,* 14; quoted in Ranz, *Printed Book Catalogue,* 24.

14. Kenneth E. Carpenter, *The First 350 Years of the Harvard University Library* (Cambridge: Harvard University Library, 1986), 70–73.

15. Ranz, *Printed Book Catalogue,* 52–53.

16. It is not clear whether Harvard's card catalogue was actually the first in America intended for the public, but it was certainly one of the earliest. Ruth Weiss claims the first was that of the Philadelphia Library Company in 1857: "The Card Catalogue in Libraries of the United States before 1876" (M.A. thesis, Graduate School of Library Science, University of Illinois, 1938), cited in Eugene R. Hanson and Jay E. Daily, "Catalogues and Cataloguing," *Encyclopedia of Library and Information Science* (New York: Marcel Dekker, 1970), 4:266.

17. The Public Catalogue, as it has always been known, still exists in row upon row of wooden cabinets located on the third floor of Widener Library at Harvard. It was preserved in part due to the furor created by Nicholson Baker over the destruction of card catalogues by libraries once the data was converted into computerized files. Baker, "Discards," *New Yorker,* 4 April 1994, 64–86. The Public Catalogue still contains many handwritten cards.

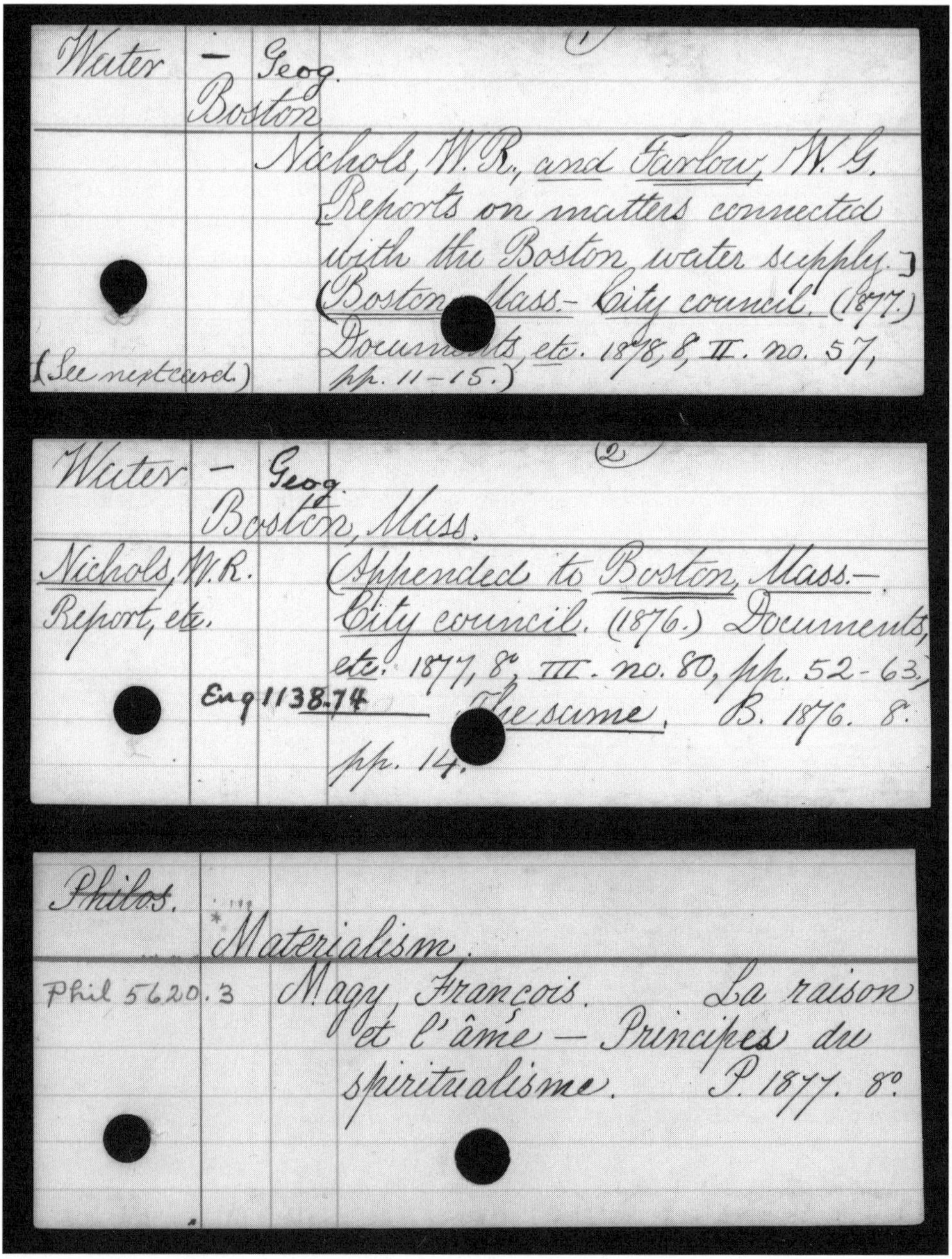

Fig. 5.1. Handwritten cards for the Harvard College Library's Public Catalogue, begun in 1862.

State Library and the Athenæum continued to issue printed catalogues in the 1870s, by the end of the century virtually all American libraries had adopted public card catalogues. They represented a revolutionary change in the way that bibliographic information was recorded and managed, and, as a fundamentally flexible and simple technology, they endured for over a century in American libraries.

Cataloguing and classification schemes were of sufficient importance to be of interest not only to men who made their living as librarians. Nathaniel Bradstreet Shurtleff, former mayor of Boston and a library trustee, wrote *Decimal System for the Arrangement and Administration of Libraries* in 1856.[18] In the 1850s and subsequent decades, reviews of catalogues and articles about libraries appeared in newspapers and in the periodical press, including the *Atlantic Monthly,* the *Nation, Norton's Literary Gazette,* and the *North American Review.* The last, for example, published in 1850 "Remarks on Public Libraries" by George Livermore, a merchant, book collector, and library trustee. The Cambridge resident argued strongly that American libraries were inadequate and that they needed to collect research materials for scholarly pursuits.[19]

Livermore was not alone. In their annual reports Harvard presidents urged donors to make funds available for a library that would make possible the advancement of knowledge. In Boston, one of those former presidents, Edward Everett, along with George Ticknor, who was long an advocate of scholarly libraries, made sure that the collections in the city's new public library would serve the researcher's need for historical and current materials in support of scholarship as well as the public's desire for light reading. With funding from a donor, Ticknor made book-buying trips to Europe, and arrangements were made with foreign agents for acquisitions of scholarly works regardless of language. Even the Massachusetts State Library, which was originally a repository for documents from the various states in America, began to collect foreign documents and special artistic, cultural, and historical works.

The catalogues for these new and growing libraries became more and more expensive. How and by whom the catalogues would be created, and how they would be paid for, was ultimately the responsibility of trustees and faculty. These men approved the entrance of women into the workspaces that had previously been all-male preserves. As we shall see, the manner in which middle-class, educated women entered libraries as workers had consequences

---

18. Nathaniel Bradstreet Shurtleff, *Decimal System for the Arrangement and Administration of Libraries* (Boston: privately printed, 1856). The system was used by both the Boston Public Library and the Massachusetts State Library.

19. George Livermore, "Remarks," *North American Review* 71 (1850): 185–220.

not only for the expansion and use of collections, but also for the economic status of women and the social organization of clerical work more generally.

The Boston Public Library

Of the four libraries, the Boston Public Library, which was the last to be established, was also the fastest-growing, and the first to hire women. The state legislature authorized the establishment of the library in 1848;[20] and although several donations of books and modest funds for acquisitions were received, not until the spring of 1852 did the city council act to set up the library. In short order, it hired a librarian, elected a board of trustees, and rented temporary quarters in a building on Mason Street, which also housed the Boston Normal School, one of the city's first public high schools for girls.[21] For librarian, the council passed over the eminently well qualified but young William Frederick Poole, formerly on the staff of the Boston Athenæum and then librarian of the Boston Mercantile Library. Instead, it chose Edward Capen, a clergyman who was then secretary of the Boston School Committee.[22]

A highly distinguished group, many with ties to the Harvard College Library, the Athenæum, and the State Library, the trustees were no strangers to library governance and catalogues. Edward Everett, who had previously served as president of Harvard and as Massachusetts governor, was selected as president of the trustees. Others included George Ticknor, a scholar and former Harvard professor; Thomas Gold Appleton, a wealthy writer and antiquarian; and Nathaniel Bradstreet Shurtleff, a physician and historian.

The trustees outlined a plan calling for four separate catalogues. These included an accessions catalogue, a shelf/alcove catalogue indicating the arrangement on the shelves, a printed alphabetical short-title catalogue with shelf numbers, and a card catalogue with full entries (including subjects). From the outset, the trustees envisioned the library as serving both the popular reading public and those readers with more sophisticated research interests, and the catalogues were devised accordingly. The printed catalogue, merely an index, was to be available for sale and readily accessible to the public on the reading room tables.[23]

---

20. Walter Muir Whitehill, *Boston Public Library: A Centennial History* (Cambridge: Harvard University Press, 1956), 13, 37.

21. Olive B. White, *Centennial History of the Girls' High School of Boston* (Boston: Samuel Eliot Memorial Association of the Girls' High School, 1952), 9.

22. Whitehill, *Boston Public Library,* 26.

23. Public Library of the City of Boston, Proceedings of the Board of Trustees, 16 October 1852, manuscript volumes hereafter cited as BPL Trustees Proceedings. The first proceedings were recorded on 31 May 1852.

The Catalogue proper of the Library . . . is in manuscript and on cards of uniform size, alphabetically and compactly arranged in drawers. . . . The number of these cards is . . . so great that they will probably never be published as a printed Catalogue. But they will always open the resources of the Library, by a complete list of its authors and subjects, with minute cross-references, and when needed, with bibliographical notes. . . . Any person who has access to the Institution may consult the Catalogue, with the aid of the Superintendent or one of his assistants, and thus learn at once whatever the Library can offer him for such researches as he desires to make, however detailed and elaborate they may be.[24]

The trustees had planned well, therefore, for the extraordinary gift in October 1852 of $50,000 from Joshua Bates, a Massachusetts-born merchant residing in London. It was for new library acquisitions.

To assist in making these catalogues, in November 1853 the trustees authorized the hiring of Misses Mary L. and Elizabeth M. Appleton at four dollars per week. This was just prior to formation of a subcommittee of the trustees in January 1854, which was after the fact "authorized to employed [sic] additional assistance, so that the card catalogues may be always kept as nearly as possible in a state of completeness and that the catalogue by short titles for the circulation of books be speedily prepared and printed."[25] In March of that year the Mason Street library, holding a collection of about 16,000 books and 1,000 pamphlets, opened its doors to the public, with general access to the collections provided by a printed short-title catalogue.[26]

In August 1854, the trustees approved hiring Miss Georgiana B. Appleton at five dollars per week (the other Appleton women's wages had been raised to this rate in January).[27] So steady was the stream of new acquisitions and gifts that the trustees rented two additional spaces.[28] In one of these, where books

---

24. Edward Everett et al., Prefatory Notice, *Index to the Catalogue of Books in the Upper Hall of the Public Library of the City of Boston* (Boston: Geo. C. Rand and Avery, 1861). Although this statement was made nearly a decade later, similar descriptions of the card catalogue, distinguishing it from other printed catalogues or indexes, can be found throughout the Proceedings of the Trustees beginning in 1852.

25. BPL Trustees Proceedings, 22 November 1853; 3 January 1854. Neither Mary L. nor Elizabeth M. Appleton is listed in W. S. Appleton, *Genealogy of the Appleton Family* (Boston: T. R. Marvin, 1874). However, it seems likely that they were related to Thomas Gold Appleton and almost certain that they were related to each other.

26. *Catalogue of the Public Library of the City of Boston* (Boston: John Wilson & Son, 1854). The preface contains the note "The following catalogue lays no claim to bibliographical merit of any sort."

27. BPL Trustees Proceedings, 26 January 1854; 15 August 1854. Georgiana Brackett Appleton, who would have been nineteen years old at the time, is listed in Appleton, *Genealogy*, 37; she was a distant cousin of Thomas Gold Appleton.

28. In 1853, the books and pamphlets numbered 10,650; in 1855 this number had grown to 29,120. Whitehill, *Boston Public Library*, 57.

from Joshua Bates were being received, Charles Coffin Jewett supervised the work of accessioning and cataloguing. Jewett, whose reputation and experience as a librarian and cataloguer was without equal, had previously worked at the Smithsonian Institution, which for a time gave promise of becoming the nation's major library, until disagreements with the Institution's secretary resulted in Jewett's dismissal. In 1858, Jewett was named superintendent of the Boston Public Library, and he oversaw the opening of the new library building on Boylston Street.

Under Jewett's direction, the library published two catalogues, the first in 1858, an abridged catalogue of the Lower Hall, which contained the most popular circulating books; and the second in 1861, for the Upper Hall (known as Bates Hall after the great benefactor's death), which held, in effect, the "research collection," including both Bates Hall circulating books and those too valuable to be used outside the library.[29]

After Jewett suffered a fatal bout of apoplexy at his desk in early 1868, the trustees selected one of their own, Justin Winsor, as the next superintendent. Like Jewett, Winsor was to become one of the most notable librarians of the century. He made his mark as an innovative administrator, who, in the course of his tenure, supervised the opening of six branch libraries throughout the city, some of which were headed by women.[30] In 1871, after unhappily contemplating yet another printed catalogue, Winsor "threw up the sponge and turned instead to a public card catalogue," in which he had entries printed on thin slips of paper and then pasted onto the cards. By duplicating entries in this way, he increased the volumes passing through the Catalogue Department from five to six thousand to twenty thousand a year.[31] From 1852 until 1877, when Winsor left to become librarian of Harvard College, seventy-four women had been employed in the Public Library, and the collection grew to 312,000 volumes. [32]

Massachusetts State Library

In 1826 an act of the legislature provided that the state publications and books belonging to the Commonwealth of Massachusetts be maintained as a library in the State House. By 1850 the library held approximately 8,000 volumes. Although small by comparison with the other libraries under discussion,

---

29. *Index to the Catalogue of a Portion of the Public Library of the City of Boston, Arranged in the Lower Hall* (Boston, 1858); *Index to the Catalogue of Books in the Upper Hall* (1861).

30. Whitehill, *Boston Public Library,* chap. 5, "The Winsor Decade," 55–102.

31. Ibid., 97; Ranz, *Printed Book Catalogue,* 40, 53.

32. Whitehill, *Boston Public Library,* 103–9.

the State Library was well supported financially. Beginning in 1850, it was overseen by a board of trustees that included George Livermore, then a member of the Athenæum's library committee and its board of trustees. In 1855, Nathaniel Bradstreet Shurtleff, also a trustee at the Boston Public Library, came onto the board. The state secretary of education, Barnas Sears, served as the *ex officio* librarian and Charles T. Jackson as the acting librarian. The library's last catalogue had appeared in 1846.[33]

Under Resolves of 1854, the library was authorized to begin preparing a new catalogue, and in November of that year the trustees "decided to employ, for a time, on trial, Mrs. Augusta Hovey, Miss Mary N. Abbot, and Miss Mary C. Snow to assist" in the work at twenty-five cents per hour. A new card catalogue "after the most approved classification," was begun, from which future printed catalogues could be produced.[34] In 1857, Mary C. Snow was appointed as a regular assistant with an annual salary of $400, and a year later a new catalogue was printed. Sarah F. Snow replaced her sister in 1859 and another assistant, Miss Caroline R. Jackson, joined her as an assistant in 1861.[35] Five years later, Miss Ellen M. Sawyer, who had been one of the first women hired by the Harvard College Library, replaced Miss Snow. Under her direction, in 1880, the final printed catalogue of the State Library appeared; the collections at that time numbered 42,000. Assisting Miss Sawyer part-time in this work was Augusta Isabella Appleton, who was employed as well by the Athenæum and was the youngest of the Appleton sisters of Portsmouth, New Hampshire, early assistants in the Harvard College Library (see figure 5.2).[36] Employing women, the step taken tentatively in 1854, had become standard operating procedure.

---

33. Jewett, *Notices*, 24–26. For purposes of comparison, the Legislature provided $300 for library purchases in 1850; in 1856 Harvard College provided $500 for its library's acquisitions. Sears would later serve as president of Brown University.

34. Transcription of Minutes of Meetings of the Committee on the Library and the State Library Board of Trustees, November 1854, Manuscript Collection 66, State Library of Massachusetts. *Report of the Librarian for the State Library for the Year . . . 1854* (Boston: William White, 1855), 27–28.

35. Minutes, State Library Board of Trustees, 5 January 1859; *Report of the Librarian for the State Library for the Year . . . 1861* (Boston: William White, 1861), [2]. It is not known if Caroline was related to the Acting Librarian, Samuel C. Jackson.

36. *Report of the Librarian for the State Library for the Year . . . 1866* (Boston: Wright & Potter, 1867), [2]. *Catalogue of the State Library of Massachusetts* (Boston: Rand, Avery, 1880), v–vi. Augusta Appleton is listed as working at the Athenæum from 1872 to 1889; *The Athenæum Centenary: The Influence and History of the Boston Athenæum from 1807 to 1907* (Boston: Boston Athenæum, 1907), 219. Appleton, *Genealogy,* 37.

Fig. 5.2. Augusta Isabella Appleton, ca. 1878. At various times in her career, Miss Appleton cata-logued materials in the Harvard College Library, the Boston Athenæum, and the Massachusetts State Library. Reproduced by permission of the Massachusetts Historical Society, Haven–Appleton–Cutter Family Photographs.

The Boston Athenæum

In 1850, the Athenæum was the largest library in Boston. Its collections had grown to 50,000 volumes and 20,000 pamphlets.[37] Incorporated in 1807 by a "society of gentlemen" who desired a library for the use of men who could afford a $300 proprietary share in the institution or an annual subscription

---

37. Jewett, *Notices*, 19–21.

of $10 per year, the Athenæum was an elite institution. The last supplement to the 1827 catalogue had been published in 1840, and the trustees appointed two committees, in 1851 and 1852, "to take measures for the preparation and completion of a new Catalogue."[38] Neither the librarian, Charles Folsom,[39] nor his assistant was up to this challenging task, in part because of the work delays occasioned by the move to a new building on Beacon Street a few years earlier.

The library committee issued a report in 1852 that recommended writing brief title entries on interleaved copies of the previous printed supplements; "Then we want the titles also written on cards from which a systematic index according to subjects can be arranged . . . for a small additional cost. The cards will be indispensable to the economical printing of the Catalogue, when funds of the Athenæum will warrant such an expense."[40] Fortunately, the library was able to hire Ezra Abbot to work on the catalogue temporarily in 1853, and from 1854 to 1856 he served as assistant librarian, before assuming the same position at the Harvard College Library. A real opportunity for progress on the catalogue seemed to present itself in 1856, when Folsom retired and William F. Poole became librarian. A year earlier Poole had expeditiously prepared a printed catalogue for the Mercantile Library Association of Boston.[41] But most of Poole's time was absorbed in purchasing books (the Athenæum had received $30,000 in 1853, following the death of Samuel Appleton, a proprietor).[42] In his twelve years there, Poole failed to produce a new catalogue, in large part because he did not adequately direct the work of Charles Russell Lowell, the assistant in charge of the project and an incurable perfectionist.[43] However, Poole began to hire women shortly after his arrival. The first of these was Mrs. A. B. Harnden, who began work in 1857. Soon after, Miss Sarah E. Gill and Miss Mary A. Bean were hired to assist Lowell in cataloguing.[44]

The realization of a new catalogue occurred during the twenty-three-

---

38. Records of the Trustees of the Boston Athenæum, 17 January 1851, 23 January 1852, manuscript volumes in the Boston Athenæum.

39. Folsom had been librarian at Harvard College from 1823 to 1826.

40. Athenæum Trustees Records, 9 February 1852.

41. *Thirty-fifth Annual Report of the Directors of the Mercantile Library Association of Boston* (Boston: John Wilson and Son, 1855). Also, Record of Meetings, Board of Directors, Mercantile Library Association, 8 January, 5 March 1855; from the Mercantile Library Association of Boston Collection in the Howard Gottlieb Archival Research Center, Boston University. Poole's assistants on the catalogue were all men.

42. *Athenæum Centenary*, 218, 70.

43. William L. Williamson, *William Frederick Poole and the Modern Library Movement* (New York: Columbia University Press, 1963), 24–44; *Athenæum Centenary*, 47–48.

44. *Athenæum Centenary*, 42. Miss Gill had previously been employed by her cousin Benjamin F. Stevens, a book agent and bibliographer, who rented a room in the Athenæum basement.

year tenure of Charles Ammi Cutter. After Lowell's death in 1870, Cutter devoted his own considerable skill and experience to this effort, and the first printed volume appeared in 1874. But as the years dragged on, Cutter had to deal with complaints from the trustees, who were concerned about not only the time lag, but the growing expense of the endeavor. Cutter seems to have anticipated this problem in the conclusion to his review of the Harvard College Library catalogue: "Yet such is the ignorance which prevails in the world about library administration, that the catalogue is hardly ever thought of by those who found libraries. Thousands of dollars are provided to procure books, and not a cent to make them useful after they are received." [45]

The fifth and final volume of the Athenæum's catalogue did not appear until 1882. Despite the fact that no books acquired after 1872 were included, it was greeted with enthusiasm and "for many years represented the culmination of the art of catalogue making." [46] Four-fifths, or $80,000 of its final cost, estimated at $100,000, was spent for the salaries of those who prepared the catalogue.[47] During the period 1857–75, twenty-nine women worked in the Athenæum. The number of women working on the catalogue and the overall cost point up that for the libraries, employing women—at a lower rate than a man would have been paid—served to keep down a major cost. After its monumental printed catalogue was finished in 1882, the library apparently relied thereafter on its card catalogue for access to its collections.[48]

Harvard College Library

The most venerable of Boston-area libraries, the Harvard College Library had been founded in 1638 and by 1850 was growing slowly, although it had amassed in its various libraries, including the student societies, a total of 84,200 volumes, impressive for that time in the United States.[49] In 1856, John Langdon Sibley was appointed librarian and Ezra Abbot assistant librarian, bringing the staff, including a janitor and the occasional help of a male clerk, to a total of four men. From the start of Sibley's tenure, acquisitions began to increase.[50] The year 1859 proved to be significant for the library

---

45. Charles Ammi Cutter, "The New Catalogue of Harvard College Library," *North American Review* 108 (1869) 129.

46. Ranz, *Printed Book Catalogue*, 75. Cutter's classic work on cataloguing is *Rules for a Printed Dictionary Catalogue* (Washington: Government Printing Office, 1876).

47. Ranz, *Printed Book Catalogue*, 38.

48. *Athenæum Centenary*, 218–20.

49. Jewett, *Notices*, 31.

50. This section on the Harvard College Library is based on Barbara A. Mitchell, " 'A Beginning Is Made': The New Card Catalogue of the Harvard College Library and the Female Labor Force,

in several ways. In February, William Gray promised $25,000 in book funds, $5,000 a year for the next five years. That annual gift amounted to roughly a tenfold increase in the funds for books, and Gray specifically requested that preference in spending it be given to purchasing currently published books.

To oversee spending the gift, a Library Council was established, chaired by Charles William Eliot, and the council requested members of the faculty to draw up lists of desiderata, which, upon review, were to be the basis for allocations among the various fields. In the meantime one agent each was engaged in England, France, Germany, and Italy to fill the orders; so, after the decision-making process, the lists had to be copied again, with the appropriate titles being sent to each agent.

Two months after the receipt of Gray's gift, to help with copying the lists of desiderata and to catalogue the "easier" books, Sibley hired two daughters of a recently deceased Harvard alumnus:[51] "Miss Caroline Louisa and Miss Ellen Maria, daughters of the late Samuel Sawyer, M.D., of Cambridge (Class of 1827) began copying lists of books to be bought, which have been brought in by Professors. Compensation six cents per hour for the present."[52] A frequent visitor who had donated newspapers to the College Library, Dr. Sawyer had received a certificate to borrow books in 1858.[53] Within a month after the Sawyer sisters were hired, they had begun to catalogue books for the "working room" catalogue; "young women began to assist in writing, cataloguing &c.," Sibley noted in his journal. Later that month a daughter of James Winthrop Harris (a male library staff member who had recently been hired for 40 cents an hour) spent several weeks inventorying the books in the alcoves with her father in preparation for the annual visit of the library overseers. It does not appear that Sibley paid Miss Harris for this work, but the next women he hired "to write &c." in March 1860 were two of Harris's daughters.[54]

A mere seven days after the Sawyer sisters began to work, the Harvard faculty approved the report of a "committee to consider the means of rendering

---

1856–1877," *Harvard Library Bulletin,* n.s. 14 (2003): 11–32. All manuscripts cited in this section are in the Harvard University Archives unless otherwise noted. Abbot, the assistant librarian at the Boston Athenæum in 1856, had considerable experience in cataloguing and was seriously considered for the position of librarian at Harvard. Sibley, however, had served as Harvard's assistant librarian since 1841 and was a Harvard graduate; Abbot's degree was from Bowdoin.

51. John Langdon Sibley, Library Journal, 11 April 1859; Abbot to Sibley, 2 May 1859, Library Letterbooks.

52. Sibley, Library Journal, 11 April 1859.

53. Ibid., 22 May 1858.

54. Abbot to Sibley, 2 May 1859, Library Letterbooks. Sibley, Library Journal, 11 June, 25 June, 12 July 1859; 13 March 1860. In ensuing years Sibley would note miscellaneous other tasks performed by the women, such as copying his library reports, writing out orders, and pasting library letters into ledgers.

the Public Library more generally accessible and useful to the undergraduates and other members of the University."[55] Among the report's recommendations was that a classified catalogue be prepared as soon as possible under Abbot's direction and that it "be exposed for general use upon one of the tables in the great hall."[56] The Harvard Corporation, Harvard's senior governing body, approved the report and asked Sibley and Abbot to submit a proposal for the type of catalogue to be implemented and the time and expense it would require.[57] Fortunately for Abbot, whose ill health often forced him to stay at home, the faculty library committee authorized the hiring of a second assistant librarian, Charles Ammi Cutter in 1860.[58] After months of fruitful discussion with Cutter, Abbot settled on a card catalogue of 2 x 5 inch cards in specially designed drawers with slanted guide blocks and buttons at the back of the drawers to prevent them from unintentionally being pulled out entirely and spilled.

As for the decision about the form and type of entries for the cards, Abbot had available for study the printed catalogues of a number of libraries, and he was aware of both the acclaim and criticism that greeted many of these in the periodical press. Harvard's last printed catalogue (1830) had been the basis, with improvements, for Jewett's catalogue at Brown (1844), but Abbot deplored the errors and inconsistencies in the 1830 Harvard catalogue, prepared "before the best methods of dealing with the numerous difficulties in cataloguing were so well settled as they are now." For form of entry in the author catalogue, Abbot proposed making entries "according to the excellent rules of Prof. Jewett and the British Museum."[59]

Abbot also proposed a subject catalogue. Of course, he was well aware of the pitfalls in determining subject classification. "Most systematic catalogues attempt a scientific management of subjects; but these arrangements, as might be expected, differ as widely as the minds that devise them." He decided upon what came to be known as an "alphabetico-classed" system in which the principal classes of knowledge and their numerous branches and sections were each arranged in alphabetical order. Essential to the utility of

---

55. Prof. Francis R. Bowen, [Report of library subcommittee], 18 April 1859, College Papers, 2d ser.

56. Faculty members were clearly appalled that no catalogue had been printed since the supplement of 1834. In fact, Abbot's title at the time of his appointment was "assistant librarian with exclusive authority in classifying and cataloguing the books." Corporation Records, no. 397, v. 9.

57. Corporation Records, 31 December 1859, v. 10.

58. Library Committee to President and Fellows, 16 May 1860, College Papers, 2d ser.

59. Abbot to President and Fellows [manuscript report, spring 1862], Treasurer's Papers, 5–6. Jewett's rules were based largely on the famous "ninety-one rules" of Anthony Panizzi, published in the British Museum catalogue of books in 1841; Hanson and Daily, "Catalogues and Cataloguing," 242–305.

Abbot's catalogue was that books would have subject entries based on their contents and not "merely by the accidental phraseology of the title." In this, and in the use of a card catalogue created expressly for the public, Abbot's plan was innovative.[60]

Abbot's proposal to the Corporation also included how and by whom the catalogue cards would be created. In 1861, he had "procured about 10,000 small cards . . . at a cost of $2.50 per thousand." He then employed one of the female assistants, for ten cents an hour, to write cards, which she eventually managed to complete at a rate of twelve and one quarter per hour. At 100 cards for an eight-hour day, 250 working days per year, Abbot calculated that "a trained and intelligent assistant" could produce 100,000 cards in four years. On the basis of this "experiment," Abbot requested that the Corporation grant him the authority "to continue the labor begun in the manner described . . . [and] to employ, in the steady prosecution of the work, the female assistant who has already been trained to it, with one or two others, as may be found expedient, at an expense of not more than $250 each per annum."[61] The plan and additional staffing were duly authorized by the Corporation, whose members probably believed that they were approving a temporary project.

Sibley soon had "five young ladies" on the library staff: Miss Caroline Louisa Sawyer; Miss Mary S. Thayer; Miss Addie T. Pedrick; Miss Louise Appleton, and her sister, Sarah Fayerweather Appleton (see figure 5.3).[62] In the first year of labor on the new catalogue, 35,762 cards were written, and Sibley could report that "the work of the Library has been carried forward with spirit and vigor."[63] During the twenty-one years of Sibley's tenure as librarian, a total of forty-seven women worked in the library.[64]

In 1868, Cutter (who had married Sarah F. Appleton five years earlier) left Harvard to become librarian of the Boston Athenæum.[65] Abbot stayed on until 1872, after which he assumed a professorship in the Harvard Divinity

---

60. Abbot, [manuscript report, spring 1862], 6.

61. Abbot, [manuscript report, spring 1862], 13–14. This document in the Treasurer's Papers is the only evidence linking the creation of the library's catalogue with the female staff. Abbot prepared another version that does not mention staffing at all, for the library's visiting committee: "Mr. Abbot's Statement Respecting the New Catalogues of the College Library," *Report of the Committee of the Overseers of Harvard College Appointed to Visit the Library for the Year 1862* (Boston: Rand & Avery, 1863), 35–76.

62. Sibley, Library Journal, July 1863.

63. Sibley, Library Journal, 31 May 1862; Annual Report, July 1862; Annual Report, July 1863.

64. The Harvard College Bursar's Journals, 1859–77, under the listing of "library," record the names of women and their monthly pay. In addition to the thirty-seven women noted by Sibley in his journal, there are ten additional women listed in the Bursar's Journals.

65. Miksa, *Charles Ammi Cutter,* 20.

Fig. 5.3. Sarah Fayerweather Appleton, 1862. A year after this photograph was taken, Miss Appleton, one of the female staff at the Harvard College Library, married Charles A. Cutter, whose distinguished cataloguing career began at Harvard. Reproduced by permission of the Massachusetts Historical Society, Haven–Appleton–Cutter Family Photographs.

School.[66] Three years before Abbot gave up his labors in the library, he hired and trained Miss Annie E. Hutchins, who later became "head of the female department of Library Assistants," and in 1873, she became the first woman to

66. In a eulogy following Abbot's death in 1884, one of his theological colleagues commented that he had "squandered his precious strength and mental powers for twenty-five years in teaching school and cataloguing books." *Ezra Abbot* (Cambridge: Harvard Divinity School, 1884), 55.

receive a salaried Corporation appointment.[67] Nowhere is there evidence that Abbot ever considered preparing another printed catalogue for the Harvard College Library. For the rapidly growing library—Sibley, by the time of his retirement at the age of seventy-three, had increased the library's collections to 164,000 volumes and a like number of pamphlets—the card catalogue was the only practical solution.[68]

The Women in the Libraries

Before women entered the Boston-area libraries as employees, they were often a source of book donations, and they visited libraries as readers and researchers. This was especially true at the Boston Athenæum, whose earliest woman proprietor was Helen Ruthven in 1829. Between that date and 1875, over one hundred and eighty women became proprietors/shareholders in the library, which entitled them to borrow books.[69] In addition, the Athenæum's circulation records indicate that women often borrowed books because a male proprietor, perhaps a father or husband, extended his privileges to them.

A number of prominent female intellectuals of the period were Athenæum patrons. The historian Hannah Adams, whose first visit was in 1829, was given free use of the library by a vote of the trustees. The educator and publisher Elizabeth Palmer Peabody, the abolitionist Lydia Maria Child, and the author and book collector Mary Lowell Putnam spent many hours in the Athenæum reading room.[70] Sibley appears to have granted access to the Harvard College Library to women scholars; viz. "Miss R. W. Brown is pursuing a course of reading & study" in the library.[71] The Boston Public Library was intended from the outset to be open to women. The original plan of the Public Library's new Boylston Street building called for a "Ladies Reading Room," but it ended up being set aside for receptions and book overflows.[72] The main

---

67. "List of Annual Salaries," Corporation Records, 1873; Sibley, Library Journal, 6 March 1873. The women whom Sibley began to hire in 1859 were the first women, other than cleaning women, to be employed by Harvard. At one point, the college president tried to get Sibley to "loan" him some of the female assistants to assist with clerical work. Mitchell, "'A Beginning Is Made,'" 31.

68. Sibley, Librarian's Twenty-second and Final Annual Report, July 6, 1877 [Cambridge, 1877].

69. Athenæum Centenary, "Chronological List of Proprietors," 126–74.

70. Athenæum Centenary, 40. An illustration in Athenæum Centenary, opposite page 130, depicts the Reading Room in 1855, and three women are included. See also Helena Toth, "Building 'Wisdom' and 'Stability': Mary Lowell Putnam's Library and Women's Book Culture in the Nineteenth Century," Harvard Library Bulletin, n.s. 14(2003): 33–48.

71. Sibley, Letterbooks, 5 March 1859, Harvard University Archives.

72. BPL Trustees Proceedings, 5 August 1862.

reading room was used by all. "This Reading-room is largely frequented, and many females avail themselves of its advantages."[73]

When the libraries decided to hire women workers in the 1850s, they apparently did not need to look far for acceptable employees. Patronage and nepotism played a large role. At least one of the Appleton women hired by the Boston Public Library in 1852 was probably related to Thomas Gold Appleton, a trustee.[74] The second woman hired by the Athenæum, Sarah Gill, had previously been employed by a book agent who rented rooms in the basement of the library. In the College Library, Sibley noted that eleven of the female assistants were related to Harvard graduates; one was a granddaughter of a former Harvard president.[75] Moreover, there are countless examples in all of the Boston-area libraries of two or more sisters being employed.

Sibley's notes about the women working at Harvard offer the best indication that they were middle class, at least in terms of the social and economic status of their families. In addition, there is ample evidence that they were well educated.[76] "Miss Thayer, Miss Pedrick & Miss Sawyer were from the Cambridge High School," Sibley noted in the spring of 1862, and "[the degree to which these women have] been highly educated is remarkable." The following year he noted with some pride the hiring of Miss Mary Eliza Allen, "who was the first scholar in last class graduated at the Cambridge High School."[77] Having previously taught at Cambridge High School, Abbot, Sibley's assistant librarian, was already familiar with the educational attainments of young women. Of the female cataloguers at work in the College Library in 1864, he wrote that "they not only possess in no ordinary degree the intellectual qualities required—quickness of perception, good judgment, and habits of

---

73. Report of the Examining Committee, BPL Trustees Proceedings, 10 November 1860. For a discussion of the planning and swift decline of ladies' reading rooms in public libraries, see Abigail Van Slyck, "The Lady and the Library Loafer: Gender and Public Space in Victorian America," *Winterthur Portfolio* 31 (1996): 221–42.

74. Of the four libraries, only the trustees at the Public Library make note of receiving employment applications. In 1858, applications for positions were received from forty-nine women, "nearly every application being accompanied with ample testimonials and recommendations." BPL Trustees Record Files, 12 February 1858. Alas, these applications do not appear in the inventory of the records held in the Trustees Room; the applications from the early twentieth century are noted as having been destroyed. Cindy S. Aron was able to base her important study of early female clerks in the federal government, who began work in 1861, on hundreds of applications retained in government files: Cindy Sonik Aron, *Ladies and Gentlemen of the Civil Service: Middle-Class Workers in Victorian America* (New York: Oxford University Press, 1987).

75. Sibley, Library Journal, 20 April 1863.

76. From their detailed applications, Aron was able to determine that the early women in government service were well educated and from middle-class backgrounds. Aron, *Ladies and Gentlemen*, 41–42.

77. Sibley, Library Journal, [spring] 1862; 17 February 1863.

accuracy—but four of them have a practical acquaintance with the Latin, French and German languages, and one of the four is also versed in Spanish and Italian."[78]

Nineteen of the forty-seven female assistants who worked in the College Library during this period were graduates of Cambridge High School, which was founded in 1847.[79] Many Boston-area high schools were established in the mid-nineteenth century (a corollary to the growth of public libraries during the period). These began as elite institutions catering to both the sons and daughters of middle- and upper-class families. The secondary school curricula in the early years tended to be classical, often intended to prepare students for college, with no gender distinction.[80] As a result, young female high school graduates often had foreign language reading skills, an important asset because of the many foreign publications in the Boston-area libraries. In 1858, the Boston Public Library trustees noted that the female staff were all graduates of the "Girls' High and Normal School [sic]"; ten years later they made it a condition of employment that female assistants be "graduates of the public schools of this city."[81]

It is likely that most of these women sought employment because of financial distress within their families.[82] The best example is the Sawyer sisters, hired in 1859 in the College Library. Four months earlier, their father, Dr. Sawyer, had died; Sibley observed in his diary that "there were many widows in Old Cambridge, on reflecting that there were two widows & seven other females without an individual of the other sex in the house lately occupied by Dr. Sawyer."[83] Letters from several women working in the Public Library request pay increases for board and, for those whose duties involved assistance to readers, suitable clothing (see figure 5.4).[84] Even if a middle- or upper-class

---

78. Abbot to [President and Fellows of Harvard College], 29 July 1864, Harvard College Papers, 2d ser., 1864. Abbot's letter was a cover letter to one by some of the women, who were seeking a pay increase.

79. William Bradbury and Elbridge Smith, *The Cambridge High School: History and Catalogue* (Cambridge: Moses King, 1882). This is the only published Boston-area high school history that includes a list of graduates and their professions and locations after graduation.

80. John L. Rury, *Education and Women's Work: Female Schooling and the Division of Labor in Urban America, 1870–1930* (Albany: State University of New York Press, 1991), 11–17.

81. BPL Trustees Proceedings, 2 September 1858, 27 October 1868.

82. Aron, *Ladies and Gentlemen,* chap. 3, "Reluctant Pioneers: The Ladies," 40–63.

83. Sibley, Private Journal, 4 January 1859. Of 114 female clerical workers in Boston in 1860, three-quarters were fatherless. Carole Srole, " 'A Position That God Has Not Particularly Assigned to Men': The Feminization of Clerical Work, Boston, 1860–1915" (Diss., University of California, Los Angeles, 1984), 228.

84. Catherine Gaffney to Edward Capen, 9 March 1868; Jennie Tyler to Charles Coffin Jewett, 12 May 1868; Caroline A. Adams and Livonia S. Norton to Trustees, 19 March 1869; BPL Trustees

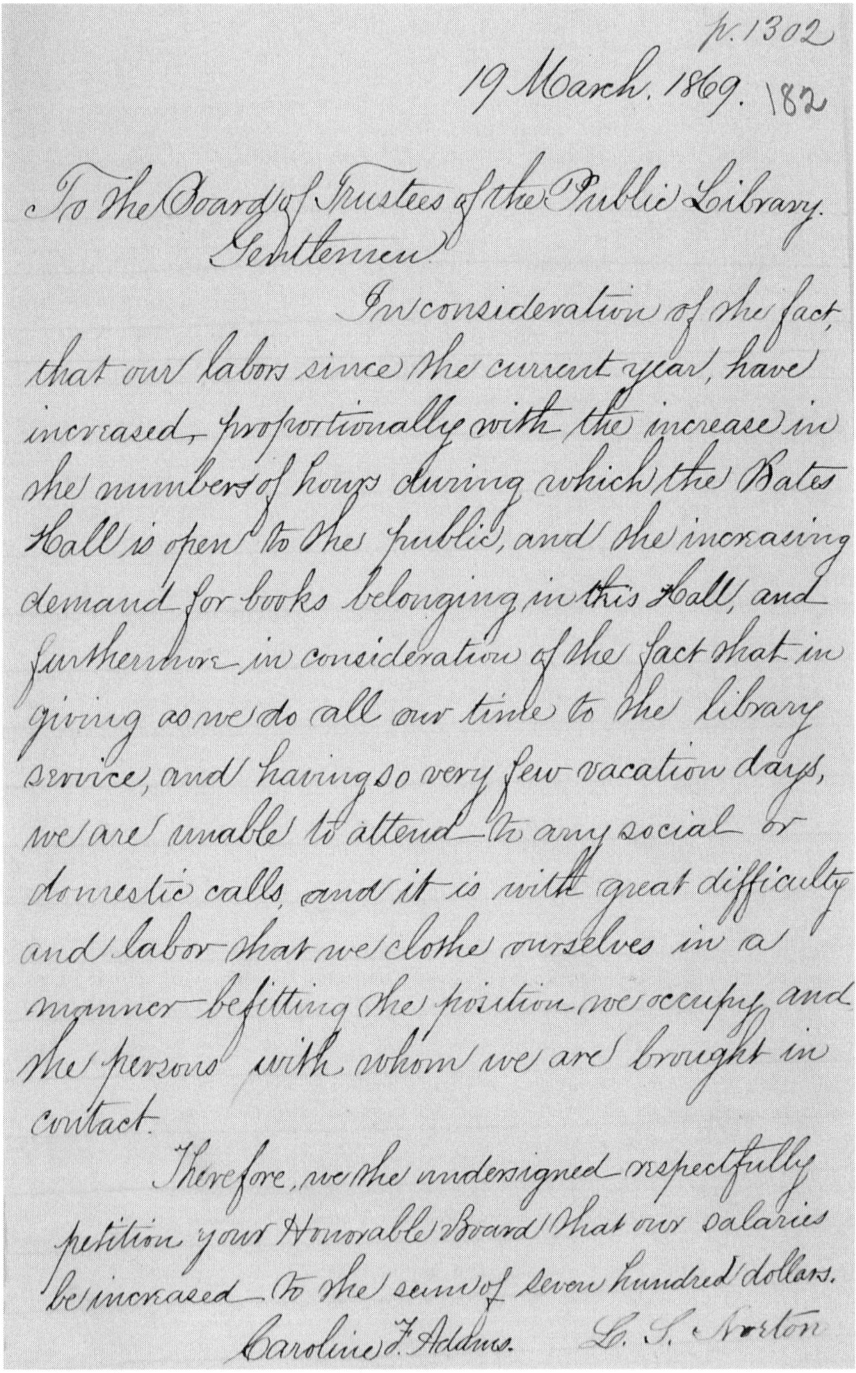

p. 1302

19 March. 1869. 182

To the Board of Trustees of the Public Library.
Gentlemen

In consideration of the fact, that our labors since the current year, have increased, proportionally with the increase in the numbers of hours during which the Bates Hall is open to the public, and the increasing demand for books belonging in this Hall, and furthermore in consideration of the fact that in giving as we do all our time to the library service, and having so very few vacation days, we are unable to attend to any social or domestic calls, and it is with great difficulty and labor that we clothe ourselves in a manner befitting the position we occupy, and the persons with whom we are brought in contact.

Therefore, we the undersigned respectfully petition your Honorable Board that our salaries be increased to the sum of seven hundred dollars.

Caroline F. Addus.   L. S. Norton

Fig. 5.4. An 1869 petition of two women library workers asking for a salary increase. Reproduced by permission of the Boston Public Library.

young woman in the Boston area did not absolutely need to earn a living, there were few appropriate avenues of employment available after graduation from high school other than teaching.

Although the great majority of the women were single, being married was not an obstacle to employment in any of the libraries. Miss Roxana M. Clark worked at the Public Library from 1859 to 1866 and resumed work from 1868 to 1876 after she had become Mrs. Eastman. Mrs. Matilda Berry Maynard and Mrs. Theresa Byington Hill served on the Harvard library staff, in addition to Sarah F. Appleton, who worked for several years after her marriage to Charles Ammi Cutter. The first woman hired at the Athenæum was Mrs. A. B. Harnden.[85] Of course, some women left their library employment for marriage, but others left for another career such as teaching, and for work at another library.[86]

Library Bureaucracies

Boston has been identified as the earliest city to begin hiring women as clerical workers, based on responses to the 1860 U.S. manuscript census, which was the first to record women's occupations. According to this source, 2 percent, or 114, of the total number of clerical workers in Boston were women. By 1880, Boston was fairly representative of other American cities, such as New York and Chicago, in terms of the number of women entering the clerical workforce. In that year women held 10 percent of clerical jobs in Boston. By 1900, that number had increased to 35 percent, and in succeeding decades women would completely dominate this labor sector.[87]

These numbers reveal that a process of bureaucratization took place, in which there was increasing demand for clerical work. Thus, Cindy Aron, in her significant analysis of the first women to work for the federal government, points out that in 1861 women were first hired to clip currency notes in the Treasury Department, but were soon performing clerical work such as

---

Record Files, v. 8, nos. 69, 97, 182. Although most women lived in family homes, a number were boarders. For information on female clerical workers living in boarding houses see Sarah Deutsch, *Women and the City: Gender, Space, and Power in Boston, 1870–1940* (New York: Oxford University Press, 2000), chap. 3, "The Moral Geography of the Working Girl (and the New Woman)," 78–114; and Oliver Zunz, *Making America Corporate* (Chicago: University of Chicago Press, 1990), 141–45.

85. Aron found that of the women applying to work in the federal government in 1862/63, 64 percent were single. Aron, *Ladies and Gentlemen,* 206, fn. 20.

86. For examples, see Mitchell, " 'A Beginning Is Made.' "

87. Srole, " 'A Position That God Has Not Particularly Assigned to Men,' " 218–28. Srole's work is based on census data and city directories. Her analysis is highly statistical and also relies on Cindy S. Aron's dissertation research.

copying and bookkeeping.[88] Angel Kwolek-Folland, in her study of the first women to work in the insurance and banking industries, notes that a female clerk was hired by a Massachusetts life insurance firm in 1866.[89] "Task specialization was [also] fundamental" to the administrative revolution.[90] Job differentiation was a key element in the expansion of the federal bureaucracy and the growth of the corporate office in the 1870s. So was it in the Boston-area libraries, where bureaucratization occurred earlier, in the 1850s and 1860s.

If the women who were working in Boston-area libraries participated in the 1860 census, it seems likely that they identified themselves as "clerks," because the nature of the work they performed was indeed clerical. As we have seen, Sibley usually recorded that the position for which women were hired in the College Library was "to write &c."; the Sawyer sisters were originally hired to copy lists of books from requests brought in by faculty. It is unlikely that the first women who began cataloguing books in the Boston-area libraries thought of themselves as "cataloguers." "Female assistant" was the title given to the women cataloguers at Harvard. By 1862, when Abbot presented his new catalogue proposal to the faculty committee, he had become "Superintendent of the Cataloguing Department," with a staff composed of a male assistant and several women devoted exclusively to this endeavor.[91]

The Boston Public Library underwent an extraordinary expansion of staff as well as collections after its initial opening in 1854. That year the staff consisted of the librarian, an assistant librarian, a watchman, and four women, with an annual expenditure for "salaries and extra help" of $2,544.[92] A mere four years later, after the move to a new library building on Boylston Street, Superintendent Jewett had twenty-one staff members, of whom eleven male and eight female staff were working on the catalogues; annual salaries amounted to $9,436.[93] Job diversification was an even greater necessity for the Public Library because it was divided into what were, in effect, two libraries—the Lower Hall and Upper Hall. The popularity of the Lower Hall reading room, which held general reference works, newspapers, and periodicals, as well as

---

88. Aron contends that the Civil War (and the unavailability of male workers) had less to do with the hiring of women than financial considerations, i.e., women could be paid less than men. However, officials used the war to rationalize hiring women who had lost husbands and fathers in the conflict. Aron, *Ladies and Gentlemen*, 70–78.

89. Kwolek-Folland, *Engendering Business*, 30.

90. Graham S. Lowe, *Women in the Administrative Revolution: The Feminization of Clerical Work* (Cambridge: Polity Press, 1987), 4.

91. Abbot, [manuscript report, spring 1862].

92. Second Annual Report of the Trustees of the Public Library, 1854, [Appendix] B, Librarian's Report.

93. BPL Trustees Proceedings, 19 October 1858.

the delivery and circulation desk, divided the female staff further into "attendants," who assisted patrons and charged out books, and "assistants," who performed clerical tasks in nonpublic areas.

The earliest mention of library "departments" in the Public Library was in 1858. Beginning the same year "young girls" between 10 and 15, who had only a grammar school education, were employed to retrieve and reshelve books in the closed stacks; they came to be known as "runners." [94] In 1865, the Committee on Administration, one of several sub-committees of the trustees, asked Jewett to produce his annual staff list, usually names and salaries only, with the actual duties of the individual staff. Unfortunately, the list usually indicates only the location of where someone worked, for example, "Desk" or "Lower Hall." But among the female staff, Roxana M. Clark appears as "Takes care of new books &c," and Lizzie Stevenson "Assists Miss Clark"; Grace Madigan is listed as "Charging books & writing." [95] Although management of personnel was ultimately the responsibility of Jewett, much of Librarian Capen's time was spent scheduling staff, accounting for absences, and handling payroll (in 1874 Capen's accounts were handed over to Addie A. Nichols, the "library auditor"). [96] Superintendent Winsor, beginning in 1869, solidified the library's bureaucratic structure, creating additional distinct departments (for instance, the Shelf Department and Binding Department). By the time he had established three branch libraries, Winsor's payroll for 1872–73 included thirty-seven employees in the "Central Library," and another nineteen in the branches. [97]

The best account of workflow in a cataloguing department of the time is that by John Fiske, Abbot's successor in the Harvard College Library. Writing in the *Atlantic Monthly,* he described it thus: Before an order for books is sent off "one of our most trustworthy assistants" ensures there are no duplicates in the library. When a box of books is received, they are "looked over by the principal assistant, with two or three subordinates," then the assistant librarian reviews them, after which, "five or six more assistants now arriving on the scene, the work of 'collating' begins." The collators are the "less experienced and less accomplished assistants." Then the principal assistant [Miss Hutchins] parcels out the books "for cataloguing," after which they are reviewed by the principal assistant and the assistant librarian [Mr. Fiske him-

---

94. Sixth Annual Report of the Trustees of the Public Library, 6 November 1858. "Miss Ross added to runners department," BPL Trustees Record Files, 10 November 1869, no. 40.

95. This is the only staff list that delineates any duties. Jewett, "Persons employed in the Public Library, 1 September 1865," BPL Trustees Proceedings.

96. BPL Trustees Proceedings, 13 October 1874.

97. Ibid., 25 March 1872.

self], then proofread by a specially trained assistant "who can be depended upon for absolute accuracy in such matters." Fiske goes on to say that he and the principal assistant write few cards themselves, only the most difficult titles, say, those in Croatian. "There is nothing especially difficult in Greek titles, save for the fact that our assistants are all women, who for the most part know little or nothing of the language." Fiske's footnote to this statement allows, "We have since, I am glad to say, found an exception to this rule, and Greek titles are now disposed of in regular course." No wonder Sibley called his female staff "an efficient corps."[98]

In the third quarter of the nineteenth century the library workplace was a fairly integrated environment, in part because of space constraints, but also because libraries in general were seen as a cultural locus where social interaction between the sexes was not inappropriate. As with office space in businesses, this would change later in the century, as more and more women entered the workplace. The greatest difference, of course, was the money earned by men and women. It is virtually impossible to give solid comparisons on wages and salaries paid to library staff during this period because of the inconsistent records of specific duties and payments in the four institutions. But it is possible to note some comparative wages paid to women within these libraries. The most striking of these is the State Library, which began paying its first female cataloguers twenty-five cents per hour in 1854, and the College Library, which began paying its first cataloguers six cents per hour five years later! In 1873, Harvard's Annie E. Hutchins received $700 per year, the Public Library paid Mary E. Joslyn $800 per year, and Ellen M. Sawyer's annual salary at the State Library was $840. In the same year, the male assistants employed by the Public Library were earning between $1100 and $1800 per year.[99]

The records of these institutions include numerous petitions for pay increases (from both men and women) and demonstrate an awareness of wages being paid elsewhere in the Boston area. Three of the female assistants petitioned the Harvard Corporation in 1864, noting "The sum paid per hour [8 and 10 cents], at a rate fixed several years since, was even then altogether disproportionate to the nature and extent of the qualifications required, and much less than that paid in other Libraries for similar labor."[100] In their peti-

98. John Fiske, "A Librarian's Work," *Atlantic Monthly* 38 (October 1876): 480–91. Sibley, Library Journal, Annual Report, July 1873.

99. Sibley was notoriously cheap; see Mitchell, " 'A Beginning Is Made.' " The Public Library salaries are listed in BPL Trustees Proceedings, 15 April 1873. The State Library trustees often gave the library's female assistants compensation in addition to their salaries; Minutes of Meetings, Trustees, State Library of Massachusetts, 13 February 1872, 21 April 1873.

100. Matilda Freeman Dana, Mary Bates Merriam, Ellen Maria Sawyer to the President and Fellows of Harvard College [29 July 1864], College Papers, 2d ser.

tion to the trustees in 1867, six of the women in the Public Library wrote "Our salary was heretofore equal to that of School Teachers, but has not been increased to the same extent."[101]

BY 1876, William F. Poole could write with authority, "there are ladies in the eastern cities who have had much experience in cataloguing, and who devote themselves to this specialty."[102] In that year librarianship was professionalized, and most would say that the profession ultimately became feminized. We now know that libraries played an important role in the development of the female clerical workforce, and in Boston and Cambridge, it was seminal. In the same way, but in the 1880s and later, "the financial industries . . . were feminized in more than the simple presence of women. The changing nature of gender in offices created a crisis for management theory, business ideology, architectural solutions to the drive for efficiency."[103]

Jewett and Winsor, in particular, brought great skill to the management of the diverse functions necessary to conduct library business, by forming an integrated staff (see figure 5.5), by creating specific bureaucratic departments, and by designing new and efficient systems, such as the acquisition and circulation of large numbers of publications. And they did this in the absence of models from the business sector in the period from 1850 to 1875. The Boston Public Library staff in 1872–73 consisted of fifty-six individuals. By comparison, the Metropolitan Life Insurance Company in New York had an office staff of fifty-four in 1889 (having hired their first female clerk in 1877).[104]

Still, the libraries' most significant contribution to the evolution of modern management in this period was the catalogue, particularly the card catalogue. This system of record management was so fundamental that it can be considered a prototypical form of technology. The link between the feminization of clerical work and technology has been treated by a number of historians.[105] Technology and its complexities have been variously defined, but several historians have viewed technological innovations as "intrinsic parts of the

---

101. Sarah E. Looke, Georgiana Philbrick, Hattie R. Cogswell, Dora Norton, Caroline F. Adams, Lydia F. Knowles to Trustees of the Boston Public Library, 8 July 1867, BPL Trustees Record Files, v. 8, no. 3.

102. William F. Poole, "Organization and Management of Public Libraries," *Public Libraries in the United States,* Part I, 490.

103. Kwolek-Folland, *Engendering Business,* 181.

104. Ibid., 30.

105. See, for example, Elyce Rotella, "The Transformation of the American Office: Changes in Employment and Technology," *Journal of Economic History* 41 (1981): 51–57; Klaus Musmann, *Technological Innovations in Libraries, 1860–1960: An Anecdotal History* (Westport, CT: Greenwood Press, 1993); Heidi I. Hartmann et al., eds., *Computer Chips and Paper Clips: Technology and Women's Employment* (Washington: National Academy Press, 1986).

Fig. 5.5. Justin Winsor and the Harvard College Library staff in the 1890s, at which point women outnumbered men. Reproduced by permission of the Harvard University Archives (HUP-SF PF Library 23, 7:1).

culture and economy of a society."[106] Its transformative nature is generally acknowledged. "Technological change alters the goods and services that are produced or the methods by which they are produced. . . . [It has] the potential to affect all areas of social life, including art and literature."[107]

In *Control through Communication: The Rise of System in American Management*, JoAnne Yates does not discount the importance of machines such as the typewriter and the photocopier in the growth and efficiency of modern businesses.[108] But all of these are simply tools with which to manage records. It is the development of the system, such as the cataloguing and classification

106. Musmann, *Technological Innovations*, 3; Daniel R. Headrick, *The Tentacles of Progress: Technology Transfer in the Age of Imperialism, 1850–1940* (New York: Oxford University Press, 1988), 5; Norman J. Vig, "Technology, Philosophy, and the State: An Overview," in *Technology and Politics*, ed. Michael E. Kraft and Norman J. Vig (Durham: Duke University Press, 1988), 15.

107. Hartmann et al., *Computer Chips*, 6–7.

108. JoAnne Yates, *Control through Communication: The Rise of System in American Management* (Baltimore: Johns Hopkins University Press, 1989), 56–63.

of bibliographic records—and access points to search and retrieve the data within those records—that is key. It is therefore more than interesting to take note of Melvil Dewey's founding, in Boston, of the Library Bureau in the 1880s to sell standardized supplies such as catalogue cards, cabinets, adjustable shelving and other library supplies. The Library Bureau soon found that its products had moved beyond libraries to appeal to a broad commercial market.[109] Catalogue cards "remained its biggest money-maker, especially after the cards were adopted by banks, insurance companies, and other businesses as a flexible means of maintaining customer records."[110] The card file was the precursor of the vertical flat filing system, which in turn gave rise to companies who proposed different methods of organizing files for record-keeping and retrieval in the late nineteenth and early twentieth centuries.

Seen within its technological, cultural, and social context, the rise of the card catalogue, and the concomitant entrance of female clerical workers into increasingly bureaucraticized libraries, was a pivotal point not only in the history of libraries. The great library catalogues, early technology systems that would endure for decades, were catalysts for an extraordinary moment of institutional growth and change.

---

109. For discussions of the Library Bureau, see ibid.; Abigail A. Van Slyck, *Free to All: Carnegie Libraries and American Culture, 1890–1920* (Chicago: University of Chicago Press, 1995), 47–54, 167–68; Musmann, *Technological Innovations,* 8–10; and Beniger, *Control Revolution,* 394.

110. Van Slyck, *Free to All,* 48.

Chapter 6

Faith in Reading

Public Libraries, Liberalism, and the Civil Religion

THOMAS AUGST

"WHY LIBRARY architecture should have been yoked to ecclesiastical architecture . . . is not obvious, unless it be that librarians in the past needed this stimulus to their religious emotions," wrote William Poole in *The Construction of Library Buildings* (1881).[1] "The present state of piety in the profession renders the union no longer necessary and it is time that the bill was filed for divorce. The same secular common sense and the same adaptation of means to ends which have built the modern grain elevator and reaper are needed for the reform of library construction."

Poole's comment on the excesses of library ornament (see figure 6.1) begs a question: what was the sacral function of the public library? Poole himself was a moving force in the new profession of librarianship, and like many of his colleagues then and now would stake the credibility of his discipline on the functional utility and managerial efficiency that came to count as "common sense" in the era of industrial progress: libraries should be designed to serve their internal functions of preservation, storage, and circulation.[2] Indeed, one response to Poole's article noted that, "thorough librarian that he is," he could see "nothing in a library but a huddle of books, which he would get into

---

1. William Poole, "The Construction of Library Buildings" (1881), cited in Kenneth A. Breisch, *Henry Hobson Richardson and the Small Public Library in America: A Study in Typology* (Cambridge: MIT Press, 1997), 219.

2. Librarians of course play many different roles across many different kinds of institutions. Pioneers in the public library movement like Poole sought, however, through the creation of the American Library Association in 1876, the development of schools of library and information science, and their public writing and speaking more generally to appropriate cultural prestige and status for their work that was accorded to the traditional professions of law, education, and medicine. See Wayne Wiegand, *The Politics of an Emerging Profession: The American Library Association, 1876–1917* (Westport, CT: Greenwood, 1986), and Michael F. Winter, *The Culture of Control and Expertise: Toward a Sociological Understanding of Librarianship* (Westport, CT: Greenwood, 1988).

Figure 6.1. The Peabody Library at Johns Hopkins University in Baltimore, completed in 1878. For William Poole, this building owed more to ecclesiastical history than to the needs of modern libraries. Photo by Michael Dersin.

as little space as possible."[3] As with the threshing of wheat, libraries must organize their services and goods on the principles of mass production, rejecting religion and feeling alike as reflexes of a pre-modern mind. In the age of mechanical and electronic reproduction, every gadget or system promises to straighten the path to secular progress. For Poole and professional elites more generally, religion itself became an emblem of culture in its vestigial form: an aesthetic and sensual pleasure in merely symbolic experience, preventing the freedom from mental bondage and social caste systems on which the progress of modern society depended. But as Henry Adams might have noted, Poole had not overcome religious superstition but given it a new outlet in the secular cult of the dynamo. Suspicious of all trappings of Catholic devotion, liberal Protestants like Poole intuitively understood faith as an essentially private experience of edification and transcendence, mediated by the individual, solitary experience of reading that for hundreds of years had animated the reformation of Christian piety.

As Poole's metaphors only begin to suggest, the modern library would adapt itself to the practical organization and management of information. The "ecclesiastic architecture" of libraries from the later nineteenth and early twentieth centuries continues to seem archaic because, in part, we have forgotten the spiritual function that institutions of public culture were meant to serve, as what James Traub recently called "secular cathedrals" of liberal society.[4] Built with bygone fads for beaux-arts and Victorian gothic design, the immense marble buildings that loom over the horizon of cities and towns across the United States attest to "religious emotions" that librarians and ordinary patrons alike associated with civic institutions at the turn of the twentieth century. In her autobiography *The Promised Land* (1913), Mary Antin describes her girlhood experience as a Russian Jewish immigrant approaching the Boston Public Library.

3. Letter from Andrew Dickson White, 15 October 1881, Daniel C. Gilman papers, Ms. 1.53, Special Collections, Milton S. Eisenhower Library, Johns Hopkins University. While writing to Gilman, White repeated an anecdote that a student had passed on to him about the impression that the physical presence of books had made upon him: "He told me that he learned at once the importance of several things which he had never before known. When I asked him for the first of these, he said: 'Silence'.... Had Yale College Library been what Mr. Poole's system would now make it, I should have had far less respect for learning, literature and for the institution that I now have." I thank Ken Carpenter for bringing this and other reactions to Poole's argument to my attention.

4. James Traub, "The Stuff of City Life," *New York Times Magazine,* 3 October 2004, 26. Neil Harris similarly describes the large private museums devoted to public culture, such as the Morgan Library, as "shrines to a secular religion that identified itself with the very pith of civilization." Neil Harris, "Collective Possessions: The J. Pierpont Morgan Library," in his *Cultural Excursions: Marketing Appetites and Cultural Tastes in Modern America* (Chicago: University of Chicago Press, 1990), 274.

It was my habit to go very slowly up the low, broad steps to the palace entrance, pleasing my eyes with the majestic lines of the building, and lingering to read again the carved inscriptions: *Public Library—Built by the People—Free to All.* Did I not say it was my palace? Mine, because I was a citizen; mine, though I was born an alien . . . My palace—mine! . . . All these eager children, all these fine browed women, all these scholars going home to write learned books—I and they had this glorious thing in common, this noble treasure house of learning. It was wonderful to say, *This is mine;* it was thrilling to say, *This is ours.*[5]

At the laying of the cornerstone for the new building of the Boston Public in 1888, Oliver Wendell Holmes declared, "This Palace was the people's own," and Antin transforms the phrase into a democratic creed. As she recalls mounting the marble steps of a public library, Antin represents a book collection as a collective resource, a "noble treasure house" over which all citizens—be they eager children, fine women, scholars, or immigrants—have an equal claim. In a democracy, the "palaces" are public spaces, not private, and nobility is achieved through the acquisition of knowledge rather than the inheritance of property.

We might interpret such declarations of civic faith as evidence of how effectively libraries were used to propagate a conservative social and economic ideology of reform.[6] As Anglo-Protestant elites in the Northeast lost their local political dominance, they founded colleges, museums, hospitals, and other nonprofit benevolent and educational institutions in order to create new channels of leadership and social control free from the interference of elected officials and the church.[7] The steel magnate Andrew Carnegie believed public

---

5. Mary Antin, *The Promised Land,* 2d ed. (Boston: Houghton Mifflin, 1969; rpt. Princeton University Press, 1985), 341. Further references to this work will be given in the text.

6. The standard histories of the public library movement remain Sidney Ditzion, *Arsenals of a Democratic Culture: A Social History of the American Public Library Movement in New England and the Middle States, 1850–1900* (Chicago: American Library Association, 1947), and Jesse H. Shera, *Foundations of the Public Library: The Origins of the Public Library Movement in New England, 1629–1855* (Chicago: University of Chicago Press, 1949). As Dee Garrison has pointed out, public libraries provided "a rich focus for expressive meaning in Victorian America" which responded to "the sense of urban crisis and chaos; the fear of immigrant intruders; the emphasis upon the family as guarantor of tradition; the discontent of women and labor; the hope that education would right the wrongs of poverty and crime; the hunger for education among the poor; the ambitious paternalistic and humanitarian motives of reformers—all were as important to the content of library ritual as the need for a contented, disciplined, and busy wage force." Garrison, *Apostles of Culture: The Public Librarian and American Society, 1876–1920* (New York: Free Press, 1979), 62.

7. Peter Dobkin Hall sketches "the reorientation of the Old Standing Order" that took place over the nineteenth century, "from an elite with public responsibilities to a group whose influence was mediated through private institutions," which included colleges, museums, libraries, hospitals, and other benevolent institutions. Peter Dobkin Hall, *The Organization of American Culture, 1700–1900: Private Institutions, Elites, and the Origins of American Nationality* (New York: New York University Press, 1982), 122, 110.

libraries were the best means for the Gospel of Wealth to serve the "permanent good" of the people because, as he put it in 1889, they stimulated "the best and most aspiring poor of the community to further efforts in their own self-improvement."[8] So too, with their formal administration as municipal institutions, libraries found themselves in the midst of explicit battles over the role of religion in public life. Orthodox and liberal Protestants fought over the opening of libraries and museums on Sundays.[9] It did not help the campaign to win tax support for libraries that elected officials tended to be Irish Catholic, and viewed all forms of public education as hostile to their faith. In 1901, for example, the Catholic hierarchy in New York briefly opposed non-Catholic libraries for its people. Its concerns were allayed only when provision was made for including a Catholic and a Jew on the board of directors of the public library.[10] In this context, as Evelyn Geller has noted, we should view the public library, like the school, as "an agency in the service of secularization, a self-conscious and controversial process of church-state separation."[11]

But what if we took Antin's profession of wonder seriously, as an expression of a historically particular secular faith, a new kind of civil religion organized around public sites and symbols of reading? And how might such an approach to the social function of symbols require us to rethink the kinds of distinctions—between symbol and function, mind and body, text and context, the individual and the collective—that helped librarians modernize the mission of public libraries, and that continue to shape scholarly definitions of culture and society? As Dee Garrison has pointed out, the librarians often spoke "in broadly religious terms" about their missionary influence; pioneers of the profession such as Charles Ammi Cutter, Charles Jewett,

---

8. Andrew Carnegie, "The Best Fields for Philanthropy," in *The Library and Society: Reprints of Papers and Addresses,* ed. Arthur Bostwick, (New York: H. W. Wilson, 1920), 35. For a study of the building of Carnegie libraries in their social and cultural context, see Abigail Van Slyck, *Free to All: Carnegie Libraries and American Culture, 1890–1920* (Chicago: University of Chicago Press, 1995).

9. On the debates over Sunday openings at the Boston Public Library that took place between 1859 and 1872, see Alexis McCrossen, *Holy Day, Holiday: The American Sunday* (Ithaca: Cornell University Press, 2000), 58–64.

10. Phyllis Dain, *The New York Public Library: A History of Its Founding and Early Years* (New York Public Library, 1972), 31. Dain notes that a "comparatively small group of philanthropic persons, who were on the boards of schools, colleges, museums, hospitals, as well as libraries, were generally members of the . . . elite (Protestant or German-Jewish) that considered practical politics dirty and most Tammany politicians vulgar and venal, an attitude also prevalent well into the twentieth century among library trustees and libraries" (33). On the public arguments and political pressures that influenced the makeup of the New York Public's board of directors, see Dain, 249–52.

11. Evelyn Geller, *Forbidden Books in American Public Libraries, 1876–1939* (Westport, CT: Greenwood, 1984), 10. As advocates "contended with dedicated adherents to older values," the professional "norm of neutrality" served to justify "a secular innovation and to protect the library from partisan control."

and Samuel Swett Green were trained for the ministry before they joined the public library movement, where like other social reformers they sought to "restructure the Christian impulse" by creating a "secular ethical system."[12] By situating Antin's idealism in the context of her own life narrative as well as the debates about social reform that accompanied the rise of public libraries, we can sketch a lived experience of institutions of reading that Poole's bifurcation of value and utility leaves obscure. As I suggest in the pages that follow, the aesthetic and spiritual experience fostered by public libraries had social uses, performing four functions traditionally served by religion: the popularization of ethical practices; the organization and differentiation of attention; the definition of community; and the promotion of scripturalism, modes of moral authority that regulate and differentiate access to textual knowledge. By serving these spiritual functions in the lives of individuals like Mary Antin, the public library made particular habits of reading central to the rituals and pieties of secular modernity—one of the "new modes of social management and self-regulation" that would define liberalism as not only a form of governance but a faith in progress.[13]

Antin's reflection is not a statement of fact, a positivist history of institutional workings, but rather a personal history of what the library meant to one patron. As such, it illuminates the new public presence and symbolic force that sites of reading had acquired in the lives of particular persons and communities by the later nineteenth century. The design and ornamentation of the Boston Public Library "generated a set of social rituals," as Sally Promey notes, that served its "cultural identification as liminal space . . . in which transformation in the status of individuals was presumed to occur."[14] Narrating both a girl's coming of age and an immigrant's conversion to what she would call the "gospel of liberty," *The Promised Land* demonstrates how the public library came to occupy this liminal space in the lives of ordinary people

---

12. Garrison, *Apostles of Culture,* 37–38. As Justin Winsor noted, the first professional gathering in 1876 was "motivated by the idea that the library was 'in essentials a missionary influence'" (37).

13. Building on Michel Foucault's late work on governmentality, scholars have recently sought to document the means by which populations of liberal democracies become self-regulating. Thus as Tony Bennett observes, liberalism entailed the historical "development of new forms of social management and regulation . . . creating frameworks in which individuals will voluntarily regulate their own behavior to achieve specific social ends," without the coercive power of the state. Bennett, *Culture: A Reformer's Science* (London: Sage, 1998), 110. For analysis of cultural formations in relation to neoliberalism, see Jack Z. Bratich, Jeremy Packer, and Cameron McCarthy, eds., *Foucault, Cultural Studies, and Governmentality* (Albany: State University of New York Press, 2003); and Justin Lewis and Toby Miller, eds., *Critical Cultural Policy Studies: A Reader* (Oxford: Blackwell, 2003).

14. Sally M. Promey, *Painting Religion in Public: John Singer Sargent's "Triumph of Religion" at the Boston Public Library* (Princeton: Princeton University Press, 1999), 153.

precisely by stimulating "religious emotions" toward particular habits, spaces, symbols, and objects of reading. Along with schools, playgrounds, museums, public parks, and other sites in the municipal landscape, public libraries in the later nineteenth and early twentieth century helped to institutionalize leisure as moral education, where individuals acquired the capacity for self-government requisite to the circumstances of a mobile and heterogeneous society. The public library in particular became a temple to a civil religion, a site not only to borrow books but also to practice devotions of self-realization that embody freedom in liberal democracies.

Freedom of Choice: Reading as Self-Ownership

Antin's exclamation on the steps of the Boston Public Library transforms an institution of public culture into a sacred shrine of democratic equality, which extends to "even" a poor Russian immigrant with an aristocratic desire for self-making, the capacious (if not grandiose) subjectivity with which many cultures have identified the exercise of power with the possession of knowledge. Whether portrayed in the enthusiastic tones of immigrant wonder or idealized by librarians and cultural reformers of the later nineteenth century, the citizen's encounter with public libraries had a paradoxical logic: individuals take personal ownership of their identity by entering public space. As her repetition of "me," "mine," "my," and "I" powerfully suggest, this young woman finds in the public library an opportunity to experience herself as an individual in newly compelling and intimate ways. "I felt the grand spaces under the soaring arches as a personal attribute of my being," Antin notes.[15] In liberal democracy, it is within the crowded spaces of public life where citizens find that being has personal attributes.

Like so many American narratives that place books in the path to self-invention — ranging from Benjamin Franklin's *Autobiography,* through the narratives of ex-slaves, to autobiographies of Richard Wright and Malcolm X — Antin's confirms a long-standing American faith that education is a means to liberty. In telling of her voyage to the "promised land," Antin invokes, like so many other immigrants before and since, a typological interpretation that maps an Old Testament narrative of Exodus onto a geographical movement from old to new world.[16] As her exclamation on the steps of the BPL only begins to suggest, however, deliverance is not only collective — the escape of

---

15. Antin, *Promised Land,* 342.

16. On the appropriation of typology to immigrant narrative, see Werner Sollars, "Typology and Ethnogenesis," in his *Beyond Ethnicity* (New York: Oxford University Press, 1986), 40–65.

Jews from persecution in the Russian Pale—but also individual: the escape of a girl from tribal superstitions and social codes enforced by religious patriarchy. In the first half of her narrative, oppression comes from outside the Jewish community, from hostile gentiles and Russian soldiers, but also from within, in the denial of education to women. No matter how poor a man was, "he was to be respected and set above other men if he was learned in the Law" (31). Not allowed to become scholars and rabbonim, girls were taught only enough to read prayers in Hebrew and follow their meaning by Yiddish translation. "It was not much to be a girl, you see," Antin observes. Without access to advanced literacy and the religious authority to which it was yoked, "a girl's real schoolroom was her mother's kitchen" (33, 34). Antin found her yearning for the "priceless ware" of "modern education" deepened by her father's alienation from religious tradition: "The rigid scheme of orthodox Jewish life offered no opening to any other mode of life" (75). Giving Antin access to learning that she had been denied during her childhood in the Pale, the public library represented a secular faith in the power of knowledge that depended on the "opening" of religious tradition itself and that rededicated the nation to its own civic ideals. Immigrants possessed a special "reverence" for learning that made them "pilgrims and voyagers for spiritual freedom," as Antin put it at a conference of librarians in 1913.[17]

Well before the Progressive Era, social and circulating libraries had assumed particular symbolic importance in defining this relationship to knowledge as "modern." In the 1798 autobiography of Stephen Burroughs, an itinerant schoolteacher and general confidence man, for example, we see that popular access to books already had become a primary reference point in the rhetoric of democratic freedom. When he arrived in Bridgehampton, Long Island, Burroughs found the community to be largely illiterate, "almost entirely destitute of books of any kind, except schoolbooks and the Bibles."[18] At some length, he recounts his efforts to remedy this general ignorance by forming a proprietary library consisting of "histories, and books of information upon secular subjects" (283). Bridgehampton's minister and judge, however, expected the

---

17. Mary Antin, "The Immigrant and the Library," *Bulletin of the American Library Association* 7 (1913): 147.

18. *Memoirs of Stephen Burroughs of New Hampshire* (New York: Dial Press, 1924). The townspeople had opposed previous effort, because it was led by the minister, Mr. Woolworth, who would be choosing books: "They generally expect the library will consist of books in divinity, and dry metaphysical writings" (281). Burroughs promised proprietors that "histories, and books of information upon secular subjects, should give the leading cast to the complexion of the library" (283). For a recent discussion of Burroughs, the controversy over the library, and the contents of the Bridgehampton Library, see Susanna Ashton, "A Corrupt Medium: Stephen Burroughs and the Bridgehampton, New York Library," *Libraries and Culture* 38 (2003): 94–120.

town library to consist of "books in divinity, and dry metaphysical writings" (281), as he puts it. They accused Burroughs of "endeavoring to overthrow all religion, morality and order in the place; was introducing corrupt books into the library, and adopting the most fatal measures to overthrow all the good old establishments" (286). The minister and judge propose books on religion and ethics, while Burroughs proposes histories and "books of information upon secular subjects."

Who shall control the reading of a community? As Burroughs represents it, this controversy over the content of the library was proxy for a more pressing contest over the moral authority of government that recapitulated the recently ended Revolution. The elites who preside over Bridgehampton are portrayed as irrational and rigid, incapable of the compromise, deliberation, or toleration expected from members of the learned professions. Flying into "ungovernable rage" when confronted with views that contradict their own, these worthies cannot be trusted to make decisions about the public good with the civility and disinterest requisite to the new republican order. As he advocated a less prescriptive, secular course of reading for the library, Burroughs grounded the constitution of social authority in the liberal values of free inquiry, natural rights, and private property: "To purchase such books with our money as we wished for was a right we inherited from nature" (291). Burroughs argues that traditional custodians of public interest—the church and the state—must defer to "the natural liberty" of men to be sovereign in their intellectual interests and literary tastes, no less than their political and economic rights: freedom itself is hard-wired in the mental and moral faculties of individuals, in the natural capacities for reason, will, and imagination. Indeed, to read books "wished for" entails a natural unfolding of the self specifically identified with a cash transaction, the right to purchase what one wants with one's money.

In tying the wishes of readers to the natural right of consumers, Burroughs's narrative dramatizes the emergence of one the central values of liberal modernity: that liberty depends upon the capacity for choice. As T. H. Breen has recently argued, the movement for American independence was made possible by the sudden expansion of the consumer marketplace. Throughout the colonies, as families of even modest means purchased the same imported teapots and fabrics, they came to share common "concerns about color and texture, about fashion and etiquette, and about making the right choices from among an expanding number of possibilities." Books too were among the new possibilities afforded by the commercial revolution of the late eighteenth century. In *The Algerine Captive* (1797), Royall Tyler's narrator is impressed, after seven years' absence from the new nation, to discover the "extreme avidity with which books of mere amusement were purchased and perused by all ranks of his countrymen." This "surprising alteration of taste" had been brought about by the spread of social libraries, "composed of books designed to amuse," which could now be found in even modest-sized inland towns, and by country booksellers, who now "filled the land" with "modern travels and novels almost as incredible" that had once been confined to the seaports and to the private libraries of gentlemen. As a result of this "surprising altera-tion in the public taste," Tyler notes, "all orders of country life, with one accord, forsook the sober sermons and practical pieties of their fathers, for the gay stories and splendid impieties of the traveler and the novelist."[19] Like Burroughs, Tyler suggests that social libraries and booksellers challenged elite intellectual hierarchies by making reading an expression of personal choice, bringing religious authority in particular into conflict with more secular tastes for goods and leisure.

Disseminated by the circulation of books no less than teapots, liberal val-ues taught ordinary women and men to locate, as Antin puts it, "personal attributes" of one's being in the exercise of taste, within material forms of exchange and impersonal forms of kinship. By opening once-genteel concern with aesthetics, comfort, and status to ordinary people, this material culture created "a realm of intensely personal experience," Breen notes, in which mid-dling sorts gained "the ability to establish a meaningful and distinct sense of self through the exercise of individual choice, a process of ever more egalitar-ian self-fashioning that was itself the foundation of a late eighteenth-century liberal society."[20] In a society increasingly oriented to individual pursuit of amusement in the marketplace, even religion could be treated as just another commodity, a mode of self-expression. "Modern" education in the liberal tradition entails not the inheritance of "good old establishments," but rather the extension of individual sovereignty over judgments as near as the book in one's hand and as distant as forms political representation.

Circulating and social libraries helped to give reading a new moral utility, identified not with adherence to theological prescriptions and professional hierarchies of learning, but with the habit of reading. As we see in the register book of a small social library formed in Taunton, Massachusetts, for example, the content of any particular book comes to matter less than the cultivation of taste as it unfolds through a diverse array of what Burroughs had discreetly

---

19. Royall Tyler, *The Algerine Captive; or, The Life and adventures of Doctor Updike Underhill: six years a prisoner among the Algerines* (Walpole, NH, 1797), 4–7.

20. T. H. Breen, *The Marketplace of Revolution: How Consumer Politics Shaped American Inde-pendence* (Oxford: Oxford University Press, 2004), xv, xvi, 55.

termed "books of information upon secular subjects" (see figure 6.2). Over a few months in 1838, William Reed moves freely among biographies *(Life of Putnam, Life of Napoleon, Baylies's Historical Memoires)*, travel and natural history *(Narrative of a Voyage to the Ocean, History of Animals)*, and fiction *(The Sketchbook, Hope Leslie, Edgeworth's Works, The Prairie)*. Where H. L. Danforth sticks almost entirely to periodicals such as the *Edinburgh Review, London Quarterly, North American Review,* and the *Museum,* Nathan Connor reads almost nothing but tales. As members wrote the title of the work and the date of the loan, they created a profile of the preferences, intensity, duration, and sequence of their leisure reading visible to friends, neighbors, and other members. Each page of the register becomes a performance of personal choice. So too, circulating libraries ranging from short-lived operations such as Caritat's commercial library in New York to large nonprofit associations such as the Philadelphia Apprentices' Library or the New York Mercantile Library repeatedly sacrificed reservations about the moral influence of books to the commercial expedience of satisfying popular demand.[21] As thousands of such libraries were formed and dissolved throughout the nineteenth century, the freedom to choose books for amusement rather than instruction—whether deliberate or casual, in imitation of or indifference to others—became integral to the fashioning of a personal ethos through the individual development of literary taste.

Like the proprietary, social, and private or commercial circulating libraries, public libraries became institutions of "modern" education by helping to popularize reading itself *as a choice,* from among books "most wished for," within the mass market for goods and leisure. The Boston Public claimed to be the first state-supported library in the world to allow patrons to take books home. As its first annual report from 1852 suggests, its trustees had perhaps learned from social libraries the importance of institutionalizing reading as a practice of leisure rather than study—of organizing their policies of collection and circulation so that, "by following the popular taste," as the annual report of 1852 put it, "we may hope to create a real desire for general reading" among "the young, in the families and at the firesides of the greatest num-

---

21. On Caritat's library, see George Reddin, *"An Early Library of Fiction* (New York: George Reddin, 1940); on the Philadelphia Apprentices' Library, see John Frederick Lewis, *History of the Apprentices' Library of Philadelphia, 1820–1920* (Philadelphia: s.n., 1924); on the New York Mercantile Library, see Thomas Augst, *The Clerk's Tale: Young Men and Moral Life in Nineteenth-Century America* (Chicago: University of Chicago Press, 2003) . For more general surveys of circulating libraries, see Haynes McMullen, *American Libraries before 1876* (Westport, CT: Greenwood, 2000), David Kaser, *A Book for Sixpence: The Circulating Library in America* (Pittsburgh: Beta Phi Mu, 1980), and Shera, *Foundations.*

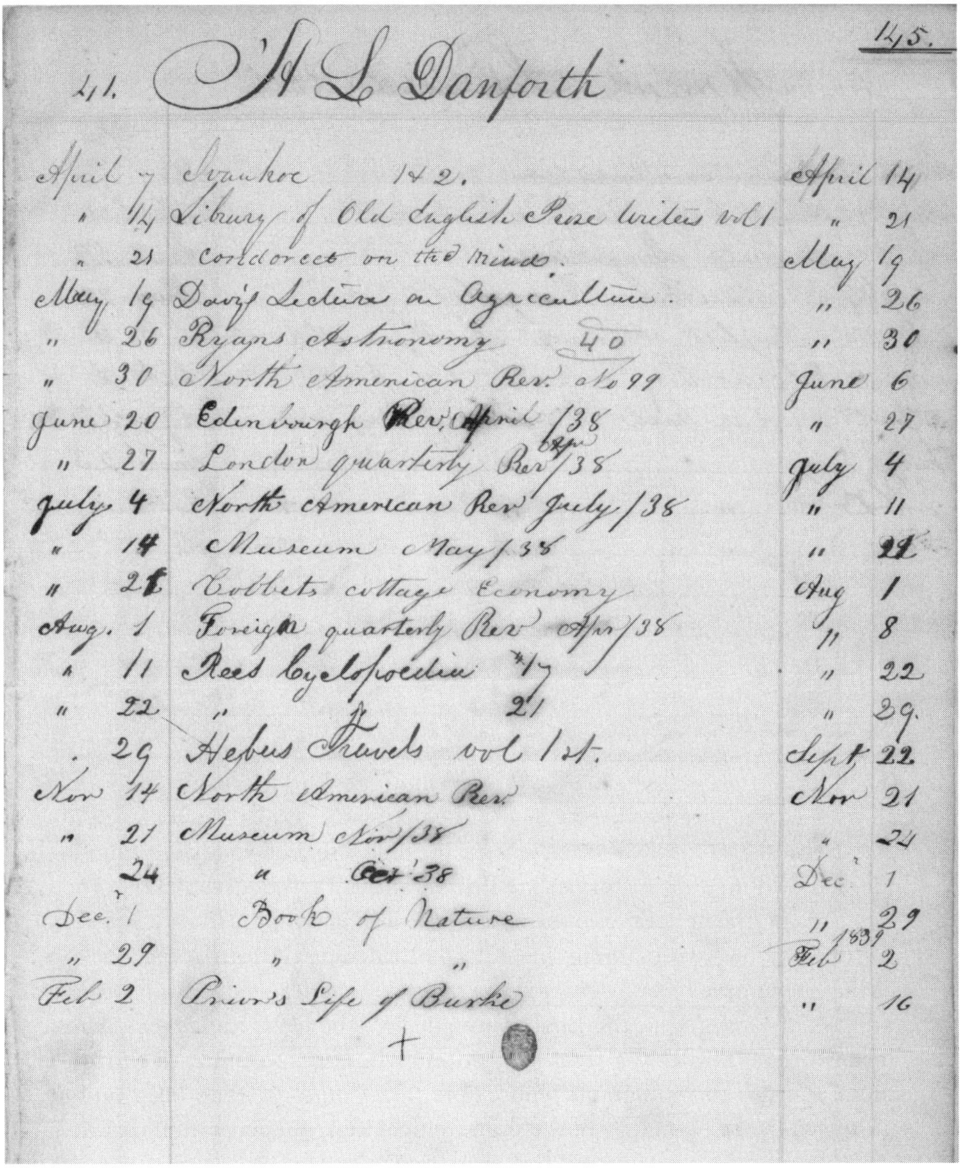

41. A L Danforth 145.

April 7	Ivanhoe 142.	April 14
" 14	Library of Old English Prose Writers vol 1	" 21
" 21	Condorcet on the mind.	May 19
May 19	Davy's Lecture on Agriculture.	" 26
" 26	Ryans Astronomy 40	" 30
" 30	North American Rev. No 99	June 6
June 20	Edinburgh Rev. April /38	" 27
" 27	London quarterly Rev /38	July 4
July 4	North American Rev July /38	" 11
" 14	Museum May /38	" 21
" 26	Cobbets cottage Economy	Aug 1
Aug. 1	Foreign quarterly Rev Apr /38	" 8
" 11	Rees Cyclopaedia 4/7	" 22
" 22	" 21	" 29
" 29	Hebers Travels vol 1st.	Sept 22
Nov 14	North American Rev	Nov 21
" 21	Museum Nov /38	" 24
24	" Oct 38	Decr 1
Decr 1	Book of Nature	" 29
" 29	" "	1839 Feb 2
Feb 2	Prior's Life of Burke	" 16

Figure 6.2. Register for the Taunton Social Library, ca. 1830s–1850s. Courtesy of the Manuscripts and Rare Books Division, New York Public Library.

ber of persons in the city." [22] From commercial and circulating libraries the Boston Public adopted the principle of purchasing multiple copies, so that "many persons, if they desire it, can be reading the same work at the same moment," "at the only time they care for it—that is, when it is living, fresh, and new. Additional copies . . . should continue to be bought almost as long as they are urgently demanded." How did the trustees defend their controversial and innovative ambition to spread "the more popular literature" throughout the city? For reading itself to become a "real desire," they argued, "as many [books] as possible" must find their way "into the home of the young; into poor families; into cheap boarding houses; in short wherever they will be most likely to affect life and raise personal character and condition." As they circulated new kinds of "popular" or "ephemeral" materials previously deemed unworthy of collection and preservation, lowered age requirements for unsupervised visits, eventually opened access to shelves, and later allowed patrons to check out multiple works of fiction at the same time, public libraries sought to popularize leisure reading among what they repeatedly called the urban "masses" with the explicit aim of transforming "personal character and condition." In this sense, as they sought to identify and respond to "real desire" for books, Boston Public and other libraries helped to make the choice of reading a secular form of ethical practice and a modern habit of self-government.

Sacralizing Public Space: The Habitat of Reading

The administration of the Boston Public Library rested with cultured elites and the managerial professional class, and the patronage was largely middle class; but the ideal public for the library, as for the public school, was the immigrant. Horace Wadlin's 1905 history of the Boston Public Library declared that there was "a duty resting upon us of extending the influence of the library, as a civic institution, towards enlarging the life and broadening the intellectual outlook of these who have recently entered the ranks of American citizenship without preliminary training in the English tongue." [23] The library was more than a means of education—"a civic institution" whose purpose was to furnish a moral breadth to immigrants whose "life" and "outlook," had been unduly narrowed by the pathology of the slum. In defending the accusation that their

---

22. *Report of the Trustees of the Public Library of the City of Boston* (Boston, 1852), 17.
23. Cited in Promey, *Painting Religion in Public,* 160. On the development of library services for immigrants, see Plummer Alston Jones, Jr., *Libraries, Immigrants, and the American Experience* (Westport, CT: Greenwood, 1999).

reading rooms harbored "loungers" and "dependents," Charles Recht in the *New York Times* in 1908 similarly linked the utility of the New York Public libraries to the moral power of habitat. The mission of reading rooms, Recht declared, was "to be the study rooms of ambitious poor men whose homes in the crowded tenements are filthy, noisy, and dark. Here, after the day's hard work, could come the eager workingman and find the books he needs and desires and learn to live instead of merely existing." The point was not simply to circulate books in the slums, as Ticknor had initially suggested in his 1852 report on the Boston Public, but to rescue the poor from the filth, noise, and darkness that kept them from answering their "needs and desires" in books. The sensory privations of poverty snuffed out the idealism and ambition that distinguish "learn(ing) to live" from "merely existing."[24]

At the very end of her autobiography, Antin returns to the steps of the Boston Public, where she enacts this distinction as a sort of cosmic revelation. After a school outing to the seashore with a science club, Antin "stood on the broad stone steps," alone as she watched a streetcar carry her friends out of sight:

> My heart was full of stirring wonder. I was hardly conscious of the place where I stood, or of the day, or of the hour. I was in a dream, and the familiar world around me was transfigured. My hair was damp with sea spray; the roar of the tide was still in my ears. Mighty thoughts surged through my dreams, and I trembled with understanding.
>
> I sank down on the granite ledge beside the entrance to the Library, and for a mere moment I covered my eyes with my hand. In that moment I had a vision of myself, the human creature, emerging from the dim places where the torch of history has never been, creeping slowly into the light of civilized existence, pushing more steadily forward to the broad plateau of modern life, and leaping, at last, strong and glad, to the intellectual summit of the latest century. (363–64)

Religions sacralize time and space, helping us form convictions about what is important, helping us to focus, train, and concentrate our attention within particular environments. They do this not merely through abstract symbols that ask us to contemplate particular concepts or meanings, but by transforming the way we perceive and comport ourselves in the physical and social world. Or, as Henry James puts it in his own 1907 account of confronting the new building of the Boston Public Library, they translate "an academic phrase" such as democracy into a "bristling fact."[25] In Antin's revelation, this

---

24. Charles Recht, "Usefulness of Public Libraries," *New York Times,* 15 August 1908, BR453.

25. Henry James, *The American Scene* (Bloomington: Indiana University Press, 1968), 249.

takes the form of a sacralization of the physical site of a library, motivated by an emotional, indeed spiritual, realization of what, exactly, liberty in the new world means for an immigrant girl: "I sank down on the granite ledge beside the entrance to the Library, and for a mere moment I covered my eyes with my hand. In that moment I had a vision of myself," Antin writes. "On the granite ledge," Antin literally *sees* herself differently, suddenly understanding with a sort of cosmic self-consciousness the relationship between her personal growth and her environment. With the humility and reverence due our most cherished deities, Antin practiced otherwise abstract civic ideals by sitting on stone, walking up a marble staircase, and whispering in the vast reading room of Bates Hall (see figure 6.3). In this sense, Antin's experience exemplified the point made by N. H. Morison, the provost of the Peabody Institute, in his defense of the Peabody Library from William Poole's criticism: "A grand hall, filled with the gathered wisdom of ages visibly set in alcoves chastely but richly ornamented, will impress the young student with a respect for books and a sense of their importance which he will never forget, and which no multiplication of 'stacks' will ever give." [26]

Especially with the City Beautiful movement in urban design and architecture, symbols of civic dignity abounded in American urban spaces at the turn of the twentieth century. At libraries, museums, and concert halls, no less than post offices, city halls, and train stations, the monumental design of public architecture transformed the sensory and perceptual experience of city life. These new institutions were among the primary vehicles in a broad, transatlantic campaign for social reform that extended liberal government into physical, social, and psychological dimensions of the urban environment. As they sought to impress citizens with "a respect for books," as Morison put it, public libraries located and organized aesthetic and moral experience of mass culture within the quotidian pathways and vistas of everyday life. This was not, of course, the same notion of culture that modern scholars have derived from the relativism of the modern social sciences, as a general way of life, but rather "norms of human perfection," as the educational reformer Matthew Arnold put it in his influential treatise *Culture and Anarchy* (1882). [27] Although committed to hierarchal distinctions of value, this definition of culture encompassed an evolutionary conception of social development that would be advanced by the modern sciences of anthropology, psychology, and economics in the later nineteenth century. For Arnold, the study of culture

---

26. University Circulars (11 May 1883), 151, Special Collections, Milton S. Eisenhower Library, Johns Hopkins University.

27. Nancy Bentley describes this relativist, anthropological concept of culture as "the web of institutions and lived relations that structure any human community." Nancy Bentley, *The Ethnography of Manners: Hawthorne, James, Wharton* (Cambridge: Cambridge University Press, 1995), 23.

Figure 6.3. "The First Landing of the Main Staircase," engraving from T. R. Sullivan, "The New Building of the Boston Public Library," *Scribner's Magazine,* January 1896, 86.

was progressive and normative; it encouraged adjustments of behavior, by which individuals might "draw ever nearer to a sense of what is indeed beautiful, graceful, and becoming."[28] By fostering the cultural tastes of their members, liberal societies would progress to higher levels of "civilization."

28. Cited in Bennett, *Culture,* 94. On the development of the concept of culture, see Raymond Williams, *Culture and Society: 1780–1850* (New York: Columbia University Press, 1958). On the reach of Arnold's work in the United States, see John Henry Raleigh, *Matthew Arnold and American Culture* (Berkeley: University of California Press, 1961). On the intellectual background of the British

As liberal reformers on both sides of the Atlantic advanced the cause of public institutions of education and recreation, they helped to develop a governmental concept of culture, associated less with personal consumption and status display than with the reproduction of moral character and the utilitarian calculus of social welfare. As Tony Bennett points out, "the most ardent advocates of public museums, free libraries and the like typically spoke of them in connection with courts, prisons, poorhouses, and, more mundanely, the provision of public sanitation and fresh water."[29] Culture meant not only the cultivation of personal taste by which, as Franklin put it in describing the influence of the Library Company, tradesmen and farmers acquired the conversational skills of gentlemen. Like the provision of sanitation or lighting, it was an investment in the general quality of life that would generate the largest benefit for the greatest number. In *Methods of Social Reform* (1883), the economist W. Stanley Jevons turned to the example of free public libraries to illustrate what he called the principle of the multiplication of utility:

> The main raison d'etre of free public libraries, as indeed of public museums, art-galleries, parks, halls, public clocks, and many other kinds of public works, is the enormous increase of utility which is thereby acquired for the community at a trifling cost. . . . If a man possesses a library of a few thousand volumes, by far the greater part of them must lie for years untouched upon the shelves; he cannot possibly use more than a fraction of the whole in any one year. But a library of five or ten thousand volumes opened free to the population of a town may be used a thousand times as much.[30]

Largely an American and British experiment, state sponsorship of public libraries and other agencies of public culture entailed enormous capital investment in the leisure and education of the working classes that had to be continually defended and justified as social engineering. Charles Recht, writing in the *New York Times* in 1908, saw the library as a duty that taxpay-

---

public library movement, see Alistair Black, *A New History of the English Public Library: Social and Intellectual Contexts, 1850–1914* (London: Leicester University Press, 1996). On the administration of education and culture as modes of liberal governance, see Ian Hunter, *Culture and Government: The Emergence of Literary Education* (Houndmills, U.K.: Macmillan, 1988), and Hunter, *Rethinking the School: Subjectivity, Bureaucracy, Criticism* (New York: St. Martin's, 1994). For comparative and multinational perspectives on neoliberal cultural policy, see Franco Bianchini and Michael Parkinson, eds., *Cultural Policy and Urban Regeneration: The Western European Experience* (Manchester: Manchester University Press, 1993); and Tony Bennett, Michael Emmison, and John Frow, *Accounting for Tastes: Australian Everyday Cultures* (Cambridge: Cambridge University Press, 1999).

29. Bennett, *Culture*, 109.
30. Cited in ibid., 108.

ers owed to the general welfare of society, a public obligation with personal benefits: "Society is under no obligation to provide necessaries, but it is under a duty to make its members orderly and educated. This is not charity — it is self-protection." Especially in an era marked by labor unrest, liberal democracies had to defend themselves from the inequalities and political instability that laissez-faire capitalism could wreak. Whatever good culture might do for particular persons, its aggregate goods became newly valuable to municipal budgets and private philanthropy. Through public baths, settlement houses, youth clubs, and park systems, as well as libraries, the state might "make" society "orderly and educated" without resorting to force. Committed to scientific and empirical models of individual and social development, and attuned to the power of the environment to shape behavior, the ideology and policies of liberalism described culture as a dynamic process by which individuals acquired a capacity for autonomy, that "learning to live" that gave one person's existence value for "society," worth collective investment and sacrifice. To conservative critics, both then and now, the expansion of liberal welfare represented a dangerous turn to socialist paternalism. Thus in 1894 did one writer, following theories of the social Darwinist Herbert Spenser, attack tax support for free libraries as a slippery slope to "a low and promiscuous communism."[31]

To align libraries with "public works" was to identify reading and leisure more generally as collective resources that, like water, must be widely distributed and managed in the interests of an entire community's health. In Jevons's accounting, the *quantity* of reading, as administered through enlightened and expert social policies, would transform the *quality* of public life. Since the incidence of libraries tended to be highest in residential areas that had lighting and sanitation, Jevons noted, "We are fully warranted in looking upon free libraries as engines for operating upon the poorer portions of the population."[32] By helping to reduce poverty and the cost of law enforcement, spending on "public works" such as free libraries would bring social and political rewards. By "operating" on the entire habitat of urban life, the circulation of books made the public library an "engine" of progressive reform, especially for ethnic immigrants, who did not have access to middle-class amenities or

31. M. D. O'Brien, "Free Libraries," in Bostwick, *The Library and Society*, 203. As O'Brien notes, "Are theatre-goers, lovers of cricket, bicyclists, amateurs of music, and others to have their earnings confiscated, and their capacities for indulging in their own special hobbies curtailed, merely to satisfy gluttons of gratuitous novel-readers? A love of books is a great source of pleasure to many, but it is a crazy fancy to suppose that it should be so to all" (209). This piece originally appeared in a collection edited by Thomas Mackay, *A Plea for Liberty* (London, 1894).

32. Cited in Bennett, *Culture*, 115.

traditions.[33] As the *New York Times* observed in 1890, "A certain number of persons within the radius of its influence will be sure to devote less time to drink, to dangerous gossip, to the perils of beer saloons and dance halls."[34] In this sense, the "palaces" that cities erected for their main libraries were merely the most visible hub of institutional networks that, through branches and circulation depots, saturated the local environment of the immigrant and working classes with books. In 1910, for example, the New York Public Library had a traveling library office that, as Phyllis Dain observed, circulated more than a million volumes at 802 "stations," including:

> public schools, playgrounds, police precinct houses, fire stations, factories, hospitals, parochial and private schools, industrial schools, churches and Sunday schools, study clubs, department stores and other places of business, the YMCA and YWCA, asylums and charitable institutions, home libraries, mothers clubs, literary societies, and study clubs and community libraries located in settlements, clubs, stores, and churches. It also distributed used books to newsboys' clubs, fresh-air homes, sailors' reading rooms, tuberculosis camps, reform schools, hospitals, mental hospitals, prisons. . . .[35]

The liberal state's administration of libraries and other institutions of public culture helped to standardize and centralize the experience of time and space. The temporal discipline imposed by public clocks helped to coordinate and direct the use of leisure in spaces like parks, museums, and libraries, which were regulated by particular hours of operation no less than the complex array of rules and informal norms that actively shaped behavior in public. Signs asked people to stay off the grass, or to not touch art; reading room policies restricted food and drink while their attendants enforced silence and order. By organizing experience according to middle-class norms of character and propriety, liberal institutions of public culture sought to transform the personalities of patrons. If the "self-governing liberal subject was master of the baser instincts and passions, a creature of thrift, energy, perseverance and, critically, reflexive evaluation of its own civility," as Chris Otter observes, then these institutions shaped the aesthetic sensibility of individuals toward the larger

---

33. As Ronald and Mary Zboray have noted, the public library formalized and centralized patterns of exchange and sociability that had characterized antebellum home libraries, translating them to monumental and bureaucratic institutions. Ronald J. Zboray and Mary Saracino Zboray, "Home Libraries and the Institutionalization of Everyday Practices among Antebellum New Englanders," in *The Library as an Agency of Culture,* ed. Thomas Augst and Wayne Wiegand (Madison: University of Wisconsin Press, 2002), 63–86.

34. "Free Circulating Library," *New York Times,* 2 March 1890.

35. Dain, *The New York Public Library,* 297.

pathology of the environment in which they moved: "Respectability involved a certain distancing, and sight, as the primary sense of distance, played a critical role in its performance." [36] The organization of civic space was not only symbolic but physical, its values embodied in the aesthetic and moral performance of new social identities. These rituals and practices transformed the otherwise anonymous experience of walking in a city or killing time into spiritual exercises in self-making that—like all modes of religion—are highly ideological and deeply personal. By walking up the marble stairs, for instance, or engaging in any number of impersonal and anonymous experiences of public culture which, because "free to all," belonged to no one in particular, one could, like Antin, craft self-conscious identities outside the realities and spaces to which many of her peers were consigned by class, gender, ethnicity, and race.

Libraries helped to sacralize public space by altering the aesthetic perceptions of ordinary people, lending to the experience of otherwise common existence moral direction and spiritual consequence. Public libraries had practical impact on how, simply put, ordinary people saw the world and moved within it. As Antin reminds us, the capacity to see beyond the narrow realities of the tenement—to be edified by the silence, cleanliness, or majesty of public "palaces"—directly shapes our ability to recognize and assert our autonomy as social actors and moral agents. "I was hardly conscious of the place where I stood, or of the day, or of the hour," Antin recalls, and it is the dislocation from her normal sense of time and place that makes possible her new birth as "the human creature," instead of a girl, an immigrant, or a Jew. Rendered in metaphors of organic growth ("emerging," "pushing," "leaping"), the conversion experience of the immigrant echoes the transcendentalist natural theology that Antin would have absorbed from her friendships with Emma and Josephine Lazarus. That conversion depends on a psychological and sensory distancing from the mundane, quotidian facts of one's actual existence, the substitution of environments more congenial to the transcendence of individuals. By "enlarging" and "broadening" the immigrant's horizons of vision and movement, as Wadlin put it, institutions of culture like the Boston Public Library helped to organize the spiritual meaning and form of individuality. Within these new public spaces, citizens could locate and perform a new kind of symbolic identity allied with the organic evolution of personality: the progress of a person, rather than a species or group.

---

36. Chris Otter, "Visuality, Materiality and Liberalism," *Social History* 27 (2002): 2.

Culture as Traffic: Reading and Social Mobility

In *The American Scene* (1907), Henry James also recounts a voyage from the old world to the new that brings him to the Boston Public Library. Written by an eminent American novelist returning stateside in 1904, after many years living in Europe, the book uses the author's encounter with the library's new building to describe how the meaning and form of culture were altered by forces of social change. James sees what had to be destroyed to accommodate the presence of so many immigrants like Mary Antin. Only a few blocks from Copley Square, he passes the Boston Athenæum, a "temple of culture," "honored haunt of all the most civilized." A gentlemen's club to which, at least in retrospect, the city had paid deference, the Athenæum was now sadly diminished: "rueful and snubbed" not only by the "brute masses" of surrounding tall buildings that hovered over it the way that roughs bullied "a studious little boy," but also by the procession of foreign born who walked by utterly oblivious of the respect expected for it from their Brahmin betters.[37] "Gross aliens," making "no sound of English, in a single instance," immigrants were in "serene and triumphant possession" of the once-homogenous city that he and other Anglo-Protestant "natives" had once thought, in its "closed order," they owned (231, 233). Once he reaches the Boston Public Library, James is overwhelmed by "the multitudinous bustle, the coming and going, as in a railway station, of persons with carpet-bags and other luggage, the simplicity of plan, the open doors and immediate accesses, admirable *for* a railway station, the ubiquitous children, *most* irrepressible little democrats of the democracy." Once private and exclusive, the old cultural order had surrendered to the noise and motion of the streets, and James searches the building in vain for "deeper depths," for "some part that should be within some other part, sufficiently withdrawn and consecrated, not to constitute a thoroughfare" (251).

Whereas the Boston Public Library provides Antin with the occasion to declare her self-ownership, it becomes for James a scene of dispossession and alienation—not merely the personal loss of the "old order" to which the Athenæum had conferred privileged access, but a diminution of value that culture suffers when its benefits are so widely distributed. James observed that the great national libraries in Paris and London, though "at the disposal of the people," kept the public at a proper distance, "there more or less under the shadow of the right waited for and conceded" (250). In their determination to be public places, however, public libraries had given themselves over to the circulation of immigrants and children, doing away with the *penetralia* essen-

---

37. James, *American Scene*, 232–33. Further page references are inserted in the text.

tial "in a place of study and meditation," by which libraries ought to resemble temples and through which the experience of culture is itself "consecrated" to "deeper depths" of the mind and spirit. According to James's calculus, the benefit of culture ought to exact humility and deference, transforming the scholar's labor into a sacred devotion undertaken in solitude and silence. Without the *penetralia* requisite for spiritual transactions of study, however, the Boston Public Library was like a "temple without altars," exemplifying "the distinction between a benefit given and a benefit taken, a borrowed, a lent, and an owned, an appropriated convenience" (249). To make culture so open to the public, without exacting obligations or debts for this access, is, indeed, to reduce its "benefits" to the divisible goods of utilitarianism. Arguing that true culture can never properly be made public, James concludes that what the Boston Public Library resembles most of all is a train station: A temple without altars, culture without prayer, movement without redemption.

Religions are, however, modes of social mobilization that allow us to cultivate the pleasures of worship within bounds of community. One of the most powerful functions of the public library, and of the liberal faith in institutions of culture it represented, was to foster a sense of social membership that defied distinctions of gender, class, ethnicity, or education that normally divide and balkanize a population. Thus while Mary Antin insists on her personal ownership of the "palace" of the Boston Public, she stresses as well the presence of other people within the civic space: "All these eager children, all these fine browed women, all these scholars going home to write learned books—I and they had this glorious thing in common, this noble treasure house of learning. It was wonderful to say, *This is mine;* it was thrilling to say, *This is ours."* [38] Liberal reformers sought to heighten this sense of community by insisting that the utility of reading in a democracy was not primarily scholarly but social, to effect an identification with others unlike oneself. When a site for the main branch of the New York Public Library was being selected, a newspaper editorial observed that "to become really a 'free public library' " required an institution to "be in easy communication . . . with every part of the city." [39] As sites of "communication" within the physical landscape of the nineteenth-century city, libraries helped to foster new experiences of community: a community not of readers sharing the same texts, but for readers sharing the same spaces—a thoroughfare organizing the movements of a heterogeneous social world. In the United States, as James puts it, "every one

38. Antin, *Promised Land,* 341.
39. "The Public Library," *New York Times,* 15 August 1895.

is 'in' everything," and "society" is "more and more the common refuge and retreat of the masses" (249).

In press coverage that attended the building of these flagship libraries, it was precisely the novelty of this social mixing that aroused the most comment from observers. In 1891 the *Boston Daily Globe* complained that the new building would eliminate the class segregation of the old Boylston building, which directed "the plain people" to the Lower Hall, stocked with more "popular" reading matter and more accessible to street traffic. To make their way to the reading room in the new building, these people would now be forced to ascend the grand staircase "with everyone else, and rub elbows with the Beacon st. swell, the teacher and all the varying classes of people who are now accommodated in Bates Hall, upstairs," the dignity and ease of their leisure spoiled by having to "brush against fine ladies and rub elbows with men who are spick and span in their fashionable clothes."[40] But, then, this was precisely the promiscuous mingling that reformers sought to achieve, since it would diffuse a moral authority of learning that remained too associated with aristocratic privilege. By bringing together individuals usually separated by neighborhood, the public space of the library allowed immigrants and the destitute to identify with their social betters, offering them examples of self-improvement and propriety necessary to their own upward mobility. In their 1891 report, the trustees of the Boston Public declared that the new Bates Hall would be "designed as a general reading-room for the whole people . . . built for the accommodation of all the citizens of Boston, without reference to so-called 'class' or condition," without any "apparent separation of the poorer users of the Library from the richer."[41] (See figure 6.4.) Through a process of mutual recognition, emulation, and identification, readers would, presumably, learn to do without the categories which kept them from seeing themselves, and being seen by others, as part of "the whole people" and "citizens of Boston."

The traffic passing through the great depot of the library would lead, presumably, upward and outward to social advancement. An article in the *Boston Evening Transcript* in 1892 offered a detailed sketch of the eccentricity and improvidence that the BPL made available to the amusement of bourgeois propriety:

> Probably the most original of the habitués of the reading room is a German by birth, his English being very bad. Every evening at 6:30 he enters the Lower

---

40. Cited in Walter Muir Whitehill, *Boston Public Library: A Centennial History* (Cambridge: Harvard University Press, 1956), 153.

41. Cited in ibid., 155.

Figure 6.4. Photograph of Bates Hall in the Boston Public Library, by Nathanial Stebbins, 1914. Reprinted by permission of the Boston Public Library.

Hall, walks over to the registration desk and looks at the clock. He then crosses the room where hangs the thermometer, at which he takes a good look. Turning, he makes a line for the thermometer in the reading-room and reads the condition of the temperature. If he is satisfied, all is well; if not, he expresses his disapproval very decidedly. He then calls for the *Pilot* and takes his favorite seat in the front of the room. At about eight o'clock he is asleep. He has not missed an evening since 1880.[42]

The library's utility as a civic space depended on the discipline and rationality with which individuals pursued their self-improvement in the company of strangers. As they proved unable to alter habits and routines fixed by poverty, however, these "aliens" turned Bates Hall into a way station on the track to nowhere. At best, many critics saw the library's investment in its public

42. Cited in ibid., 153.

status—the elaborate building as well as the stunning artwork by John Singer Sargent and others—as a detraction from its core functions, as when another habitué of the reading room in 1895 observed, "within the space of one hour, a troop of eleven women tourists, two bands of school-girls personally conducted by their mistresses, besides scores of sight-seers of all ages, alone or in groups of varying numbers." [43] At worst, the fear of outsiders in the temple of culture—children and immigrants, the homeless and tourists—became outright fear of physical and moral contamination, as with the idea that books circulated in the slums would spread cholera to the suburbs, like pathogens of class breakdown.

In both their aggressive marketing campaign to justify public taxation for library services, and their monumental designs of entrances, staircases, catalogues, reading rooms, and entrances to buildings, libraries helped to identify a modern public, "the People," with a new kind of social space. This public was not, as Benedict Anderson argued in his theory of modern nationalism, a virtual community, effected by the symbolic "imagination" of readers who, through novels and newspapers, entered into a shared sense of territorial and temporal simultaneity. Nor was it an anonymous "public sphere" constituted by the mass circulation of texts. It was, rather, a physical space where social difference became visible, a larger theater of the heterogeneous diversity that characterized nineteenth-century cities but was otherwise obscured by the residential, occupational, and commercial segregation of the population amongst slums and street-car suburbs, "downtown" business and vice districts, crowded ethnic tenements and single-family middle-class homes. If James laments the busy, crowded movements within the library's halls as a distraction from the traditional mission of culture, Antin argues the opposite: libraries should foster reading not as a refuge from the crowded spaces of public life, but rather as a means of transport within it, a hub for traffic in social identities.

In its simultaneous unity and diversity, the community that worshiped at the public library was made of *individuals* rather than social types. Patrons *might* learn to see their "so-called" differences of "class" and "condition" not as determined by environment, but as the outcome of their own initiative and self-motivation in moving across public institutions of education and culture. As the first report of the Boston Public had pointed out in 1852, a large public library would consummate the public school system by giving students means to achieve "the farther progress of education, in which one must be mainly his own teacher." [44] As the 1914 report of trustees similarly observed, the library

---

43. Cited in ibid., 176.
44. *Report of the Trustees of the Public Library of the City of Boston, July 1852* (Boston, 1852), 8.

"educated only in response to individual wants and demands. Everything that is done is done in response to requests from individuals who ask for that which they each want most," in contrast to education in schools "imposed on those who receive it."[45] The public library would grow and expand, accordingly, as individuals consummated their otherwise abstract faith in freedom by taking responsibility for their own self-improvement, by practicing self-culture. So, too, a 1913 article about immigrants and public libraries correlated the foreigner's "insatiate" reading habits and "appetite for knowledge" with his rapid escape from the ethnic ghetto: "the ultimate success of the immigrant in New York may be measured by the distance he moves from lower Manhattan."[46] In this context, reading is less a solitary process of meditation and study, what James suggests to be a "deep" space of moral and intellectual communion, than a prosaic vehicle for physical and social mobility, a normative and institutional means of "civilization" and "uplift."

Fiction and the Scriptures of the Modern Self

Antin's romance of public life, and James's alienation from it, both bear witness to the historical emergence of institutions and values of print culture—particular ways of thinking about and acting upon the benefits of reading and embodying them in symbolic and functional forms of social life. What, James asks, is the value of reading, and of culture more generally that has made such unholy alliance with the quotidian movements of mass society? Even if one conceded "to the New Land the fact of possession of everything and convenient under heaven," of "all the accessories and equipments, a hundred costly things, parks and palaces and institutions, that the earlier community had lacked" (248), the city seemed to James "to have no capacity for the uplifting *idea,* no aptitude for the finer curiosity, to envy the past." With its grand spaces and elegant furnishings, the Public Library "was committed to speak to one's inner perception still more of the power of the purse and of the higher turn for business than of the old intellectual, or even of the old moral, sensibility" (248, 249). Facilitating social transactions with the dispatch and efficiency of business, new institutions of public culture fostered access at the cost of transcendent value, "the uplifting *idea*"—reformatting the meaning of culture for a country whose main formula, as James lamented, was "to make so much money that you won't 'mind,' don't mind anything" (237).

What James minds, of course, is what he perceives to be profound changes

---

45. Promey, *Painting Religion in Public,* 147.
46. Carl Ackerman, "The Bookworms of New York: How the Public Libraries Satisfy the Immigrant's Thirst for Knowledge," *The Independent,* 23 January 1913, 199, 201.

in where and how Western culture does its thinking. With the displacement of an "old" intellectual and moral sensibility by a liberal imperative of "not minding," the value of reading shifts from the object of study and the attention the individual reader brings to it—in the transcendental, Kantian emancipation of spirit or insight through cultivation of Mind, in how we pretend that any institution can "speak one's inner perception"—to the diffusion of books and their social benefits among a population. In James's offhand observation, we see a distinction about the value of collecting books, one best encapsulated by the difference between "knowledge" and "information." If librarians in the nineteenth century believed in the moral hierarchies and universal value of books that contribute to "knowledge," they would by the twentieth century prefer to speak in a value-neutral fashion about "information" as a resource, like water or electricity. The concept of information implies technological problems of quantity and distribution, rather than epistemological and hermeneutic problems of discerning God's design, for instance, or preserving scientific and moral truths for future generations. Between minding and not minding the presence of children and immigrants as they overran the archive, then, lies a perennial conflict between elitist and democratic arguments about whether the circulation of texts multiplies the social welfare or erodes the quality of culture. Where does the moral authority of a text lie: in the "good" that follows from the individual's apprehension of elusive but uplifting ideas (from which the social world can only be a distraction), or the "goods" that flow from management of commodities across ever larger populations and territories? As texts cease to be quasi-sacral objects, linking readers to a seemingly timeless realm of Mind, do they become just another form of currency, an increasingly antiquated "medium" of traffic on the information superhighway?

Religions promote their social power by fostering the moral authority of the written word, honoring certain texts and particular ways of engaging those texts as testaments to truth, spirit, tradition, or history. The "modern education" that public libraries helped to bring about entailed not only the creation of new physical and social contexts for reading—as a mode of self-directed leisure, linked to the reform of public space and the circulation of new forms of social identity—but a change in the attitudes that citizens of liberal societies assume toward the material forms and practical utility of knowledge. For the professional librarians and reformers who so often assumed a "missionary" tone as "apostles of culture," the modern library would institutionalize a new scripturalism, in which the material forms of reading were altered so as to cultivate public faith in secular ideals of individual and collective progress. The "highest and best influence of the library," as William I. Fletcher observed in *Public Libraries in America* (1899), "may be summed up in the single word culture, although abuse has perverted the idea into something like cant. No word so well describes the influence of the diffusion of good reading among the people in giving tone and character to their intellectual life." What made reading good, and retrieved the concept of culture from the tendentious abstractions of cant, were its practical effects in "counteracting the attractions of saloons and low resorts of all types," and awakening "a dormant fondness for reading and culture" among boys and young men in particular who lacked "home and school opportunities." As Fletcher suggests, it was the taste for reading as an activity, and not the value we impute to particular books, that we should count as culture: not objects, preciously guarded in museums, in collections, or in the expertise of learned professionals, but the processes of social evolution by which a people's "intellectual life" acquires "tone and character." Echoing advocates of educational reform like Matthew Arnold, or social scientists like Jevons or G. Stanley Hall, library professionals understood culture as a hierarchical, progressive movement of "a people" from barbarism to civilization.

But can the act of reading offer the "highest and best influence" we call culture regardless of the content of reading? Especially striking in Fletcher's formulation is the proposition that social groups can have an aggregate "intellectual life" which, as Bridgehampton's minister and judge no less than Henry James recognized in their defenses of an "old order," must inevitably challenge traditional forms of moral authority.

> While books, even good books, are not always entitled to be called means of grace, whoever will look candidly at the matter will clearly see that only narrow and dwarfed ideas on spiritual subjects and a distorted form of religious life can consist with poverty of resources in mind and intellect. None are more impressed with the need of culture to lay a basis for large, tolerant, and truly Christian views and practices than those who endeavor to show the meagre and stunted intellects of the masses the Way, the Truth, and the Life. Not that their salvation is to begin with culture, but in order that religion may be all that it should, the enlargement and development of the higher human faculties obviously should precede.[47]

Despite his qualifications, Fletcher was arguing that the "means" of reading *was* grace: that salvation lay in liberation of the "meagre and stunted intellects of the masses" from "narrow and dwarfed ideas on spiritual subjects." Once separated from particular doctrines and the literal authority of scripture,

---

47. William Isaac Fletcher, *Public Libraries in America,* 2d ed. (Boston: Little, Brown, 1899), 38.

however, the "enlargement and development of the higher human faculties" became its own faith, a process of reflection and judgment that might as easily lead away from *a priori* certainties of "the Way, the Truth, and the Life"—toward spiritual and aesthetic pluralism, many ways of cultivating the "tone and character" of one's own life—rather than to that of any savior. In this way do mechanisms of circulation and communication that bring otherwise distant people close de-center the prescriptive authority not only of the church but of literal modes of reading, attachments to particular words, on which it depends. To read in liberal culture is to enter networks of meaning, many paths to multiple truths.

The fate of social and public libraries alike in the nineteenth century depended entirely on their willingness and capacity to multiply their traffic in books. And in no aspect of their collection or circulation policies did libraries do more to liberate nineteenth-century concepts and institutions of culture from paternalistic "cant" than in the mass circulation of fiction.[48] As they obsessively tabulated statistics on circulation, the annual reports of these institutions consistently found that patrons borrowed novels more than any other kind of reading, and did so at a rate that far exceeded the percentage of fiction held by collections. In its statistics of circulation of twenty-four public libraries in 1874–75, for example, the 1876 *Special Report* documented that in libraries ranging from California to Ohio to Virginia, "English prose and fiction, and juvenile" constituted more than half of the works in circulation for all of the libraries, and more than 70 percent at twelve of the libraries. So too, well before its move to new quarters, at least 70 percent of the works that circulated from the Boston Public Library's "Lower" Hall were "prose fiction for adults and youths."[49] At the turn of the century, writers and speakers often asserted that two-thirds of the circulation of public libraries could be attributed to "juvenile fiction and fiction."[50]

The public library's accommodation of the novel was made possible by the expansion and diversification of the print marketplace. Fletcher argued in an early piece in the *Nation* that when read within the broader context of the print market, library statistics showed that readers preferred to borrow rather

---

48. On changing attitudes toward fiction among librarians, see Garrison, *Apostles of Culture;* and Garrison, "Immoral Fiction in the Late Victorian Library," in *Victorian America,* ed. Daniel Walker Howe (Philadelphia: University of Pennsylvania Press, 1976). Also see Esther Jane Carrier, *Fiction in Public Libraries, 1876–1900* (New York: Scarecrow Press, 1965), and Carrier, *Fiction in Public Libraries, 1900–1950* (Littleton, CO: Libraries Unlimited, 1985).

49. "Library Reports and Statistics," Bureau of Education, *Public Libraries in the United States of America: Their History, Condition, and Management, Part I* (Washington: GPO, 1876), 820–21.

50. James Angell, "The Use of the Public Library," in Bostwick, *The Library and Society,* 429.

than buy fiction: "Many families buy and read historical, religious and other standard literature and send to the library for fiction." The gradual emergence of dense networks of literacy—through the domestication of literary practices, the expansion of non-classical literary curricula in secondary and higher education, and the proliferation of agencies of "middlebrow" taste in the print market—helped to insulate and guide readers from the "pernicious" and "promiscuous" tendencies of "blood and thunder" tales or "sensation" fiction that they could obtain, without adult supervision, in the penny press or Beadle's dime libraries.[51] Through the scribbled notations on catalogue cards, guides to "home-reading," personal assistance to patrons, programs with schools, and myriad other schemes, public librarians actively sought to shape the tastes of their patrons. Both commercial circulating libraries and public libraries contributed to the emergence of modern aesthetic values for judging the moral influence of fiction. As Robert Snape points out, the fiction question was concerned not with whether novels should be provided in public libraries, but "with the distinctions between different types of novels, and with literary merit and moral standards."[52] As Justin Winsor, the superintendent of the Boston Public, wrote in the 1876 *Special Report,* "Libraries do not do their whole duty unless they strive to elevate the taste of their readers, and this they can do, not by refusing to put within their reach the books which the masses of readers want, but by inducing a habit of frequenting the library, by giving them such books as they ask for and then helping them in the choice of books," and "conducting them" to higher forms of literature. "Multitudes of readers need only to be put in this path to follow it."[53]

By both appealing to and directing the habit of reading for leisure, public libraries helped to legitimize fiction as a medium of "modern education." William Poole pointed out at the 1876 conference of librarians that the "great mass of readers prefer to take their knowledge" from fiction, which treats actual events and lives, natural laws and physical phenomena, and "other subjects, mental, moral, sentimental and divine."[54] As they defended circulation policies, librarians argued that fiction did not have to overturn the role of religion and morality, as the elites of Bridgehampton had feared, but could

---

51. For a description of this literary landscape and an analysis of its relation to development of middle-class character, see Augst, *The Clerk's Tale.*

52. Robert Snape, *Leisure and the Rise of the Public Library* (London: Library Association, 1995), 30.

53. Justin Winsor, "Reading in Popular Libraries," in Bureau of Education, *Public Libraries in the United States of America,* 432. On freedom of reading and censorship, see Geller, *Forbidden Books.*

54. Cited in Fletcher, *Public Libraries in America,* 34.

give them forms of expression and authority more suited to a new democratic order. The Apprentices' Library of Philadelphia, for example, noted in its 1871 report that "works of fiction that portray well-drawn characters, the virtues that constitute a pure and upright life, convey to the reader eternal truths" that "can be more effectually taught by example than by precept." By fostering identification with the realistic example of fictive persons and situations, the "better class of novels" avoided what its 1880 report called the "injurious tendency" of fiction to give "absurdly unreal views of life" and to "promote a love of excitement and adventure and discontent with regular habits of industry."[55] Even when, like so many early leaders of the library profession, Fletcher held his nose at what the public wanted, he argued that their desire for fiction was natural, a "craving for that romance in literature which is missed from life" that the public library was obligated to meet, lest the public seek satisfaction in less "wholesome and ennobling" channels of amusement. "To the masses of the people, hard-worked and living humdrum lives, as well as to those lapped in luxury and pining for something to kill time, the novel comes as an open door into an ideal life, in the enjoyment of which, even in fancy, one may forget the hardships or the tedium of real life."[56]

The mass circulation of fiction in public libraries helped both to standardize and to personalize the very concept of morality, substituting psychological norms of individual development for prescriptive virtues and vices that had previously governed traditional moral and religious training. The new social sciences in the late nineteenth century and the marginalization of theology in the university helped to rationalize morality itself as a process of organic growth. As one sociologist observed in 1908, "Virtue no longer consists of literal obedience to arbitrary standards set by community or church but rather in conduct consistent with a growing personality."[57] One might argue, though, that this version of "growing personality" was itself modeled on the narrative and representational strategies that made the popularity of the novel, as Ian Watt pointed out some time ago, coincident with the emergence of Western individualism. As a genre, of course, the novel evolved in ways designed to appeal to the imagination—a concept that, as it was shaped by faculty psychology and romantic aesthetics, increasingly emphasized the subjective nature of reading. Learning to see characters as "round" rather than "flat," as

---

55. Lewis, *History of the Apprentices' Library of Philadelphia*, 64.

56. Fletcher, *Public Libraries in America*, 31–32.

57. Cited in David Kennedy, *Birth Control in America: The Career of Margaret Sanger* (New Haven: Yale University Press, 1970), 68.

persons rather than types, readers also came to understand identity itself in distinctively "modern" terms that mirrored the autonomy and ambiguity of their choices and actions.[58] Achieving unprecedented popularity as a medium of entertainment, novels made available to mass audiences the personal histories and emotional depths of individuals.[59]

In large part through the mass circulation of fiction, then, public libraries multiplied the paths away from the literal Truth of traditional moral or religious instruction, in ways that allowed ordinary readers to interpret universal truths from the examples of real life—whether actual or imagined, a character's or one's own. Mary Antin never mentions what she read, but *The Promised Land* in effect transforms her life into a fiction, reimagining an immigrant's story as a distinctively American romance of self-discovery. "I was born, I lived, I was made over," Antin declares in the preface. "I could speak in the third person and not feel that I was masquerading. I can analyze my subject, I can reveal everything; for she, and not I, is my real heroine" (xix). Antin recalls walking through the library's courtyard daydreaming that she was "a Greek of the classic days," finding that there, "everything I read in school . . . was real to me," and casting herself as the protagonist of a "romance more thrilling than poet ever sung" (342, 343). In both her teenage reading and her adult writing, then, Antin applied to her actual life the power of fiction that James Angell, president of the University of Michigan, had praised in 1904, to "give us vivid pictures of life" and "a reality to history."[60] In this sense, *The Promised Land* itself exemplifies the influence of popular novels to encourage "the prevailing infirmity of our time which seems to substitute sensibility for morality," as Josiah Quincy lamented in his comments about the effects of free libraries (1875).[61] In Antin's hands, as with so many romancers of the public library throughout the twentieth century, a literary sensibility of the utility of imagination—that "distinctively modern faculty"

---

58. On the genre of the novel and individualism, see Ian Watt, *The Rise of the Novel: Studies in Defoe, Fielding, and Richardson* (Berkeley: University of California Press, 1957). On the representation of character in novels and its relation to new forms of interiority fostered by the growth of consumer culture, see Deidre Shauna Lynch, *The Economy of Character: Novels, Market Culture, and the Business of Inner Meaning* (Chicago: University of Chicago Press, 1998). On the uncertainty of identity in market culture, see Jean-Christophe Agnew, *Worlds Apart: The Market and the Theater in Anglo-American Thought, 1550–1750* (New York: Cambridge University Press, 1986).

59. On the permutations of liberal individualism in relation to American literature, see Gillian Brown, *Domestic Individualism: Imagining Self in Nineteenth-Century America* (Berkeley: University of California Press, 1990), and Cyrus R. K. Patell, *Negative Liberties: Morrison, Pynchon, and the Problem of Liberal Ideology* (Durham: Duke University Press, 2001).

60. Angell, "The Use of the Public Library," in Bostwick, *The Library and Society,* 429.

61. Josiah Quincy, *Protection of Majorities and Other Essays* (Boston, 1875), excerpted in Bostwick, *The Library and Society,* 59.

which Colin Campbell defines as "the ability to create an illusion which is known to be false but felt to be true" — itself furnishes American self-making its secular morality.[62] A few contemporary reviewers detected in Antin's story what the *Yale Review* called a "programme of the extreme individualist" that often veered into what the *Hebrew American* described as "an orgy of egotism," setting, as Oscar Handlin notes, "the goal of self-expression as the supreme good."[63] But then, it is precisely the essentially romantic devotion to self-expression and the quasi-spiritual search for self-fulfillment that, with the onset of the consumer revolution of the late eighteenth century, made individualism the creed of a modern middle class.[64]

Making transcendent goods of citizenship feel true for herself, Antin bears spiritual witness to the practical power of imagination to individualize and personalize the realities of immigrant life. Blurring first and third person, Antin's autobiography offers itself as a scripture to the civil religion. In *They Who Knock at Our Gates: A Complete Gospel of Immigration* (1914), Antin argued that prejudice against immigrants represented a heresy against the "Gospel of liberty," the "holy order" of citizenship, that sustained its sacred truth through typological imagination that identifies not only present immigrants with the past pilgrims, but also native self with foreign others.[65] "Go from the public school to the public library, from the library to the social settlement, and you will carry away the same story in a hundred different forms," Antin observes, because each story enacts the same "American confession of faith," a "recital of the doctrines of liberty and equality" (47, 6). Whether written down and added to the voluminous canon of American immigrant literature,

---

62. Colin Campbell, *The Romantic Ethic and the Spirit of Modern Consumerism* (Oxford: Blackwell, 1987), 78: "The individual is both actor and audience in his own drama, 'his own' in the sense that he constructed it, stars in it, and constitutes the sum total of the audience." Antin's memoir in general repeatedly emphasizes the subjective nature of memory and the role of daydreaming and romance in her recollections.

63. Cited in Werner Sollars, "Introduction," *The Promised Land* (New York: Penguin), xxxii; Handlin, "Introduction," *The Promised Land* (Princeton: Princeton University Press, 1969), xii.

64. As Campbell argues, the emergence and veneration of the imagination were crucial to romanticism and the development of the hedonistic ethics of modern consumer culture more generally. As it was propagated through novel reading and urban bohemianism, "romanticism provided that philosophy of 'recreation' necessary for a dynamic consumerism: a philosophy which legitimates the search for pleasure as good in itself and not merely of value because it restores the individual to an optimum efficiency." Campbell argues that romanticism inspired the modern "philosophy of self-expression and self-realization most commonly attributed to Freud," and that provided "ethical support for that restless and continuous pattern of consumption" (201). For an anthology of comments on public libraries by American writers, see Susan Allen Toth and John Coughlan, *Reading Rooms* (New York: Washington Square Press, 1991).

65. Mary Antin, *They Who Knock at Our Gates: A Complete Gospel of Immigration* (Boston: Houghton Mifflin, 1914), 11, 27. Further references to this work are indicated in the text.

or merely seen by sympathetic librarians and teachers, the vivid and various *stories* of immigrant experience can, as did the four gospels of the New Testament, awaken an evangelical "sensibility" of "our faith as Americans." During political campaigns for immigrant restriction in the 1910s, that sensibility had been dulled by "commissions and committees," perverted by "experts and statisticians"(9), or prejudiced by "tyranny of phrases," catchwords, stereotypes, slurs, and slogans (34). Read as the founding law of "our national gospel" rather than a "a bombastic political manifesto" excusing a "gigantic land-grab"(27), Antin declares, "the Declaration of Independence, like the Ten Commandments, must be taken literally and applied universally"(14).

Antin applies the literal creeds inscribed on the library by making it the literary stage for her self-realization. On its steps and inside its walls, the heroine finds her true identity, that true self "made over" by the common spiritual inheritance embodied in reading that is "Free To All." At the very end of her memoir, sitting on the steps of the Boston Public, Antin writes:

> I am not tied to the monumental past, any more than my feet were bound to my grandfather's house. . . . The little house in Polotzk, once my home, has now become a toy of memory, as I move about at will in the wide spaces of this splendid palace, whose shadow covers acres. No! It is not I that belong to the past, but the past that belongs to me. . . . Into my hands is given all [of America's] priceless heritage, to the last white star espied through the telescope, to the last great thought of the philosopher. (364)

Antin's emancipation represents, finally, a freedom from history—from the facts about one's origins that otherwise bind us to the "monumental past." At a monument to public culture, knowledge of the universe and America's heritage alike become a personal possession, "given" into an immigrant's hands. At the public library, Antin has gained license to "move about at will" in the public space of memory, to rewrite history as her own story, in a way emblematic of liberalism: "I don't belong to the past, but the past belongs to me." And indeed, as *The Promised Land* became a major bestseller, Antin's own story became, if only for a short time, a widely circulated gospel for the civil religion; The *New York Sun* reported that Antin's name led all "the books most called-for at the various libraries."[66] In 1928, selections from it were published separately in the Riverside Literature Series, which suggested that one theme for written class-work be "Mary Antin's Faith in America."[67]

---

66. Cited in Sollars, "Introduction," *Promised Land,* xxxii.
67 *At School in the Promised Land or the Story of a Little Immigrant* (New York: Houghton Mifflin, 1928), vi.

Used as a text for civics classes as late as 1949, *The Promised Land* offered
students and would-be citizens personalized revelation of the cosmic power
of education to "open doors" to possible futures and potential lives.

In his memoir *Men and Women* (1888), Thomas Wentworth Higginson, who had himself served as a director of railway and telegraph companies,
turned, like William Frederick Poole and Henry James, to the metaphors
of networks, systems, and machinery to explain the free library's role in the
advance of modernity: "The simple truth is that the creation of a system of
such libraries is like the creation of great railway system; it must be an evolution, not a creation outright." Precisely because no one can "now foresee
what fifty years of development will do," the "essential thing in managing
libraries . . . is to have faith in the community in which one lives" by welcoming an unknown future, embracing hope in progress.[68] Mary Antin sought
to make her own story a personal testament to this faith, to defeat fear of
social change by writing a spiritual autobiography of an immigrant's conversion to the civil religion of democracy. As they used the new infrastructure
of public culture to achieve their own social mobility and self-advancement,
she argued, immigrants would vindicate not only the institutions and laws of
liberal governance, but the trust in individual freedom that constituted the
secular gospel of modernity.

In our own time, the role of religion in public life has assumed new promi-
nence in political debates, and tax support for public goods such as education
and transportation, first built in the Progressive Era, has come under attack.
Yet a 1996 poll found that the "American public agrees wholeheartedly with
the library leaders" that an impressive physical space "is part of the library's
identity." That millions of dollars continue to be spent on the erection of
library buildings in cities such as Seattle and Minneapolis, and that millions
are spent to expand and renovate marble and limestone monuments like the
Boston Public Library, suggests that libraries "may occupy an almost sacred
place in the American community psyche," even as the Internet and home
computer have assumed many of their functions in the dissemination of
information.[69] While their aesthetics are more modern or postmodern than

---

68. Thomas Wentworth Higginson, *Men and Women* (New York, 1888), excerpted in Bostwick,
The Library and Society, 65, 66.

69. Laura Weiss, *Buildings, Books, and Bytes: Libraries and Communities in the Digital Age*
(Washington, DC: Benton Foundation, 1996), 26, 15. The attachment to buildings was viewed by 65
percent of respondents as a high priority, third after hours and programs for children and purchasing
new public library books; 84 percent of African Americans thought it important for libraries to
spend money in this way.

ecclesiastical, these civic buildings suggest that one of the primary social functions of the public library remains symbolic: the staging of freedom in the local, often mundane struggle of individuals to craft a meaningful identity for themselves amidst routine paths and standard choices of mass society. Although scholars have for some time been concerned with interpreting the ideological meanings that lie beneath the norms inscribed on the walls and mission statements of cultural institutions, Mary Antin's narrative reminds us that reading in liberal society can be a moral devotion, characterized by values of literalism, sincerity, and idealism. However banal they perhaps have become to professional (and typically secular) critics of American modernity, the seeming "truths" of the liberal creed — "Free to All" — are newly revealed to individuals as they walk up a staircase, select one book rather than another, sit in a reading room, or find a dignified space for repose and reflection.

In the early twentieth century, the personal histories of immigrants and children like Mary Antin helped to create faith in the public library as an engine of middle-class formation, and in liberalism more generally as the path to modern progress. In representing the seemingly organic growth of children and the immigrant's special capacity for physical and social mobility, *The Promised Land* argued that the library and other institutions of public culture "made" Americans by fostering the individual's universal and innate drive for adaptation and evolution — for self-making that might continually redeem a fallen society from its own realities.

Chapter 7

Domesticating Spain

1898 and the Hispanic Society of America

Elizabeth Amann

I FIRST visited the library of the Hispanic Society of America in November 1996. At the time, I was working on Góngora's *Solitudes,* a dense and allusive poem of the Spanish Baroque, and wanted to consult several seventeenth-century commentaries in the library's collection. A doctoral candidate at Columbia, I had only the common student's knowledge of the institution: I had been told that it was an excellent resource for medieval and early modern studies and that it was conveniently located a few stops north on the IRT subway. When I arrived at the 157th Street station on a blustery Saturday, I walked south on Broadway through a Dominican section of Washington Heights and then turned west into the courtyard of the Audubon Terrace. Entering through its iron gates, I saw on my left the façade of the Hispanic Society, Escorial-like in its austerity, and on my right a similar building (now Boricua College), decorated with statues and bas-reliefs on Spanish themes. Prominent among the latter was a forlorn Don Quixote celebrated in kitschy quatrain:

> Shall the deeds of Caesar or Napoleon ring
> More true than Don Quijote's vapouring?
> Hath wingéd Pegasus more nobly trod
> Than Rocinante stumbling up to God?

In between the two buildings, several neighborhood children were playing baseball. A sign for an exhibit held three years before blew in the wind.

When I entered, I was shown to a cryptlike reading room and promptly brought the commentaries on Góngora. The space was dark and windowless, and for the few hours I read, no one else entered. Leaving, I briefly toured the museum of the society, known for its collection of Goya, El Greco, and Velázquez. Like the shipwrecked hero of the *Solitudes,* I was again a lone visitor. Except for a silent guard who followed me from room to room, the halls were empty. The final room I entered, dedicated to murals of rural life by the impressionist painter Joaquín Sorolla, doubled as the gift shop. Here, an elderly Castilian woman sold a series of pamphlets about Spanish culture published by the institution, many from the 1920s and 1930s. As I browsed through booklets about wedding costumes in La Alberca and women's coiffure in Candelario, the saleswoman, happy to have a visitor, began to tell the story of the society, a romantic tale about a monopolist's son who fell in love with Spain and honored it with a library and museum.

In the middle of the conversation, we were startled by footsteps. As I looked around to see who was there, my interlocutor laughed.

"Son los pasos de él," she said.

"¿De quién?"

"De Mister Huntington."

("Those are his footsteps." "Whose?" "Mister Huntington's").

The Hispanic Society of America and the Generation of 1898

What one learns from a brief survey of the pamphlets in the gift shop is that the Hispanic Society of America was founded in 1904 by Archer Milton Huntington (1870–1955), heir to the Central Pacific Railroad fortune and a relative of Henry Edwards Huntington (the founder of the Huntington Library and Art Gallery in San Marino, California). Huntington was trained to carry on the family business but was drawn more to arts and letters than to trade. A dilettante and compulsive collector, he decided against a university education, schooled himself in countless fields and hobbies (Arabic, surgery, bookbinding, ironwork, numismatics, archaeology, poetry), and acquired many notable collections, to some of which he later dedicated museums or institutions. Principal among these interests was his love of things Spanish, inspired by a boyhood fascination with *The Zincali* and *The Bible in Spain,* popular, romanticized accounts of Iberia by the nineteenth-century adventurer George Borrow. In 1892, Huntington began traveling regularly to Spain and went on to publish a travelogue, *A Note-Book in Northern Spain* (1898), an English translation of the epic poem *The Cid,* and many books of verse on Spanish themes. His most impressive tribute, however, is undoubtedly the Hispanic Society itself. As an institution, it was utterly unprecedented: a library and museum dedicated entirely to the study of a cultural other. In its early years, the institution flourished, attracting prominent artists, writers, and scholars and amassing a considerable library. Intellectuals of the teens and twenties regarded it as a major cultural center in New York.

What one learns from a brief visit to the society today is that the moment of this eminence is long past. Gloomy and desolate, the institution seems tomblike and stands in stark contrast to the vibrant Dominican neighborhood in which it is located. In recent years, it has been a center of controversy due to its refusal to establish dialogue with the Hispanic community around it and to elitist statements by a president, Theodore Beardsley. Interviewed for an article in *ARTnews* in 1993, Beardsley dismissed the idea of an outreach program or involvement with the local community: "You're talking about a very low level of culture. You're talking about maybe literacy. . . . You don't even have to go to the Caribbean resentment of Spain to explain the total lack of interest." [1] He went on to remark, "The land with the view of the Hudson and the fresh air is too good for these non-tax-paying slums." His comments led to a series of demonstrations in 1994 organized by "Dominicanos contra la Difamación" (Dominicans against Defamation) and several other Dominican groups. [2] Given the founder's philanthropic vocation and his desire "to promote the public welfare by actively advancing learning," Beardsley's insistence that "We're not into social welfare" is startling. [3] Paradoxically, the institution has become something opposed to its origin precisely by attempting to remain faithful to it.

The decline of the society in recent years—its movement from spoon-in-mouth to foot-in-mouth—and the irony of its current relation with its community make it a particularly interesting case study in the history of American libraries and cultural institutions. At the time of its foundation, its neighborhood, Washington Heights, was an affluent and growing section of Manhattan. When the IRT subway line was opened in 1904 and extended into Inwood in 1906, many immigrants, mostly German and Eastern European, moved to the area, which led to a boom in the construction of residential housing. Huntington's selection of the Audubon Terrace for several of his projects was part of this development. He followed the trend of the moment, the movement uptown. The Hispanic Society too was a product of its time. It is a typical example of the large, civic-minded institutions that philanthropists constructed in the late nineteenth and early twentieth century and which came to define the urban landscape. In its conception, it is not dissimilar to the Pierpont Morgan, the Newberry, or the Huntington: it is a part of a larger turn-of-the-century phenomenon of institutions of "culture" founded and endowed by capitalists. Huntington, in this sense, resembles

---

1. Robin Cembalest, "Change the Board and Get Rid of the Director," *ARTnews,* September 1993, 152–59.

2. Robin Cembalest, "Confrontation on 155th Street," *ARTnews,* April 1994, 49.

3. Cembalest, "Change the Board," 153.

Adam Verver, the philanthropist and collector of Henry James's *The Golden Bowl.*

What is unique about the society and what makes it an illuminating case study is historical irony. As Harlem became overcrowded after World War II, many Puerto Ricans and African Americans migrated to the neighborhood and have been followed in recent years by Dominicans. What was a "Frankfurt on the Hudson" became "Quisqueya on the Hudson." The Hispanic Society was now surrounded by a thriving Hispanic community. The common heritage of the institution and the residents, however, served only to emphasize the differences between them. The presence of the immigrants has revealed the anachronisms of the society, the incompatibility of its antiquated notion of "culture" with an increasingly multicultural world. The society's vision of Spanish reality, when confronted with the reality itself, was clearly only a projection.

In the 1993 article in *ARTnews,* Robin Cembalest carefully traced the institutional problems (rigid bylaws, secretive practices, limited outreach, among others) that led to the society's decline and discredit. What I would like to suggest in this essay is that the current situation of the society may be attributed not only to these practical factors but also and perhaps more fundamentally to the vision of Spain and the conception of "culture" that the library and museum attempted to project. In order to understand the development of the institution, it is necessary to reconstruct its conception of the cultural other it purported to represent and to situate this vision in its historical context.[4]

My argument in what follows will be twofold. First, I will show that Huntington's Hispanic Society should be read in light of certain intellectual discourses and tropes that circulated in Spain in the 1890s and that have come to be identified by Hispanists with the generation of 1898. The best-known figures of this group, conventionally limited to those born between 1864 and 1875 (Huntington himself, we should recall, was born in 1870), are Miguel de Unamuno, José Martínez Ruiz (pseudonym, "Azorín"), Pío Baroja, Antonio Machado, Angel Ganivet, and Ramiro de Maeztu. Although many Hispanists

---

4. Huntington never defined explicitly his vision of Spain and the Hispanic Society. As Michael Codding notes in his contribution to *Hispanic Society of America: Tesoros* (New York: Hispanic Society of America, 2000), what little we know about Huntington's opinions and intentions "remain[s] largely anecdotal or [has] been gleaned from his *A Note-Book in Northern Spain* (New York, 1898) and his later poetry" (18). An extremely secretive man, Huntington burned many of his diaries and much of his correspondence. In attempting to reconstruct his conception of Spain, I have relied on his travelogue and poetry as well as statements by colleagues and the early studies and lectures he sponsored.

have problematized the generational label and the association of these figures with the political crisis of 1898, their writings do coincide in a few important ways. First, all of them are concerned with the "problem of Spain," the problem of accounting for the nation's decline from imperial grandeur (particularly after the disastrous Spanish American War) and of locating a "nucleus" of Spanish identity. This question had been debated by Spanish intellectuals for more than a century, but the figures of this generation adopted a somewhat different approach. Earlier writers had attempted to identify a Spanish essence or flaw by scrutinizing the nation's past, particularly the biographies of its politicians, kings, and rulers. What distinguished the thinkers of '98 was that they looked instead to the humble, untold, anonymous lives of the Spanish people. They turned from the history of Spain to what Miguel de Unamuno called its "intrahistory," the simple, profound spiritual values of the *pueblo* that were transmitted over centuries from one generation to the next.[5] In what follows, I will argue that Huntington's approach to his collection echoed this project and many of the tropes it introduced into Spanish thought.[6] Tracing the intellectual and literary genealogy of the institution will show that the Hispanic Society was informed by the same historical context as '98 thought: the colonial crisis of 1898 and its outcome.

Though Huntington's institution clearly reiterates the tropes of 1898, we will see that it puts them to different uses. In their original, Spanish context, the strategies and tropes of the '98 writers formed part of a project of self-study: though this did involve a certain fetishization of the masses, the intellectual ultimately sought to immerse himself and to find his own identity in the common people and their collective unconscious. In the case of Huntington's archive, in contrast, these discourses were invoked to represent a cultural other, a nation that had only recently posed a military threat and whose

---

5. The concept derives in part from the German notion of *Volkgeist*. For a discussion of the notion of intrahistory and its origins, see J. W. Butt's "Unamuno's Idea of 'Intrahistoria': Its Origins and Significance" in *Studies in Modern Spanish Literature and Art Presented to Helen F. Grant,* ed. Nigel Glendinning (London: Tamesis, 1972), 13–24. Unamuno elaborates the idea in the essays of *En torno al casticismo* (1895; rpt. Madrid: Alianza, 1986).

6. Scholars have occasionally noted the connection between this generation and Huntington's thought. In "The Library of the Hispanic Society of America," for example, María Luisa López-Vidriero notes in passing that "[Huntington's] concern with 'the soul of the nation' was close to the tense patriotism of the Spanish intellectual movement known as the 'Generation of 1898' " (*Tesoros,* 40). See also Felipe Garín and Facundo Tomás, "Joaquín Sorolla y la generación del 98: El debate después de la modernidad," in *Sorolla y la Hispanic Society: Una visión de la España de entresiglos* (Madrid: Museo Thyssen-Bornemisza, 1998). The importance of '98 discourse for the articulation of the society's own vision of Spain, however, has not been studied. As much of the writing on the institution is produced or authorized by the institution itself, the objectivity of the archive's and Huntington's representation of Spain is rarely placed in question.

defeat marked a decisive moment in the history of American imperialism. The second movement of my argument will be to show that in the Hispanic Society of America the discourses of 1898 are subordinated to an imperialist and often Orientalist project.[7] Where the '98 intellectuals attempted to answer the question "who are we?", the HSA uses the same tropes to address a different problem: "who is the cultural other against whom we define ourselves?" The discourses of 1898 are deployed here not so much to understand as to contain and project upon the cultural other.

The Intrahistoric Archive

In the introduction to his travelogue from 1898, *A Note-Book in Northern Spain,* Huntington begins by posing the "problem of Spain" and, like the '98 writers, rejects standard historical explanations:

> How often the question is asked as to the causes which have brought Spain down from her ancient position in the affairs of Europe, and it is a question not impossible to answer, though the great cause is probably to be found in a direction different from that which is generally supposed. Pride, a weak monarch, a dissolute court, religious intolerance, all these are admirable starting points from which to prove a nation's decline. But Spain has been by no means unique in the possession of these requisites. (5)

For Huntington, as for the '98 thinkers, political and historical factors are "mere effects," the cause of which (he goes on to explain) must be located in the "spirit" of the people (5). Huntington's writing resembles that of the generation of 1898 not only in the questions it raises but also in its genre and method. The travelogue or the impressionistic essay on landscape was one of the hallmarks of the generation. As Herbert Ramsden has noted, '98 was a "generation of *excursionistas,*"[8] of walkers: these writers often hiked through the Spanish countryside and recorded their impressions. Huntington's approach and sources were also similar to the ninety-eighters': like them, he privileged the wisdom of the commoners he met in his travels.[9] Influenced

---

7. On the notion of Orientalism, see Edward Said, *Orientalism* (New York: Vintage Books, 1979). Said uses this term to refer to the process by which the Westerners constructed a vision of the Orient that allowed them to define their own culture against the East.

8. H. Ramsden, *The 1898 Movement in Spain* (Bristol: Manchester University Press, 1974), 141.

9. In her biography of Huntington, *Archer Milton Huntington* (New York: Hispanic Society of Society of America, 1963), Beatrice Gilman Proske, one of his early disciples in the society, notes how greatly Huntington valued the perspective of the common people: "It was the Spaniard whom he sought across the length and breadth of Spain from La Coruña to Barcelona, over to the Balearic Islands, and around the coast to Cádiz. He spoke with all he met along the roads, in uncomfortable

by the determinism of Taine, the '98 writers attempted to read the spirit of Spain's people in its landscape and endlessly evoked the stark, melancholy countryside of Castile and the stoic solemnity of the shepherds and peasants who dwelled in it.[10] In the opening words of the *Note-Book,* Huntington adopts a similar stance: "In Spain it is less the 'color' and 'romance' of which we hear so much, than the strange, sombre setting of it all—the wonderful, melancholy landscape, unvaried, sullen, monotonous to-day, to-morrow ablaze with a fiery life; impetuous, restrained, indifferent, responsive. Look deep enough into its heart and you may read the heart of the Spaniard" (1). Huntington asks the same questions and looks to the same intrahistoric sources—the ways of the commoners, the spirit of the landscape—as the '98 writers.

This emphasis on intrahistory may still be observed in the halls of the Hispanic Society. As I mentioned before, Huntington dedicated an entire room to murals of Spanish rural life by Joaquín Sorolla. Though this painter's work was often strikingly polemical (as in his 1899 "A Sad Inheritance," a painting of children infected from birth with deforming venereal diseases), Huntington commissioned him to celebrate the everyday life of the common Castilian, Galician, or Valencian. The murals represent collective festivals and laborers at work (a bullfight, Holy Week in Seville, shepherds, fishermen, peasant picnics, harvests, dancing). Surveying the modern paintings in the society's recent publication about its collection, *Tesoros,* one is struck by how many are representations of rural Spanish types or landscapes: the pages are filled with items such as "Sevillanas" (Sevillian girls) by Francisco Iturrino or "Tipo segoviano" (Segovian type) and "The Family of the Gypsy Bullfighter" by Ignacio Zuloaga y Zabaleta. Much of the collection, moreover, is dedicated to common crafts such as tile work, festival costumes, ceramics, glass-blowing, ironwork, and pottery. The emphasis of the society is on the countryside and its intrahistoric traditions (landscapes, crafts, and folklore) rather than the cities of Spain: figures of the urban vanguard such as Picasso, Dalí, and Miró are notably absent. As the project of the organization is to *represent* the cultural other, the latter—international names and often nonrepresentational artists—can have no place.

Though Huntington's preoccupations and approach are similar to those of

---

inns, and felt an affection and respect inspired by their 'pride and grave dignity' that gave warmth to all his future work" (3). Michael Codding, similarly, concludes, "Through personal interaction with individuals from all levels of Spanish society, and in particular those of the countryside, Huntington felt that finally he had discovered the soul of Spain in its people"; see *Tesoros,* 28.

10. For an excellent discussion of the Generation of 1898 and its reception of Taine, see Ramsden's *1898 Movement in Spain.*

the generation of 1898, his conclusions always bear the mark of his American and capitalist upbringing and the emergence of U.S. imperialism. When he asks why Spain has lost "her ancient position in the affairs of Europe," he ultimately concludes that "the cause is the absence of that which has developed the great nations of the earth, the cause on which civilization rests, the great primitive developing agency—the trading spirit" (5). Spain is positioned here as a pre- or unhistoric realm (it lacks the developmental principle or "cause") against which Huntington can define American difference. As in much Orientalist writing in which the East is fetishized as a fantastic land of origins and the Arabs presented "as if [they] had not been subject to the ordinary processes of history,"[11] Spain in this description precedes or escapes historical development. Huntington's intrahistoric vision removes Spain from the international arena of political, financial, and historical agency.

The Spanish House

Huntington's assessment of Spanish history rests on a complex series of oppositions. On the one hand, as we have seen, he attempts to project an intrahistoric vision of Spain: he presents it as a country lacking the developmental principle that would make it a historical player. At the same time, however, he must in some way account for the Spanish past: its imperial age, its tumultuous history in the nineteenth century, and its continued involvement in international affairs through 1898. In the opening of the *Note-Book,* Huntington makes a gesture toward this past in a discussion of common foreign conceptions of Spain and its character:

> Our knowledge, largely had at second hand, colored with antipathy of race or religion, too often produces an attitude of contempt, pity, or aversion. . . . Yet she cares less for what you may think of her than does any other nation in Europe, and you can force her to accept fewer of your ideas than any other. It has been a tradition with her that people beyond the Pyrenees are not friendly people, and she is not prone to look within and discover the cause of their dislike. The United States has taken her the sewing machine and the Life Insurance Company, and she has welcomed the latter at least. She likes gambling games, and will even not refuse to take a hand with Death himself. (3)

At first, Huntington seems to counter overly subjective and biased visions of Spain with a more objective account, but what follows immediately is a daring personification: Spain is represented as a testy and irrational woman

---

11. See Said, *Orientalism,* 230.

(note the repetition of the female pronoun), who, not unlike Wharton's Lily Bart, rejects domesticity (the sewing machine) and embraces a dangerous and ultimately fatal path of gambling and speculation. Untamed and indifferent to others' opinions, Huntington's Spain is a fascinating *femme fatale*. As the argument develops, it becomes clear that this image of gambling womanhood is a metaphor for Spain's recent past and an explanation for its decline:

> With the absence of trade goes the absence of a knowledge of the outside world, and, though a certain general knowledge was brought back by the Europe-conquering soldiers of Charles and Philip, it was a knowledge of how easily gain could be made *in the old way,* rather than a stimulus to the merchant.
>
> Without the logical traditions of buying and selling, raised up through generations, Spain could hardly avoid the errors of government which the want of such traditions brings. She could scarcely hope not to become the victim of each and every scheme for a financial millennium, as a nation, which we are all accustomed to smile at when played in the more self-evident form of personal charlatanry. And most of all, the dignity of work had been lost. The Spanish laborer pitied himself—and was pitied. (6)

In explaining Spain's history and particularly its decline, Huntington's metaphor scapegoats a gullible and illogical female who is too ready to speculate and whose profligacy compromises the common Spaniard.

At this point, the argument returns to its initial claim to proffer a truer representation of Spain. Beguiled or disgusted by the testy and unfeminine woman that is Spanish history, most foreigners (Huntington claims) fail to recognize the inner essence of Spain, its intrahistoric character as represented by the Spanish laborer or commoner. This shift in focus is accompanied by a new metaphor. As Huntington turns from history to intrahistory, he moves from gambling womanhood to a domestic male:

> But few, I know, cross the threshold of the Spanish house to find how good a man at heart the owner is. He is proud, it is true, and does not much favor the stranger, but it is the pride of a reserved nature, not of a weak one. We must be slow in our judgement of this man. Let us both be charitable; what he thinks, as what we think, is the growth of a thousand years. (7)

The Spanish "house" in this passage is associated not with history but with intrahistory, with a way of being and thinking that has evolved among the people over hundreds of years. The radical shifts of the gambling woman's fortune and of Spanish history are opposed to this stable, unchanging identity, the inner essence of Spain and the inside of its house. The rest of the *Note-Book* will be primarily an exploration of this "house," of the intrahistoric customs and traditions of the common Spaniard. The underlying opposition of the passage echoes the distinction between history and intrahistory that dominated '98 thought.

At the same time, however, it departs radically from this model. What is perhaps most striking about this passage is Huntington's inversion of gender roles. Where we might expect that Spain's tumultuous imperial history would be identified with a male figure (as its protagonists were generally soldiers and kings) and its domesticity with women, Huntington reverses these conventional associations. Spanish history is a *femme fatale,* while its intrahistory is a domesticated male. This way of representing the problem of Spain serves not merely to describe the essence of Spain but also to position it in relation to the United States. On the one hand, by representing the historical Spain as an irrational *femme fatale,* Huntington constructs the cultural other in a such a way that American models of economy and domesticity can be defined against it: he stages an encounter between the American sewing machine and the Spanish death wish. At the same time, this inversion of gender roles is a strategy of containment: by feminizing the imperial legacy of Spain and relegating its men to the domestic sphere, Huntington disarms his object of study.

Culture as Domestic Duty

If the discussion of the problem of Spain in the *Note-Book* inverts gender roles, however, Huntington's solution, his own idealized "Spanish house"—the Hispanic Society—restores them through a division of labor that recalls '98 attitudes. One of the most publicized features of the institution was Huntington's early decision to place college-educated women in librarian, curatorial, and executive positions. Although this staffing policy reflected the broader trend of the feminization of American librarianship during the latter half of the nineteenth and beginning of the twentieth century[12] and was motivated by economic considerations (female employees could be paid much less than their male counterparts), Huntington's decision seems to have been informed in part by a vision of womanhood that recalls the '98 association of intrahistory, woman, and the *hogar* (home). The image of the *hogar* was of central importance in the writings of the generation of 1898. For Miguel de Unamuno and Pío Baroja among others, the domestic sphere was the space through which intrahistory was transmitted from one generation to another. The agent of this transmission was almost always the domestic

---

12. Dee Garrison has explored this phenomenon in *Apostles of Culture: The Public Librarian in American Society, 1876–1920* (New York: Free Press, 1979).

woman and particularly (in Unamuno's work) an idealized mother figure: the woman privileged by the '98 writers was gifted with an instinctive and nonintellectual wisdom that allowed her to inspire and perpetuate a sense of spiritual community.

Huntington assigned a similar role to his female employees. Without belittling the laudable achievements and dedication of these women, it is important to note how Huntington conceived of their function. As one of them, Beatrice Proske, later recalled, he "thought that women would be good museum workers because they were good housekeepers." [13] The domestic metaphor is telling: the type of research that these female employees were assigned suggests that Huntington conceived of his society as a house or *hogar* where Spain's intrahistoric traditions might be preserved and transmitted through the patient, meticulous labor of women. Among the publications of the early female staff are titles such as *Hispanic Lace and Lace Making, Catalogue of Laces and Embroiderers,* "Barcelona Glass in Venetian Style," "The Golilla: A Spanish Collar of the Seventeenth Century," "Spanish Dress Worn by a Queen of France," "Women's Festival Dress: Candelario, Salamanca," "Women's Costume: La Alberca, Salamanca," and "Women's Coiffure: Candelario, Salamanca." Although a few of these studies deal (always in a descriptive rather than interpretive way) with major artists such as Velázquez, the emphasis of this work seems to have been placed on accurately recording the dying intrahistoric (and largely female) customs of Spanish provincial life. The focus of these studies is the crafts of Spain, traditions transmitted from generation to generation. "Women's Coiffure: Candelario, Salamanca," a pamphlet about a hair-do cultivated in a single village of Spain, is a typical example: the only justification for the research or claim as to its importance is the anonymous author's observation that "this coiffure is said to have persisted for at least five generations." Like the woman privileged by '98 thought, these female librarians and curators became the keepers of the house in which intrahistory was preserved and transmitted.

The vision of women's role in the Hispanic Society, in a sense, is a corrective to the *femme fatale* of Spanish history. It is the vision that (quite literally) supports Huntington's idealized Spanish house. Inscribed on one of the society's pillars is a sentence by María de Maeztu y Whitney, an educator and early lecturer at the institution: "While woman is absent during the hours of spiritual labor, she cannot ask (as feminism does) for the *right* to culture, which, as a task to achieve, is not a privilege that one conquers but rather a duty that one fulfills" (my translation). Etched on the supporting pillar and

---

13. Cembalest, "Change the Board," 155.

covered in glass, the words serve as a motto for the society's staff and visitors. It identifies the cultural activity of Huntington's "house" as a domestic duty that preserved the intrahistoric and spiritual legacy of Spain: the political and the imperial were subordinated to the patient labor of traditional, spiritual womanhood.

As this framed graffito suggests, the society's conception of itself as an extension of the Spanish *hogar* served not only to perpetuate the intrahistoric tradition and spiritual identity of the cultural other but also to contain and depoliticize it. The institution's domestic vision of scholarship—archive-keeping as a house-keeping—suggests an innocent, tidy, and ideologically neutral field, but it is ultimately founded on exclusions: a silencing of politics and history. This tendency to exclude and depoliticize and the subtext of 1898 are reflected in the history of the library itself. In the early years, Huntington snapped up from the Spanish peerage many preexisting collections, which became the foundation of the society's holdings. As Luisa López-Vidriero observes, the Spanish government, devastated by the costs of the war of 1898, was not in a position to buy the great private collections still on the market. In a sense, thus, some of the holdings of the library were part of the war booty. While Huntington did try to avoid depleting Spain of its cultural patrimony—he preferred to buy objects that had already left the country—the ease with which he acquired these was a consequence of the war, of the fact that the national government and cultural institutions were not in the bidding. Later developments at the society also strangely reflect the context of its inception. In 1927, Huntington realized that the space of the institution was insufficient to its holdings and decided to limit its focus. The criterion by which he did so is telling. Rather than dedicate the collection to a specific discipline, genre, or period (the library's strength, for example, is manuscripts and books from before 1701), the founder decided to divide the material geographically: the HSA would continue to acquire material about Spain and Portugal, while a fund was established at the Library of Congress for publications about Latin America. This transferal of the former colonies from the Spanish "house" to a U.S. government institution mirrors the international situation after 1898. Just as Spain was unequal to the burden of its colonies, Huntington's Spanish house was, in the words of Beatrice Proske, "not equal to the burden of an increasing volume of publications beyond the boundaries of the mother countries, Spain and Portugal."[14] The exclusion further depoliticized Huntington's Spanish house. By severing Spain and Portugal from the rest of the Hispanic world, the society not only cut Spain

---

14. Proske, *Archer Milton Huntington,* 20.

off from its imperial past but also alienated the institution from its surrounding community.

Don Quixote's Vapouring

If there is a hero from the imperial past in the imagined Spain of the society, it
is the Don Quixote depicted in bas-relief across the terrace and memorialized
in Huntington's poetry:

> Can truth or history such beauty keep
> As vast reality of visions deep?
> Shall deeds of Caesar or Napoleon ring
> More true than Don Quijote's vapouring?
> Hath wingéd Pegasus more nobly trod
> Than Rocinante stumbling up to God? ("A Rocinante," *Collected Verse*)

In these verses, the influence of '98 thought on the society's projection of
Spain is again clear. Miguel de Unamuno, one of the main figures of this
generation, embraced Don Quixote as the hero of an alternate reality that
transcended the bleak actuality of Spain. Just as Huntington's verses privilege
the imaginary over the historical hero, Unamuno insists that Don Quixote's
feats are as praiseworthy and real as those of his living contemporaries:

> To exist is to do works, and hasn't Don Quixote worked, and done work on
> the spirit just as actively and livingly as the knights errant who preceded him
> did theirs, just as actively and livingly as so many other heroes whose historical
> reality need not be verified by a Don Álvaro Tarfe? . . . The great Captain, or
> Francisco Pizarro or Hernán Cortés, led their soldiers to victory, but it is no less
> true that Don Quixote has sustained the souls of energetic fighters, filling them
> with spirit and faith, consolation on defeat, moderation in triumph.[15]

Unamuno's vision of Don Quixote, like Huntington's, emerges from the
romantic reading of Cervantes' novel. Figures such as Byron and the Swiss
historian J. C. L. Simonde de Sismondi identified with its hero, whom they
considered not a buffoon but a misunderstood poet. Read thus, the novel was
not farce but tragedy: for Sismondi, it was "le livre le plus triste qui ait jamais

---

15. Miguel de Unamuno, *Ensayos* (Madrid: Publicaciones de la Residencia de Estudiantes,
1917), 2: 112–13, my translation. References to this work appear henceforth in the text. Unamuno
added a footnote to remind his readers who Álvaro Tarfe is. Between the publication of the first
and second parts of *Don Quixote,* a sequel by another author (Avellaneda) began to circulate. In
Cervantes' Part II, Don Quixote encounters a character named Álvaro Tarfe, who claims to have met
Avellaneda's Don Quixote. Cervantes' Don Quixote obliges him to swear before the mayor and town
clerk that he is the real Don Quixote.

été écrit," and for Lord Byron, "Of all tales 'tis the saddest—and more sad / Because it makes us smile." Unamuno's reading follows the romantic interpretation in that it champions the knight, reasserts his heroism, and defends him against Cervantes' spoof. Here, however, Don Quixote is no longer the hero of romantic individualism misunderstood by the majority but rather "the collective soul individualized, the one who, feeling more in tune with the people, feels in a more personal way; the prototype and result, the spiritual node of the people" *(Ensayos* 2:113). This vision is clearly related to Unamuno's notion of intrahistory. Like the ideal '98 intellectual, Don Quixote has a special connection with the people and the essence of Spain. In another essay, this spiritual depth is attributed not to his male author (whom Unamuno disdained as narrow-minded) but rather to a feminized community: "if Cervantes was the father of Don Quixote, his mother was the people of which Cervantes formed part" (5:220). Don Quixote emerges from the womanhood that nurtures and transmits the spiritual and intrahistoric values of the people. Unamuno's reading thus inverts the romantic interpretation: where the latter presents the one (Don Quixote as poet) abused and misread by the many, the former presents the many (Don Quixote as collective spirit) abused and misread by the one (Cervantes).

Huntington's reading of Don Quixote has affinities with both the romantic interpretation (he writes of the "beauty" of the knight's "visions deep") and Unamuno's revision of it. For both Unamuno and Huntington, Don Quixote's adventures become a quest for the Sacred. Unamuno, whose thought was influenced by Kierkegaard, came to regard Don Quixote as the ideal Christian hero, a model of the leap to faith. Huntington, similarly, represents Don Quixote's steed as "stumbling up to God": Don Quixote embodies the struggle to believe despite the disillusionments of reality. Like Unamuno, moreover, Huntington creates an opposition between Don Quixote and history: heroism is transferred from a real to an imaginary plane.

This transferal is a recurrent motif in Huntington's projection of Spain. In the poem "El Romancero," Huntington again privileges dreamt over actual adventures:

> Take back your deeds of the hour that bleeds
> And give us the deeds of dreams,
> We cannot live
> On the bread you give
> Not truth—but the truth that seems! *(Rimas* 38)

In Huntington's Spain, ideal heroic action takes place not in reality or time ("the hour that bleeds") but in fiction and dream ("the truth that seems").

This motif attests to the influence of '98: Unamuno, in his *Cancionero*, opposes the *mendrugos* (the crumbs) of Spain's past (particularly, the Inquisition) to a spiritual bread associated with both Don Quixote and God.[16] It is important, however, to distinguish between Huntington's and Unamuno's use of this motif and bread imagery. Where in Unamuno the bread and the "deeds of dreams" hold forth the possibility of regeneration (it is a Eucharistic bread), in Huntington they shift Spanish heroism and aggression into a past conditional: Spanish adventurers are described as wielding "the sword of the unknown Lord / Who rules in the might-have-been" *(Rimas* 39). After 1898, it would be difficult to read these verses without knowing the Lord who rules the actually-is. The emphasis on the imaginary here is not (as in Unamuno) a prescription for Spain's regeneration but rather a testimony to its defeat and disarmament.

In Huntington, thus, the transferal of heroic action from the real to the imaginary serves as a strategy of containment, and in much of his writing it echoes Orientalist tropes. As Edward Said observes in *Orientalism* (170), nineteenth-century travelers to the East often projected an "Orient of memories, suggestive ruins, forgotten secrets, hidden correspondences": Nerval wrote of a "pays des rêves et de l'illusion" (cited in Said 182). Huntington, similarly, emphasizes the dreamlike nature of his object of study: "The imagination has wings in this place," he writes in the *Note-book,* "Soon one is breathing the unreal" (2). In a poem titled "España," he evokes "A land of ethereal distances and dreams," and in "El Romancero," he describes how the Spanish adventurers "seek romance / Or the land of Prester John." The reference to Prester John, a legendary Eastern ruler and a standard figure on the "Oriental stage" (Said 63), suggests the Orientalist and fantastic nature of Huntington's projection of Spain. In displacing the cultural other to an imaginary sphere, Huntington resorts to an Orientalist strategy of containment: he disarms Spain, relegating its military agency to a past conditional, and projects it as an ethereal and unreal place.

This strategy of containment and Orientalist inflection may be detected in the Hispanic Society's portrayal of Don Quixote. Though Huntington's reading clearly coincides with Unamuno's in celebrating Don Quixote's heroism as an alternative to feats of historical figures, it is important to note that the real leaders to whom Unamuno opposes the imaginary knight are heroes of

---

16. Miguel de Unamuno, *Cancionero, diario poético* (Buenos Aires: Hispanic Institute in the United States, 1953). For an analysis of Unamuno's emplotment of Spanish history, see Amann, "Restyling History through Image: Unamuno's *Cancionero,* " *Revista Hispanica Moderna* 52 (1999): 46–59.

Spain (Columbus, Pizarro, and Cortés), while those in Huntington's poem are not (Julius Caesar and Napoleon). Furthermore, where Unamuno's historical figures helped to expand the Spanish empire, Huntington's created empires that encompassed and invaded Spain. Huntington, that is, projects the opposition between real and imaginary heroism, between history (actual feats) and intrahistory (spiritual quest) across international borders and places Spain in the position of the colonial subject. The visual representation of Don Quixote in bas-relief that illustrates Huntington's verses reinforces this defeatedness: his lance is broken, and it is difficult to imagine a knight of sorrier countenance. Together the image and the cited verses project a forlorn, beaten figure who pathetically stumbles along. Their tone is far removed from the New Testament optimism of Unamuno's writings, which propose *Don Quixote* as a Spanish Bible (*Ensayos* 5:214) and represent his birth as a sort of immaculate conception in reverse. If Don Quixote is for Unamuno the key to the regeneration of Spain and a return to its intrahistoric essence, the emphasis in Huntington's vision is his failure, and any hope conceded lies only in the world of "dreams."

The society's portrayal of Don Quixote involves not only a representation of Spain as the defeated other but also an Orientalist projection. It is revealing that the bas-relief of Don Quixote is juxtaposed to another of Boabdil, the last Moorish ruler in Spain, who is represented gazing back (in 1492) at the empire he has lost. If one considers the society in the light of 1898, it is difficult not to read this as an allegorical representation of Spain's own position vis-à-vis its former empire. The society, that is, sets up parallelisms between the Christians of the Reconquest and the Americans, on the one hand, and between the defeated East and the Spain of 1898. Spain becomes the Orient against which America may now define itself in its imperialist age. The juxtaposition of Don Quixote and Boabdil, both defeated warriors, suggests that the two images comment on one another: the consolation for the loss of empire (represented through the Moorish ruler) is "Rocinante stumbling up to God." Reading the visual display as a text (from left to right), we move from 1492, the birth of Spanish empire, to Don Quixote, a clear substitute for and anticipation of the history of 1898, a fiction that compensates for the loss of empire. Spain's imperial past is visually contained by two images of defeat.

Disinterring Spain

It is precisely this defeatedness that allows for Spain to become an object of study. In an essay titled "The Beauty of the Dead," Michel de Certeau observes that popular literature emerged as an object of investigation only after it was considered almost extinct. Only when it no longer seems an ideological threat do scholars begin to "go about preserving ruins, or . . . see in it the tranquility of something preceding history, the horizon of nature, or paradise lost."[17] These words might describe as well the Hispanism of Huntington's society. It is only after 1898 and the defeat of Spain that its project and projection become possible. As de Certeau points out, this type of study is inherently circular:

> As early as Henri Marrou's fine and penetrating "Introduction à la chanson populaire française," it has been said that, in the last instance, "the folksong owes its distinctive character to the popular halo it has in our eyes." What then is the meaning of this phantom that designates the origin and at the same time conceals it, this 'halo' that reveals while 'covering over'? . . . these studies of popular culture take as their object their own origin. They pursue across the surface of texts, before their eyes, what is actually their own condition of possibility — the elimination of a popular menace. (120)

The images of Spanishness Huntington's archive projects are similarly a halo, a ghost that at once points to and conceals the condition of possibility of the Hispanic Society: the war of 1898 and the death of an empire. Like the popular studies de Certeau examines, the HSA is a monument to the "beauty of the dead."

This preoccupation with death is an undercurrent of both the '98 intellectuals' attempt to recover intrahistory and the project of the Hispanic Society. In Unamuno's novel *San Manuel Bueno, Mártir,* the hero, a modern intellectual who is terrified by his own mortality, longs to return to the unproblematic faith and intrahistoric values of the people.[18] The site of this lost simplicity is a feudal village that has long been covered by a lake. Manuel's longing to return to the intrahistoric is an archaeological desire, a desire to unearth something dead.

Huntington's project resembles Manuel's in two respects. First, it emerges from an archaeological project: in 1898 Huntington went to southern Spain to participate in an excavation, which was interrupted by the outbreak of the war. In his poetry, he memorialized his experience exhuming Roman corpses: "Those months we opened sixty graves, / Brushing the Roman dust away, / To gather fragments that had held / Loved memories of a faded day. / There lay the ring upon her breast, / Just where her faded hands had crossed, / The

---

17. Michel de Certeau, *Heterologies: Discourse on the Other,* trans. Brian Massumi (Minneapolis: University of Minnesota Press, 1997), 119.

18. Miguel de Unamuno, *San Manuel Bueno, Mártir y tres historias más* (Salamanca: Almar, 1978).

golden presence of her soul— / But not the gold of earth—was lost" (50).
Huntington's archival project involved the transferal of these dead "fragments" from Spain to New York: an entire room of the society, for example,
is dedicated to tombs and effigies from the Monastery of San Francisco de
Cuéllar.

A second similarity between Manuel's and Huntington's projects is that
both seem to react against time, decay, and mortality. Just as Manuel's fascination with the underwater village is informed by his fear of death, the
Hispanic Society is an attempt to create a timeless, otherworldly realm that
resists the changes, politics, and turmoil of history. Critics of the institution have often noted that Huntington's archive seems a fortress against the
present. Determined to project his will into eternity, Huntington wrote the
bylaws of the institution in such a way as to eliminate any departure from his
original vision and intentions. This attempted self-immortalization (in one
poem, Huntington evokes Horace's *Exegi monumentum*) has worked against
the modernization of the institution: as Cembalest reports, the society has
resisted innovations such as e-mail, fax machines, photocopiers, proper climate control for its collections, and even elevators (the building has eight
stories) because the founder was once trapped in one.[19] The image of Huntington imprisoned in the elevator is an apt metaphor for his society: both
he and it struggled to rid themselves of the constraints of time and mortality
but were ultimately entombed within them. The halls are still haunted by his
footsteps.

The projects of Huntington and Unamuno's Manuel are similar in that
they are both archaeological fascinations with and reactions against the
finitude of temporal existence. What distinguishes them, however, is the
relationship between self and other in each. Manuel longs to join his voice to
those of the villagers as they recite their credo: what the '98 intellectual (and
particularly Unamuno) desired was a fusion between himself and the people.
Huntington, in contrast, does not seek to merge but rather to project his
voice upon the dead he exhumes. The dominant trope of his writing and his
society is prosopopeia: he gives a face and voice to the other he represents.[20]
If Manuel's longing is experienced as a suicidal impulse to immerse himself in
the lake and join its dead community, Huntington's gesture is much closer to
Chateaubriand's at the pyramids: he seeks to inscribe his name on the tomb

---

19. Cembalest, "Change the Board," 155.

20. In his verse, Huntington is fascinated by the dead and often projects voices upon them. One
poem, for example, is titled "Song of Spain's Ghost" (Archer M. Huntington, *Collected Verse* [New
York, 1953], 282). Another, "Spanish Wanderer," evokes "Sleepers who stir not ever to waken / The
sea their timeless tomb; / Angel of Death has gathered here / War flowers of holiest bloom" (283).

of the dead Orient. His society seeks to overcome death by projecting it onto the cultural other. It can only remain alienated from the living present, the Hispanic community that now surrounds it, the actual voices of the other.

What is imagined in *San Manuel Bueno, Mártir* is an integration of self and other. The relation between self and other in Huntington's society is somewhat more complex. It is perhaps best described by the equivocal phrase that Derrida explores in *Archive Fever:* "L'un se garde de l'autre." [21] This phrase suggests both a conservation of and a distancing from the other: it can mean "One keeps some of the other" or "One guards oneself from the other." In the Hispanic Society of America, the dialectic between self and other that Derrida describes is projected across international borders: Huntington's archive is at once an attempt to contain and to ward off the cultural other that is Spain.

---

21. Jacques Derrida, *Archive Fever: A Freudian Impression,* trans. Eric Prenowitz (Chicago: University of Chicago Press, 1995).

Chapter 8

Women Writers and Their Libraries in the 1920s

Karin Roffman

During the same period in the early 1920s, the poet Marianne Moore and the novelist Nella Larsen—both yet to publish their first major works—were assistant librarians at different branches of the New York Public Library. Moore worked at the Hudson Park Branch downtown; Larsen worked at the 135th Street Branch uptown. Both authors managed the children's sections of their libraries, reported to the same central administrator (Miss Annie Moore), and took the examination offered by the central library as a tool for promotion. The geographical distance between the two library branches, however, signals the different literary worlds the two authors are viewed as inhabiting. Greenwich Village was the center of the burgeoning modern art movement; Moore wrote an unpublished account of spending her days in the library and her evenings at readings with other modernist poets in Lola Ridge's apartment. The Harlem Renaissance was centered at the 135th Street branch; Arna Bontemps, Langston Hughes, and others published accounts of that library as the first stop for artists arriving in Harlem. As authors, Moore and Larsen (see figures 8.1 and 8.2) are never discussed together; as librarians, however, both are mentioned in the same volume of New York Public Library minutes.[1]

This essay argues that for modern women writers, authorship and librarianship were related critical experiences. Through their writing, Moore and Larsen similarly question how institutions develop and how individuals respond to different systems of organizing knowledge. A shared preoccupation with systems of knowledge production drives their work and can be traced back to their early responses to library training. Because libraries

---

1. Marianne Moore is mentioned on pages 12 and 14, and Nella (Larsen) Imes on page 378 (New York Public Library Minutes: Committee on Circulation, Volume 21: 1921, New York Public Library, Manuscripts and Archives, RG5).

Figure 8.1. Marianne Moore in 1925. Reproduced by permission of the Yale Collection of American Literature, Beinecke Rare Book and Manuscript Library.

offered alternative forms of education to the university for early twentieth-century women, women writers used libraries for work and study—and critiqued their experiences in those spaces—as male writers used and critiqued their experiences in universities. T. S. Eliot's rejection of Harvard graduate school in order to write poetry, Ezra Pound's endorsement of Eliot's decision, William Carlos Williams's overtly anti-academic essays, and Wallace Stevens's lyrical undercutting of his white-collar day job have helped to define a modernist poetics (and a circle of central modernist writers) closely connected to a critique of the modern university. Because women's library education is viewed as less culturally central than the university, women's participation in a key discussion on the relationship between American institutions and modern writing has been largely ignored. Because women's thoughts about libraries are found in private journals, letters, unpublished notes, poetry, and prose — not in public speeches and widely read essays like those of their male counterparts — their analyses have not been recognized as marking a cohesive modern experience nor have connections been made between their library

Figure 8.2. Nella Larsen in a photograph presented to Carl van Vechten. Reproduced by permission of the Yale Collection of American Literature, Beinecke Rare Book and Manuscript Library.

training and their writing. By illustrating intellectual connections between the works of Marianne Moore and Nella Larsen — two writers whose common interests have never been discussed — this essay explores how study of women's work in libraries and other cultural institutions might uncover a shared modernist ideology among a diverse group of early twentieth-century women writers.

In current criticism, modern women writers' literary and historical engagement with libraries is *always* dismissed as unimportant. This critical legacy is largely due to a triumvirate of early twentieth-century cultural critics — George Santayana, Van Wyck Brooks, and Malcolm Cowley — who established a powerful and seemingly permanent vocabulary for reading institutions as gendered spaces by the 1920s. In speeches, journals, and books, they challenged the future of American institutions, attacking libraries as symbolizing the nation's un-modern, anti-intellectual, and feminine institutions.

Early twentieth-century debates about America's intellectual and institutional weaknesses are succinctly summed up by George Santayana's speeches on gentility. Santayana's 1911 address at the University of California at Berkeley officially vocalized resentment toward what he called "The Genteel Tradition" in literature. He gave a name and a description to a type of writing he associated with "the American woman." [2] Van Wyck Brooks's *America's Coming-of-Age* (1915) developed Santayana's claims and argued that American culture was in a period of crisis.[3] Malcolm Cowley later described Andrew Carnegie as the embodiment of a divided American personality:

> The two sides of Puritanism might be united in a single man, Andrew Carnegie, who made a fortune by manufacturing armor plate and then spent it in promoting peace by impractical methods and in building libraries where the men in his rolling mills, who worked twelve hours a day and seven days a week, would never have time to acquire culture. . . . "Culture" was regarded as a foreign accomplishment to be learned and exhibited like golf or table manners, almost a commodity to be bought like a new Keats manuscript for Mr. Morgan's library.[4]

This image of a man who wants to have business concerns (during the week) and culture (on Sunday), but whose mind has so divided the two ideas that

---

2. George Santayana, "The Genteel Tradition in American Philosophy," in *The Genteel Tradition: Nine Essays,* ed. Douglas L. Wilson (Cambridge: Harvard University Press, 1967), 40. He called American women: "all genteel tradition."

3. Van Wyck Brooks, *America's Coming-of-Age* (New York: B. W. Huebsch, 1915), 3–35.

4. Malcolm Cowley, "The Revolt against Gentility," in *After the Genteel Tradition,* ed. Cowley (New York: Norton,, 1936), 18.

it cannot fully grasp an idea of "culture" as containing both, is the principal image, according to Cowley, Brooks, and Santayana, of America's lack of intellectual breadth and intensity and of the poor quality of its institutions. Cowley chose as an exemplum of this unfortunate tradition the man whose philanthropy helped create more than one thousand public libraries across the United States. It was not only Carnegie, but the libraries forever linked to his name that Cowley and other critics held responsible for keeping America from developing culture.

For Moore and Larsen, the particular experience inside libraries both informed and transformed the writing process. They learned from books that they found in these spaces, but they also learned firsthand about the structures and systems through which understanding occurs. Library training, unlike the experience of attending a university, emphasized operations of an institution. By working in the library, women writers were studying specific ways institutions structure and shape knowledge. They independently recognized that gendered attacks on libraries diminished the possibility that women's work inside those spaces could be taken seriously and that these institutions were increasingly being read in ways that shaped the historical record about themselves. As women writers such as Moore and Larsen critiqued the increasing authority these institutions were being given to organize knowledge, they offered alternative models for the future of institutions and culture.

While organizational systems by which materials are classified, arranged, and shelved would not seem necessarily to inspire any particular kind of writing, for Moore and Larsen they led to new ways of thinking about forms of knowledge as determining paths of thinking. They recognized the ways that their own writing was also being classified—through gender, race, and class biases—in part by observing the processes through which cultural institutions categorized information. In her writing, each woman imagined new ways to create knowledge and new ways to learn through a process of observing systems of social control, and then critiquing and resisting their institutionalization. Both Moore and Larsen recognized the possibility of challenging cultural authority through imaginative questioning and a dedication to discovering new ways to learn.

Developing Critique of the Library Profession

Both Moore and Larsen were initially excited by their work in libraries, but they became increasingly disillusioned with their jobs. While a waning of interest might be a natural part of many kinds of daily work, they recognized broader implications in their dissatisfaction with library training.

Figure 8.3. New York Public Library, Hudson Park branch, Greenwich Village, decorated for Old Home Week celebration, spring 1913. Reproduced by permission of the New York Public Library.

Their critiques challenged the institutional identity the public library had worked to establish in the early twentieth century and became part of an anti-institutional ideology in their writing.

Moore's interest in the library profession began while she was working as a secretary for Melvil Dewey in 1910 and continued during her work as an assistant to librarians at the Hudson Branch of the New York City Public Library between 1921 and 1925 (see figure 8.3). Though Moore's published writing does not overtly emphasize the importance of these early experiences, unpublished letters from the period and a later unpublished novel and auto-biography reveal that she thought seriously about library work and considered pursuing a career as a librarian. New York Public Library records from the early 1920s provide documentation that Moore took its library examination. This test was required for application to library school and for promotion within the library branch system (Larsen took the same exam). Although Moore's scores qualified her for both opportunities, after her promotion she chose to leave library work. The fact that she prepared for the difficult exam, however, shows her consideration of library work as a possible profession. Her subsequent writing suggests that part of her rejection of the library was a rejection of its requirements and ideas about professionalization.[5]

By the time Moore began to work for Dewey in 1910, he was a controversial figure, but she liked him immediately. Dewey had been forced out of the establishments that he had created—the professional library school at Columbia and the American Library Association—and had instead created a network in Lake Placid to promote his ideas.[6] He employed dozens of people to work for what was largely a consultation business. Moore observes Dewey and, in a letter home a few days after she arrives in Lake Placid, she explains why he fascinates her:

> Mr. Dewey has the walls lined with files . . . an engraving of a rebellion or school romp. I hadn't time to look at it. He has revolving bookcases of files, neatly labeled, perhaps only one bookcase and an extent of deck along the wall in front of the windows . . . and just in front of his chair in the corner where the windows stop, a bookcase set on the desk full of ordinary books. He has a wonderful command of English. He has a horror of Britticisms (MCT) [for M. Carey Thomas of Bryn Mawr] kind and yet the most finished individual style I have ever heard. Hence, contact with him is liberalizing. He is very droll. . . . He certainly is a dream as far as personality goes. He might be unpleasant, self-contained but very drastic and I am pleased to know that he has the idea firmly in his mind that I wish to please him. He gave me half a dozen letters tossing over the originals from the authors to be filed when I had copied his letters in carbon on the backs. They are very liberal and have every device imaginable to facilitate work and yet are economical.[7]

Moore appreciates Dewey's combination of efficiency and economy. As Louise Collins has noted, Moore continued Dewey's practice of copying letters sent out onto the backs of original letters received in her private correspondence

---

5. Although Moore generally gave the impression that the public library job was simply a part-time relatively unimportant experience for her, the New York Public Library Minutes: Committee on Circulation show that she took the exams for promotion on January 5, 1921, passed the test, and was promoted to grade two. Nella Larsen took the same test the same year, with the same result. During the period that Moore worked at the Hudson Park Branch, that branch is mentioned three times in the Library Minutes, for sewage issues, an employee's fall, and problems with the children's room floor (New York Public Library, Manuscripts and Archives, RG5).

6. Morris Longstreth, *The Adirondacks* (New York: Century, 1920), 231–58. Longstreth explains that Dewey was accused of anti-Semitism by his colleagues and forced out of Columbia and the library association. Dewey continued to categorize guests at his Lake Placid Club, dividing them into "classes" and excluding Jews.

7. Marianne Moore to Mary Warner Moore, 10 July 1910, Marianne Moore Collection, The Rosenbach Museum and Library (hereafter cited as MRML).

and particularly when she became editor at *Dial* magazine.[8] Dewey had been part of the movement that created "a growing belief that knowledge itself should and could be used more efficiently."[9] She describes his spare office decorations as an extension of the ideology of efficiency he brought to cataloguing and other facets of modern librarianship. Moore sees a connection between his ideology, his aesthetic, and his "wonderful" use of language, and she is attracted to him:

> Mr. Dewey is an HM* (*HM = handsome man) a Dream or anything favorable that you wish to call him. He called me in before dinner to give me some letters. . . . He was in a flannel shirt and slippers. Explained his attire said he couldn't stand the slightest restriction about his neck or across him. He talked to me a little while said I wasn't to be worried if I got things wrong at first. He said he knew shorthand was a thing which required years of practice and he would try to go slowly and spell the names but that I wasn't to be frightened etc. if I didn't get them. He asked me what my specialty was in college said that Miss Seymour said I had done very well in the work she had given me—got everything very accurately and was very promising. He didn't use that word but conveyed the idea. Mr. Dewey's room is ideal.[10]

Dewey represents an ideal of knowledge to Moore—at first. She praises his "finished" style (personal and literary), his "complete" presence, his "liberal" attitudes; his combination of certainty and style impresses her. Her letters home about this first job suggest the extent to which systems of knowledge and the use of language are connected in her mind. She admires Dewey—the premiere organizer and system-maker of late nineteenth-century thought—a man who recognizes, perhaps, a like-mindedness in Moore, and he clearly encourages her attraction.

Yet Moore's job with Dewey is exploratory and brief. She embraces his aesthetic principles as "ideal" at the same time that she also begins to think more critically about terms she associates with him such as "finish" and "complete"—words and ideas that will become importantly undercut in her early poems. When Dewey moves permanently to Lake Placid in 1906,

---

8. Louise Collins, "Marianne Moore, Melvil Dewey, and Lake Placid," in *Marianne Moore: Woman and Poet,* ed. Patricia Willis (Orono: National Poetry Foundation, 1990), 54. Examples from Moore's editorship are in the Dial/Scofield Thayer Papers, Beinecke Library, Yale University. Other than brief descriptions of Moore's work with Dewey in biographies, this is the only essay I have found that considers Moore's experiences in Lake Placid in relation to the development of her poetic principles such as efficiency, compression, and precision.

9. John Cole, "Storehouses and Workshops: American Libraries and the Uses of Knowledge," in *The Organization of Knowledge in Modern America, 1860–1920,* ed. Alexandra Oleson and John Voss (Baltimore: Johns Hopkins University Press, 1979), 374.

10. Marianne Moore to Mary Warner Moore, 10 July 1910, MRML.

he is determined to make his center "the nation's model rest and recreation community based on Protestant values and Victorian standards of social conduct."[11] These are values familiar to Moore and help explain her initial attraction: it is the order, of a collection of books no less than a room, that lends completeness and finish their erotic charge. Yet she also recognizes these values as the achievements of patriarchal control that she plans to remain free of as she imagines other personal and professional models of organization. In letters home over the next few weeks, however, Moore would critique Dewey's system of work. She complains that he does not stick to regular hours of employment or give her intellectual work to do. Moore develops ideas about the connections among systems, knowledge, and language that she first notices by observing Dewey, suggesting that in leaving Dewey's club she begins to experiment with creating a more personal system of values and standards and an individual poetic language.

Moore's job at the Hudson Park Branch of the New York Public Library cements in her mind critiques of institutions and institutionalized systems (for example, catalogues, categories, classification, and organizational tools) that she first began to develop as an assistant to Melvil Dewey. Moore later recounts her initial excitement and subsequent misgivings about this library position. In her unpublished autobiography, she compares her initial enthusiasm for working in the library to a developing feeling that it is an authoritarian space.[12] She describes working at the Hudson Public Library, which she was first attracted to in part because of its convenient location across from her house and its proximity to the books that she loved. The librarian of this branch, Miss Mary Leonard, asked Mrs. Moore to be allowed to place Marianne on the staff. At first the job seemed exciting and convenient. Moore was asked to give her opinion on the value of certain books as serious works or as entertainment. She liked the job, but found that it interrupted the flow of what she generally chose to read. Still, she was happy to be around books. Yet a growing dissatisfaction led her eventually to leave. At first she found that her opinions were not particularly sought after or taken seriously. She discovered also that those in positions of authority such as Frederick Hopper, who was in charge of the main branch, or Miss Anne Carol Moore, who was in charge of children's books, did not value her opinion specifically because she had not been to library school. Moore had taken a course in library economics at Bryn

---

11. Wayne Wiegand, *Irrepressible Reformer* (Chicago: American Library Association, 1996), 50.

12. This is a point that Paul Valéry also makes in reference to the new authoritarian museum culture. In the essay "The Problem of Museums," he begins by suggesting that the "no smoking" signs and the signs directing one to check one's coat and umbrella are signs of the museum's authority and ultimately affect the type of relationship one can have with it. Paul Valéry, "The Problem of Museums," *Arts* 34 (March 1960): 40–41 (first published in 1923).

Mawr, and she felt that, along with her intelligence, that should have been sufficient to allow her to recommend books to children. She found, though, that the assumption that you could not work in a library without a degree from library school was pervasive.[13] Many years later, she still sounds rather bitter about the extent to which she was not allowed to express an opinion at the library due to her lack of official training credentials. In the next paragraph, Moore reveals how different her evenings were from her days: readings at the home of Lola Ridge where the future of modern poetry was being discussed and where her opinions were asked and listened to often and freely.

Moore's initial expectation that library employment would be not only a continuation but a deepening of the patron's search for knowledge is quickly dispelled. Moore is disappointed that other librarians are not interested in her thinking and ask her to do easy and mechanical work. Her confusion over library work, however, reveals the library's continued struggle into the 1920s with its identity as a profession. While Dewey had declared in "The Profession" (1876) that a new era of librarianship had arrived, Moore's reaction to her job suggests that Dewey's early statements were not entirely realized:

> The time has at last come when a librarian may, without assumption, speak of his occupation as a profession. . . . The time *was* when a library was very like a museum, and a librarian was a mouser in musty books, and visitors looked with curious eyes at ancient tomes and manuscripts. The time *is* when a library is a school, and the librarian is in the highest sense a teacher, and the visitor is a reader among the books as a workman among his tools. Will any man deny to the high calling of such a librarianship the title of profession?[14]

Dewey establishes a clear line of demarcation between the library's dusty past and its modern, gleaming future, between the library's pre-1876 attitudes and its post-1876 plans for success. Generally, historians have agreed with Dewey's assessment. This often-quoted essay has been used as a sound bite to illustrate the clear distinction between two eras in library development. In his influential essay "Storehouses and Workshops: American Libraries and the Uses of Knowledge," John Cole makes much of Dewey's image of the new visitor to the library as a "workman among his tools," a phrase that idealizes the library's new attitude about itself as a living, functional space. Cole's essay chronicles the library's development from a "storehouse," a space interested primarily in the accumulation of materials, to a "workhouse," a modern space invested in an idea of itself as an information center through the increased use

---

13. Paraphrased from Marianne Moore, "Autobiography: Coming Home," 48–52 (Unpublished, n.d., MRML).

14. Melvil Dewey, "The Profession," *American Library Journal* 1 (30 September 1876): 5–6. (The *American Library Journal* became the *Library Journal* the following year.)

of its materials by patrons. Cole argues that the library became a more modern and useful space by the end of the nineteenth century.[15] But though the library itself was changing, the new image of librarianship with "specialized methods acquired in professional training [that] always include more than rule-of-thumb procedures or routinized skills" did not necessarily describe the realities of library work, especially for the thousands of women who would occupy the lower ranks of the profession.[16]

For all the supposed intellectual freedoms of a library, Moore found it a rather rigid place to work and rather bureaucratic in its conception of its own future. In an unpublished novel, "The Way We Live Now" (1967), she negatively characterized librarians as people who behave like policemen, and who use organizational systems in place of creating original ideas or genuine analyses of history. Specifically identifying Oxford, which she had visited during her trips to England, as a society that seemed to guard and label knowledge more than it used it, Moore recognizes the library as both a place of intellectual freedom and a potential prison. Librarians behave as authorities even more than do policemen, an act of self-aggrandizement that Moore generally does not admire.[17] In Moore's desire for intellectual openness, she gravitates toward libraries as places for freedom and learning, but she finds her experience inside them disappointing. In the poems she was writing for *Observations* (1924) at the same time that she worked at the Hudson Park Branch, she explores the possibilities for art to transcend or resist the kinds of institutional pressures that inhibit freedom or possibilities for knowing. She would at the same time celebrate the energy required to build these institutions and seek to harness that energy for the production of art.

During the early 1920s, Nella Larsen trained at library school and also worked as a librarian at the New York Public Library's 135th Street branch (see figures 8.4 and 8.5). As the first black woman accepted into the New York Public Library School, however, Larsen had experiences that went even further than Moore's in highlighting some of the problems inherent in the library system.[18] Under the direction of Superintendent Ernest Reece, the Library School used an educational model based largely on Melvil Dewey's

15. Cole, "Storehouses and Workshops," 371.

16. Robert D. Leigh, *The Public Library in the United States: The General Report of the Public Library Inquiry* (New York: Columbia University Press, 1950), 187.

17. Paraphrased from Marianne Moore, "The Way We Live Now," 253 (unpublished, 1967, MRML).

18. Larsen complained about the school's attitude toward black people in the "Author's Statement" for Alfred K. Knopf, 24 November 1926. In the Alfred A. and Blanche Knopf Collection, Harry Ransom Humanities Research Center, University of Texas Libraries. Discussed in Thadious Davis, *Nella Larsen, Novelist of the Harlem Renaissance: A Woman's Life Unveiled* (Baton Rouge: Louisiana State University Press, 1994), 147–51.

Figure 8.4. New York Public Library, 135th Street branch. Reproduced by permission of the New York Public Library.

Figure 8.5. Reading Room of the 135th Street branch, with librarian Ernestine Rose at her desk. Reproduced by permission of the New York Public Library.

ideas about library training. Reece contended in school documents and in his later publications on library education that the library is a form of technology and the librarian is an "operator" of the library machine, and he aimed to improve the organization and the long-term efficiency of libraries through his administration.

Ernest Reece embraced Dewey's librarian training program to modernize libraries. Arguing that "the librarian need not discover knowledge nor create books . . . [rather] make the content of books more available than otherwise it would be," Reece underlined his assumptions about knowledge during Larsen's year in library school.[19] In these later books, reflecting on his work in the 1920s, he noted: first, that in library training gaining knowledge and operating it are two different functions and that they can be separated; second, that librarians would want to learn to operate knowledge; third, that one

19. Ernest Reece, *The Curriculum in Library Schools* (New York: Columbia University Press, 1936), 3–6.

can learn how to operate knowledge. The aim of his method was for libraries to experiment in "simplifying and cheapening routines . . . to methodize an aggregate of tasks," in part through the ability of graduating librarians to continue to organize and increase the management efficiency of libraries.[20] To demonstrate his commitment to Dewey's methods, Reece required the library school students to study Dewey's ideas through the purchase of five textbooks which would be used for the entire school year.[21]

To an open-minded writer such as Larsen, Dewey's explanations for decisions on how to classify knowledge were problematic. Throughout the *Decimal Clasification* (1922) textbook, Dewey explains that classification should provide "practical usefulness" and be flexible; his examples, however, clearly show the degree to which he felt his system of classification was totalizing and finished. For example, he explains in a section called "new subjects" that new topics will arise in the future. While acknowledging incompleteness as an inherent aspect of his program, the paragraph actually argues for the completeness of his system. Dewey writes that "a new topic is always closely related to sum existing hed," [22] and he offers evidence for the ways new information can be categorized using his already prepared model. His system would strive to account not only for all present and past knowledge, but also for all future knowledge.[23]

Given Larsen's introduction to classification systems, it is not surprising that her novels suggest that she was increasingly skeptical of any institutions that produce comprehensive systems of knowledge. Larsen had completed library school and was nearing the end of her career as a librarian by the time

---

20. Ibid., 12–19.

21. The five required textbooks are: American Library Association, *Catalogue Rules* (New York: ALA, 1908); American Library Association, *List of Subject Headings for Use in Dictionary Catalogues, 3d edition* (New York: ALA, 1911); C. A. Cutter, *Rules for a Dictionary Catalogue, 4th edition* (New York: ALA, 1904); Melvil Dewey, *Decimal Clasification,* 8th, 9th, 10th, or 11th eds.; and A. B. Kroeger, *Guide to the Study and Use of Reference Books* (Chicago: ALA, 1917).

22. Melvil Dewey, *Decimal Clasification,* 11th ed. (Lake Placid, 1922), 14.

23. Other students at the Library School voiced concerns about what they saw as the school's overemphasis on the Dewey decimal classification system. An undated special report was filed in the early 1930s based on student evaluations of the courses. The evaluations are composed between 1928 and 1933, a few years after Larsen left and after the school had been absorbed by Columbia, but most of the courses and faculty remained the same. In the comments about the "classification" course—"LS 211"—students complained about the overuse of the Dewey system, and showed an understanding of some of the limits of the system. Examples are: L. B. Pratt, 1928, who writes that there should be "more comparison and study of classification systems other than Dewey"; R. A. Miller, 1930, who writes that "in place of the sanctity of D.C. [Dewey Classification] should like to see substituted theory that modifications are necessary and that nothing is finally learned," and B. M. Franz, 1933, who asks for "less emphasis on D.C." and "more on L.C." The New York Public Library Library School Records, box 14, Columbia University Rare Book and Manuscript Library.

she wrote her first novel, *Quicksand* (1928). For her protagonist, she created a character who rejects all systems of knowledge as flawed and who seeks entirely other ways to learn — outside of libraries, schools, and any other systematized forms of knowledge production. Helga Crane eventually acknowledges that there may be no position outside of institutions from which to learn, but as a result of Larsen's career within those places, Helga comes to her questions about institutions, systems, and knowledge production with the sophistication of someone who has been on the inside of spaces that claim only to exhibit or "operate" knowledge, but are actually in the business of manufacturing it.

An Anti-Institutional Ideology

Moore's complicated institutional aesthetics developed from contradictory reactions to her early work experiences. In essays published in the 1920s, Moore defines her poetic vision with such clarity that it is tempting to ignore her tendency to contradict these definitions in other essays. While in a few essays she praises "precision," "explicitness," and "order," in other essays she criticizes "experts," "monuments," "collections," and "synthesis." In a 1925 essay on the influence of museums and libraries on children's creativity, for example, Moore quoted Denman Waldo Ross's definition of beauty as "a supreme instance of Order, intuitively felt, instinctively appreciated."[24] She liked to entertain both points of view simultaneously — that examples of order are both beautiful and destructive — as she suggested in a 1927 review of several new poetry anthologies:

> Academic feeling, or prejudice possibly, in favor of continuity and completeness is opposed to miscellany — to music programs, composite picture exhibitions, newspapers, magazines, and anthologies. Any zoo, aquarium, library, garden, or volume of letters, however, is an anthology and certain of these selected findings are highly satisfactory. The science of assorting and the art of investing an assortment with dignity are obviously not being neglected, as is manifest in "exhibitions and sales of artistic property," and in that sometimes disparaged, most powerful phase of the anthology, the museum.[25]

Moore defines an anthology as something worthwhile at the same time that she undermines this very definition. Her long and confusing first sentence

---

24. In Patricia Willis, ed., *The Complete Prose of Marianne Moore* (New York: Viking, 1986), 152. Other essays and reviews in which Moore also includes examples of these words are "Dress and Kindred Subjects" (596–600), "Ideas of Order" (329–31), and "Idiosyncrasy and Technique" (506–18).

25. *Complete Prose of Marianne Moore,* 182.

suggests that continuity and completeness are properly opposed to miscellany. The rest of the paragraph undoes this notion. Moore eventually argues that the seeming disorder and lack of completeness in miscellany can be "highly satisfactory" in certain contexts, including the libraries and the museums that inspired the essay. She tosses off this anti-establishment (or at least anti-academic) analysis of the benefit of incompleteness and disjunction with the charming tone of one who agrees with the establishment.[26] A closer reading of this essay, however, suggests that Moore more likely holds a singular view.[27]

Moore was fond of lists, anthologies, and indexes, but disliked classification systems, organizational principles (particularly those in museums and libraries), and experts. While it might seem as though lists and classification systems are the same (since they both involve principles of selection), Moore's poems show why this is not the case. Her poems repeatedly unmake the lists that they make, and her lists are never allowed to become systems of thinking or ways of organizing thoughts. This tendency is both a poetic device and an ideological one. It allows Moore to admire libraries without having to commit herself to adhering to their systems of organizing or presenting knowledge. Almost every Moore poem offers some obstacle to learning and some ingenious form of resisting or circumventing it. Moore saw libraries as exercising useful types of social control. Since one of her poetic realizations is that measures of control often inspire creativity, she is as grateful for structures of authority as she is resentful of them.

Moore's ideas about both creating and undoing classification systems are exemplified by the unusual index that she composed for *Observations*.[28]

---

26. Moore's conciliatory tone is one explanation for the way her essays tend to be read as statements of her aesthetics of order rather than as critiques of this aesthetic. For example, Louise Collins discusses Moore's aesthetic as "precision of phrase, deliberateness, and a concern with categorizing" in "Marianne Moore, Melvil Dewey, and Lake Placid," in Willis, *Marianne Moore: Woman and Poet,* 53–60. My analysis of Moore's experience working for Melvil Dewey suggests that Moore became less enamored of the job the longer she worked for him. By the time she writes *Observations,* she critiques his aesthetic of categorization and classification as exclusionary and not conducive to thinking creatively. I argue that her late poems resist and undo his aesthetic of order.

27. In a letter to her mother from Lake Placid, Moore wrote: "I am not much of a stenographer. My value is miscellaneous." Her use of the latter word suggests some attachment to the ideas and values embedded in her definition of it. Marianne Moore to Mary Warner Moore, 24 July 1920, MRML.

28. Although *Observations* (1924) was Moore's second published volume of poems, she considered it her first. H.D. and Bryher, without Moore's knowledge, published *Poems* in 1921. Although she was grateful to them, in letters she also clearly stated that she wished they had not done so. She considered *Observations* her first book, so much so that in her unpublished autobiography, "Coming Home," she fails even to mention the publication of *Poems.* In a letter to Bryher, 7 July 1921, Moore writes: "You say I am stubborn. I agree and if you knew how much more than stubborn I am, you would blame yourself more than you do, on having put a thing through, over my head. I

Moore uses indexes in later volumes to list titles of poems or first lines, but in *Observations* she uses the index to emphasize specific words, groups of words, and ideas. Her interesting choices of words to index (and not to index) draw attention to seemingly minor words and phrases in the poems and offer another level of direction and, perhaps, misdirection in reading them. For example, Moore indexes many—though not all—of the animals mentioned in the poems. "Alligator," "ant with stick," "antelope," "bear, tailed," "bears," "cockroaches," are only some of the many animals that are indexed. Yet other terms that are central to poems, such as "octopus," "human," "intellectual," "evidence," are not listed. The index, which she worked on extensively with her mother, must have been fun to compose. It is both a list of words in a poem and a seeming system (one might imagine important words and concepts get listed), but an almost impossibly idiosyncratic one. In *Observations,* the index has no apparent organizational plan, a system without evident guiding principles or definition.

In her early poems, Marianne Moore considers how poetry can continually reshape thinking. These ideas eventually become central to "Poetry":

> *Poetry*
> I, too, dislike it.
> Reading it, however, with a perfect contempt for it, one discovers in
> it, after all, a place for the genuine.[29]

Moore asserts that rejecting any system of thinking—and she views a poem or any work of art as an organized system—enables one to learn and to discover what is "genuine" in it. Moore's process of revisions embodies an

---

had considered the matter from every point and was sure of my decision—that to publish anything now would not to be to my literary advantage; I wouldn't have the poems appear now if I could help it and would not have some of them ever appear and would make certain changes; if Mr. Thayer contributed 'When I Buy Pictures,' I cannot understand why he did not send 'A Graveyard' with it as it is certainly the better of these poems in the July *Dial.* Despite my consternation, the product is remarkably innocuous. I should have used *Observations,* I think, as a title but I like *Poems. . . ."* In *The Selected Letters of Marianne Moore,* ed. Bonnie Costello (New York: Knopf, 1997), 164.

29. This version of "Poetry," from Moore's *Complete Poems* (1967), is the best known of the poem's many versions for the obvious reason that it is the one still seen most often in print. In addition to the different versions of "Poetry" published in *Poems,* the two versions in *Observations* (1924 and 1925), *Selected Poems, Collected Poems,* and *Complete Poems,* there is also the version from *Others* 5 (1919) and the copies that exist with Moore's penciled corrections (for example, the Beinecke Library copy of *Poems* that Moore gave Louis Untermeyer in which she pencils in changes on a few poems, including "Poetry"). Robin Schulze's recently edited *Becoming Marianne Moore: The Early Poems, 1907–1924* (Berkeley: University of California Press, 2002) includes a facsimile of *Observations* as well as some of the original publications of the poems. Schulze's book will eventually change how readers of Moore think about the different versions of her poems and may put older versions back into circulation in the next few years, but this has just started to happen.

aesthetic of resisting permanence and completion.[30] Through multiple revisions of "Poetry" over fifty years, she allowed no final version of the poem to exist as complete. Even in the last published version, Moore included a footnote that contains a longer version of the same poem. This reference to another version undoes the implied permanence of the published version, forcing the reader to continue to think about the poem as unfinished. Her aesthetic of resistance is also an aesthetic of creation, since her poems and index participate in a process of experimenting with established systems (like a published poem or the index to a work) and offer possibilities for their alteration and reimagination.

Moore's *Observations* (1924) directly questions whether institutions are capable of change. She imagines that the ideal institution includes within it the possibility of transforming itself indefinitely. "Marriage" articulates the institutional environment inhabited by the poems in the volume:[31]

> This institution,
> perhaps one should say enterprise
> out of respect for which
> one says one need not change one's mind
> about a thing one has believed in,
> requiring public promises
> of one's intention
> to fulfill a private obligation.

---

30. One of the subjects that has been brought up repeatedly in Moore criticism over the last ten years is the difficulty of discussing Moore's texts because there are multiple versions of the same poems and essays due to her extensive revisions of previously published works. Robin Schulze's "'The Frigate Pelican''s Progress: Marianne Moore's Multiple Versions and Modernist Practice," in *Gendered Modernisms: American Woman Poets and Their Readers,* ed. Margaret Dickie and Thomas Travisano (Philadelphia: University of Pennsylvania Press, 1996), argues that "the question of why Moore's work remains so undervalued in relation to her peers is complex, but . . . Moore's role in the development of modernist practice and her position in literary history generally have been difficult to assess because of the slippery and unstable nature of her texts" (118). While Schulze is referring mainly to Moore's practice of revisions, her comments also resonate with Moore's penchant to contradict, deny, or omit what she has written before. This practice of revising or unmaking (or remaking) a statement is a philosophical as well as textual practice for Moore in *Observations.*

31. Readings of "Marriage" generally are extremely helpful in working out the meanings of phrases and the contexts for quotations in the long, complicated, and difficult poem. Most readings, though, contend that Moore was writing only about the subject of marriage. As in almost all Moore poems, she was writing about marriage, and she was writing about other things, too, that the word "marriage" and the idea of it made her remember. For helpful essays on "Marriage," but ones that do not consider the poem metaphorically or historically, see David Bergman, "Marianne Moore and the Problem of 'Marriage,'" *American Literature* 60 (1988): 241–54; and Heather Cass White, "Morals, Manners, and 'Marriage': Marianne Moore's Art of Conversation," *Twentieth Century Literature* 45 (1999): 488–510. Margaret Holley, *The Poetry of Marianne Moore: A Study in Voice and Value* (Cam-

Moore's anxiety about "marriage" is also an anxiety about the relationship between institutions and creativity. In letters to H.D., Bryher, and Robert McAlmon while writing "Marriage," Moore objects to Bryher's marriage to McAlmon because "your daily intellectual formula and Robert's were not the same."[32] For Moore, the intellectual formula was the process by which one could continue to be creative. Moore loved libraries; much as she was smitten with Dewey's room at Lake Placid, she felt attraction to institutional formulas that—especially for women—could result in the compromise if not suffocation of creativity. If any institution placed limits on this process, she felt it should be circumvented.[33] In her own life, Moore sought to make the rooms in which we live fit the creative impulse, rather than to fit one's work into the order of existing systems, however seductive. She sought to organize her private life in close proximity to both the library and burgeoning bohemian modernism, using her understanding of each space and ideals to critique the other through the creation of a new poetic world—one aware of the limits and the necessity of order.

NELLA LARSEN'S body of work also recalls and reassesses her work as a librarian. Though they never met or read each other's works, Larsen's novels argue for an anti-institutional ideology similar to Moore's, suggesting ways that art might provide possibilities for questioning and resisting entrenched systems of thinking and learning. In *Quicksand* (1928) Larsen uses a library to think more broadly about the process by which ideas become institutionalized as culture—a process which preoccupies her characters Helga Crane, Clare Kendry, and Irene Redfield in *Quicksand* and her second novel *Passing* (1929). Library school made clear to Larsen, if she did not know it already, that an archive is a technology that produces a certain form of knowledge based, in large part, on what it excludes. Library school made clear that the ideology of an institution is visible in the ways its spaces are organized—for example, adhering to Dewey's classification system so that all works by black authors are categorized under "slavery—326," or having no number available for books by gay writers. Larsen's female characters understand that the produc-

---

bridge: Cambridge University Press, 1987), 56–57, notes that "Marriage," "An Octopus," and "Sea Unicorns and Land Unicorns" were written simultaneously, with phrases from one draft of a poem entering a draft of a different poem.

32. Moore, *Selected Letters,* 158 (Marianne Moore, letter to Bryher, 3 May 1921).

33. Moore, *Selected Letters,* 120. Laurence Stapleton, however, argues that the impetus for the poem was a conversation, quoted in her notebook, that Moore had with Alfred Stieglitz about his marriage to his first wife, as he uses the word "institution" to describe marriage. Laurence Stapleton, *Marianne Moore: The Poet's Advance* (Princeton: Princeton University Press, 1978), 40–41.

tion of knowledge is always also the production of new methods or theories of exclusion because, consciously or not, the ideology of the specific institution is repeated in the larger culture. These characters can perceive knowledge to be a mode of exclusion in large part because they work in libraries and schools, in institutions of mainstream culture whose authority depends on the ability to exclude them, and they recognize that this exclusion is part of a larger social problem. These novels argue that the new emphasis on requiring "professional" status to work in educational and cultural institutions simply gives institutions the ability to claim a meritocratic right to discriminate.

Larsen emphasizes Helga Crane's intellectual quest from the opening paragraph of *Quicksand.* Restless, dissatisfied, intelligent, and visionary, Helga discerns hypocrisy everywhere, although she notices it primarily in the places she thinks it most certainly should not be — in the schools, libraries, and intellectual programs that she works at and believes in at first. Rejecting each new job and responsibility she receives for offering anti-intellectual and unimaginative solutions to critical social problems, she becomes increasingly despairing about the possibility of finding a space from which to create a new, productive form of knowledge. Her sudden move back to the South at the close of the book is another step in her series of efforts to find knowledge that will free her, both intellectually and imaginatively, from old and familiar ways of thinking about issues of race, class, and gender. While Helga Crane has very few of the characteristics of the usual hero, she is unwavering in her commitment to independent thinking.

Fittingly, Larsen's *Quicksand* begins with a question.[34] As the epigraph to the novel, Larsen uses the last four lines of Langston Hughes's "Cross," a poem about a child thinking about his future:

> My old man died in a fine big house,
> My ma died in a shack.
> I wonder where I'm gonna die,
> Being neither white nor black?

Although critics have generally discussed this epigraph in terms of the interracial relationship that seems central to both the poem and the novel, these last four lines set up those interrelationships within a larger area of territory for the novel — the relation between knowledge and identity.[35] In the complete

---

34. All references to Larsen's novels are to *The Complete Fiction of Nella Larsen,* ed. Charles R. Larson (New York: Anchor Books, 2001) (hereafter cited parenthetically in the text).

35. Recent criticism on the epigraph is rather divided as to how to read the poem in relation to Larsen's novel. In the 1970s and 1980s, Larsen criticism stressed the image of the "tragic mulatto" in reading *Quicksand.* In the late 1980s and early 1990s there was a backlash against these readings.

poem, it is clear that the father is a rich white man and the mother is a poor black woman. In the four lines that Larsen includes, however, the races of the rich man and the poor woman are left out. Instead, the emphasis is on the child, and the fact that a child's natural sense of "wonder" at the world can be transformed into specific anxieties about race, class, and gender: Who will the child turn into? Will he be more like his mother or his father? What race and what economic condition will the child inhabit in the future? At the same time, the poem ends with a question mark, a punctuation mark that leaves open the possibility of an answer, or the possibility of more questions. The last four lines of the poem suggest that the child's desire to know something might be more important than any specific information he is given. Larsen's novel is not so much an answer to the child's question as a meditation on the question itself, and on the institutions that exist to answer such questions. In the world that the novel imagines, the ability to ask a question is a precondition of knowledge and an art that most adults have lost or forgotten in the effort to show that they have answers. By beginning a novel with a question about wondering, Larsen creates a space of open-ended possibilities for knowing that Helga Crane will spend the entire novel trying to find and inhabit. Helga attempts to open up questions about the development of identity—what children become—that are usually foreclosed by norms of race, gender, and class.

Helga begins the novel as a schoolteacher, an unquestionably intelligent and determined woman. Over the next twenty-four hours, as she at first ambivalently considers leaving her teaching position at Naxos and then abruptly resigns during her conversation with the principal, Dr. Anderson, it becomes clearer that her ire is directed at "this great institution" much more than it is directed at the South or at the white preacher. "This great institution" is not Naxos, or simply "Negro Education" in the South, but American ideas about education in general. Helga recognizes that the institutionalization of education that has unwittingly created the ideology of Naxos *and* the white preacher has shaped the modern South as well:

Articles in the last six or seven years treat the passage quite differently: In "Nella Larsen's *Quicksand: A Narrative of Difference*," *CLA* 4 (1997): 458–66, Yves Clemmen argues against seeing the image (or the novel) as a tale of the "tragic mulatto." Barbara Johnson argues just as passionately that "Nella Larsen herself suggests that her novel should be read through the grid of the mulatto figure" (253) in her essay "The Quicksands of the Self: Nella Larsen and Heinz Kohut," *Female Subjects in Black and White: Race, Psychoanalysis, Feminism,* ed. Elizabeth Abel, Barbara Christian, and Helene Moglen (Berkeley: University of California Press, 1997), 252–65. George Hutchinson's essay "Nella Larsen and the Veil of Race," *American Literary History* 9 (1997): 329–49, returns to the subject of the mulatto, but with the benefit of "the best recent criticism . . . particularly feminist themes" (329).

> It was, rather, the fault of the method, the general idea behind the system. Like her own hurried shot at the basket, the aim was bad, the material drab and badly prepared for its purpose. This great community, she thought, was no longer a school. It had grown into a machine. (39)

Helga understands that Naxos is not the problem that she is trying to name; the problem is much deeper, more embedded and more difficult to identify, but it has to do with the "ideas behind the system" and the meanings of words such as "method," "aim," "system," and "purpose." Throughout the early sections of the novel, Helga repeatedly tries to articulate something that she feels strongly — that individual desires are in conflict with institutional goals.

At Naxos, on the evening that the novel begins, the constant, slightly irritated sensation of personal insignificance that Helga has felt throughout two years of work there suddenly becomes obvious. She realizes that the school is not a human thing made up of individuals with ideas, but rather is an inhuman system — "a machine," as Ernest Reece had described the library during Larsen's training — a piece of technology that rejects "ideas" in favor of methods or anything regulated, repeatable, and directed. Once Helga can articulate this recognition (as she does at length in Dr. Anderson's administrative office), she no longer wants to work at Naxos. While it may seem as though Helga's tirade is against the school's hypocritical policies, her actual decision to leave the place occurs only after she has learned for herself how knowledge is produced there. The school is a machine; knowledge is manufactured; methods and aims go in and systems come out; these systems produce more methods and aims; and no new knowledge is ever created. This realization gives her the power to reject Naxos, a power that she claims she lacked before when she first recognized that "she was powerless" (40).

In leaving Naxos, Helga upends her seemingly stable life of jobs, institutions, and connections, and embraces the notion that there is a power to be found in a state of uncertainty or not knowing. She applies for a job in a library, and she is angry though not ultimately surprised when she learns the reasons for her rejection:

> She would find work of some kind. Perhaps the library. The idea clung. Yes, certainly the library. She knew books and she loved them. . . . After a slight breakfast she made her way to the library, that ugly gray building, where was housed much knowledge and a little wisdom, on interminable shelves. The friendly person at the desk in the hall bestowed on her a kindly smile when Helga stated her business and asked for directions. . . . Outside the indicated door, for half a second she hesitated, then braced herself and went in. In less than a quarter of an hour she came out, in surprised disappointment. "Library training" —

"civil service" — "library school" — "classification" — "cataloguing" — "train-ing class" — "examination" — "probation period" — flitted through her mind. "How erudite they must be!" she remarked sarcastically to herself, and ignored the smiling curiosity of the desk person as she went through the hall to the street. For a long moment she stood on the high stone steps above the avenue, then shrugged her shoulders and stepped down. (62)

Helga's brief but thorough analysis of her experience illustrates her increas-ingly sophisticated understanding of how institutions operate. Larsen's train-ing in library school is evident in the very specific list of terms that she includes as the reasons the library offers for why Helga cannot work there. Each term, "library training," "civil service," "classification," is set off by quo-tation marks and dashes to emphasize that Helga hears them clearly and that she distinguishes between their institutional and intellectual requirements. Helga's sarcastic thought, "How erudite they must be!" is a protest against a place that "housed much knowledge and little wisdom." Seeing knowledge appropriated by the library as a passive concept (it is "housed"), Helga's analy-sis can be traced back to Larsen's library training and specifically to Reece's ideas about the operation of knowledge.

Helga's rejection of the library's professional vocabulary is also a recogni-tion that institutions organize and present information (in part, through pro-fessional requirements and specialized vocabulary) for public use in ways that profoundly shape cultural understanding. Helga's more skeptical and ques-tioning attitude toward all institutions and institutionalized thinking drives the rest of the novel. She is clearly attracted to the power and authority that institutions carry within them, but wonders whether an individual's desire for freedom is ultimately compromised in adhering to any system of thinking. In Helga's quest for intellectual openness — what she defines as the ability to think for herself — she joins the race movement, leaves America, falls in love, gets married, moves back to the South, and has children. In moving from one episode to the next, *Quicksand* argues that freedom requires not only intel-lectual desire but the individual will to resist all institutions, all systems, and all statements (even one's own).[36] Thus, the seeming contradictions at the

---

36. Helga has resisted marriage and motherhood. When she sees James Vayle, her ex-fiancé and fellow teacher from Naxos, at a party in Harlem, his argument for wanting to marry makes her angry and makes her want to reject him all over again (which she does). He claims that "the race is sterile at the top. Few, very few Negroes of the better class have children, and each generation has to wrestle again with the obstacles of the preceding ones: lack of money, education, and background. I feel very strongly about this. We're the ones who must have children if the race is to get anywhere" (132). James misunderstands Du Bois's ideas about the "Talented Tenth" (which Du Bois explains in *The Negro Problem: A Series of Articles by Representative American Negroes of Today* [New York: Pot and

end of the novel (the succumbing to religious ecstasy, the return to the South, the acceptance of marriage and motherhood, and the willingness to stay) are necessary steps in personal formulas of freedom. That this goal can never be reached is a failure neither of the novel nor of Helga Crane's quest, but of how we conventionally define freedom.

Helga learns that the freedom and happiness she desires, which she imagines as an experience of greater knowledge and insight, can only be realized in an ongoing process of trying to distill knowledge from experience. As a result, her "final" destination in the novel, which includes the South, marriage, religion, motherhood—all the things she has previously rejected—is as important a part of her quest and as necessary a part of the process by which she learns as all of her previous rejections and resistances. In the final section of the novel, Helga is miserable—married to a man she does not love and unable to leave because of another pregnancy. Yet the conclusion is not entirely bleak. Helga, even in her weakened state, thinks about the possibility of a future. The quest that she began when she left the South at the beginning of the novel continues. As the novel ends we recognize Helga in difficult but familiar territory: attempting to transcend the social and cultural structures that she is temporarily trapped within.

Moore and Larsen: The Ideal Cultural Institution

Both Moore and Larsen continued to think about the relationship between individuals and institutions, authors and archives. Moore's early poems look forward to her final creation of an ideal cultural institution. Moore's glacier in "An Octopus" is a massive object transformed and undone by the end of the poem. This is a metaphor for the intellectual process that she had always imagined needed to occur in order to know something. The intellect needed to unmake and reshape itself in order to continue to think.

In her will, Moore's final written work, she designed her own institution. In poems such as "To a Snail" and "The Paper Nautilus," she had imagined different kinds of shelters; she wrote about animals that carried around their

---

Company, 1903], 31–75). James's restatement of Du Bois's ideas is self-serving. Du Bois does encourage those with money and access to elite opportunity to have children, but he does this as part of a larger plan to promote a vision for the possibilities of education and intellectual achievement. Helga's sympathy for some of Du Bois's ideas (which she expresses while working for Mrs. Hayes-Rore) makes her that much more angry at James for misstating them. The scene is particularly interesting because, although Helga's reaction to James's speech about marriage is quite bitter, it is also the point at which the novel introduces the last of the social institutions that Helga will reject (and then join): marriage and motherhood.

own houses, and she praised these animals for having homes that are movable, efficient, and aesthetically pleasing. In choosing a place to deposit her papers, Moore created a shelter not for herself, but for her possessions. In 1968, Moore declined an offer from the University of Texas to buy her papers. She considered donating her things to Bryn Mawr, but shortly before her death she instead sold her papers to the Rosenbach Museum and Library in Philadelphia.[37] Her will establishes a new space for the "Marianne C. Moore Room"—the objects taken from her 1960s New York City apartment—to be placed inside the Rosenbach museum building, a privately owned townhouse built in the 1860s near Rittenhouse Square; another section of the same building will hold her manuscripts and other papers. In this way, she created her own museum and library within a modest building on a street of private homes.

The seeming anti-monumentality of Moore's library is reinforced by its mobile nature. While the townhouse does not move, Moore's possessions inside of it do. Despite many comments to the contrary, Moore had an enormous number of possessions.[38] The objects are divided among the museum, the archive, and the library. As a result, objects that inspired poems (Elizabeth Bishop's gift of a paper nautilus that inspired the poem of that name) or were inspired by poems (both E. E. Cummings and H.D. gave Moore artistic renderings of a yellow rose after she wrote the poem "Injudicious Gardening") are in the Marianne C. Moore Room, while the various working drafts of those poems are in the archive, and the versions in the published volumes are accessible on the shelves of the library.

This space resists any kind of easy identification; it is not simply a library, an archive, or a museum, yet it is all of these things. To understand Moore and her work, one must move among the rooms taking up questions about the differences between these spaces, and being unable to see any one object, work, or idea as finished. In "Of Other Spaces," Foucault writes:

> The idea of accumulating everything, of establishing a sort of general archive, the will to enclose in one place all times, all epochs, all forms, all tastes, the idea of constituting a place of all times that is itself outside of time and inaccessible to all ravages, the project of organizing in this way a sort of perpetual and indefinite accumulation of time in an immobile place, this whole idea belongs to our modernity. The museum and the library are heterotopias that are western culture of the nineteenth century.[39]

---

37. Marianne Moore, will dated 1967, MRML.

38. "My favorite possessions? I am not a collector, merely a fortuitous one." *Complete Prose of Marianne Moore,* 598.

39. Michel Foucault, "Of Other Spaces," *Diacritics* 16 (1986): 26.

Moore chooses a nineteenth-century space, but reinterprets it through a twentieth-century, gendered perspective. She does not treat the library or the museum as an immobile place, or as a heterotopic space set apart from other spaces (the townhouse does not stand alone on the street or in the neighborhood; the library does not stand alone from the archive or museum). Rather, she gives to the building attributes of modern movement by creating necessary (and natural) movement within it. This mobility, this continuous loop of information, is a final mode of resisting "finish" in what is, literally, the rooms of her life and work. Moore creates the antithesis to Melvil Dewey's room in Lake Placid that she first so admired. Instead, Moore, writing her final work during the civil rights movement and the women's movement, creates a mobile, flexible, sociocultural space that will continue to circulate between systems of thought and experience without ever settling into one model of expression. She admires the spectacle of institutions (enough to create one), but she also resists institutionalizing her life or her work in any one way.

Like Moore, Larsen argues through the writing of *Quicksand* that learning occurs more powerfully not in the arrival into knowledge—which often results in the creation of systems that limit and exclude—but in the process of attempting, and failing, to arrive at certain knowledge. Larsen's desire for knowledge is the simplest explanation of her choice to train as a librarian; and her disappointment in her experience as a librarian provides the most straightforward explanation of why she quit. She began her librarianship by bragging about how much she studied and the languages she practiced for the library's required examination, but once she had left the library worried about having to return to a job that did not "suit" her.[40] The daily logs that she carefully filled out for several months as the 135th Street children's librarian show evidence of both these feelings: while Larsen initially filled in details about what books she read to children in nearby schools and other evidence of her community outreach work, she later included less information on the forms.[41] Her attention had turned by this point to beginning *Quicksand,* a new outlet for learning and, as her letters to Carl Van Vechten attest, an effort that she was certain would yield nothing but the persistent feeling of not knowing what she was doing—her favorite kind of challenge.[42]

---

40. Nella Larsen Imes, letter to Carl Van Vechten, 29 September 1926; Nella Larsen Imes, letter to Carl Van Vechten, 26 January 1928. Beinecke Rare Book and Manuscript Library, Elmer Imes Manuscripts.

41. Box 2, Folder 3, October 1924–June 1925. New York Public Library 135th Street Branch Collection, Schomburg Center Records 1921–1948. Schomburg MSS.

42. There are many examples of Larsen's comments about not knowing how to write. One example is Nella Larsen Imes, letter to Carl Van Vechten, 7 December 1926. Beinecke Rare Book and Manuscript Library, Elmer Imes Manuscripts.

Like Moore's, Larsen's body of work also resists completion; it requires readers to ask what they believe about her work and why, and to consider their own knowledge and systems of beliefs in relation to hers as always incomplete. Because Larsen's corpus is so small, critics tend to consider seriously all of her published works (including letters to the editor, games for a children's magazine, reviews of others' works), and they have to analyze and categorize their own values about these seemingly lesser works in comparison to her published novels. Because Larsen used many pseudonyms (and variations of her name) during her career, it is possible (and, some argue, likely) that not all of her published stories have been found, and critics writing about her recognize and openly admit that their knowledge of her is necessarily incomplete.[43] Because she did not participate in any collecting or cataloguing of her own, the process by which it has been discovered and analyzed has involved the works and ideas of others, thus ensuring that her thoughts and beliefs do not stand alone.[44] While becoming increasingly fed up with librarianship as a career in the late 1920s, as she became more successful as a writer, Larsen considered the connections between the two professions—what librarians and libraries *do* to writers (and vice versa), and the consequences of archiving and collecting works. As much as aspects of these ideas appealed to her, she resisted the desire to join one profession or the other or to make any final statements about what she knew and how she came to know it.

Library work links the lives and works of Marianne Moore and Nella Larsen. Their reflections on the modernization and professionalization of libraries shaped their view of institutions, which in turn shaped their literary ideas and expressions. They sought to resist the institutionalization of ideas and thinking, both through writing and through the reflection on physical spaces that hold written works. Moore and Larsen shared one ideal vision: that their writing would invite new perspectives, challenging our systems of knowledge, never resting easily wherever we might seek to place it.

The kind of thinking and writing about institutions that emerged from

---

43. The names she used at various points included: Nellie Larson (given name), Nella Imes (married name), Allen Semi (married name backwards), Nella Larsen, and Nella Larsen Imes.

44. Larsen's friend Carl Van Vechten, on the other hand, actively and eagerly catalogued his own work and collections. Larsen knew this because she saved clippings of reviews of his works for him to place inside scrapbooks in the 1920s (particularly about the publication of *Nigger Heaven* in 1926). Van Vechten's cataloguing of his collections of letters, documents, and books, which he eventually gave to the Beinecke Library and which he thought seriously about and wrote excitedly about in letters to Langston Hughes in the 1930s and 1940s, has raised questions at the Beinecke about whether to keep collections' classification systems intact when they are transferred to a library. Van Vechten created a system whereby he divided his collection into writings by African Americans, and writings by everyone else. As a result, in order to know where to look for something in his collection at the Beinecke, one must first know the race of the person with whom he corresponded.

their library experience is similar to but distinct from the anti-institutional poetics of male modernists. Because Moore and Larsen understood both the intellectual ideals and the practical operation of the library, they were in a unique position to discover firsthand how institutions classify knowledge — a view of institutions that male modernists did not have. This specific knowledge led them to recognize ways in which they wished to transform those spaces. Women writers understood that the organization of knowledge in libraries, as models of Enlightenment rationality, would never fully include them, but as products of socially and culturally conscious minds of the twentieth century, institutions could potentially be transformed by creating new systems through which to organize knowledge. To do this, Moore and Larsen sought to create a kind of art that challenged static thought, reimagined the bounds of intellectual quest, and undid traditional organizational systems of thought such as indexes and narrative closure. While their aesthetic rebellion was understood in only limited ways by fellow modernists, the complexity of their efforts continues to produce new readings and new possibilities for interpreting their thinking.

Chapter 9

The Library as Place, Collection, or Service

Promoting Book Circulation in Durham, North Carolina, and at the Book-of-the-Month Club, 1925–1945

JANICE RADWAY

ON JANUARY 1, 1929, Clara Crawford, the librarian of the Public Library in Durham, North Carolina, officially submitted her annual report to the board of trustees. Although she was expected to report only on the previous year's accomplishments and to state the library's future needs, Crawford used the five-year anniversary of her appointment to summarize the great strides the Durham library had made during her tenure. Indeed, Crawford claimed, "During this time the work has taken on new character and power both as to the extent of city and county territory covered by book distribution and the kind of service rendered to the community as a whole." She would justify her claim, she suggested, by elaborating the four objectives that had governed the Durham library's recent development and the measures that had been taken to realize them.[1] She noted accordingly that the library had pursued "(1) more and better books; (2) a larger and better qualified library personnel; (3) more intensive and specific extension of library facilities; [and] (4) lastly, the enlargement of library building accommodations to meet the demands of extended use."[2]

As a small municipal library in the American South, the Durham institution had developed considerably later than similar libraries in the Northeast and even in the Midwest. Nonetheless, its development history and the contemporary challenges it faced in serving its community were characteristic of small libraries across the country.[3] Indeed, like most of its peer institutions in

---

1. Clara Crawford, *Durham Public Library, Annual Report, 1929,* 1.
2. Ibid., 2.
3. For an extended discussion of the history of reading and print culture in relationship to a small municipal library in the Midwest, see Christine Pawley, *Reading on the Middle Border: The Culture of Print in Late Nineteenth-Century Osage, Iowa* (Amherst: University of Massachusetts Press, 2001).

the twenties, Durham sought to expand book circulation, to promote reading, and to improve the selection of books it was able to offer its patrons. Crawford reported, however, that she and her staff felt constrained in their task by the low level of financial support from the city and county governments. Accordingly, she detailed the creative measures that had to be taken in order to increase and better the library's holdings as well as to bring more Durham citizens into the building.

The report indicates that Crawford and her staff sought constantly to wean their adult clientele away from their preference for popular fiction and that they tried to alter both the patterns of use and the function the library performed in the lives of its patrons by increasing their holdings in quality fiction and nonfiction. At the same time, the Durham library staff placed new emphasis on serving children and eventually followed the national trend of creating a reading room dedicated to their special tastes and needs. Although Crawford and her staff also worked constantly to refine the way their building served library patrons by altering the use of space and by attempting to make the building an attractive and alluring destination, they also sought to dislodge the library's functions from the building that housed them in order to extend its services to rural residents, laborers at their place of work, and individuals recuperating in the hospital.

In effect, the staff labored constantly to resolve certain tensions in the very concept of the library.[4] They were troubled in practice over whether to emphasize the library as place, that is, its material presence as a building in a given locale, or its more functional existence as a set of services oriented toward the needs and interests of readers. They worried as well about how much to stress the library's depository function or its status as a device for the circulation of books. Finally, they struggled to balance their role as educators and champions of high culture with their desire to serve more patrons with quite different tastes and desires. There was a limit, however, to how far Clara Crawford and her assistants would go in serving what they took to be the Durham community. In fact, it is important to point out that Crawford's report elided a central social fact about the city of Durham. At the time, the city actually housed *two* libraries, one for its white inhabitants, the other for its "colored" citizens. Clara Crawford's report made no mention of the existence of the Durham Colored Library or of the particularities of its social location. Neither did it mention the somewhat different way in which the Durham Colored Library approached the questions of community service, book collection, or the practice of offering reading advice.

---

4. For a discussion of the multiple functions of the library, see Thomas Augst, "American Libraries and Agencies of Culture," *American Studies* 42 (2001): 5–22.

In the years between the two world wars, many municipal libraries wrestled with the problem of how to understand the very concept of the library itself as well as how to order their own institution, and they did so in a rapidly changing environment for print culture. The decade of the twenties, in particular, was characterized by the extension and consolidation of newspaper reading among the American population, by the further growth of mass-market, consumer-oriented magazines, and by the creation of a new middlebrow cultural formation produced by the wedding of a consumer-oriented sales operation to an evangelical interest in recommending better cultural materials to more individuals.[5] Foremost among such middlebrow initiatives was the Book-of-the-Month Club, which was organized in 1926, only two years after Clara Crawford assumed her position in Durham as the city's white Librarian.[6] Like Crawford, the Book-of-the-Month Club's founder, Harry Scherman, sought to expand book circulation and to raise the level of taste within the population. Significantly, however, Scherman did so to make a financial profit. A former advertising man who had an instinctive understanding of the mechanics and possibilities inherent in a system of mass production, distribution, and consumption, Scherman seemed to realize that to sell more books, he would need, in some sense, to de-materialize and de-localize the very act of book acquisition itself.

In a sense, both the Book-of-the-Month Club and the Durham Public Library were wrestling with the same problem, the problem of how to foster connections between books and readers. Durham's library tackled this problem the traditional way by physically drawing some portion of a preconstituted community to a particular book-reading space established within that community and by offering it both a particular collection of books and advice about how to make use of it. Scherman, on the other hand, set out to access a much more dispersed audience of book readers through the vast network of the U.S. postal system. Because he could not rely on geographic proximity to gather his readers, he had to find some other way to consolidate them as a group as well as the means to persuade them that he had something useful to offer. Scherman proposed to gather his readers as a set of subscribers to a

---

5. On the history of the newspaper, see Michael Schudson, *Discovering the News: A Social History of Newspapers* (New York: Basic Books, 1978); on the rise and development of the mass-market magazine, see Richard Ohmann, *Selling Culture: Magazines, Markets, and Class at the Turn of the Century* (London: Verso, 1996); on the formation of middlebrow culture, see Joan Shelley Rubin, *The Making of Middlebrow Culture* (Chapel Hill: University of North Carolina Press, 1992).

6. For a history of the Book-of-the-Month Club, see Janice Radway, *A Feeling for Books: The Book-of-the-Month Club, Literary Taste, and Middle-Class Desire* (Chapel Hill: University of North Carolina Press, 1997). The account of the club given here is a redaction of the arguments made in this earlier book.

regularized book distribution scheme in part because he believed strongly that the book publishing industry was failing at the business of book distribution. The reason, he suggested, was that they persisted in relying on the mediating institutions of the bookstore and the library.[7] The relatively small number of both, he argued, automatically capped sales and thereby limited reading. Scherman proposed to increase book sales by expanding the pool of potential readers. He would do so by addressing the population en masse through the use of national advertising and a brand-name marketing scheme. Scherman promised all who subscribed to his service that he would automatically send them a book a month. Though he called his operation a "club," thereby evoking the image of chummy local gatherings and community spaces, in fact, the library Scherman constituted was not a place but a carefully selected collection of books assembled to address widely dispersed readers gathered by certain shared desires and tastes.

As I have argued elsewhere, Scherman and the Book-of-the-Month Club were swiftly attacked for standardizing book reading as well as readers themselves.[8] Cultural critics feared that agencies like the club were relentlessly stamping out individual and geographic particularities and contributing to processes of massification. They worried, especially, that an organization like the Book-of-the-Month Club would spell the demise of the community library and the local bookstore. Though it can certainly be argued that the club and other middlebrow agencies did contribute to the creation of what would soon be called "the culture industry," a set of businesses that redundantly circulated selected texts through multiple media like print, radio, and film, it is also the case that bookstores survived, as did local libraries. Little has been done, in fact, to think about local library practices in tandem with schemes like the Book-of-the-Month Club. Indeed, it would be instructive to compare book practices at the club with those followed contemporaneously by a range of different libraries to see whether the club actually produced increased standardization of reading. Such a broad survey is beyond what can be attempted here.

---

7. It was common in the decade of the 1920s to find laments in the pages of *Publishers Weekly* about the inadequacies of contemporary book distribution. In 1930, in fact, the National Association of Book Publishers commissioned Orion B. Cheney to write the first formal report ever to be published on the book industry. They were prompted to do so by a significant drop in book sales brought on by the Depression. Cheney's report, *Economic Survey of the Book Industry, 1930–1931* (New York: Bowker Books, 1931), was issued the following year and, to the chagrin of many in the trade, indicted the industry for relying on the "I shot an arrow into the air theory of publishing," and for assuming that the book audience would always be small and select.

8. For a full account of the criticism of the club, see Janice Radway, "The Scandal of the Middlebrow: The Book-of-the-Month Club, Class Fracture, and Cultural Authority," *South Atlantic Quarterly* 89 (1990): 703–36. See also Radway, *A Feeling for Books,* chap. 7, 221–60.

I would, however, like briefly to review how the Book-of-the-Month Club addressed its subscribers and selected its books, precisely so as to compare such practices with those adopted in Durham at the white library as well as at its black counterpart. Such a comparison, it seems to me, will suggest, that the specificities of geography, locale, and community continued to matter significantly in Durham even though, apparently, the city's librarians attended to the new middlebrow authorities and even subscribed to the Book-of-the-Month Club. At the same time, both at the city white library and at the Durham Colored Library, librarians adopted book collection and recommendation practices that tended to address their patrons as the club did, that is, as individuals with specific interests and tastes. Though they continued to think of themselves as educators and evangelists in the cause of bringing high culture to the outpost of Durham, North Carolina, they also moved, as the club did — in the interest of circulating more books to more people — to acknowledge the existence of different reasons for reading. Attending to how this actually worked both in Durham and through the club will enable us to track the way a desire for augmenting book circulation contributed to increased interest in the diversity of readers and the variability of their reading purposes and tastes. This, in turn, should help us to think more clearly about the complexity of libraries as particular spaces, as collections of books, and as services oriented to the needs of multiple readers.

When Harry Scherman set out to sell new books by mail, he contested certain common assumptions of the publishing industry as well as the library profession about the nature of books and reading. At the same time, he challenged some of his culture's most cherished assumptions about the special, transcendent qualities of literature and art. In doing both together, he threw the weight of his organization behind the cause of the circulating book, that is, the desire to get more and different books to more and varied readers.[9] To do so, he found it necessary to create an evaluative practice that foregrounded readers and their multiple reasons for reading rather than authors or the properties of the texts they created. Although the club was initially famous for its reliance on an older Arnoldian language of the universal and the best, over time it acted to serve a range of readers with somewhat different reading tastes.

As Scherman formulated his plans in the early 1920s for what would become the Book-of-the-Month Club, trade book publishers argued that advertising was of limited value in increasing book sales. Since each book

9. On the development of "the book bound for circulation" and its difference from the self-consciously "literary" book, see Radway, *A Feeling for Books,* chap. 4, 127–53. Much of the account given here is drawn from this chapter.

was wholly distinct and individual, industry analysts reasoned, it was prohibitively expensive to advertise every book published. Additionally, since each unique book appealed to its own distinct and different audience, it was virtually impossible to identify that audience ahead of time or to advertise in all the venues it might peruse. All that could be hoped was that a publishing house's books might, on the basis of early reviews and recommendations, make their way to bookstores and libraries where they then might be offered to readers by knowing booksellers or librarians. In effect, the industry and the library profession foregrounded the singularity of the book as a distinct text and material object and viewed book audiences as unique collections of individuals assembled serially through the mechanism of face-to-face interaction and personal advice from groups gathered locally at the bookstore or library.

Scherman approached the whole problem differently. He believed many more people could be persuaded to become book readers if they were given better access to books as well as to the kind of advice that would explain not the particulars of a book's content but how it would address readers' interests, desires, or needs. To promote greater access, it would be necessary to eliminate the bottleneck effect created by the relatively small number of bookstores and libraries in the United States. Scherman proposed therefore to bypass both in the interest of augmenting book buying. He would gather potential readers together not materially but in mediated fashion through the use of nationally oriented advertising campaigns and a mail-order subscription scheme. Something like a subscription scheme would be necessary, Scherman reasoned, because, to make a profit from selling books, one needed to get them continuously and predictably to a stable number of individuals who could be counted on to make regular purchases. His subscription operation would require individuals to contract with his organization for a specified period of time in order to receive automatically one book each month. Those books would be sent out all over the country through the aegis of the American postal system. The subscription mechanism thus gathered an audience together in much the same way mass-market magazines did, that is, not literally, in space, but in dispersed and mediated fashion through the channel of communication opened up by the practice of regularized, serial distribution.

Scherman realized, however, that to persuade people to contract for his distribution service, he would need to substitute something for the social advice and personal recommendations that were thought to govern transactions in bookstores and libraries. In effect, since he intended to send out neither "steady sellers" nor classics but new books, he was asking potential subscribers to buy their books sight unseen. He proposed, therefore, to sell a promise along with his membership through the use of a carefully crafted advertising campaign. In mailings directed at known book readers (who were expected to influence others), and in advertisements placed in all the important book-review periodicals, he would promise potential subscribers that the "new" books they received each month would prove to have specific reading uses and a sure value in the future. Not only would they enable their buyers to keep up with what was most current in a rapidly changing and intensely "modern" culture; they would also enable those who purchased them to demonstrate their cultivation and acquaintance with the best that was being published at the moment. To underwrite that promise, he hired a group of well-known experts and asked them to select a title every month from the trade's projected offerings. That title would then be sent to his subscribers as "the best book" published that month.

In effect, Harry Scherman trademarked a set of disparate and discrete books by offering them publicly as the singular product of a distinguished committee (see figure 9.1). The particular form of renown enjoyed by the individuals selected for this committee, which he publicized continually in his advertising campaign, then conferred a specific identity on the books selected. Understandably, Scherman did not choose the vaudeville, stage, and movie stars usually associated with celebrity testimonials. Instead, he tapped well-known literary authorities including the well-respected and best-selling novelist Dorothy Canfield, and Henry Seidel Canby, the editor of the increasingly important *Saturday Review of Literature*. The other members of the first selection committee included Heywood Broun and Christopher Morley, two respected literary journalists, and William Allen White, the editor of the *Emporia Gazette*. Quickly dubbed "The Book-of-the-Month Club Judges," this group enabled Scherman to combine a modern advertising and commodity sales operation with a more traditional approach to the question of literary value and book recommendation and use. By featuring the judges individually in his ads with small cameo portraits, Scherman aped the kind of personal recommendations and advice he was effectively trying to render obsolete through his automatic distribution system. At the same time, the notion of "the best" evoked the critical principles of Matthew Arnold and an approach to books that privileged authors, the idea of originating genius, and the notion of transcendent, universally established excellence.

These nods to an older form of cultural circulation and an older aesthetic economy did not satisfy cultural commentators or literary critics. In fact, they claimed that Scherman's judges functioned only as a marketing device. They could not be objective or protective of supposedly universal standards of literary excellence, the club's critics charged, because they would be required to choose books that would make a profit. Serving reader taste, in their view,

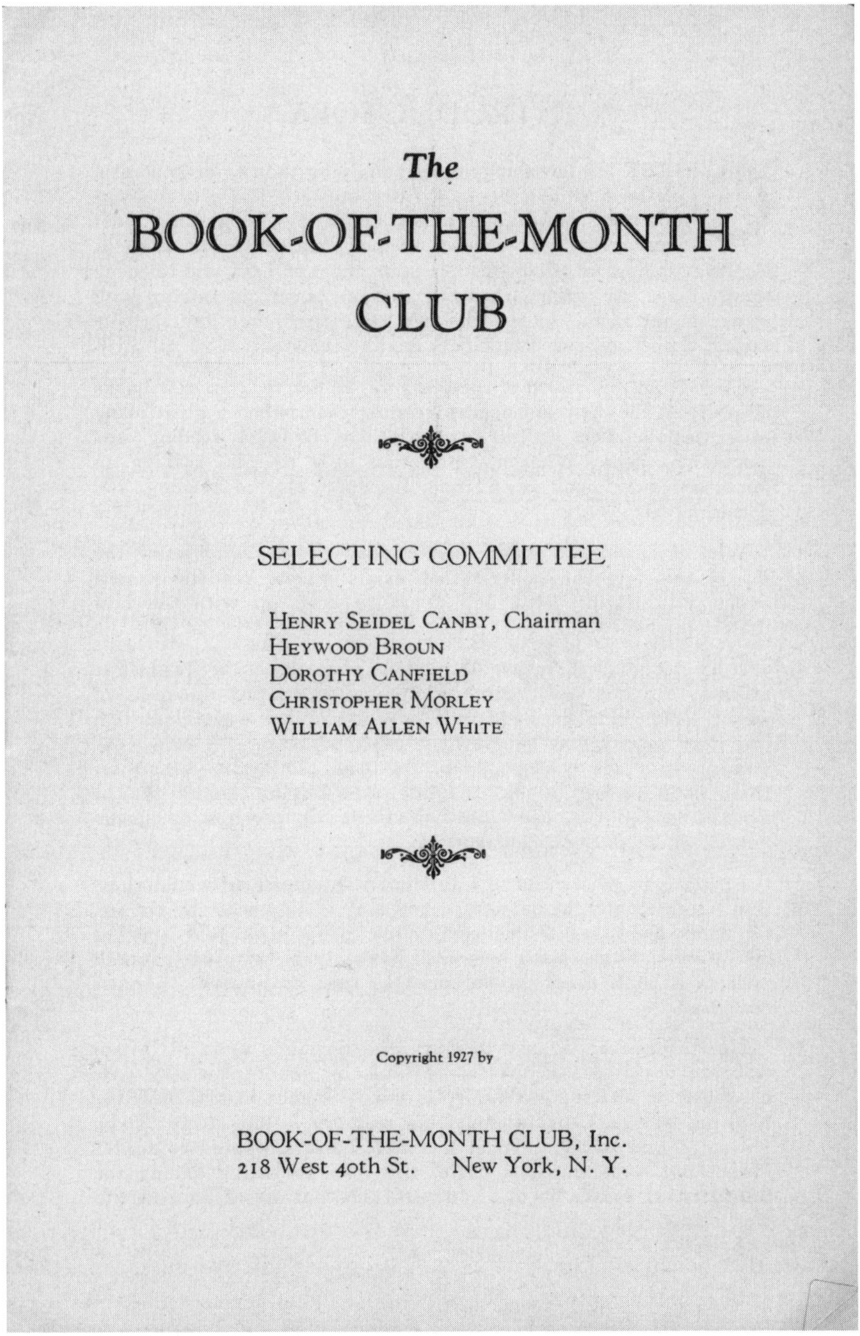

The

BOOK-OF-THE-MONTH CLUB

SELECTING COMMITTEE

HENRY SEIDEL CANBY, Chairman
HEYWOOD BROUN
DOROTHY CANFIELD
CHRISTOPHER MORLEY
WILLIAM ALLEN WHITE

Copyright 1927 by

BOOK-OF-THE-MONTH CLUB, Inc.
218 West 40th St. New York, N. Y.

Figure 9.1. Book-of-the-Month Club pamphlet announcing the original "judges."

would lead only to the distribution of mediocre books. To counter the criticism, Scherman insulated the judges from the business end of the operation and told them they should feel free to select the books they thought the best. This was not a risky decision, however, because Scherman had selected individuals who had already proved themselves interested in promoting reading and getting more books to more people. They pronounced themselves interested in the taste of "the general reader," a taste they defended by concomitantly declaring that most high literary fiction, literary modernism, in effect, was a "special taste," comprehensible to only a few well-educated, well-informed individuals. As a consequence, despite their repeated assertions of their allegiance to the idea of "the best," in practice, the judges actually elaborated a system of evaluation that privileged readers and their differing aims, intentions, and desires rather than the features or qualities of texts themselves. They emphasized how books could be *used* by their readers rather than how specific textual properties qualified a book for placement in the literary pantheon. The club positioned itself as a service to readers even as it masqueraded as a library of the best (see figure 9.2). As Henry Canby, the chairman of the panel, put it, "the best book is worth nothing at all if it never finds a reader." [10]

Because the goal of the larger Book-of-the Month Club operation was to see to it that the right books found their way to the right readers, the evaluative system the judges worked out in the early years of the club's operation sought to match reader desires and taste with books' differing potentials. The judges worked, first, to clarify for themselves *why* people read books rather than, say, listened to the increasingly ubiquitous radio or turned to newspapers and magazines for entertainment and information. Then, they tried to understand why people chose *particular* books to read. Finally, they tinkered with the best ways to describe books so that their relevant features would be made known to readers with preformed tastes, desires, and needs. The judges conceived their business less as a process of evaluation and judgment than as one of definition and sorting. Their job was to read all the books submitted by the trade, to imagine who might find such books interesting or useful, and then to evaluate how well particular books might satisfy the individuals most likely to select them. Since the publishers had been instructed by Scherman to send all different kinds of books, the judges quickly realized they could not compare apples to oranges or oranges to grapefruits. Not all books were "literary" books, and even "literary" books differed in form, function, and intent. As Henry Canby put it:

---

10. Henry Seidel Canby, *American Memoir* (Boston: Houghton Mifflin, 1947), 357.

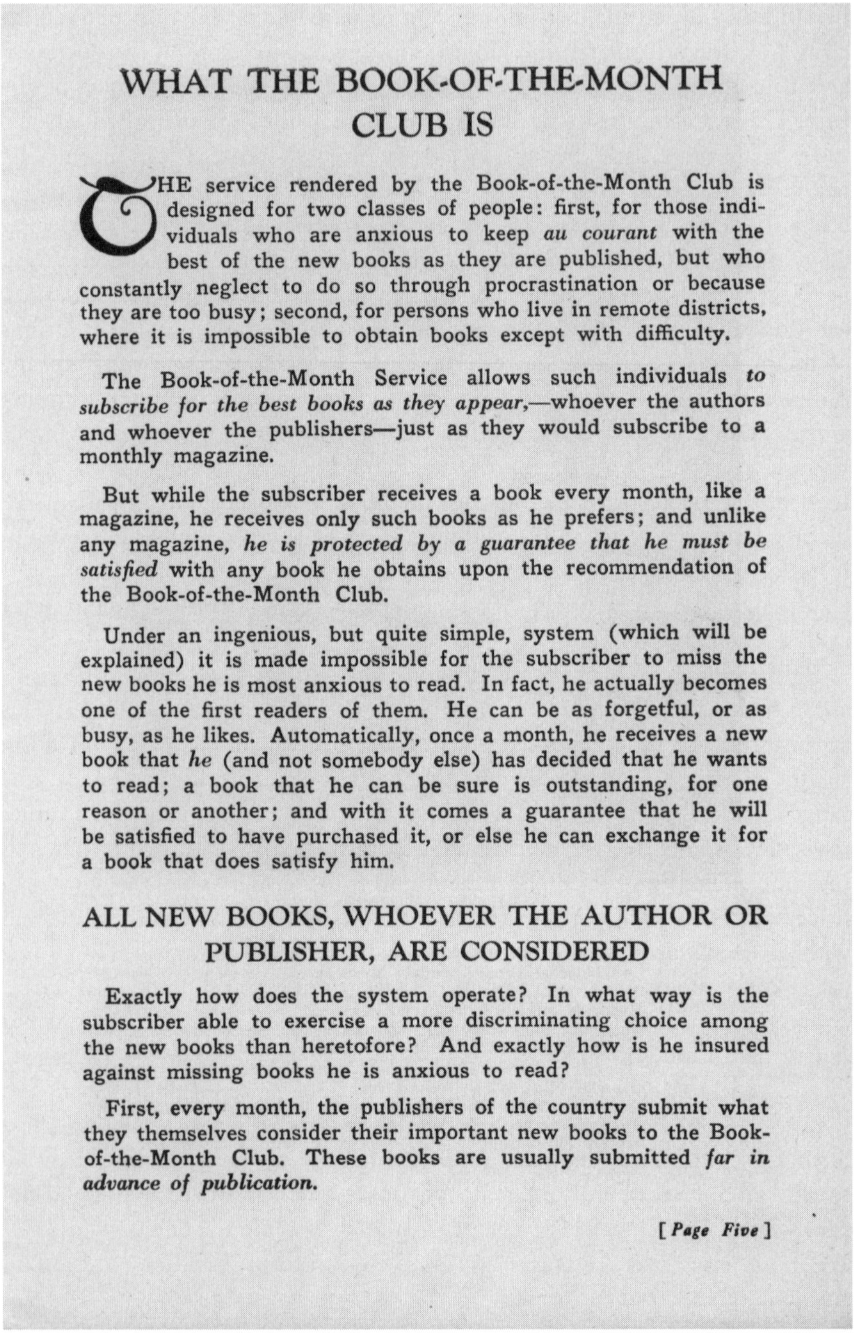

WHAT THE BOOK-OF-THE-MONTH
CLUB IS

THE service rendered by the Book-of-the-Month Club is designed for two classes of people: first, for those individuals who are anxious to keep *au courant* with the best of the new books as they are published, but who constantly neglect to do so through procrastination or because they are too busy; second, for persons who live in remote districts, where it is impossible to obtain books except with difficulty.

The Book-of-the-Month Service allows such individuals *to subscribe for the best books as they appear,*—whoever the authors and whoever the publishers—just as they would subscribe to a monthly magazine.

But while the subscriber receives a book every month, like a magazine, he receives only such books as he prefers; and unlike any magazine, *he is protected by a guarantee that he must be satisfied* with any book he obtains upon the recommendation of the Book-of-the-Month Club.

Under an ingenious, but quite simple, system (which will be explained) it is made impossible for the subscriber to miss the new books he is most anxious to read. In fact, he actually becomes one of the first readers of them. He can be as forgetful, or as busy, as he likes. Automatically, once a month, he receives a new book that *he* (and not somebody else) has decided that he wants to read; a book that he can be sure is outstanding, for one reason or another; and with it comes a guarantee that he will be satisfied to have purchased it, or else he can exchange it for a book that does satisfy him.

ALL NEW BOOKS, WHOEVER THE AUTHOR OR
PUBLISHER, ARE CONSIDERED

Exactly how does the system operate? In what way is the subscriber able to exercise a more discriminating choice among the new books than heretofore? And exactly how is he insured against missing books he is anxious to read?

First, every month, the publishers of the country submit what they themselves consider their important new books to the Book-of-the-Month Club. These books are usually submitted *far in advance of publication.*

Figure 9.2. The Book-of-the-Month Club's appeal for subscribers.

There is — to take the novel — the story well calculated to pass a pleasant hour but able to pass nothing else — there is the story with a good idea in it and worth reading for the idea only; there is the story worthless as art but usefully catching some current phase of experience; and there is the fine novel which will stand any test for insight, skill, and truth. . . . Now it is folly to apply a single standard to all these types of story. It can be done, naturally, but it accomplishes nothing except to eliminate all but the shining best.[11]

The project at the club, therefore, was to multiply gauges and evaluative standards. The judges sought to ask what every book was useful for, even lesser books with modest aims and intentions.

In effect, Henry Canby and his colleagues treated all books that came to them as instances of multiple, differentiated types, that is, as examples of different classes or genera, each with its own peculiar functions and uses. Is this serious fiction, they asked themselves, or hammock literature? Is this a sea saga or a small woman's novel? Is it popular or academic history? Is it literary criticism or literary biography? Only then did they ask, is it *good* literary biography? Does it fail as an entertaining yarn? Will it satisfy readers who will select this title because they desire a particular kind of reading experience?

The Book-of-the-Month Club judges focused on the diversity and variety of the literary field, on its ability to produce many different kinds of books with different features and aims. In spite of Harry Scherman's ritual repetition of the claim that the club sent out "the best book of the month," in practice the judges claimed that this sort of hierarchical grading was an impossible task. As a consequence, their work contested the structure of the literary field as it had developed in the years between 1870 and 1900.[12] During that time, the literary field was increasingly conceived as a homogenous space, shaped something like a pyramid, with the apex occupied by high literary fiction while everything else, including nonfiction, journalism, and popular fiction, was ranged below. In contradistinction to this, the judges categorically differentiated books from each other on the basis of their potential functions and potential appeal to readers. Some additional comments by Henry Canby are useful in giving a sense of how differently the judges envisioned the struc-

---

11. Henry Seidel Canby, *Definitions: Essays in Contemporary Criticism* (New York: Harcourt, 1922), 297.

12. For an account of the transformation of the literary field during this period, see Michael Warner, "Professionalism and the Rewards of Literature: 1875–1900," *Criticism* 75 (1985): 1–28. See also Gerald Graff, *Professing Literature: An Institutional History* (Chicago: University of Chicago Press, 1987); Richard Brodhead, *Cultures of Letters: Scenes of Reading and Writing in Nineteenth-Century America* (Chicago: University of Chicago Press, 1994); and Nancy Glazener, *Reading for Realism: The History of a U.S. Literary Institution, 1850–1910* (Durham: Duke University Press, 1997).

ture of the literary field. He wrote: "[It] is sometimes necessary to remind the austerer critic . . . that there are a hundred books, of poetry, of essays, of biography, of fiction, which are by no means of the first rank and yet are highly important, if only as news of what the world in our present, is thinking and feeling. They cannot be judged, all of them on the top plane of perfect excellence; and if we judge them on any other plane, good, better, best, get inextricably mixed." Canby, for one, was willing to judge books on other planes and thus to contest the very idea of good, better, and best judged upon one set of criteria. He continued: "There is no help except to set books upon their planes and assort them into their categories—which is merely to define them before beginning to criticize."[13]

The very concept of different planes constructs a view of the print or literary universe *not* as an organic, uniform, hierarchically ordered space but rather as a series of discontinuous, discrete, and noncongruent worlds. Each of these worlds, whether history, current affairs, travel writing, science, or nature writing, was peopled by its own inhabitants, ideally by expert writers and by the readers who turned to them for specific enlightenment, pleasure, and illumination. Where the role prescribed for the critic in the former literary world was that of Olympian, omniscient judge, the role occupied in the kind of world inhabited by the Book-of-the-Month Club judges was more that of an adviser or mediator, someone who could facilitate a connection between readers and the books (and authors) that would most satisfy them.

Given the fact that the Book-of-the-Month Club was remarkably successful at attracting and retaining subscribers—indeed, the club never lost money after its first year of operation, even during the Depression—it seems clear that its patrons were satisfied by the service it offered. It is worth asking, then, about the identity of its clientele. Although little data survives about the first members of the Book-of-the-Month Club, it is possible to determine that a majority of them were college graduates or had at least some college education. A fair number of them were professionals—doctors, lawyers, dentists, and teachers. Significantly, Harry Scherman once noted as well that a goodly number of secretaries and clerks also subscribed—in fact, the membership of the club in the early years was close to 60 percent women.[14] Given that figure, it seems likely that the wives of professionals were also well represented in

---

13. Canby, *Definitions,* 298.

14. The best discussion of the club's first subscribers is contained in a Columbia University Oral History Project interview with Edith Walker, who oversaw the process of acquiring new members. See "The Reminiscences of Edith Walker," 877–78, in Oral History Research Office, Butler Library, Columbia University, The Book-of-the-Month Club. Director, Allan Nevins; interviews by Lewis M. Starr, 1955.

the subscription roles. In any case, it seems clear that the club drew its clientele from a fast-developing class fraction in the United States in the interwar years as well as from those who wanted to be associated with that group. I am thinking here of the group we tend to call white-collar workers, that is, people who labored for a salary not with their hands but with their minds. Often referred to at the time as "brain workers," these individuals are now considered to be part of what is called the professional-managerial class.[15] They labored in many different fields, marshaling information, relying on their training as specialists in particular disciplines and arenas, coordinating social services, cultural production, educational work, and facilitating the bureaucratic and managerial work necessary to the smooth functioning of the increasingly complex and integrated American economy.

Although these individuals commanded a certain form of expertise in their own narrow fields and could read technical material on the job, their pleasure reading, apparently, was of a more general nature. At least the books sent out by the Book-of-the-Month Club would suggest so. The club aimed for the person they called "the general reader," the "average intelligent reader," in Harry Scherman's words, a nonspecialist who consulted books for information, who turned to them for advice and assistance as well as for pleasure. Kenneth Burke once suggested that people like these treated books as "equipment for living," that is, as volumes with practical utility and pragmatic applications even if the end they had in mind was only the provision of an interlude of pleasure.[16] To satisfy readers like these, the judges selected and sent out a range of books in many fictional genres, biography, current events, popular history and science, nature books, and travel writing. Although they sometimes recommended high literary fiction, once the club went to an alternate operation where the subscriber could substitute for the book-of-the-month, they tended to stick with what was called midlist fiction, that is, nonexperimental fiction that was at once readable and yet discernibly literary in its aspirations. The club also offered a wide selection of reference volumes and popular guides and handbooks.

---

15. On the rise of "brain workers" and their status as a new class, see Barbara Ehrenreich and John Ehrenreich, "The Professional-Managerial Class," in *Between Labor and Capital,* ed. Pat Walker (Boston: South End Press, 1979), 5–45. See also Richard Ohmann, *Selling Culture,* and his *Politics of Knowledge: The Commercialization of the University, the Professions, and Print Culture* (Middletown, CT: Wesleyan University Press, 2003).

16. Kenneth Burke, *The Philosophy of Literary Form: Studies in Symbolic Action,* rev. ed. (New York: Vintage Books, 1957), 253–62. For an extended discussion of how contemporary reading groups tend to use their reading as "equipment for living," see Elizabeth Long, *Book Clubs: Women and the Uses of Reading in Everyday Life* (Chicago: University of Chicago Press, 2003).

I have already alluded to the fact that the Book-of-the-Month Club was remarkably successful at attracting subscribers. It also made a significant splash in the public arena as booksellers, literary critics, and cultural authorities widely debated the significance of its intervention in the literary field. Indeed, the club was enormously controversial. As indicated before, many claimed that it would standardize cultural fare in the United States and stamp out literary diversity. When the judges selected a particular book title, it was often reported as news by national newspapers. Most of the titles offered by the club were reviewed in one or more of the major book-review organs of the time or discussed on popular radio shows like *Information, Please!* Harry Scherman was able to demonstrate after only a few months of operation that rather than depress bookstore sales, club selection actually boosted them and even tended to augment sales of an author's earlier publications. As librarians also discovered that their own patrons would come to the library requesting the current Book-of-the-Month Club selection, they learned quickly to watch the club's catalogue and to ensure that they had several copies on hand. Many actually became subscribers to the club for their libraries. It should also be noted that many Book-of-the-Month Club selections eventually made their way into film format because film producers saw them as hot commercial properties; they assumed that in acquiring them they were also acquiring a guaranteed audience.

It seems clear, then, that the Book-of-the-Month Club was at least a contributing factor to the emergence in the United States of what has been called "the culture industry," that is, a complex and differentiated apparatus for cultural production and distribution.[17] Although this apparatus was highly complex and internally competitive, it also tended to circulate redundantly, through many different forms and nodes, a relatively small body of cultural materials that reached many more Americans than had been possible previously. Although some saw this as a positive development and connected it to rising high school graduation rates and college attendance, others worried that middlebrow authorities like the club were destroying standards and ruining high literary culture as well as homogenizing literary taste and readers themselves by privileging only a few books, thereby excluding diverse materials from the marketplace.

In this context, it is worth remarking again that although the club presented itself as a mechanism for assembling a library of "the best new books," in fact, as a commercial enterprise and consumer-oriented service, it actu-

---

17. For the classic definition of the culture industry, see Max Horkheimer and Theodor Adorno, *The Dialectic of Enlightenment* (New York: Herder and Herder, 1972).

ally privileged readers and their interests more than it worried about literary quality. Indeed, it is significant, that within a year of its founding, the club moved away from its policy of automatically dispensing one book a month and allowed its subscribers to substitute for the selected title from a list of recommended books drawn from a range of genres. To inform subscribers about these books, the club created its own periodical, part review and part catalogue, designed to inform potential buyers about what they might expect from a given book. Though the short descriptions written by the judges and other club officials described certain textual features of the books themselves, they also took pains to sketch out the sort of reader who might find such a book useful or pleasurable. In the end, what the club aimed to do in order to generate its profit was to match books with the people who aimed to read them for particular purposes. I think it fair to say, then, that despite its name and its advertising efforts to evoke the image of a library of the best, the Book-of-the-Month Club was reader driven, in however mediated a form, precisely because Scherman and his partners aimed to make a financial profit from augmenting book circulation as much as possible.

Despite the opposition of the literary elite, more and more print-culture agencies in the interwar years also sought to augment cultural consumption. Indeed, they focused with energy on what might be called the audience problem, that is, the problem of how to access potential readers through outreach, extended distribution, and cultivation of audience interests and attention. This was as true within the library profession as it was in commercial publishing sectors. Although librarians had been troubled for years by conflicts over their appropriate goals, aims, and intentions, they, had, increasingly, begun to enlist more systematically in the cause of the circulating book. It is true that the years between 1870 and 1900 were characterized by the fiction debates, that is, by largely conservative arguments about the moral respectability of fiction and therefore about its proper place in the library.[18] Because a significant number of librarians thought of themselves as educators and as providers of cultural uplift, they labored hard to direct their patrons' attention both to the classics and to substantial works of nonfiction. Some even instituted restrictive circulation policies at their institutions that controlled the number of fictional titles patrons could check out. Despite this conservative tendency, however, this period was also characterized within the world of librarianship by a desire to promote book circulation of all kinds.

This trend had initially gathered steam in 1876 when Melvil Dewey

---

18. On the subject of the fiction debates in libraries, see Dee Garrison, *Apostles of Culture: The Public Librarian and American Society, 1876–1920* (New York: Free Press, 1979).

introduced his new decimal-based scheme for book classification and cataloguing at the first organizational meeting of the American Library Association (ALA) during the centennial exposition in Philadelphia.[19] Before Dewey
introduced his system, in small libraries books had generally been shelved on
the basis of their date of acquisition. Although various finding aids were used
to direct readers to relevant books, this shelving mechanism separated books
of like subject matter from each other and thus made browsing impossible.
Dewey's decimal scheme, which divided printed knowledge into ten areas that
could be infinitely divided into subclasses through the use of Arabic numerals, both grouped like books together and provided for the infinite expansion
of every category.[20] In effect, Dewey's scheme assumed that books were in
dialogue with each other, that knowledge production was ever progressing,
and that readers were individuals with previously established topical interests
and reading desires who needed easy access to books. Thus his scheme made
the practice of browsing in the book stacks potentially worthwhile. Still, it
would take some time before the majority of libraries fostered this kind of
social circulation in the cause of circulating more books.

By 1879, when the ALA adopted a motto also drafted by Dewey — "The
best reading for the greatest number at the least cost" — the profession officially had committed itself to the potentially conflicting ideals of cultural
uplift and cultural outreach at the same time.[21] Even when librarians agreed
that they had a duty to make books available to a larger and more diverse
audience, they could not agree among themselves about what constituted
"the best reading" or who should determine its character. Although ALA
members debated among themselves about what experts should be consulted,
few thought patrons themselves should be left to pursue their own tastes or
interests. The fiction debates raged within the ALA for years because librarians worried that they were bringing patrons into their libraries who wanted
only to read the most melodramatic and salacious fiction. They hoped that
restrictive fiction circulation policies would prompt library-goers to turn to
more serious reading material. At the turn of the century, though, even as
the ALA recommended that only 15 percent of a library's collection should

---

19. On Melvil Dewey, see Wayne Wiegand, *Irrepressible Reformer: A Biography of Melvil Dewey*
(Chicago: American Library Association, 1996).

20. On Dewey's decimal system and its relationship to the rise of specialization in knowledge
production in the United States, see John Higham, "The Matrix of Specialization," in Alexandra
Oleson and John Voss, *The Organization of Knowledge in Modern America, 1860–1920* (Baltimore:
Johns Hopkins University Press, 1979), 3–18.

21. Melvil Dewey, "Origin of A.L.A. Motto," *Public Libraries* 11 (1906): 55; cited in Wayne
Wiegand, "The American Public Library: Construction of a Community Reading Institution,
1876–1924," in *A History of the Book in America,* vol. 4, ed. Carl Kaestle and Janice Radway (Chapel
Hill: University of North Carolina Press, forthcoming).

be devoted to fiction, most public libraries found that "fiction — especially popular fiction — averaged 75 percent of circulation."[22] Library patrons apparently had their own ideas about what libraries were useful for and their own opinions about what books were pleasurable to read.

By the time Andrew Carnegie became interested in library development and commenced funding public libraries, the focus on fostering book circulation had increased substantially. Between 1890 and his death in 1919, Carnegie gave $41,000,000 to construct 1,679 public library buildings in 1,412 communities in the United States.[23] At the heart of virtually every one of those buildings was the circulation desk, the central node from which the librarian could monitor the stacks and the reading room, supervise both library workers and patrons, and assist the public in its quest for information and books to read. Carnegie library plans were highly standardized, in fact, and they tended to be quite different from earlier library layouts, which had featured lots of nooks and crannies, private trustees' meeting rooms, and closed stacks. As Abigail Van Slyck has noted, earlier plans tended to articulate the message that "mere mortals were not welcome in every part of the library," which was often understood as "the holy of Holies."[24]

Andrew Carnegie's ideas about appropriate library plans reflect the development of what one librarian called "the modern library idea," that is, the notion of a library devoted to public service and characterized by "public support, open shelves, work with children, cooperation with schools, branch libraries, traveling libraries and library advertising."[25] In keeping with this view, Carnegie libraries tended to be open, well-lit spaces that featured rooms devoted to public service. The central placement of the circulation desk emphasized the librarian's authority and enabled her to exert control over everything going on around her. The desk thus foregrounded the librarian's professional status even as it installed the public and the activity of book circulation at the very heart of the library.

Oddly enough, despite the fact that the physical layout of libraries and the profession as a whole tended to emphasize circulation and interaction with the public, neither did much to foster an extended interaction between the professional librarian and the various readers who came for advice. Where other professions placed great emphasis on the professional/client interaction and called for office spaces with private rooms for leisurely consultation and treatment, librarians and the architects who served them tended to cluster

---

22. Wiegand, "The American Public Library."

23. Ibid.

24. Abigail A. Van Slyck, *Free to All: Carnegie Libraries and American Culture, 1890–1920* (Chicago: University of Chicago Press, 1995), 18.

25. Ibid., 25.

professional spaces downstairs and in out-of-the-way spaces. In doing so, they required readers to ask for assistance, a potentially embarrassing act, in public, in the open, in the middle of the busiest part of the library. Despite the growing emphasis on the circulation of books and the serving of readers, some libraries and librarians found it difficult to rein in their own forbidding authority as people who knew better. In effect, then, they remained ambivalent about whether the library was a depository and a pedagogical institution or a distribution mechanism and a sophisticated form of consumer advice.[26]

In fact, it was not until the mid-1920s that the ALA even commissioned its first study of circulation activities in the library. It did so as part of a larger curriculum study that was designed to review library school curricula and to write appropriate texts to be used within them. The first volume in the series was published in 1927 by Jennie M. Flexner, Head of the Circulation Department in the Louisville Public Library. Her study, *Circulation Work in Public Libraries,* was clearly designed to give circulation work a more prominent place within the profession by construing it as a complex task requiring special expertise, a particular personality type, and a calling to serve the public.[27]

It is evident that Flexner was attempting to counter a view of circulation work as being little more than routine bureaucratic labor. Although she acknowledged the importance of charging books efficiently, keeping track of their borrowers, and managing to induce those borrowers to return books when they were needed, she also tried to foreground the more subtle aspects of the librarian/reader interaction. In characterizing the sort of person who would make a good circulation assistant, she noted that "[he] will need to be a thoughtful student of practical psychology." She continued:

> He should learn to treat each reader as an individual whose request is an important matter. He will cultivate in the reader's mind the thought that personal service from the library to the borrower is the end and aim of the institution and its staff. He must likewise gain a fine skill in breaking through that reticence which is frequently found in the reader when he comes to the library desk. The borrower, as he appears here, is frequently singularly lacking in self-confidence. He may feel that behind the desk is a person who knows the books and the rules to which he must conform in drawing them, and he may hesitate to display ignorance by asking questions.[28]

---

26. This was initially pointed out to me by Wayne Wiegand in conversation. For a full elaboration of his argument, see Wiegand, "The American Public Library."

27. Jennie M. Flexner, *Circulation Work in Public Libraries* (Chicago: American Library Association, 1927).

28. Ibid., 5.

It is not hard to understand why library patrons might have felt fearful even when the profession was trying to convince its public that the library was an attractive, appealing, and welcoming place. What with strict enforcement of the rule against talking, closed stacks in some libraries, the profession's continuing embarrassment about fiction and popular literature, and its stern promotion of the classics and serious reading, it is no surprise that some people continued to feel inferior and ill informed in the library. Indeed, one can easily conjure the image of someone seeking information about automobile repair, say, or a good novel to read as a distraction from economic worries, who might have hesitated to ask for advice with a long line of people waiting to check out books. Flexner stressed again and again throughout her book that, to counter such fears, circulation librarians and their assistants ought to respect every patron's desires and tastes and treat every request in a forthcoming way. Still, she observed repeatedly that it was also the duty of the librarian to steer the patron to better books whenever possible.

Jennie Flexner's volume did not address the question of how librarians were to determine what constituted the better books. She did not need to since this was a major component of library education at the time. Library students spent long hours learning how to draw on the expertise of other professionals in specialized fields in order to identify and select appropriate books for their collections. Like the judges at the Book-of-the-Month Club, librarians increasingly envisioned the world as one comprised of special domains presided over by knowing experts who could be relied on to serve the general populace. Wayne Wiegand, a prominent historian of the library profession, has suggested, however, that librarians' respect for the authority of experts was so great that they tended to discount their own knowledge of readers' tastes. As a consequence, they deferred to the judgment of others. When they surveyed specialized journals in many different fields and scanned their reviews for advice about the best books to buy, what they often found were recommendations designed to serve professionals in the field. Consequently, the books given high praise were often too dense, too narrowly focused, or two difficult for the general reader. Librarians thus had to be taught to look as well to the country's new middlebrow authorities.[29]

In a well-known text, *Living with Books: The Art of Book Selection,* written for Columbia University's Studies in Library Service, Helen Haines recommended that after turning first to the ALA's *Catalog* series, to *Booklist, Book Review Digest,* and *Bookman's Manual,* librarians ought to develop the habit

---

29. See Wiegand, "The American Public Library."

of scrutinizing major review periodicals.[30] Most of them had been created in the teens and the twenties to promote book reading and to serve the new, college-educated professional audience. Among the most prominent were the *New York Herald Tribune's* book review section and the *Saturday Review of Literature,* whose editor was none other than Henry Seidel Canby.[31] Amy Loveman, Canby's assistant at the *Review,* assisted him in deciding which books should go to the Book-of-the-Month Club judges for consideration as the best book of the month. The two organizations, in fact, were tightly entwined. In relying on Canby's judgment and that of his colleagues, librarians tended to accept the middlebrow understanding of the serious general reader and to buy those books that Canby and company suggested would satisfy the intelligent generalist. Although Haines cautioned librarians that they must also learn to evaluate the reviewers, she noted that "in spite of contradictions and stultifications in judgment, there emerge from the mass of current criticism a certain consensus of opinion concerning the literature of the day, and a certain indication of its trends, tendencies, and qualities, that must be known and heeded in book selection and supply."[32] She admitted further that though "personal tastes and personal opinion must always infuse individual criticism, even of the highest caliber . . . the standards supported by such editors and reviewers as Dr. Canby, the van Dorens, Llewellyn Jones . . . and many others, are establishing a current criticism that honestly seeks to denote the qualities and defects of current literature and is helping to improve literary expression in form and to clarify and strengthen its ideals."[33]

Haines's book was published in 1935. Canby had been editor of the *Saturday Review* since its founding in 1924. Obviously, the fame he enjoyed just eleven years later was sufficient for Haines to feel it unnecessary to provide his first name or to identity him further. Although one might think this a function of her position and the fact that she was writing for a professional audience, it is worth pointing out that in her 1931 Annual Report of the Durham Public Library, Clara Crawford also approvingly quoted "Dr. Canby."[34] She assumed that the library's trustees and the town and county officials for whom the report was written would recognize Canby's name and the authority of his critical pronouncements. It seems possible to suggest, then, that

---

30. Helen E. Haines, *Living with Books: The Art of Book Selection* (New York: Columbia University Press, 1935).

31. On the creation of *Books,* the review section of the *New York Herald Tribune,* see Rubin, *The Making of Middlebrow Culture,* 34–92.

32. Haines, *Book Selection,* 94.

33. Ibid., 97.

34. Clara Crawford, *Durham Public Library, Annual Report, 1931,* 3.

the middlebrow culture then being promoted by the *Saturday Review* and the Book-of-the-Month Club, as well as by more and more libraries around the country, had made inroads in Durham, North Carolina, too. In fact, in 1937, one of the ten women's reading clubs operating in Durham was actually named The Book-of-the-Month, testifying perhaps to adoption among some, at least, of the imperative to read regularly and thereby to keep up with the pace of modern life.[35]

It is impossible to draw a detailed portrait of the day-to-day struggles of Durham's librarians or their relationships with their patrons, since few of the library's internal records survive, including those tracking either acquisition or circulation. Consequently, it is equally difficult to provide an account of how much of the Durham library's collection was affected by middlebrow cultural agencies like the Book-of-the-Month Club. Still, the few records that do remain, plus annual reports from the teens through the forties, indicate that Durham's library emerged and developed out of the very struggles that had troubled the larger profession. Accordingly, the records tend to suggest as well that just as the library profession and other print-culture agencies sought deliberately to increase book circulation and reading in the twenties and thirties, so, too, did Durham. As Durham's librarians did so, they placed increasing emphasis on their institution's service to its readers. Indeed, it is quite clear that, like Jennie Flexner and Helen Haines, Durham librarian Clara Crawford thought seriously and systematically about how best to address readers' tastes. Still, even as she did so, she continued to worry about her responsibilities as a cultural pedagogue. To the trustees, as a consequence, she reported assiduously each year about how successful she had been at steering her increasing numbers of patrons to better books. The imperative to increase circulation, it would seem, proved something of a challenge to older ideas about the library as an edifying collection. To address the specificities of local taste, libraries like Durham found it necessary to adapt to the preferences and demands of potential patrons. In some cases, this necessitated a deviation from the library's mission of cultural uplift and an exploration of other possible ways to serve the community. In comparing how Durham's white and black libraries approached this challenge, we should be able to see how geographical and social specificities continued to matter even at a moment when a nationally oriented middlebrow culture was being consolidated and distributed through an increasingly integrated culture industry.

Conceived by civic-minded women of the local elite in 1895, the Durham

---

35. The Library Committee of the Literary Clubs, minutes, 19 February 1937, in clipping scrapbook, Durham Public Library.

library was organized, supported, and initially funded by prominent citizens including Julian S. Carr, the founder of Blackwell's Durham Tobacco Company, the Durham Cotton Manufacturing Company, and the First National Bank; Dr. Edwin C. Mims, an English professor at Trinity College, soon to be renamed Duke University, and a member of the Canterbury Club; and George C. Watts, a prominent physician.[36] Together with their wives, these men raised subscription funds to establish the library, petitioned the state legislature for a charter, and donated the land for the library's first building. Despite the prominent role played by this Durham elite, however, most of the founding donations supporting the library were small (less than $100) and came from local organizations like the Durham Graded School, the Durham Music Company, and the Durham Band. This testifies, it would seem, to a broad range of support for the creation of this new civic institution.[37] Although the charter was granted by the state in 1897 and the building opened in 1898, it was not until 1911 that Durham hired its first professional librarian, Mrs. A. F. Griggs, who set about reorganizing the Durham library according to what was then called "the modern library idea." She expanded the library's book stock, attempted to reach the area's rural residents through the acquisition of a bookmobile (at the time, one of only six in the United States) and pushed the city to seek funds from Andrew Carnegie for a modern building.[38] Under her direction, the campaign successfully garnered a Carnegie donation of $32,000; and, in 1921, after pledging to fulfill the endowment's requirement of ongoing municipal support, Durham dedicated its new library building. The colonial revival edifice was erected according to a standard Carnegie plan featuring the centralized circulation desk, public stacks, a reading room, and downstairs space devoted to offices but earmarked for future expansion.

Despite the fact that Griggs promoted the modern library idea of increasing book circulation and providing better service to readers, it is well worth pointing out that the Durham library appears to have been founded as a way to leaven the image of Durham as a rough manufacturing town in the rising New South. In his master's thesis on the history of the Durham library, Walter Martin High reports that in 1888, Durham was significantly snubbed when the Baptist Female University would not locate there in spite of the fact

---

36. For details about the library's founding, see Walter Martin High III, "A History of the Durham Public Library, 1895–1940" (masters in library science thesis, University of North Carolina at Chapel Hill, 1976). See also "The Durham County Library and Its Community," Prepared by the Staff of the Durham County Library, February, 1977–June, 1979, in Miscellaneous File, "History," Durham County Library.

37. High, "History," 8.

38. Ibid., 39.

that Durham had offered twice the amount of financial support proffered by any other town. Apparently, the Baptist commission "felt that Durham was a culturally unfit place in which to 'risk the lives' of young females during their formative years."[39] Creating a library, Durham's prominent citizens argued, would testify to the city's cultural as well as economic leadership and would prove to potential developers that it was something more than a dirty industrial city with sordid ideals. Surviving records do not enable one to say with any specificity how the library pursued the goal of demonstrating Durham's cultural refinement on a daily basis. Still, it does seem clear that in its early years the library thought of itself primarily as an educational institution. Indeed, High notes that contemporary accounts reported constant use of the library by high school students and city and county teachers. At the same time, apparently, five women's literary clubs prepared their programs using library materials and donated their purchases to the library at the end of the year. Similarly, in an article titled "Rural Library Extensions," for the *North Carolina Library Bulletin,* Lillian Griggs chronicled her efforts to get books to farmers, who, she believed, "had far greater appreciation of good literature than did city residents."[40] This is sketchy evidence, of course, but it does tend to suggest that Griggs and her assistants continued to think of their job at least in part as raising the level of taste in Durham by promoting the best that had been thought and said.

When Lillian Griggs left the Durham library in 1923 to become secretary and director of the North Carolina Library Commission, Clara Crawford succeeded her. Professionally trained like Griggs, Crawford was especially interested in the promotion of reading among children. At the same time, she sought continually to improve the services the library offered to its adult patrons and tried to persuade the trustees to hire additional librarians to do the job professionally. She encountered considerable opposition along the way. In 1928, for instance, one trustee argued for the dismissal of the children's librarian, suggesting that a library should be a collection of permanent books rather than have many librarians.[41] Similarly, in 1931, at the moment when the library's appropriations were halved by the County Commission as a result of the Great Depression, several county commissioners sought to eliminate the bookmobile entirely because they felt residents should come to the library if they wanted books. Others, apparently, justified the reduction

---

39. Ibid., 17.

40. Lillian Griggs, "Rural Library Extensions," *North Carolina Library Bulletin* 2 (1915): 96, quoted in High, "History," 28.

41. Board of Trustees, Durham Public Library, "Minutes," 15 October 1928. "Miscellaneous" File, Durham Public Library.

in spending by suggesting to the local newspaper that "Books, we got enough books, and what does anybody want with any more? Those than can afford em, buy 'em. Those as can't ain't got any business with 'e." [42] Durham's citizens, it would seem, agreed neither about the usefulness of a library nor about the character of the patrons it should serve.

Clara Crawford's annual reports from the twenties and thirties indicate that she sought to justify the library's request for county and city funds by pointing constantly to the educational role the library played in the community and to its successes in elevating the taste of Durham's citizens. She was especially keen to dispel the notion that library going was frivolous or bound up only with the pursuit of pleasure. Indeed, in 1931, she expatiated at length about the book "as a machine to think with," and attempted to inform the trustees about how professional librarians make decisions about what books should be acquired. Observing that the librarian must not limit herself to stocking "the most sensational titles" reviewed in the Sunday supplements, Crawford suggested, "she must watch her stock of standard classics which are in constant demand by high school and college students, she must follow the output of the publishers and try to acquire those volumes which she believes of permanent value to mankind and those which she anticipates her public will need or enjoy at some future time." [43] It was in this context that she approvingly quoted Dr. Canby and his views about "the really important new books of 1931." Suggesting that a librarian needed to have sufficient funds at her disposal to acquire "the less heralded and more serious new books," she reported to the trustees that Canby believed those books had been written by psychologists, economists, philosophers, historians, and biographers. Crawford suggested further that such books were read by "serious readers" and that *their* interests, especially, needed to be addressed by the library's future acquisitions. Her comments suggest that, like the Book-of-the-Month Club, she believed that the library should serve serious general readers first and attempt to steer them to the best books published each year, if not each month.

Still, it is important to note that Crawford conceded in her report that 77 percent of the Durham library's patrons actually read fiction. [44] Although her comments reveal a certain nervousness about this fact, in elaborating upon it she demonstrated significant sensitivity to the character of her patrons and to the complexity of their reasons for choosing the books they did. Crawford thus repeated the same older aesthetic and pedagogical views used to market

42. High, "History," 58.
43. Clara Crawford, *Durham Public Library, Annual Report, 1931*, 3.
44. Ibid.

the Book-of-the-Month Club yet, like the club, she also moved carefully to respect and attend to the tastes and needs of those who actually came to her for advice. Indeed, she assured the trustees that the group of fiction readers "includes every type of citizen from the University professor who has spent his day teaching and thinking upon the economic problems of the world and now wishes to forget them in an engrossing mystery story . . . ; to the tired workman who has fed some piece of material into a machine, and another just like, and another and another until the whistle released him from his monotonous task, and now he too wishes to forget them all in the thrilling silence of the jungle punctuated only by the cries of wild beasts as they come to the ears of a man–no, a superman–who must strangle them with his bare hands to save himself." Here Crawford attempted to dispel the idea that fiction reading was purposeless and even an immoral activity indulged in only by the uneducated. Fiction reading, too, she suggested, is a worthwhile, even necessary, instrumental activity. She continued:

> Such books have their place upon the shelves of a tax supported library whose aim is to meet the reading needs, as far as it is financially able, of every man, woman, and child in that community. In this time of depression, recreational reading plays a vital part in maintaining the morale of the community. Never so often as in recent months has the staff been asked repeatedly, 'to recommend a book so interesting that I will forget everything else.' To the librarian this oft repeated request is not monotonous because every single reader means by that 'so interesting' something entirely different from what his fellow meant, and the adviser finds it an exciting psychological game to fit to each reader the exact kind of books he wants.[45]

Despite her defense of recreational reading, however, it is clear from Crawford's comments elsewhere that she and her colleagues continued to be somewhat ambivalent about the importance of fiction at the Durham Public Library. In 1935, for example, she reported to the trustees that she believed it was peculiarly the obligation of Durham's library, surrounded as it was, by "great university libraries," "to concern ourselves in attracting whenever and however possible the nonreader, also in serving and stimulating many men, women, and young people who have not yet come to any sort of 'purposeful reading' but are still completely satisfied with 'recreational reading of a far from meritorious character.' "[46] Evidently, despite the pressures of the Depression, she still felt that there was greater worth in nonfiction, more

---

45. Ibid., 4.
46. Clara Crawford, *Durham Public Library, Annual Report, 1935*, 4.

serious books, and purposeful reading. As late as 1940, when much of the stigma attached to fiction had faded in the national context, Crawford still foregrounded the library's success in increasing its circulation of nonfiction books. She noted that in 1920, of the 33,000 books circulated, 95 percent was fiction. By 1930, she added proudly, circulation had climbed to 184,000 volumes, only 74 percent of which was fiction.[47] Even with the increase, it seems pretty clear that in the interwar years most Durham library patrons used the library to facilitate recreational reading and that most of the recreational reading they selected was fiction.

These statistics may reflect the fact that fully half of the Durham library's patrons were children. In 1932, for example, 35 percent of the patrons used the Children's Room and another 14 percent were young people under the age of 21. Thus, only 51 percent of Durham's library patrons were mature adults. Of those, 36 percent were men and women who worked with their hands, 28 percent earned their livelihood by their brains, and another 36 percent were women who gave "homemaker" as their occupation.[48] In her 1932 report, Crawford noted that it was extremely difficult to determine who read what, but she nonetheless recounted the results of a small study she made of the circulation records for 60 nonfiction volumes. She discovered that of the 424 persons who had checked out these books, 14 percent were readers under 20, 5 percent were men and women who worked with their hands, 53 percent earned a livelihood with their brains, and 28 percent were homemakers. Crawford concluded that "the brain worker, although numerically smaller than the other adult groups, is more interested in adding to his or her educational qualifications through reading."[49] Although the statistics are very spotty and merely suggestive, this does tend to imply that while middlebrow culture, with its many biographies, outlines, and omnibuses, may have made its way into Durham, its consumption and use may well have been concentrated in only a small segment of the population. This seems even clearer when you recognize that in 1935 the library's 12,000 active borrowers (who checked out an average of 14 volumes each) represented only 27 percent of the white population.

Still, Crawford and her assistants constantly sought to expand the book-reading population in Durham and to serve the tastes of those who did not share in the valorization of the serious and the educational. Although they worked to make books available to the laboring classes by establishing out-

47. Clara Crawford, *Durham Public Library, Annual Report, 1940,* 6.
48. Clara Crawford, *Durham Public Library, Annual Report, 1932,* 6.
49. Ibid.

posts in mills and manufacturing plants, their principal form of outreach was to the county's rural population. Indeed, it was the rural character of the population and the somewhat primitive nature of the state's educational system that most troubled those involved in early state library efforts. In the June 1928 issue of the *North Carolina Library Bulletin,* for example, Edgar W. Knight observed: "We are among the poorest if not the poorest book market in the United States, and in public libraries we rank near or at the bottom of the list. This condition is the result of the state's failure to provide schools for the instruction of its children. At no period in its history has North Carolina had an adequate education system." He continued: "Reading is habit and is established just as other habits—such as smoking, bathing, or bacon for breakfast. It satisfies. North Carolinians learn to smoke before they learn to read. The tradition of tobacco is stronger than the tradition of reading." [50]

Only a few years later, in 1932, the state Library Commission noted that fully 62 percent of the state's population lived on farms or in small towns where there was no library service at all—despite the fact that many of the larger city libraries had, like Durham, instituted bookmobile service during the twenties. Although Durham's bookmobile was stocked with a wide variety of books, the city librarians apparently recognized that their rural clientele wanted not only fiction but fiction of a decidedly different kind than the sort they would have preferred to put in the hands of their readers. In an article from the *Raleigh News and Observer,* which ran on an August Sunday morning in 1925, Miss Petty, the bookmobile librarian, observed of a recent trip: "We always tried to pick a shady spot for our truck, and in Ramseur we were fortunate enough to secure a resting place by the village well. They had phoned ahead from Franklinville that we were coming, and a good crowd gathered. I sat on the brick curb and dispensed Billy Sunday, Zane Grey, stories of operas, and 'Peter and Polly' to boys with lint on their clothes from the cotton mills. Busy mothers with five or six children to select for, men from the bank and nearby stores, and a few people just passing through stopped to see what the excitement was about, and remained to borrow a few books." [51] She noted further that, in many cases, Zane Grey was the only author's name the farmers recognized. Their wives seemed to prefer love stories "of the Southworth-Holmes" variety and looked for books by Gene Stratton-Porter and Grace Richmond. Rural readers seemed to prefer much more popular

---

50. Edgar W. Knight, "North Carolina and Libraries," *North Carolina Library Bulletin* 7 (1928): 65–66.

51. "Miss Kiwanis Roams Country Roads," *Raleigh News and Observer,* 7 August 1925, Clipping Scrapbook, Durham Public Library.

literature than the middlebrow fare that was making its way into the homes of Durham's more urban middle class. And that popular literature was not necessarily up-to-date. Durham's most rural, least educated readers, it would seem, did not wish to use the library to appear either cultivated or modern; rather, given easier access to books, they sought relief from lives of hard, nearly constant labor in the easy-to-read stories of the mass-market press. And Durham's librarians apparently were willing to override the valorized tastes of their profession in order to serve the needs of those readers in all their geographic and social specificity.

What they were not willing to override, however, were their region's strictures against the mixing of the races. At no time in the period under investigation here did the white city library ever serve Durham's African American inhabitants; this despite the fact that, according to Booker T. Washington, Durham had "the sanest attitude of white people toward the black" that he had ever seen in the South.[52] Indeed, segregation was such an integral part of life in the South at this time that Durham's dominant business infrastructure was profoundly racialized, as were its middle-class cultural institutions. Because these businesses and institutions involved and would serve only whites, they were duplicated by parallel organizations designed to serve the region's black population. At the time, Durham was noted for the prosperity and success of its black middle class, a fact that prompted W. E. B. Du Bois to call the city the "Negro business mecca of the South."[53] This was due in part to the activities of a small group of professional men who had been raised by free landowning blacks. Doctors, lawyers, and businessmen, they were instrumental in the founding of the North Carolina Mutual and Provident Association, one of the first black insurance companies in the country, as well as a range of other Negro businesses.[54]

It was, in fact, Dr. Aaron McDuffie Moore, a Shaw University graduate, Durham's first black physician, and one of the three founders of the North Carolina Mutual and Provident Association, who first conceived of a library for Durham's black citizens "where children could come and

52. Booker T. Washington, "Durham, North Carolina: A City of Negro Enterprise," *Independent* 70 (1911): 642–50.

53. Quoted in Beverly Washington Jones, *Stanford L. Warren Branch Library: 77 Years of Public Service, A Phoenix in the Durham Community* (Durham: Durham County Library, 1990), 19. For Du Bois's extended remarks on Durham see "The Upbuilding of Black Durham," *World's Work* 23 (1912): 334–38.

54. On the history of the North Carolina Mutual Life Insurance Company, see Walter B. Weare, *Black Business in the New South: A Social History of the North Carolina Mutual Life Insurance Company* (Durham: Duke University Press, 1993).

read good literature."[55] He established such a library in 1913 at the White Rock Baptist Church, one of the oldest in the black community and home to an increasingly wealthy and educated congregation. The library opened that year with 799 volumes, some of which had been donated by Dr. James Edward Shepard, president of the National Religious Training School and Chautauqua, now known as North Carolina Central University. According to Beverly Washington Jones, the historian of what would later be named the Stanford L. Warren Branch Library, denominational differences kept this first early library from being used by the broader black community.[56]

Through the efforts of one of Moore's business partners, John L. Merrick, and with the financial support of one of the city's most prominent white citizens, James B. Duke, the library was moved in 1916 to a newly constructed building at the corner of Fayetteville and Pettigrew Streets. It was officially chartered by the state of North Carolina in 1918 as the "Durham Colored Library Association" and given monthly financial support by the city of Durham. Located in the Hayti area of the city, which Du Bois noted was home to "a group of five thousand or more colored people, whose social and economic development is perhaps more striking than that of any similar group in the nation," the library aimed both to educate a broader range of patrons and to serve their needs.[57] Although Moore suggested that the library was organized for "the purposes of placing good wholesome reading matter in the reach of our Negro boys and girls and thereby to train them into the habit of this class of reading," he also conceived of the library, as he and his partners did of North Carolina Mutual itself, as an operation "with a soul and a service." He noted additionally, then, that the library "was especially designed to help those who are not able to select and purchase books for themselves."[58]

Moore's comments suggest, of course, that his attitudes toward literature and his conceptualization of the library's mission were similar to those familiar middle-class views expressed by the white-dominated library profession as well as by those who ran Durham's library for whites. Indeed, the Durham Colored Library would conventionally collect and display the best that had been thought and said in the past, and it would extend that tradition to those who might not have grown up with it in their homes. Yet it is important to point out that the collection practices at the library suggest that Moore and those who worked with him had additional hopes for the library as a

55. Jones, *Stanford L. Warren Branch Library,* 19.
56. Ibid., 20.
57. Quoted in ibid., 19.
58. Ibid., 20.

somewhat different sort of institution, one that might counter the dominant culture's disparaging view of the Negro. Indeed, the Durham Colored Library soon began to amass a significant collection of books written by, for, and about African Americans. It is not clear whether this move originated with Moore himself, with Shepherd, with Hattie B. Wooten, the first librarian, with Stanford Lee Warren who succeeded Dr. Moore as president in 1923, or with his daughter, Selena Warren Wheeler, the second librarian, who served from 1932 to 1945. Selena Warren has herself suggested to Beverly Washington Jones that many of the 799 volumes in the original collection "dealt with Black life and history." [59] Whenever the collection was begun, the very fact of its existence suggests that, from very early on, the library's founders construed its mission in complex fashion. Conventionally middle class in their outlook from one perspective, from another they were acutely aware of their putative difference from the dominant white majority as well as of the disadvantages their race suffered because of that difference. The library's founders thus sought to create a specially focused collection that would redress the effects of such difference by contributing to the constitution and future consolidation of a proudly self-conscious, race-based community.

In its desire to acquaint its patrons with the classics of the dominant culture, the Durham Colored Library offered the usual touchstones of literature and the standard reference volumes of the period. At the same time, in its efforts to inform its citizens about their own cultural heritage and the literary traditions of colored Americans, it continued to collect what was then called, "race literature." According to Victoria Earle Matthews, race literature should not be thought of simply as books on "race matter." Rather, she noted, "By Race Literature, we mean ordinarily all the writings emanating from a distinct class . . . a general collection of what has been written by the men and women of that Race: History, Biographies, Scientific Treatises, Sermons, Addresses, Novels, Poems, Books of Travel, miscellaneous essays and the contributions to magazines and newspapers." [60] At once acknowledging the significance of race and seeking to suggest that it need not constrain black Americans by limiting them to writing only about race, Matthews and those who shared her views sought to claim that all of human knowledge was open to the Negro for exploration and discussion.

This expansive and inclusive definition of race literature was envisioned so as to counteract what many believed were the regrettable effects of literacy

---

59. Ibid., 22.
60. Victoria Earle Matthews, "The Value of Race Literature: An Address Delivered at the First Congress of Colored Women of the United States, July 30, 1895," *Massachusetts Review* 27 (1986): 170.

upon African Americans. Indeed, after struggling vigorously to acquire the literacy so long denied them, African American readers discovered that they had managed to gain access to books that regularly perpetuated stereotypes of black Americans even when not recommending their continuing subordination. A self-conscious "race literature" would challenge such stereotypes *and* enable African Americans to lay claim to all of human thought. Race literature would thus contribute to racial uplift, but it would also function as a form of resistance to dominant views and additionally begin the process of transforming them. As early as 1900, in fact, Daniel Murray, an assistant librarian at the Library of Congress, collected close to 1,400 books in a "Bibliography of Negro Literature," which was presented as the Negro Exhibit at the Paris Commission in 1900. Fueled by the advocacy work of people like Du Bois and Carter Woodson, this body of literature was expanded in the teens, twenties, and thirties. In an *ABC for Negro Boys and Girls* that was included in her 1925 book, *Charming Stories for Young and Old,* Alice Howard articulated the goals of this literature in the following way:

> I feel safe in saying that every child in the United States between the ages of three and ten receives among its toys and especially at the Holiday season, an A, B, C Book, many of which are a reflection of the child of color. In almost every instance N stands for Nig, a black dog or cat; Ned, a Negro boy, a waiter, and so on. First-hand observation of these facts shows the urgent need and place in the home for a book of this class, which our boys and girls need not be ashamed of. Race pride is legitimate and praiseworthy. It is developed through knowledge and understanding of the history, traditions, achievements, and characteristics of the race. Things that have been looked upon as a detriment and drawback can through the right teaching to our children be turned into an asset and thus lay the foundation for the love of, and the loyalty to our Race.[61]

There is no way of knowing whether Durham's children could find Alice Howard's book at their library. Even if they could not, though, it seems clear that they found others much like it, books like *Africa and the Discovery of America,* donated in 1925 by the Beta Phi Chapter of Omega Psi Phi Fraternity. Books like this one were written to encourage black Americans to use their literacy and wisdom for community building as well as for emancipatory functions. No doubt the writer Pauli Murray was not alone in her ability to use the Negro collection as a source of inspiration as well as a fund of knowledge, something she mentioned in her autobiography, *Proud Shoes.*[62] Apparently, Durham's black citizens used the collection heavily. Indeed, in

---

61. Quoted in Violet J. Harris, "African-American Conceptions of Literacy: A Historical Perspective," *Theory into Practice* 31 (1992): 277.
62. Pauli Murray, *Proud Shoes: The Story of an American Family* (New York: Harper, 1956).

1942, Selena Warren recommended to the board of trustees that the Hattie B. Wooten Browsing Room be used to house "the collection of books on the Negro and by Negro authors," because "these books were [disappearing] from the Main Reading Room and because many of them were already out of print and could not be replaced."[63] The collection, clearly, was of use to many who came in contact with it. Selena Warren felt that it would do greater service to Durham's black community as a permanent, noncirculating collection.

Given the sketchy evidence that survives about readers and reading from this era, it is difficult to tell how Durham's black citizens were changed by the library or what they used their reading to do. Did they turn more regularly to the Negro Collection and periodicals like the *Journal of Negro History* than to the *Encyclopedia Britannica,* purchased in 1927, or to the Book-of-the-Month Club selections, which were regularly received at the library on Fayetteville Street during the late 1920s?[64] How deeply were they affected by what they read? Did they aspire merely to middle-class respectability and to acceptance by white society, or were their goals more emancipatory and activist? It is difficult to know. We do know, though, from the minutes of the library's board that, in 1933, they at least discussed "the attitude of the Librarian at the City White Library," and "it seemed to be the consensus of opinion among those members present that it was wise for our people to continue to go there and ask for books which could not be obtained from our library in order that the proper officials of the County and City might see the need of increasing the appropriation for the Durham Colored Library."[65]

Accommodation to segregation? Perhaps. But also deliberate confrontation and a desire to bolster the resources of what had clearly become by then an important community institution housing many reading clubs, civic meetings, children's story hours and movie Saturdays, activities for teens, and support for those involved in adult training courses. Small wonder, then, that at the 1940 dedication of the library's new building, which was named after Stanford L. Warren, ceremonies opened with the singing not of the *Star Spangled Banner* but the *Negro National Anthem.*[66] Throughout the forties and fifties, in fact, the Stanford L. Warren Library sponsored a Book Review Forum featuring prominent speakers from the black community, including Dr. John Hope Franklin and Pauli Murray. In 1944, the library also hosted

63. Jones, *Stanford L. Warren Branch Library,* 8, 30–31.

64. This information is drawn from a file of miscellaneous receipts, notes, letters, and committee minutes in possession of the Stanford L. Warren Branch Library, Durham County Library.

65. Board of Trustees, Durham Colored Library, Minutes, 15 January 1933.

66. Program, Dedication Ceremony, Stanford L. Warren Branch, Durham Public Library, 14 April 1940. In possession of the Stanford L. Warren Branch, Durham County Library.

an exhibition of selected paintings by contemporary Negro artists, including works by Romare Bearden and Hale Woodruff. The exhibition was heavily attended.[67]

In spite of the lack of acquisition and circulation records, then, these few sketchy details, which survive in miscellaneous records still kept at the Stanford L. Warren branch of the now integrated Durham County Library, suggest that Durham's black library did indeed help to provide an important space for community formation and that it did promote a certain race consciousness among the city's black population. Whether it also helped to promote community organizing and to foster the sort of political consciousness that burst on the scene in the late 1940s and 1950s and led eventually to the galvanizing sit-ins only sixty miles away in Greensboro, is difficult to say. It is perhaps ironic to note, however, that those resistant and oppositional sit-ins took place at a lunch counter in a Woolworth's five and ten cent store, one of the earliest chains for mass distribution in the United States and the very one Harry Scherman had sought to exploit in order to dispense the fruits of his first effort to enlarge the audience for books. In 1916, in fact, he had created something called the Little Leather Library, a collection of twenty-five-cent classics he sought to sell through the many Woolworth's stores stretching out across the nation. Although his enterprise was highly successful, it was his realization that he would soon exhaust the list of titles generally recognized as classics that pushed him to conceptualize the Book-of-the-Month Club as a way of selling even more books to more readers. His initial emphasis on automatic distribution, of course, did not much acknowledge the variability of readers' desires or tastes. As we have seen, however, Scherman's desire to reach more and more readers soon pushed him to adapt to the facts of what might be called reading diversity. His was a commercially generated desire, to be sure, but it did spur him and his organization to think hard about how to service readers and their multiple motives for seeking out a book to read. In that, he was not all that different from the nation's librarians, who sometimes had to forgo their own desires to instruct and to leaven taste in order to move their books off dusty shelves. Geographic and social diversity, and the variability in taste that both promoted, whether economic, gendered, or race-based, continued to matter in the United States even amidst increasing efforts at mass distribution. Whether such diversity declined over time is a matter for a longitudinal and much more complex investigation than could be attempted here.

---

67. Jones, *Stanford L. Warren Branch Library,* 9.

Chapter 10

Blood and Thunder on the Bookmobile

American Public Libraries and the Construction of "the Reader," 1950–1995

CHRISTINE PAWLEY

In 1967, Bob H. took a new job: he became a bookmobile driver for the Door County (Wisconsin) Library. Bob, a Wisconsin native, had worked for twenty-one years on the West Coast where he was parts manager for a car dealership, before deciding to move back to the Door Peninsula. While job-hunting, he spotted a classified ad: the county library was looking for a bookmobile driver. In the early 1950s, the county bookmobile had been staffed by both a driver and a professionally trained librarian, but since 1953 funding shortages had forced the library to roll the functions of both positions into one. Now the driver was expected not only to take the vehicle to all parts of the county, but also to stock it with books, advise readers on their choices, and even select materials for purchase. "Well, why not try it?" Bob reflected: "I like books and I've always been an avid reader. I can remember walking five miles when I was a little kid to get to a place where I could get books." [1] Although untrained and with no experience in library work, Bob took to his new job like a duck to water. "It was the best job I ever had," he reminisced. A major factor was his longtime fondness for reading. "Bob was a reader to start with," the library director Jane Livingston Greene explained. [2] For Bob, his experience in the car company was perhaps more relevant than Greene realized. "I had a parts department, and a book department, it was similar to it as far as putting things in different places," he pointed out. But it was his reading habit that made the bookmobile a natural environment for

---

This research was carried out with support from the Wisconsin Historical Society through an Amy Louise Hunter Fellowship, and from the University of Iowa through an Old Gold Summer Fellowship and an Arts and Humanities Initiative Grant.

1. Interview with "Bob H.," Door County, Wisconsin, 13 March 2001.
2. Interviews with Jane Livingston Greene, Sturgeon Bay, Wisconsin, 13 March and 25 May 2001.

him. "I fell right into it like a kid in a candy car with all [those] books," he said. "Which one am I going to read [next]?"

Scholarship in the history of reading tends to focus on two elements— readers and texts—in attempting to uncover answers to questions of who read what, how, and why, and although texts have tended to absorb the lion's share of scholarly attention, readers are catching up.[3] So far, however, few researchers have paid much attention to the social and institutional mechanisms that link specific readers with specific texts, assuming, perhaps, that once certain texts are "available" in a reading environment they make their way into an individual reader's hands through a classical mechanism of supply and demand—that readers simply exercise individual preference in deciding to pick this title rather than that. For millions of "ordinary" Americans from the mid-nineteenth century on, their local tax-supported public library has been a major source of books. But libraries are not neutral depositories of printed materials—a kind of black box in which readers and texts "only connect." Libraries are social systems, the outcome of the intended and unintended actions and policies of those who work in and for them, and of their users. And since their beginning in the 1850s, free public libraries have purposefully set out to shape readers' choices of material. In other words, librarians have tried to construct readers, and thereby produce a particular kind of reading identity.

To begin to understand these shaping mechanisms, historians of readers and reading need to consider both libraries' official policies and practices, and the unofficial ways in which librarians and readers implemented and experienced them. A persistent controversy has revolved around the quality of reading materials that public libraries provide and the reading habits that public libraries thereby encourage. In the nineteenth century, early leaders of the nascent profession of librarianship debated the desirability of reading fiction,

---

3. Robert Darnton, "History of Reading," in *New Perspectives on Historical Writing,* ed. Peter Burke (University Park: Pennsylvania State University Press, 1992), 142; Jean-François Gilmont, "Protestant Reformations and Reading," in *A History of Reading in the West,* ed. Guglielmo Cavallo and Roger Chartier (Amherst: University of Massachusetts Press, 1999), 224. For recent general works on the history of reading in North America and Europe, see Jonathan Boyarin, ed., *The Ethnography of Reading* (Berkeley: University of California Press, 1992); Steven Roger Fischer, *A History of Reading* (London: Reaktion Books, 2003); Carl F. Kaestle, Lawrence C. Stedman, et al., eds., *Literacy in the United States* (New Haven: Yale University Press, 1991); Yvan Lamonde and Sophie Montreuil, eds., *Lire au Québec au XIXe Siècle* (Saint-Laurent, Québec: Fides, 2003); Martyn Lyons, *Readers and Society in Nineteenth-Century France: Workers, Women, Peasants* (Houndmills, U.K.: Palgrave, 2001); Alberto Manguel, *A History of Reading* (New York: Viking, 1996); and Barbara Ryan and Amy M. Thomas, eds., *Reading Acts: U.S. Readers' Interactions with Literature, 1800–1950* (Knoxville: University of Tennessee Press, 2002).

many strenuously opposing it.[4] But over subsequent decades much of this opposition evaporated, to the extent that by the middle of the twentieth century most librarians were at least resigned to novel-reading as pervasive and mostly harmless, and by the end of the century many actively embraced it. Yet the journey from condemnation to acceptance of popular reading materials in public libraries progressed neither smoothly nor evenly. This essay elaborates on some of the ways in which readers and public librarians collaborated and contended over the construction of the ideal reader, as well as on the professional discourse of librarians. In particular, it focuses on official policies and unofficial reading practices of participants in a rural Wisconsin library and bookmobile service during the 1950s and 1960s, drawing on oral interviews and institutional records to uncover what it meant to be "a reader" for the librarians and patrons who were most extensively involved. Although published and archived documents provide the foundation of this research, it was the interviews with approximately twenty-five former patrons and librarians that provided insights that would otherwise have been irrecoverable. Contact with the present-day director of the Door County Regional Library provided the first contact, and others snowballed from there. Now aged between fifty and ninety, these residents of Door and Kewaunee County were happy to reminisce singly and in groups: their memories have provided a rich resource.

Bookmobile driver Bob H. may seem an unlikely representative of a profession eager to stress an educative, high-culture role for the public library, but library director Greene's pragmatic decision to hire him, not only to drive the bookmobile but also to select and recommend the books that it carried, needs to be seen as part of a movement that represented a radical change in how many public librarians conceived of their jobs, their patrons, and the reading materials that they provided for their communities. The Door County bookmobile service started in 1950, at a time when 23 percent of Wisconsin's population lacked free library access, and rural literacy rates were also low. Selecting contiguous counties, the Wisconsin Free Library Commission (WFLC) secured public funding to bring library services to the region, resulting in the Door–Kewaunee Regional Library Demonstration of 1950–52 — part of a nationwide movement to improve library service to rural areas. A key component was the "library on wheels" — a bookmobile that made regular stops at crossroads and one-room schools. But at the November 1952 general election, after a three-year period during which library circulation increased by 160 percent and local children achieved a measurable improvement in reading, voters

4. For details of this debate during the latter part of the nineteenth century, see Esther Jane Carrier, *Fiction in Public Libraries, 1876–1900* (New York: Scarecrow Press, 1965).

determined in a referendum whether to continue county funding. Republican Party Cold War rhetoric that linked anticommunism with fiscal conservatism persuaded Kewaunee County electors to vote down the library. Argued one library foe, "If we are called upon to reimburse a military commensurate with an all-out war effort, the tax burden will be great enough without also having to pay for a bookmobile service." [5] Door County residents, on the other hand, voted in favor of continuing the library, so although Kewaunee County rural service halted abruptly, the Door County bookmobile continued its rounds. When in 1967 the original 1950 vehicle finally wore out, county supervisors planned to eliminate the service; but vociferous library supporters changed their minds, and it was not until 1995 that Door County bookmobile service terminated.

During the twentieth century, bookmobiles were perhaps the most widespread and visible embodiment of library "outreach," but they were not the earliest method by which Wisconsin's librarians distributed reading materials beyond the library's walls. At the end of the nineteenth century, WFLC founders Lutie Eugenia Stearns and Frank Avery Hutchins established a system of "traveling libraries" that consisted of up to one hundred volumes housed in a "strong book case which had a shelf, double doors with a lock and key, a record book for loans, printed copies of the few simple rules, borrowers' blanks, and so complete a line of equipments that it could be set up anywhere on a table, a box or a counter and managed as an independent library." [6] In addition to collections for general public use, the WFLC also provided traveling libraries for lumber camps, tuberculosis sanitoria, orphanages, and readers of Norwegian and Danish, German, Yiddish, Polish, and "Bohemian" (Czech). As Hutchins reported in the WFLC's first *Biennial Report,* "About one-third of the libraries are kept in post offices, one-half in farm houses, one at a small railway station, the remainder in small stores." [7] A local volunteer managed each library, overseeing the borrowing process, keeping simple records, and corresponding with the commission. Stearns

---

5. Open letter from Frank W. Wessely to Supervisor Ray P. Fulwiler, *Algoma Record-Herald,* 26 March 1953. For a fuller account of this political process, see Christine Pawley, "Reading *versus* the Red Bull: Cultural Constructions of Democracy and the Public Library in Cold War Wisconsin," *American Studies* 42 (2001): 87–103.

6. Frank A. Hutchins, *Free Traveling Libraries in Wisconsin: The Story of Their Growth, Purposes, and Development; With Accounts of a Few Kindred Movements* (Madison: Wisconsin Free Library Commission, 1897), 6. Stearns and Hutchins modeled their service on the system of traveling libraries established by Melvil Dewey in New York State during the 1890s; see Wayne A. Wiegand, *Irrepressible Reformer: A Biography of Melvil Dewey* (Chicago: American Library Association, 1996), 148, 203.

7. Reprinted in Hutchins, *Free Traveling Libraries in Wisconsin,* 82.

later recalled that she often delivered the traveling libraries herself "by stage, sleigh, buggy, wagon, passenger coach and caboose, wearing out five fur coats in succession. . . . During the winter I would secure a black bear-skin to wear over my fur-lined muskrat coat. . . . I would get a three-seated sleigh, remove the last two seats, and fill the space with books."[8] Such intrepidity mirrored that of other women librarians in the early twentieth century. Anne Hadden, for instance, traveled by horseback and mule to deliver books in remote areas of California's Monterey County, as did Mabel Wilkinson in Wyoming, and during the 1930s "pack horse librarians" distributed books in rural Kentucky, funded by the Works Progress Administration.[9] In 1914, after changes in the Post Office's rules for parcel post, the WFLC also introduced a system of sending books by mail upon written request from state residents.[10]

The first bookmobile service in the United States is credited to Mary Titcomb, librarian of the Washington County Free Library, Hagerstown, Maryland. In 1904 Titcomb arranged for traveling library collections to be exchanged by the library's janitor, Joshua Thomas, by means of a hired wagon and horse. In 1905, however, she sent Thomas out in a wagon specially converted to carry 250 books. Since this vehicle resembled "a cross between a grocer's delivery wagon and the black hearse of the village undertaker," some farm families "were reluctant to use . . . the 'dead wagon,' " but over time the service proved popular. When the first vehicle was destroyed in a railroad crossing accident, the library board commissioned a replacement.[11]

Attempts such as these to provide services "outside" the library contrast with the late nineteenth- and early twentieth-century emphasis on library buildings. From the middle of the nineteenth century on, American public library advocates urged the importance of providing physical space, not just to house materials but for readers to read them.[12] The strongest impetus for

8. Lutie E. Stearns, "My Seventy-five Years: Part I, 1866–1914," *Wisconsin Magazine of History* 42 (1959): 216.

9. Denise Sallee, "Reconceptualizing Women's History: Anne Hadden and the California County Library System," *Libraries and Culture* 27 (1992): 351–77; Joanne E. Passet, *Cultural Crusaders: Women Librarians in the American West, 1900–1917* (Albuquerque: University of New Mexico Press, 1994); and Jeanne Cannella Schmitzer, "Reaching Out to the Mountains: The Pack Horse Library of Eastern Kentucky," *The Register of the Kentucky Historical Society* 95 (1997): 57–77.

10. Christine Pawley, "Advocate for Access: Lutie Stearns and the Traveling Libraries of the Wisconsin Free Library Commission, 1895–1914," *Libraries and Culture* 35 (2000): 434–58.

11. Eleanor Frances Brown, *Bookmobiles and Bookmobile Service* (Metuchen, NJ: Scarecrow Press, 1967), 14–15. For details about Mary Titcomb and the Washington County Free Library, see also Deanna Marcum, "The Rural Public Library at the Turn of the Century," *Libraries and Culture* 26 (1991): 87–99.

12. Sidney Ditzion, *Arsenals of a Democratic Culture: A Social History of the Public Library Movement in New England and the Middle States from 1850 to 1900* (Chicago: American Library Association, 1947), 30.

public library construction came from the Carnegie Corporation. Considered "the most influential philanthropic program in American history," the Carnegie program funded the building of over sixteen hundred public libraries in the United States between 1886 and 1917 in partnership with grant-seeking communities.[13] In various ways, the design of these buildings reflected contemporary values that related not only to reading, but also to the library users and employees themselves. As Abigail Van Slyck explains, although Carnegie Corporation officials discouraged "monumentality" in favor of building efficiency and functionality, urban central libraries still often consisted of "large, rectangular blocks of granite or marble" that were "modeled on the great cultural institutions of a previous generation." Such buildings effectively segregated middle- from working-class readers and restricted the latter's access to both "the full extent of the building" and "the full range of its symbolism."[14] Smaller branch libraries catered more effectively for working-class readers, but here too, building design facilitated the librarian's control over reading practices. By centrally positioning circulation desks with a view over radial stacks, for example, library designers "mimicked the planning devices of prison architecture, particularly those of Jeremy Bentham's Panopticon."[15]

Reading rooms were considered an essential component of public library buildings, and served to control how, where, and what different groups read. Reading rooms reserved exclusively for women were not uncommon in public libraries during the late nineteenth century, and some librarians even considered them "an absolute necessity for encouraging respectable women to venture into the public library."[16] Reading rooms were also designed to uphold racial segregation. The Carnegie Library of Gainesville, Texas, for instance, included a basement reading room for the black population, served by a separate entrance that protected white patrons from encounters with African American readers.[17] And reading rooms were also enlisted in the maintenance of class distinctions. On the one hand, some argued that reading rooms—especially those devoted to newspapers and periodicals—encouraged library "loafing" by working-class men. Newspaper reading rooms were sometimes situated close to the front door, in the basement or on the second floor, to minimize interaction among supposedly working-class periodical readers and

---

13. Theodore Jones, *Carnegie Libraries across America: A Public Legacy* (New York: John Wiley, 1997), 130.

14. Abigail A. Van Slyck, *Free to All: Carnegie Libraries and American Culture, 1890–1920* (Chicago: University of Chicago Press, 1995), 90–91, 98–100.

15. Ibid., 120.

16. Abigail A. Van Slyck, "The Lady and the Library Loafer: Gender and Public Space in Victorian America," *Winterthur Portfolio* 31 (1996): 221–42.

17. Van Slyck, *Free to All*, 158–59.

middle-class book-reading patrons.[18] Some on the other hand argued that library reading rooms were themselves a way of forestalling undesirable, or even criminal behavior. In 1896, following a violent assault by six young men on a sixteen-year-old girl, concerned residents of Iowa City, Iowa, claimed that a public library would be "a destroyer of street loafing" by keeping "boys and girls off the streets."[19]

By offering extramural services, librarians hoped to extend the public library's beneficial influence in areas where no permanent physical facilities existed. They carefully selected traveling library collections to appeal to the reading tastes of the communities served, while upholding the high standards demanded by library authorities.[20] But as a consequence, they also relinquished control of not only the spaces where people read, but how and even what they read. Whereas public library reading room rules encouraged reading in silence in the company of others who were similar in age, gender, and class, reading outside the library allowed more freedom in the use of library materials. Not only could readers choose where to read, but they could also read library books out loud to others, and could pass their reading materials on to friends and family, so that (for example) books intended for children might be read by adults, and vice versa.

Building design was only one of the ways in which late nineteenth- and early twentieth-century public libraries attempted to control reading practices. Public libraries also adopted several organizational devices to control what and how their patrons read. While throughout the nineteenth century almost all librarians condemned the reading of fiction, they differed as to the appropriate professional response. A few diehards called for a library regime of total abstinence. "I could tell of one young woman of my acquaintance, of fine education," warned William Kite of the Germantown (Pennsylvania) Free Public Library in 1877, "who gratified a vitiated taste for novel-reading till her reason was overthrown, and she has, in consequence, been for several years an inmate of an insane asylum."[21] Most librarians took a less drastic

---

18. Van Slyck, "The Lady and the Library Loafer," 227. For discussion of numerous aspects of periodicals in American libraries, including the location of periodical reading rooms, see Charles Johanningsmeier, "Welcome Guests or Representatives of the 'Mal-Odorous Class'? Periodicals and Their Readers in American Public Libraries, 1876–1914," *Libraries and Culture* 39 (2004): 260–292.

19. Lolly Parker Eggers, *A Century of Stories: The History of the Iowa City Public Library, 1896–1997* (Iowa City: The Iowa City Public Library Friends Foundation, 1997), 5.

20. Librarians did not always support culturally authoritative collection building, however. Lutie Stearns, for example, frequently rejected professional prescriptions (Pawley, "Advocate for Access," 449).

21. William Kite, "Fiction in Public Libraries," *Library Journal* 1 (1877): 277–78. Although Kite is a much-cited example of this extreme viewpoint, Esther Carrier, *Fiction in Public Libraries,* 363, comments that in fact he was the only librarian who actually called for total abstinence.

position, pointing out that the taxpaying public had a right to determine how their tax dollars were spent, even though they themselves deplored especially the "inveterate" or "persistent" reading of fiction. Wrote Mellen Chamberlain in 1883, "We may believe that the trustees have no right to expend the public money for the mere amusement of the people; but, if the people think differently, trustees must yield to their wishes or leave."[22]

Yet others actually saw some advantages to fiction. Writing in 1879, Samuel Swett Green, of the Worcester (Massachusetts) Public Library, supported even "sensational" fiction if it gave "young persons a taste for reading." After all, he argued, "it is certainly better for certain classes of persons to read exciting stories than to be doing what they would be doing if not reading."[23] Any reading, Green implied, was better than no reading, especially if it encouraged people to climb a ladder of progress. Moreover, the poor would undoubtedly get up to no good unless safely diverted by an entertaining book. Library leaders' reading ideology was thus embedded in an underlying matrix of class relationships in the urbanizing world of late nineteenth-century America.[24] Gender relations, too, contributed to leading librarians' construction of the ideal reader. Middle-class women were assumed to be the principal readers of fiction (though actual evidence suggests that men, too, read novels in large numbers).[25] Moreover, librarianship is a profession stratified by gender; early public library leaders were all men, and even today, although women predominate in clerical and middle-management jobs, men still occupy executive positions in disproportionate numbers. The strictures of late nineteenth-century library leaders aimed not only at counteracting supposed female reading patterns, but also at shaping the professional practices of the — mostly — women who actually came into face-to-face contact with patrons.[26]

To control the content of patrons' reading and steer them toward more worthwhile materials, librarians established routine procedures. These

---

22. Mellen Chamberlain, "Report of Fiction in Public Libraries," *Library Journal* 8 (1883): 209.

23. S. S. Green, "Sensational Fiction in Public Libraries," *Library Journal* 4 (1879): 348–49 (345–55).

24. Values clashed between those who cast patrons primarily as students or strivers, and those who felt obliged to meet the taxpayers' demands. Whereas the former stressed transforming immigrants into "American citizens" and promoting social mobility, from the latter position it was but a small step to defining the reader as consumer, a contradiction that inheres in library rhetoric to this day. For a discussion of this contradiction in the context of early twentieth-century public library development, see Pawley, "Advocate for Access," 434–58.

25. Christine Pawley, *Reading on the Middle Border: The Culture of Print in Late-Nineteenth-Century Osage, Iowa* (Amherst: University of Massachusetts Press, 2001), 104–11.

26. Van Slyck details ways in which the interior design of Carnegie libraries cooperated with library practices to produce gendered space, in which women librarians were channeled into low-level routine tasks; see especially *Free to All*, 160–73.

included limits on the number and kinds of books borrowed, closed stacks, standardized selection, and a personal advice system called "Readers' Advisory." The so-called two-book system was one of the first such devices. Many early public libraries issued only one book at a time. However, some librarians complained, most patrons consequently borrowed only novels. According to the two-book system, libraries allowed a second to be borrowed, provided it consisted of "solid literature." [27] Closed stacks were another controlling procedure. Larger libraries generally used closed stacks, and at an 1877 conference most librarians spoke out against opening the shelves to patrons.

As more and more experimented with the system, however, they found that neither chaos ensued, nor books vanished. [28] During the Progressive Era, although librarians still aimed at producing a non-fiction-reading public, they were beginning to relax circulation and shelf access policies. In 1910, Arthur E. Bostwick, a former president of the American Library Association (ALA), reported, "Open access, though a suspected and doubted experiment fifteen years ago, is now practically universal in America in all but large city libraries." [29] And by the late 1920s the practice of restricting adult borrowers to one or two books had ended. "The period of years is short since one volume each of fiction and non-fiction was considered a fair and liberal portion for a borrower," wrote the librarian Jennie Flexner in 1927. "A reasonable number of books, fiction or non-fiction, is usually allowed on any borrower's card." [30] Yet liberal access policies did not necessarily reflect an underlying shift toward a less paternalistic reading ideology. "Many public-library readers betray the symptoms of intellectual youth," Bostwick told his readers. "They are fond of narrative; they like simple words and ideas clearly expressed and easily apprehended; they like, above all, plenty of action. . . . [I]nstead of frowning upon them, the librarian must be prepared to humor them, to select books that satisfy such desires and are at the same time good literature." [31] Even adult readers, Bostwick implied, needed to be led, like children — indeed they *were* children in terms of their reading practices.

At the same time that shelf access was opening up, increasingly professionalized and standardized selection procedures provided more control over

---

27. E. A. Birge, "The Effect of the 'Two-Book System' on Circulation," *Library Journal* 23 (1898): 93–101.

28. Laura M. Janzow, "Open Shelves," in *The Library without Walls: Reprints of Papers and Addresses,* ed. Janzow (New York: H. W. Wilson, 1927), 151.

29. Arthur E. Bostwick, *The American Public Library* (New York: D. Appleton, 1910), 38–39.

30. Jennie M. Flexner, *Circulation Work in Public Libraries* (Chicago: American Library Association, 1927), 99.

31. Bostwick, *American Public Library,* 126.

what appeared on the shelves. In small libraries during the nineteenth century, library trustees rather than librarians had often undertaken book selection. In 1900 John Cotton Dana, a leading librarian, still listed among trustee duties the "general direction of choice and purchase of books." [32] But by 1920 he was arguing that although "trustees are the responsible managers of the library, the librarian is their expert executive. . . . They should leave to him . . . [the] choice of books." [33] At the same time, commercial companies were producing aids to professional selection. In 1898 the Minneapolis publisher H. W. Wilson started the comprehensive trade catalogue *Cumulative Book Index.* In 1905 he introduced *Book Review Digest,* followed in 1909 by *Children's Catalog* and the *Standard Catalog for Public Libraries* in 1918. Professional and state commissions also contributed to the standardization movement. In 1893, the ALA published its first selection guide for public libraries.[34] Other selection aids followed fast. In 1902 the Wisconsin Free Library Commission's *Suggestive List of Books for a Small Library* instructed selection committees to remember that the tax-supported public library should provide "books that give pleasure." But at the same time, the commission warned, the public library had a duty to "train" readers to choose better and better books.[35]

At the middle of the twentieth century, some library leaders continued to stress their predecessors' reading values. In 1949 the WFLC published "A Partial List of Series Not Circulated by Standard Libraries" that represented "the type of book not approved for purchase with library funds nor for placing on the shelves of any public or school library in Wisconsin." [36] This list

---

32. The term "trustee" refers to library board members; John Cotton Dana, *A Library Primer,* 2d ed. (Chicago: Library Bureau, 1900), 18. In the small Iowa community of Osage in the early 1890s, for example, a subcommittee of the Library Committee selected books for the library on the principle of meeting local demand, perhaps even choosing them from mail order catalogues of companies like Montgomery Ward and Sears Roebuck. The result was a considerable preponderance of fiction, including many titles that professional librarians did not approve; see Pawley, *Reading on the Middle Border,* 77–91.

33. John Cotton Dana, *A Library Primer,* 1920 ed. (Boston: Library Bureau, 1920), 13–14.

34. *Catalog of "A.L.A." Library: 5000 Volumes for a Popular Library* (Washington: Government Printing Office, 1893). See also Wayne A. Wiegand, "Catalog of 'A.L.A.' Library (1893): Origins of a Genre," in Delmus E. Williams et al., *For the Good of the Order* (Greenwich, CT: JAI Press, 1994), 237–54.

35. *Suggestive List of Books for Small Library Recommended by the State Library Commissions of Iowa, Minnesota, Wisconsin, Nebraska, Idaho and Delaware* (Madison: Wisconsin Free Library Commission, 1902), 3–4. In 1905 the ALA started a serial publication, *Booklist,* that appeared several times a year and included not only a "current buying list of recent books" but also "brief notes designed to assist librarians in selection." (*A.L.A. Booklist,* 1, nos. 1– 2 [1905]): 2).

36. *Weeding the Library: Suggestions for the Guidance of Librarians of Small Libraries* (Madison: Wisconsin Free Library Commission, 1949), 9. This pamphlet was found in the archives of the Algoma (Kewaunee County) Public Library.

included some of the nineteenth century's most popular authors—including Horatio Alger, Oliver Optic, and Pansy—as well as twentieth-century series books: the Bobbsey Twins, the Oz books, and Nancy Drew.[37] Yet at the same time, it was clear that librarians were failing in their attempts to shape public library readers according to late nineteenth-century standards. In 1949, the communications researcher and former librarian Bernard Berelson reported to the Public Library Inquiry the results of a 1947 national survey of public library users, along with a summary of all studies of library book use and users published since 1930.[38] "Although no one knows exactly just how to define 'quality' in popular reading," he argued, "everyone acknowledges that the public library circulates many titles which would not qualify as 'good' by any generally accepted literary standard." Neither was he shy of specifying these not-so-good titles; "Mystery and detective stories, love and romance fiction, adventure and western stories, recent novels widely publicized but of little literary distinction, popularizations of current affairs characterized by sensationalism and easy dogmatism rather than by dispassionate and qualified analysis—these and similar books are widely circulated by the public library."[39]

During the 1920s and 1930s, in addition to systems for controlling what appeared on the shelves, public librarians developed a new system for influencing what readers took off the shelves. This was the "Readers' Advisor." The 1935 *Enoch Pratt Free Library Staff Instruction Book* described a Readers' Advisor as one who "interviews the patron seeking individual help in directed reading and study, and attempts to stimulate continuity and purpose in his reading, whether for cultural, recreational or practical needs."[40] And while some public libraries were employing professional Readers' Advisors to help patrons develop their own reading programs along approved lines

---

37. L. Frank Baum created the Oz series, though others contributed to it. Multiple authors employed by the Stratemeyer Syndicate wrote the Bobbsey Twins and Nancy Drew series, under the pseudonyms Laura Lee Hope and Carolyn Keene.

38. Bernard Berelson, *The Library's Public* (New York: Columbia University Press, 1949), 137. The Public Library Inquiry was a major study of American public librarianship conducted in the late 1940s by a team of social scientists headed by a University of Chicago political scientist, Robert D. Leigh. It published its findings in seven volumes that included *The Library's Public* by Bernard Berelson; *The Public Librarian,* by Alice Bryan; *The Public Library in the Political Process,* by Oliver Garceau, studies on government publications, the book industry, and the information film, plus *The Public Library in the United States,* by Robert D. Leigh. For a recent analysis of the PLI, see Douglas Raber, *Librarianship and Legitimacy: The Ideology of the Public Library Inquiry* (Westport. CT: Greenwood Press, 1997).

39. Berelson, *The Library's Public,* 128.

40. *Enoch Pratt Free Library, Staff Instruction Book: Methods and Practices Concerning the Staff and the Service in the Various Departments and Branches* (Baltimore, MD: Enoch Pratt Free Library, 1 November 1935), par. 632.

at no charge, ventures like the Book-of-the-Month Club and the Modern Library were helping to construct the "middlebrow" reader by distributing "expert" advice to an expanded group of book buyers on a commercial basis.[41] As Megan Benton explains, the period between the two world wars saw the expansion of book culture as a market commodity. Although book ownership had "traditionally bestowed a certain elite cultural credential," a new focus on consumption led to " 'domestic bookaflage,' the selection and presentation of books in one's home to project the cultural persona that others would perceive."[42] Purchase of books for the home required space for their display, and during the first half of the twentieth century American domestic architecture began to accommodate this growing practice. Whereas before 1900 home book collections were typically housed in a specific room often called a library, study, or den, after the turn of the century books spread out over the house, from the parlor to the bedrooms.[43] To some extent this colonization of the home by books reflected an increased book availability arising from the nineteenth-century industrialization of book production, but it also reflected changes in reading practices facilitated by a revolution in domestic heating and lighting technology. The introduction of electric lighting and central heating made it possible, perhaps for the first time, for the less wealthy to read, for example, in bed. No longer were families confined on dark winter evenings to sitting as a group around the kitchen or dining table, where the light from a single lamp served to illuminate the activities of young and old alike, whether they were reading, studying, mending clothes, or doing the household accounts. Thus the practice of reading by ordinary Americans shifted away from specialized spaces like library reading rooms, or for the more affluent—and usually male—a study at home. Increased "leisure" time that resulted from reductions in working hours meant that middle- and working-class people not only had more time to read, but also could enjoy reading in the park or at the beach. Increased commuting time boosted reading on trains (already a standard practice), trams, and buses.[44]

41. Joan Shelley Rubin, *The Making of Middlebrow Culture* (Chapel Hill: University of North Carolina Press, 1992); Janice A. Radway, *A Feeling for Books: The Book-of-the-Month Club, Literary Taste, and Middle-Class Desire* (Chapel Hill: University of North Carolina Press, 1997); Jay Satterfield, *The World's Best Books: Taste, Culture, and the Modern Library* (Amherst: University of Massachusetts Press, 2002).

42. Megan Benton, " 'Too Many Books': Book Ownership and Cultural Identity in the 1920s," *American Quarterly* 49 (1997): 270.

43. Linda M. Kruger, "Home Libraries: Special Spaces, Reading Places," in *American Home Life, 1889–1930: A Social History of Spaces and Services,* ed. Jessica Foy and Thomas Schlereth (Knoxville: University of Tennessee Press, 1992), 94–95.

44. Ronald J. Zboray, *A Fictive People: Antebellum Economic Development and the American Reading Public* (New York: Oxford University Press, 1993), 69–82.

Although book studies scholars often portray this expansion of book ownership as a "popularization" of book culture, it was a movement still largely confined to the middle-class minority. As Benton argues, the working classes were still likely to own few books beyond "a family Bible and a collection of well-worn devotional works, and perhaps a small number of reference books such as almanacs, dictionaries, schoolbooks, and cook books."[45] Even in the 1940s and 1950s, books were in short supply in rural Door County homes. Gerry G., a former rural schoolteacher, for example, recalled that in his own family there were no books or newspapers at all. He himself found a way to fill the gap, even in the days before the advent of the bookmobile; his parents, who owned a small cheese factory, would drop him off once a week at the public library when they went to town to sell their products.[46] For the majority of working and rural families, then, there was little alternative to the public library; and since public library buildings were almost always located in towns and cities, the bookmobile (like its forerunner the traveling library) provided rural families with a unique opportunity to read.

In 1949, to persuade Wisconsin's legislature to fund the Door–Kewaunee Regional Library, state library officials stressed the public library's importance in furthering democracy by forming an educated citizenry. But to the librarians who worked most closely with rural residents, the most important feature of their work was in creating a reading identity among the region's young people. "On the bookmobile, we really raised a generation of readers," recalled former library director Greene.[47] To local librarians like Greene, the distinction between good and bad reading that library authorities like Bernard Berelson continued to maintain took a distant second place to the importance of simply encouraging reading as a habit. Providing what borrowers wanted to read took precedence over providing what was considered good for them. Initially, as noted earlier, the bookmobile staff consisted of a driver-cum-clerk (always male) and a professional librarian (usually female), but this arrangement proved expensive. After state funding ended in 1952, a more cost-conscious policy entailed that the driver not only drove and issued books, but also selected titles for purchase, chose which volumes to carry, and advised readers on their choices.

How did Bob select books? Here he took on the persona of the library professional. "Well I read a lot of reviews, you know, which we got in the library," he remembered. "You've got your *Booklist* and all that . . . and I was a great

---

45. Benton, "'Too Many Books,'" 274.
46. Interview with Gerry G., Algoma, Wisconsin, 9 January 2002.
47. Interview with Jane Livingston Greene, Sturgeon Bay, Wisconsin, 23 October 2000.

one for *Kirkus Reviews.*[48] He always looked, too, for newspaper reviews. "In fact I've gotten the *Chicago Tribune* all my life—the Sunday paper and their book section . . . is pretty good." Bob was folded into the professional library community both through his adoption of expert collecting practices, and through attending librarians' monthly meetings to discuss book selection. But he also listened to what he called his "customers." "Women loved the love stories," he said, "and men, they kind of kept away from them. Westerns, I would say, the men were more into westerns, and mysteries, and historicals. . . . Biographies I had to carry a few of those along. . . . [I]f I'd get a new biography in, why, they'd scarf it up, you know."

Bob set no limits on how many books patrons could borrow. People could check out "just as many as they could carry, right, and I wasn't always too strict about if they forgot to bring one back." Patrons often entered into discussions about books on the bookmobile, forming impromptu reading communities as they made their choices. "We had a lot of the women do that," Bob commented. " 'I just had this, can you give that to her this time?' You know, it worked that way, [and] then actually the children were that way too. A lot of them were good readers. 'My girlfriend wants to read this, this time, can she have it—can we have it back or renew it?' " But as time went on, Bob found himself supplementing the official titles he had so carefully selected from reviews and other sanctioned sources, with less official materials. "Towards the end . . . well, people were donating so many of them paperbacks, I'd go through and pick out a lot of fiction out of them. . . . Well, I had some of the ladies that liked [those] romances, then I'd have a box of those and they could just take them, and . . . I'd write on the slips five or six paperbacks. If they brought them back, okay. If they didn't, it was okay [too] because they were donated to start with." Thus bookmobile practice blurred the cultural distinctions that library professionals officially still supported.

Some Door County residents enjoyed other opportunities for reading not sanctioned by the library. Former bookmobile patrons Marlene and her sister Delores remembered reading comic books as children in the 1950s: "Our neighbors across the street . . . were from Chicago. . . . [T]heir father was a janitor in the Chicago apartments, and he would collect all the comic books. . . . [T]hose boys had boxes and boxes full. . . . [W]e would read the comic books all the time. Not that we could ever buy any because we didn't

---

48. *Kirkus Reviews,* which provides reviews of books in advance of publication, was founded in 1933 by Virginia Kirkus, formerly head of the children's book department at Harper & Bros. At first Kirkus made her bimonthly bulletin available only to subscribing bookstores, but two years later libraries were also able to subscribe.

have any money to buy them, but we sure got to read them from Ed and Joe."[49] The children understood perfectly that teachers, librarians, and even their parents considered this reading "inferior." Were there comic books on the bookmobile? "Oh no," said Delores emphatically, and "Oh definitely not," said Marlene. As parents themselves, they adopted a more liberal policy, though, for reasons that local librarians like Jane Livingston Greene—and even nineteenth-century authorities like Samuel Swett Green—would have approved. "Some people's philosophy was if they were reading a comic book they were reading junk," said Delores. "But I let [the children] read that book. If you were learning to read, what difference . . . if it's a comic book, because that might get you interested in reading something else."

As managerial discourse seeped into librarianship during the Progressive Era and gathered momentum in the interwar years, an increased stress on "performance" encouraged librarians to blur the distinction between good and bad reading. Individual public library directors had long been in the habit of recording numbers and categories of books circulating for publication in their annual reports, and to back up requests for local financial support. Whereas these earlier circulation reports often distinguished between fiction (by implication undesirable reading) and nonfiction (better), now these distinctions faded before a new need to maximize library use irrespective of quality. In 1921 the ALA accepted the principle of seeking federal funding for public libraries, though it was another seventeen years (1938) before the organization opened a Washington, D.C., office with the purpose of lobbying Congress. To bolster requests for federal assistance, library leaders' public rhetoric relied heavily on quantitative measurements of library use that focused on sheer numbers of circulating materials, while avoiding issues of reading quality. Not until 1956, with the passage of the Library Services Act, did the ALA finally get what it wanted; but in the meantime it had escalated the volume of its efforts in ways that affected the library profession's practices, and consequently, its values.

In 1943, for example, an ALA pamphlet entitled *The Equal Chance: Books Help to Make It* argued, "Books are the universal medium of education whether in school or outside—books to find the facts behind the news reel or broadcast—books to fit us for a job, or help us to find it—books to explain the economic picture and the world changing before our eyes—books for our children—books to enjoy." And yet, the pamphlet pointed out, books were more readily available in some areas than in others: "There are thirty-five million people in the United States who have no public libraries within reach. Of these thirty-five million citizens, thirty-two million live in small

---

49. Interview with Marlene and Delores, Door County, Wisconsin, 23 May 2001.

villages or in the open country, and having few books of their own, they are deprived of a basic means of education." Nowhere in this pamphlet does a distinction appear between worthy and unworthy books: reading—any reading—was to be valued, the authors implied. A key component of appeals for federal funding had become "statistics," as the ALA used carefully chosen numbers to back up its argument: "Realizing that difference in ability to pay for maintaining libraries accounts for many of the gross inequalities in library service, one is not surprised to learn that the state of Arkansas with $248 per-capita income spends only 5¢ per capita for public library service and reaches with it only 44 per cent of its population, while California with $734 per-capita income spends 84¢ per capita on the city and county libraries which serve 98 percent of its residents." *The Equal Chance* ended with several pages of charts and tables: "The statistical data on the following pages will enable you to compare your own state with other states, in order to estimate what your state has accomplished." First and most prominent was a table displaying circulation data per capita in public libraries in forty-eight states and the District of Columbia.[50] Clearly, if gross circulation figures were to form the foundation for an argument in favor of federal funding, and since fiction consistently accounted for 70 to 80 percent of circulation, reading fiction was now something to promote rather than frown upon. Linking funding to the managerial concept of performance favored a less discriminatory approach; indeed, a rapid turnover of books boosted the all-important statistics and thus contributed to the library's financial health.

In the early 1950s, the Door–Kewaunee Regional Library, too, paid careful attention to circulation and other use statistics, and employed these in an effort to persuade voters as well as county and state officials of the library's value to the community, and thus to continue funding it. In a publication summarizing the Demonstration's impact, the WFLC printed tables that displayed circulation data, reported on the results of specially commissioned evaluative surveys, and even calculated the time and cost of each title circulated.[51] Clearly, WFLC staff believed that the quantitative evidence that this "scientific" approach employed would count for more than librarians' impressionistic judgments about the quality of patrons' reading in persuading legislators and voters of the library's worth. And after all, numbers did translate into resources. Although in 1952 the numbers of Kewaunee County voters did not add up to continuing support for the regional library, in Door

---

50. *The Equal Chance: Books Help to Make It* (Chicago: American Library Association, 1943).

51. *The Idea in Action: A Report on the Door–Kewaunee Regional Library Demonstration, 1950–1952* (Madison: Wisconsin Free Library Commission, 1953), 26–37.

County numbers worked in the library's favor both in 1952 and again in 1967, when a barrage of protest—a "rebellion" according to one former patron—persuaded the Door County supervisors to retain the bookmobile.[52]

Although the official Door–Kewaunee Demonstration report, focusing mainly on quantity, avoided the issue of the content of patrons' reading, the picture that emerges from conversations with Bob and other library staff and patrons is one that at least in part valorizes those practices that many library leaders a century earlier had been so keen to denigrate. According to these members of the mid-twentieth-century Wisconsin library community, a "reader" was defined as one who read many books, who primarily read fiction, and who made little practical distinction between those materials sanctioned by the library and those that were not. In raising "a generation of readers," library staff encouraged children and adults to read often and to follow their desires—at least up to a point. And by the end of the century some official library practices originally aimed at supporting a high-culture, professional, ideology of reading, had been converted to a "populist" purpose. In 1982, at about the time that the study of popular culture was achieving legitimacy in the academy, the publisher Libraries Unlimited produced a volume targeted at Readers' Advisors.[53] The author, Betty Rosenberg, taught a library class at the University of California that took a revolutionary perspective on reading. *Genreflecting: A Guide to Reading Interests in Genre Fiction* (now in its fifth edition) focused on precisely those categories that librarians formerly considered so objectionable: Westerns, Thrillers, Romances, Science Fiction, Fantasy, and Horror. Rosenberg's advice "Never apologize for your reading tastes" became codified into "Rosenberg's first law of reading."[54] Publication of *Genreflecting* signaled that a reading identity practiced by generations of library users was now legitimate, and that though still controversial, reading "genre fiction," had become a mainstream practice in American public libraries.

Scrutinizing the public library's history reveals that library leaders, despite articulating their ideology of the ideal reader in their professional writings, and attempting to impose it by means of organizational and physical structures, were not necessarily successful. The reading public did not passively

---

52. Interview with Gayle G., Sturgeon Bay, Wisconsin, 23 May 2001.

53. For an overview of the cultural studies debate over "Cultural populism," see John Storey, *An Introduction to Cultural Theory and Popular Culture,* 2d ed. (Athens: University of Georgia Press, 1998), 202–29; and Betty Rosenberg, *Genreflecting: A Guide to Reading Interests in Genre Fiction* (Englewood, CO: Libraries Unlimited, 1982).

54. Diana Tixier Herald, *Genreflecting: A Guide to Reading Interests in Genre Fiction,* 5th ed. (Englewood, CO: Libraries Unlimited, 2000), xiii.

accede to the official library ideology. Research into historical readers in specific localities can provide an important corrective to "top-down" analysis that over-privileges a monolithic interpretation of cultural authority. Such studies foreground readers' own choices and influences on local library practice—influences that sometimes reinforced and at other times subverted official policies and goals. Local librarians, too, might diverge widely from authoritative recommendations; articles published in professional journals are not necessarily an accurate guide to actual practice. And "official" policy itself was never unified or uniform. Even in the nineteenth century, the rhetoric on reading in public libraries was divided, as library leaders attempted to balance competing ideologies while promoting the health of this always financially challenged institution. By investigating both the library profession's rhetoric and the experiences of specific reading communities, historians can show that reading as a cultural practice, and the associated identity of "reader," emerge in diverse forms from a complex set of environments. In its own small way, the Door County bookmobile itself represented contested terrain. In selecting reading materials, Bob relied on the one hand on the stalwarts of standard professional collection development: *Kirkus Reviews, Booklist,* and the *Chicago Tribune.* On the other, he was happy to "dilute" the collection with donated romances, mysteries, and westerns—paperbacks that patrons often returned, but sometimes did not.

Five years after the publication of *Genreflecting* validated the library practices that he had been putting into operation for years, Bob retired from the bookmobile. He would rather have kept working, but the old van leaked fumes and affected his health. "I really enjoyed it—I wouldn't take a million dollars for it," Bob said. "I loved the people and I loved the kids. In fact I loved the kids when I quit more than anybody." And the Door Peninsula readers missed him, too. "My customers . . . they come up to me, 'Hi Bob . . . I sure wish you were on that bookmobile again!' You know, I got a lot of that. . . . [W]hen I'd go into town, or see somebody, why it was, 'Oh you've got to get back on that bookmobile, you've got to get it together, we can't find no books, you know.'" For nineteenth-century library leaders, Bob would have had all the "wrong" characteristics for a library professional; an inveterate or persistent fiction reader himself, he would also have been excluded by his class from the ranks of library authorities, and by his gender from the ranks of library assistants. Yet to Door County readers, Bob was the perfect Reader's Advisor—patient, friendly, knowledgeable, flexible—but never judgmental. And ironically, it is Bob's brand of populist readership rather than the library authorities' professional reading identity that today provides the popular support that permits the public library's survival. Walk into any public library, and you will find prominently displayed—often on supermarket-type revolving carousels—large quantities of popular fiction. Shelved by genre, these romances, mysteries, horror stories, and books of science fiction constitute one of the library's biggest "selling points." An enormous range of commercially produced printed reference tools, along with websites and electronic databases like *NoveList* and *What Do I Read Next* provide librarians and patrons with detailed information on authors, titles, characters, and story lines that help match readers with their favorite type of book. The very existence of these guides, websites, and databases constitutes a form of cultural authority that itself provides a justification for popular materials in the library. Such materials have formed a solid base of library use for over a century—but in the early twenty-first century librarians no longer need to feel guilty about them.

Chapter 11

Toward a New Cultural Design

The American Council of Learned Societies, the Social Science Research Council, and Libraries in the 1930s

Kenneth Carpenter

In the late 1920s, the scholarly world was experiencing signs of a publishing crisis. Would the philanthropic foundations continue to provide sufficient subsidies to cover rising costs? At the same time, scholars were experiencing needs for source materials that libraries were unable to provide, and libraries, in addition, were finding that many of their existing holdings were crumbling. American learned societies in the humanities and social sciences responded. Through their umbrella organizations, they formed a joint committee, which to this day continues to be the only instance in which scholars of many sorts took a long and hard look at what might be called the infrastructure of academia. The committee was active throughout the 1930s, almost all of that time chaired by the visionary historian Robert C. Binkley (see figure 11.1).

The Joint Committee on Materials for Research initially focused on these problems of scholars and libraries, with emphasis on the possibility that the new technologies of reproduction, in both paper and film, could solve them by creating a new pattern of communication. They could, Binkley envisioned, diffuse among libraries the source materials for research, and then inexpensively disseminate the results of the scholar's work, even assist in the note taking and document gathering inherent in that process.

As the decade progressed, Binkley came to see wider possibilities for the developing technologies. He came to believe that they could create a new cultural design. With use of the new technologies, every town, many families even, would find that individuals were able to research, write, and then disseminate histories within the small, interested circle. Or, towns could have their published poet; that art would then be public, just as were music and visual art, through local bands, choral societies, and art shows. Binkley also anticipated collaboration in scholarship, with some individuals pursuing

Figure 11.1. Robert Cedric Binkley. Reproduced from a photograph by Frances W. Binkley.

research not to write it up themselves, but to aid professional historians. High school teachers, especially, he envisioned, would become researchers. The web would also be furthered by local historical societies using the technologies to record their holdings and even to disseminate copies.

Binkley wished to further what he called "history for a democracy." [1]

---

1. Robert Binkley, "History for a Democracy," *Minnesota History* 18 (1937): 1–27. This was presented on January 18, 1937, before the Minnesota Historical Society. Page numbers in parentheses refer to *Selected Papers of Robert C. Binkley*, ed. Max H. Fisch (Cambridge: Harvard University Press, 1948).

"History," he wrote, "nourishes the spirit of any institution." It creates "a conception of relationship with . . . [the] past," and furthers "a feeling that our present activity has some meaning in the scheme of time" (198). Binkley's development of the implications of historical knowledge was, as the title of his essay indicates, stimulated by fear of the spread of totalitarian regimes. He was, however, explicitly opposed to a purely celebratory history of democratic institutions, to the inculcation of any particular view of the past. Such a history would resemble that of the fascist regimes. He urged, on the contrary, that "investigators [must be] free to follow wherever the evidence leads them . . . even if it should be discovered that the heroes of democracy were villains, and that the institutions of democracy did not function as the well-wishers of democracy would have preferred" (201). It was not a nationalistic history that he wished, but rather a history that would "nourish and sustain . . . the value of the individual personality and the protection for him of a maximum zone of freedom" (202), within the framework of "groups of all kinds, organized in all ways" (202). Indeed, he saw the "federative organization of society" (202) as protecting the freedom of the individual against a centralized state. It was not the group that had to be protected against an excess of individualism, but rather the group that was necessary to maintaining the freedom of individuals—to the end, Binkley explicitly stated, that the "people" rule themselves. They "must act with a keen respect for facts, for knowledge, for enlightenment. They must be willing to get together on the common platform of discovered truth, wherever that platform may be" (202). In other words, it was the process that was crucial.

Binkley saw three kinds of history as preserving these values. One was a "history of individuals," that is, family history. The history that would preserve our federative structure was local history, and the "history that will preserve the basis of government by ourselves is history written by ourselves" (203), which, he noted, "implies participation in scholarship," since that induces "respect for truth and understanding of the methods by which it is investigated" (203). The amateur was thus a vital part of the web of scholarship. As he wrote in his conclusion to "History for a Democracy," "Let us therefore have history of the people, by the people, and for the people." Or, as he concluded his essay "The Cultural Program of the W.P.A.," in which he called for the schools to use documentary materials in teaching, "ultimately, the American people will be more conscious of the possibilities of the democratization and enrichment of our culture."

Although Binkley did not, he might have applied an expression employed by Horace Mann in his third (1839) report as Massachusetts Commissioner of Education to describe the important function of libraries: formation of "a powerful, and exemplary people."[2] Binkley stood in a line that in fact went back beyond Mann to the early days of the Republic, and through him and the Joint Committee on Materials of Research, the American Council of Learned Societies (ACLS) and the Social Science Research Council (SSRC) attempted in the third decade of the twentieth century to change both American scholarship and American society.

THE ACLS and the SSRC did not have in mind such a broad agenda when they created the Joint Committee in 1929, and the Joint Committee began with attention to scholarly problems. These were, however, not so much signs of weakness as of the transformation of scholarship in the 1920s. The Great War marked a divide. In its aftermath the United States moved from being an outpost of scholarship into a leading role—in the minds of some, even the nation primarily responsible for maintaining the traditions of Western culture. Thus, as early as May 1919, the American Association of University Professors drafted a plan for an International Catalogue of Humanistic Literature, and the Carnegie Endowment for International Peace was asked for $50,000 for an "International Congress for the purpose of laying plans to produce an Apparatus of Scholarship that would be of value to the scholars of the world in the field of the Humanities to supplement the International Catalogue of Scientific Literature now being revised by the Royal Society of London."[3] The bibliography was never undertaken, but humanistic scholarship and international peace were clearly linked in this call for a humanistic project that was analogous to one in the sciences. Implicitly, the letter states, balance must be maintained in the world of learning, and that had been lost. The Carnegie Endowment, on January 28, 1919, had appropriated $5 million to the National Academy of Sciences, which placed the National Research Council, established in 1916 during the war, on a permanent basis. It became the second foundation-funded institution devoted to scientific research, the first being the Rockefeller Institute for Medical Research, established in 1901. The message was not lost on the Carnegie foundations. Both the Carnegie

---

2. *Common School Journal* 2 (15 April 1840): 120. Binkley did not need to read Horace Mann to come by his views; they were experientially derived. His father, a high school teacher, one-time secretary to Joaquin Miller, was also a published poet who learned Chinese and built up a working library for Chinese studies. Also crucial may have been the experience of driving from California to New York in 1927. In that era before the interstates, the Binkleys experienced firsthand town after town. Fisch, in two paragraphs obviously based on an interview with Mrs. Binkley, recounted the trip and the conversation; see Fisch, "Robert Cedric Binkley: Historian in the Long Armistice," *Selected Papers,* 11–12.

3. Letter from Yale's Secretary to the "Carnegie Peace Foundation," 26 May 1919; Yale Librarian Papers, Box 5, folder 43 (RU, 19ND–A–233).

Corporation and the Carnegie Foundation for International Peace supported the American Council of Learned Societies.[4] A few years later, in 1923 (incorporated 1924), the social scientists, following the earlier examples, formed the Social Science Research Council, with major support again coming from foundations, especially those of the Rockefellers.

The foundations, besides assisting learned societies, had two major possible ways to further the advance of knowledge. One was to create, outside universities, research institutions devoted to humanistic or social science studies, as they had done in the sciences. The Brookings Institution is an example of such an institution, but the foundations also decided to support research in universities. They recognized that universities were no longer only teaching institutions serving undergraduates. They had changed, in part thanks to funding for pensions and salaries as well as to gifts for endowment from the various Carnegie and Rockefeller foundations, donations that also stimulated support from individuals. With both stronger finances and a new sense of their mission, the major universities could be partners of the foundations in creating new knowledge.[5]

The emphasis on research created a need for subventions for publishing the results of research. The need was brought to the attention of the foundations, as in the December 1926 "Report of the Advisory Group" of the Rockefeller-funded General Education Board, which called for "general subventions to periodicals, and series of monographs, [plus] special aid for the publication of individual books."[6] They did support publication, but the learned societies were uneasy about whether subventions would continue. Today's crisis in scholarly publishing is not a new phenomenon. The anomaly was the post–World War II era when scholarly publishing flourished, thanks to the expansion of well-funded libraries and to the growing number of academicians.

Just as increased funding for research led to manuscripts worthy of publication, it also created a need for source materials as well as access to an ever-

---

4. It was officially formed on February 14, 1920, at a meeting in the office of the Institute of International Studies, an organization funded by the Carnegie Endowment. That meeting was chaired by the institute's director, Stephen P. Duggan, who was also involved in the bibliography.

5. Roger L. Geiger, *To Advance Knowledge: The Growth of American Research Universities, 1900–1940* (New York: Oxford University Press, 1986; New Brunswick, NJ: Transaction Publishers, 2004) is crucial to understanding this period, especially chaps. 1, 3–5. No indication has been found that foundations turned to universities because they possessed in libraries the tools of scholarship. See also Frederick P. Keppel, *The Foundation: Its Place in American Life* (New York: Macmillan, 1930), where the discussion on pp. 87–88 indicates consideration of the two options for foundation efforts to advance knowledge.

6. In Yale Librarian Papers, box 37, folder 413, General Education Board.

wider range of scholarly monographs and journals. The problem was acute. Except for some traditional fields in which the need was for a limited body of currently produced publications, such as classical and medieval studies, few libraries had adequate research collections. Even for publications issued in the United States, no library equaled the comparable holdings of, say, France's Bibliothèque nationale, which had long been the beneficiary of copyright deposit in a highly centralized nation. No union catalogue, not even on cards, then existed, so a scholar could not determine if and where a particular book was held, without turning to colleagues and librarians. The possessing library might lend, but otherwise the option was either travel or a photostatic copy, if the library had one of those quite new machines. The great microfilm collections, which brought together holdings from many libraries, did not then exist, let alone today's online versions. The scholar in 1929 would only just have been able to determine where a file of a journal might exist, thanks to the *Union List.* Library directors, both professional librarians and faculty library directors, had long been aware of the inadequacy of collections. With exceptions, particularly at the Library of Congress, the New York Public Library, Harvard and Yale, and some specialized libraries, the accepted wisdom was that the necessary research materials could be brought to this country only by dividing up collecting areas. For example, Library X would emphasize Spanish literature, while Library Y built Italian. Library directors could not implement such coordination. Even if a few directors had sufficient power and money to participate, their numbers were small. In almost all institutions, funds were controlled by a faculty library committee whose main function was to divvy them up among the academic departments. To set some aside for a national plan would have required a consensus impossible to reach, and, of course, librarians themselves were eager to have their allocation for reference books or for special purchases be as large as possible.[7]

---

7. The problem, with concrete examples, was spelled out by Princeton's librarian, James Thayer Gerould, in a letter of 25 January 1932 to Robert C. Binkley. It reads in part: "The primary task of every library is to meet the current demands of its constituency, demands, which, in most of them, are seldom fully met. No library can, or should, accept a program which would make it impossible for it to meet reasonable requests for books from the men actually on the ground. So long as the universities which the libraries serve do not delimit their fields, so long as they do not recognize the necessity for the development of American scholarship on a national basis, so long as we maintain institutional particularism, no very significant results can be expected. Every effort thus far made to secure cooperation, except as the plans have been related to institutions within particular cities, has failed. A committee of the Modern Language Association which, for several years, has been attempting to secure agreements as to the distribution of Spanish periodicals, was compelled, at its last meeting, to confess its powerlessness and to ask for discharge. A similar attempt of the psychologists, a number of years ago, and efforts which I personally have made to distribute the responsibility for

The problem of collections was, in fact, intellectual as well. What appropriately constituted library materials, and what did scholars really need? Scholarly monographs and journals, both current and back files, were indisputably desirable, as were editions of the works of canonical authors and most kinds of earlier printed source materials for historians, especially if obtained by gift. But manuscripts? Ephemera? Material in fields not taught? Material published outside the book trade, such as state and municipal publications? Some such material for the social scientist was outside the ken of the humanistically trained librarian, who was accustomed to serving the social scientist who pursued traditional historical and a priori approaches. Some social scientists who sought to develop general laws that would result in improved conditions of life wanted to obtain "knowledge and understanding of the natural forces that are manifested in the behavior of people and of things," and they were not sure they needed libraries very much at all. Beardsley Ruml, the powerful director of the Laura Spelman Rockefeller Memorial, was one such, and an influential 1924 report that he commissioned advocated field work and statistics.[8] Others did emphasize materials,[9] and a major statement was made at the August–September 1929 meeting in Hanover, New Hampshire, of the Council of the SSRC. It drew up a list of "ultimate objectives" and detailed the "specific policies and procedures" for obtaining them.[10] Seven methods were listed, followed by specifics. The seven, which "came to be reverently referred to . . . as The Seven Roman Numerals,"[11] were:

---

the purchase of files of the French and German local historical, archaeological and literary societies, have had no result. Everywhere there is a recognition of the importance of the task, but there is equal unanimity in the claim that there are no funds which can be used for the purchase of books that are not in immediate demand."

8. For a discussion of Ruml's role and of Lawrence K. Frank's report, "The Status of Social Science in the United States," see Geiger, *To Advance Knowledge,* 149–56.

9. Librarians and scholars, as well as foundations, were concerned. For example, the Laura Spelman Rockefeller Memorial requested a report on "what is being done for the collection and preservation of material of all sorts that may serve to illustrate and record the various phases of contemporary life"; and the Association of American Universities sponsored a study of libraries (George A. Works, *College and University Library Problems, a Study of a Selected Group of Institutions Prepared for the Association of American Universities,* 1927). In 1926, two of the five committees of the SSRC were the Committee on Publication of an Index and Digest of State Session Laws and the Committee on Abstracts of Social Science Periodical Literature, which was also working with a League of Nations subcommittee seeking to develop a "plan for a general analysis of social science literature."

10. Council of the SSRC, *Fifth Annual Report, 1928–1929* (November 1929), Appendix B, 42–46.

11. Elbridge Sibley, *Social Science Research Council: The First Fifty Years,* 162, which is available online, following Kenton W. Worcester's *Social Science Research Council, 1923–1998* (New York, 2001), on the SSRC website.

I. By improvement of research organization
II. By development of personnel
III. By enlargement, improvement and preservation of materials
IV. By improvement of research methods
V. By facilitation of the dissemination of materials, methods and results of investigations
VI. By facilitation of research projects
VII. By enhancement of the general appreciation of the significance of the social sciences.

Two of the seven, numbers 3 and 5, have to do with materials, and the "specific policies and procedures" spelled out under those headings demonstrate a keen understanding of relevant issues relating to materials: [12]

III. Enlargement, Improvement and Preservation of Materials

Since scientific progress in all fields is conditioned by the existence of a constantly enlarging body of research materials and by its availability to investigators, one of the primary duties of the Council is to promote such objects and to concern itself with the improvement and preservation of research data. In carrying out these purposes the following courses of action are appropriate:

A. Initiating and participating in plans for making more comparable and more widely serviceable the classifications of social and economic data, for making more precise the significance of the data, and for otherwise improving such records

B. Helping to lay out a plan for the nation-wide development and coördination of existing archival collections and for the building up of new research collections along special lines at strategic scholarly and geographical centers

C. Initiating and participating in plans for constructing union finding lists and calendars of the resources of existing research libraries, with particular reference to their social data, so as to make them more available to scholars

D. Initiating and participating in plans to discover, select, edit, publish, or otherwise reproduce basic data in the social sciences, which are difficult of access to students or likely to perish

E. Calling to the attention of individuals and of governmental, business and other institutions and agencies the importance of preserving their records for future analysis and study

F. Encouraging the adoption and widespread use of those varieties of paper and other materials used in the making of records which promise a maximum durability

---

12. I have been unable to determine who was responsible for the detailed plan laid out in roman numeral III.

G. Initiating, encouraging and participating in plans to develop the research uses of historical, industrial and social museums; and encouraging the building up of new collections with these purposes in mind.

V. Facilitation of the Dissemination of Materials, Methods and Results of Investigations

Social research is directly aided by the publication and distribution of the results of investigations to research workers and by opportunities for fruitful contact among investigators. The following types of activity are appropriate to these ends:

A. Publication:
1. Encouragement in all types of publication of (a) the prompt issuance of advance summary notices of research results for the information of other workers in the same field, following the practice of the natural sciences; and (b) the making available in some form of the full data on which published reports are based
2. Study through conferences and other means of the service rendered currently by social science journals, including the problem of adequate technical reviewing
3. Possible development under the Council of a reprint and bulletin service similar to that of the National Research Council
4. Encouragement of the assembly of research abstracts in specific fields of research
5. Study of the need for monograph series in various fields of inquiry
6. Representation to the universities of their responsibility in making doctoral dissertations generally available
7. Coöperation with State and Federal agencies in the more prompt dissemination of the results of investigations made under tax-supported auspices
8. Study of the problem of the publication of social science material including textbooks, by university presses and commercial publishers in so far as such publication affects the range and adequacy of the material made available
B. Interchange of information through conference and other informal means:
1. Development of ready informal interchange of points of view, research experience and data among (a) the departments, including the pertinent natural sciences, in a given university; and (b) research agencies of all kinds, including commercial agencies in a given geographical location
2. Development of formal conferences, including (a) active coöperation with the various associations in their Christmas meetings, and (b) the sponsoring of carefully planned meetings of workers on a given problem at centers at which active work on this problem is going forward.

The SSRC Council also voted to ask the ACLS to join in forming a commit-tee.[13] The ACLS agreed, and the first meeting of the Joint Committee was held on February 17–18, 1930, at SSRC offices in New York. It was chaired by Dr. Solon J. Buck, superintendent of the Minnesota Historical Society. The other initial members were N. S. B. Gras, professor of business history at the Harvard Business School (also involved with the Mediaeval Academy), Clark Wissler of the American Museum of Natural History; Waldo G. Leland, per-manent secretary of the ACLS; Harry Miller Lydenberg[14] of the New York Public Library; Arthur H. Quinn, professor of English at the University of Pennsylvania; and Robert C. Binkley, professor of history at Western Reserve University.

Binkley could not make the meeting, but he contributed in advance of it a four-page, single-spaced memorandum, "Possibilities for Enlargement, Improvement and Preservation of Research Material." It began by noting three research problems in chemistry and technology—paper manufacture, paper preservation, and "miniature photography and projection"—that, "if solved . . . will affect much of the practical development of policy." Binkley's evident capacity for hard and thoughtful work continued to be demonstrated, and in September he was appointed secretary of the committee; then in 1932, after Buck asked to be relieved of the chairmanship, Binkley was selected chairman. He continued in that role until his death from cancer of the esoph-agus in the spring of 1940.

Binkley was, along with Lydenberg, his closest colleague on the commit-tee, a pioneer in concern about preservation. Although the American Library Association had established a committee to look into paper quality in 1912, concern about paper had not gone beyond the doors of libraries. Lydenberg changed that. He wanted scientific research, and when the National Research Council argued that research into paper quality was a library problem, Lyden-berg retorted that librarians were not scientists, that the chemistry of paper was a problem for scientists.[15] He was instrumental in getting the Carnegie

---

13. The precise steps in setting up the new committee are unclear. The *Fifth Annual Report,* covering 1 July 1928, to 1 September 1929, records the existence of a Joint Committee on Enlarge-ment, Improvement and Preservation of Data, a name that Robert S. Lynd, permanent secretary of the SSRC, used in a letter to Harry Miller Lydenberg, on 7 January 1930, when the new committee should have been formed (NYPL Archives, RG6, ser. 2, box 3, Lydenberg: December 1929–Febru-ary 1930). The only difference between the membership of the two committees is that Quinn and Binkley had been added. It is possible that changing the name was crucial, since the use of "data" has a definite social science ring.

14. Lydenberg's official title was Reference Librarian, a term that then meant he was head of the Reference Library at 42nd Street.

15. New York Public Library, Director's Office, Edwin Hatfield Anderson papers, Series 1: Gen-eral correspondence, 1915–1928, Box 12, National Research Council folder.

Corporation to make a grant of $10,000 on October 15, 1929, to carry out the scientific work. Lydenberg may also have been behind the ACLS Council considering, on January 26, 1929, "the imminent danger of the loss of much manuscript and printed material through disintegration of the paper on which it was printed."[16]

Lydenberg and Binkley had in fact met over the issue of preservation.[17] In 1927, Binkley, then an instructor at New York University, sent his undergraduates to the New York Public Library to comb through the library's holdings of Public Record Office publications on the Spanish armada; and the student use was so heavy that it was brought to the attention of Lydenberg, perhaps by Keyes Metcalf, who was then Lydenberg's deputy. Lydenberg got in touch with Binkley and asked him to come by to talk over the problem his assignment was creating. Years later, Lydenberg recorded that Binkley's "first words when we met showed intensity, zeal, appreciation of the other man's point of view, willingness to adjust himself to conditions, and at the same time confidence in his cause and insistence on its rightness. That first impression grew more attractive the longer I came to see and talk with the man."[18]

For Binkley, this encounter made vivid the "problem of reconciling maximum use of research materials in the present, with their preservation for future generations"[19] and he, ever the historian, was stimulated to look into the question historically. The result was "The Problem of Perishable Paper," delivered at the First World Congress of Libraries and Bibliography, held in Rome in June 1929.[20] He wrote that upon the first introduction of writing, durable materials had been used. This meant that libraries were able to serve the twin goals of disseminating texts and preserving them. No conflict existed between those two goals — not until the second half of the nineteenth century. Binkley was well aware of the irony of the timing of the introduction of wood-pulp paper. "The nineteenth century made us more conscious of our duty to history." We came to "understand that an accurate knowledge of

---

16. ACLS *Bulletin* no. 11 (June 1929): 38.

17. Although it may be that Lydenberg suggested Binkley be appointed to the committee, Binkley's appointment may have been a result of his earlier acquaintance with Robert T. Crane, who succeeded Lynd as permanent secretary. Binkley had studied under Crane at Stanford, and that relationship is indicated by the fact that Crane was one of the few people to address Binkley as "Bob." Binkley never used Crane's first name in correspondence. Crane's support was, in any case, crucial in the work of the Joint Committee.

18. Fisch, "Robert Cedric Binkley," in *Selected Papers,* 12, quoting from Lydenberg's memorial statement in American Council of Learned Societies, *Bulletin* no. 33 (October 1941): 56–59.

19. Fisch, "Robert Cedric Binkley," 12–13.

20. This paper is published in Primo Congresso Mondiale delle Biblioteche e di Bibliografia, *Atti* (Rome: Libreria dello Stato, 1931), and reprinted in Binkley, *Selected Papers,* 169–78. Binkley attended the conference as representative of the Hoover Library.

all aspects of our past was essential to clear thinking upon the present. And having thus taught us the value and sanctity of all records, it began to print its records upon highly perishable paper!" Now the two duties diverge, because the writing materials are no longer durable. The librarian of today, is, as a result, "unable to do what . . . [earlier generations] have done, for the records of our time are written in dust" (170–71).

After putting forth the need for research on paper quality and for working out a means whereby publishers would produce some copies of printed material on durable paper, Binkley turned to salvaging what was already in libraries. He concluded that the cost-effective way was by reducing a photographic reproduction to "microscopic proportions and reading it by projection or by some other optical device" (177). That paper was delivered before a learned audience concerned primarily with books and libraries, but as early as January 1929, right in the period when Lydenberg was striving to obtain scientific assistance on the problem of poor paper, Binkley had also written for a scientific and more popular readership. In that essay in *Scientific American,* he proposed as a solution, "photographic copying . . . on a reduced scale, to be read back again with a magnifying glass or by projection on a screen."[21] That paper was condensed in *Reader's Digest* in February 1929, the month after its appearance in *Scientific American,* thus showing both the novelty of the topic and the belief that it would be of interest to an audience beyond the learned.

Binkley was not the first to advocate photographic copying, but he was perhaps the first to urge "reduced-scale photographic copies" and to call for "coördination of the salvaging efforts of the libraries of the world" (178). Although microphotography was then known,[22] by 1930 it had barely been mentioned with respect to libraries. Photography had, however, entered into the world of libraries in the second decade of the twentieth century,[23] and by 1921 at least a few librarians had the idea of using photography for col-

---

21. In this essay, Binkley also likened the process of deterioration to "slow fires": "That is to say, the decomposition of wood-pulp paper is chemically identical with the burning of a log in the fireplace, except that the process goes on at a lower temperature, and takes a longer time." C. Binkley [sic], "Do the Records of Science Face Ruin?" *Scientific American* 140 (January 1929): 29.

22. Allan B. Veaner, ed., *Studies in Micropublishing, 1853–1976: Documentary Sources* (Westport, CT: Microform Review Inc., 1976), 81–99.

23. Mentions in Harvard annual reports document this point. In the 1914–15 *Reports of the President and Treasurer of Harvard College* (p. 149), the acting dean of the Harvard Law School, Austin Wakeman Scott, wrote about "probably" photographing occasional laws by the "new photostatic process, at a moderate expense," wording that suggested a future direction. In the 1920–21 *Report* (p. 229), the librarian of Harvard College, William Coolidge Lane, wrote that the Harvard College Library was supplying photostats made by the photostat operator of the Massachusetts Historical Society. In the 1920s, Harvard libraries began to record gifts of photostat copies; see the searchable file of annual reports at http://hul.harvard.edu/huarc/refshelf/.

lection building—even doing so cooperatively, albeit on a small scale. The Newberry Library, as early as June 1921, distributed a list of titles that it was considering obtaining as photographic reproductions. It asked in part for bibliographical information on the books, as well as for locations of copies (there was not yet a National Union Catalog), but the goal behind publishing the list was larger. The Newberry sought to determine whether other libraries might wish "to co-operate in the enterprise to obtain prints for their own collections."[24] It noted that the Modern Language Association had appointed a committee to look into the question of photographic reproductions. An attempt was even made, by Frederic Ives Carpenter, a professor of English, to summarize American thinking and activities at this time. This 1921 essay included a "suggestive letter," dated July 5, 1921, of George Parker Winship whose responsibilities in the Harvard Library included the Widener Memorial Rooms and the Treasure Room. In his letter Winship went beyond the idea of buying copies of various books in a number of areas. His vision was that libraries would, after acquiring a collection of originals, systematically use photography to complete the holdings of those materials.[25] A programmatic step was taken by scholars, in that the photographs obtained via the committee of the Modern Language Association, mentioned in the Newberry pamphlet, were being centrally deposited at the Library of Congress. Then the librarians involved undertook to make these photographs, as well as others, available through a union list of them. Their 1929 catalogue recorded about one thousand titles reported by libraries across the country, including the ninety-six deposited in the Library of Congress through the MLA.[26]

Besides exploring photography as a means to acquire materials, scholars and librarians were also beginning to see a role for photography in disseminating the products of scholarship. Thus, the American Council of Learned Societies *Bulletin* no. 8 (October 1928) contained "An Inexpensive Method

24. See *Proposed Photographic Reproductions of Rare Books and Manuscripts* (Chicago: Newberry Library [1921]), i–iii.

25. Frederic Ives Carpenter, "The Photographic Reproduction of Rare Books," *Papers of the Bibliographical Society of America* 15 (1921): 35–46. It was also reprinted and distributed separately. The Winship letter is on pp. 41–42.

26. *A Union Catalog of Photo Facsimiles in North American Libraries: Material So Far Received by the Library of Congress,* comp. Ernest Kletsch, Curator of Union Catalogs of the Library of Congress (Yardley, PA: F. S. Cook & Son, 1929). Interest in photographic reproductions of manuscripts was not confined to this have-not nation across the Atlantic. Indeed, the British took another step toward systematic effort by surveying library policies and facilities for copying in countries around the world. The answers to the August 1921 questionnaire that the British Foreign Office had distributed were compiled and printed as *Photographs of Manuscripts: Reports from His Majesty's Representatives Abroad Respecting Facilities for Obtaining Photographs of Manuscripts in Public Libraries in Certain Foreign Countries* (London: Stationery Office, 1922).

of Reproducing Material Out of Print."[27] No author's name is attached to the essay, which describes a "method known variously as the zincographic, planographic, or off-set process." It records that the United States Government Printing Office established early in 1927 a zincographic department for producing out-of-print material,[28] and it concludes by stating that the Executive Offices of the ACLS can supply "names of concerns . . . samples, and the most recent quotations." If the GPO could use the process for out-of-print material, it could also do so for new publications.

Although only a few pioneers envisioned that printing from raised type would lose its monopoly as a means of disseminating substantial numbers of copies of a text, handwriting had long since lost its monopoly in making individual copies. The typewriter was by then common in libraries,[29] and it could be used to create masters for duplicating or making multiple copies. Among the many processes, some, such as the hectograph and mimeograph, had been developed in the 1870s and 1880s.[30]

It was inevitable that someone would see the possibility of microcopying text and then projecting it for the scholar to read. The first such proposal seems to have been Robert Goldschmidt and Paul Otlet's *Sur une forme nouvelle du livre: Le livre microphotographique,* Institut international de bibliographie, publication no. 81 (Brussels, 1906).[31] Although this publication was available in the United States and the Institut international de Bibliographie was itself well known—and controversial—in the 1920s, it may be that the example of the cinema was more important in drawing attention to the possibilities of microphotography. In fact, the term "projecting" was used to describe what machines for reading microfilm would do, and the film itself that was employed for "micro-copies" or "film-slides," was initially the same film used in movies.

---

27. "An Inexpensive Method of Reproducing Material out of Print," ACLS *Bulletin* no. 8 (October 1928): 11–15.

28. The essay, in mentioning that the GPO had reproduced a sixty-page brochure on Joseph Pennell for the Library of Congress, emphasized that zincography could be used by libraries and scholars for current publications.

29. It seems that typewriters came to be adopted in library work in the 1890s and 1900s. Thus, the University of Rochester Library acquired its first typewriter in 1898; see http://www.library. rochester.edu/. Penn State bought its first typewriter for producing catalogue cards in 1902; see http://www.libraries.psu.edu/tas/cataloging/dept/history.htm.

30. Many machines are described and pictured at http://www.officemuseum.com/copy_machines .htm. The website is based on a variety of printed works, among them Barbara Rhodes and William W. Streeter, *Before Photocopying: The Art & History of Mechanical Copying, 1780–1938* (New Castle, DE: Oak Knoll Press, 1999), and T. A. Russo, *Office Collectibles: 100 Years of Business Technology* (Atglen, PA: Schiffer, 2000).

31. A translation appears in Veaner, ed., *Studies in Micropublishing,* 100–108.

Because Binkley linked preservation and the reproduction of texts, including microfilm reproduction, he was an ideal member of the Joint Committee. More than that, though, Binkley—the scholar and former librarian—saw the possibility of newly developing technologies for disseminating source material. He knew firsthand that printed materials, even those of recent times, can be exceedingly rare and worthy of preservation and dissemination. Binkley had, immediately after the war, assisted in France in collecting material on the war on behalf of Herbert Hoover. Then, while pursuing a doctorate in history, he worked as reference librarian from 1923 to 1927 in the Hoover Library on War, Revolution, and Peace, which preeminently among American libraries was collecting modern source materials.

The year after receiving his Ph.D., 1928, Binkley published an article in *Historical Outlook,* "Revision of World History," in which he argued that historical writing changes in response to the interests of successive periods and that archival policy should take into account successive shifts—ideas that were not then truisms a decade before the Society of American Archivists was formed. In 1929, the thirty-one-year-old was also a rising star in the historical profession. Not only was he highly productive as a scholar; his "Ten Years of Peace Conference History," published in the December 1929 issue of the *Journal of Modern History,* had, according to its editor, "aroused more comment and evoked more praise than any other contribution to the *Journal.*" Binkley began his teaching career at New York University. When Sidney B. Fay moved to Harvard from Smith in 1929, he suggested Binkley as his successor, calling him "the most promising man in the field of modern European history." Binkley spent a year there before moving to Western Reserve in the fall of 1930, where he repeatedly returned after teaching stints at Harvard (1932–33) and at Columbia (1937–38).[32]

Binkley the observer of the academic world also saw that the developing technologies of reproduction could make it possible to publish for the ever-smaller scholarly communities that Binkley the historian saw as an inevitable consequence of the development of academic disciplines. The advent of printing, argued Binkley, enabled the "moderately wealthy man" to afford "a fairly complete collection of the materials he desired" (181).[33] And since what the individual scholar desired was identical to what others also wished, the means of reproduction of texts meshed with the needs of the scholarly world. As, however, learning markedly advanced in the eighteenth century, special-

---

32. Fisch, "Robert Cedric Binkley," is the source of the biographical information about Binkley.

33. Robert C. Binkley, "New Tools for Men of Letters," *Yale Review,* n.s. 24 (1935): 519–27; rpt. in *Selected Papers,* 179–97.

ization also developed. Then, in the nineteenth century significant change took place in the economics of book production and distribution. Cheap and abundant paper was introduced about midcentury, and that, combined with mass literacy, altered the economics of book production, making large editions necessary in order to absorb the costs. In this world, the scholar could easily obtain what everyone else also wanted, but "the body of documentation that was once the common ground of all learning and culture [had] . . . lost its cohesion," and scholarly publications had become a "relatively unimportant element in the total bulk of publication" (182). The scholar's problem came to be to get what no one else (or only a few) "would think of looking at" (182). Subsidies to publishers served only to alleviate the problem, not solve it.

To Binkley, the general framework of two types of materials applied as well to libraries. Some holdings, ideally, were identical in all libraries, as is implicit in a work such as C. B. Shaw's *A List of Books for College Libraries* (New York: Carnegie Corporation, 1931), to which he referred. Others, even though printed, more nearly resembled archives in their rarity. He termed these "special collections" and stated that they required a new approach: "The great generation of librarians now passing away saw the problem of internal library administration solved. We will have to think of library systems rather than separate libraries. That generation dealt chiefly with two classes of material passing through our hands. They knew only one way of acquiring a book — to purchase it, and only one way to service it — to lend it. . . . Our problems will be far more intricate than theirs, and also, I believe, far more interesting."[34] Binkley envisioned a number of methodologies within a world of library systems, but foremost was, as with scholarly production, the employment of new technologies to reproduce material.

Since Binkley viewed technologies as essential to solving the problems of scholars and libraries, to gather information about them and to make it available were priorities. His first effort was *Methods of Reproducing Research Materials: A Survey made for the Joint Committee on Materials for Research of the Social Science Research Council and the American Council of Learned Societies* (Ann Arbor: Edwards Brothers, Inc., 1931). The 139-page book, with various inserted reproductions, had on its title page a statement that immediately let the reader know what was in hand: "This edition published by Edwards Brothers, Ann Arbor, by the photo-lithographic process from author's own manuscript, pica double space typescript, reduced one-half."

---

34. Robert C. Binkley, "The Reproduction of Materials for Research," in *Library Trends: Papers Presented before the Library Institute at the University of Chicago, August 3–15, 1936,* ed. Louis Round Wilson (Chicago: University of Chicago Press, 1937), 225–36; rpt. in *Selected Papers,* 224–35. The quotation is part of the concluding paragraph.

Only one hundred copies were printed. Most of these, the author wrote, were for those who had assisted him in preparing the book. Although he did not say so, he probably wanted to demonstrate the feasibility of printing in small numbers at low cost. The 1931 edition was, in effect, an internal document, meant to inform those involved with the two Councils and to obtain their support for his ideas. Binkley, characteristically, assumed he would have it, and he promised a subsequent edition for wide distribution. It did appear, in 1936, in an edition of 1,500 copies,[35] also published by Edwards Brothers. The 1936 publication had a slight but important title change. Two words were added, so that the title read *Manual on Methods of Reproducing Research Materials.* That suggestion of a detailed handbook was accurate. In this edition, he worked out the cost structure of each method of reproduction in relation to number of copies, and through rich detail, including 55 tables, 73 illustrations, and even product samples, he made utterly convincing the case that new and viable means of reproduction existed.

Covered was standard printing from raised type; the Multigraph process; photo-offset; the standard typewriter as well as the Varityper and Electromatic typewriter; carbon paper copying; the hectographic process, both gelatin and liquid; mimeograph techniques; blueprinting, photostating, and allied techniques, including the Dexigraph; the issue of non-Roman characters, tabular matter, diagrams, and illustrations, including photoengraving, half-tones, Photogelatin or Collotype; Intaglio processes, Aquatone and Pantone, Dermaprint, photosensitive paper processes; paper permanence; binding, vertical filing, and film storage; reduced-scale photographic and photolithographing, including Peters' Miniature Abstracts and Theses, the Fiske method, Filmstat reproduction, Bendikson procedure, the Van Iterson device, the Folmer Graflex Recording Camera, and the True-Vue apparatus; microcopying and projection reading; photographic and projecting apparatus, including the Cinescopie and Photoscopie, E.K.A. camera and Lemare Ampligraph, Leica and Contax equipment, the Argus, Ansco Universal Still-Film Copying Camera, Ludwig camera, Matson camera, Filmograph and Kennedy cameras, Draeger camera, Folmer Graflex camera, Recordak bound-book copying cameras, Recordak camera, Newspaper Recordak, and, of course, projector reading machines, as well as projector-and-enlargement equipment.[36]

---

35. The number comes from Alan Marshall Meckler, *Micropublishing: A History of Scholarly Micropublishing in America, 1938–1980* (Westport, CT: Greenwood Press, 1982), 23 and his n. 22, citing box 67 of the ACLS Records at Library of Congress. The number, writes Meckler, was increased from 1,000 because of demand.

36. Binkley was also aware that print's monopoly of the means for mass communications was past. Although he envisioned that other media could have a role in scholarly communication ("Television may render long-distance reading a possibility" [177]) and in special areas of research (folk

All of these methods were tested, and all were considered from the stand-point of aesthetics and legibility, as well as costs. Even large-scale microfilming received its test: the 315,000 pages of the records of the Agricultural Adjust-ment Administration and the National Recovery Administration, filmed under the supervision of T. R. Schellenberg, the Joint Committee's executive secretary. Unforeseen problems arose, and these were duly reported.

The section on microfilm also reported on the Bibliofilm Service, which provided on-demand copying in the library of the U.S. Department of Agriculture, and Binkley noted that the Library of Congress, the New York Public Library, Yale, and the Huntington had all installed cameras, as had the Preussische Staatsbibliothek. He dealt with the issue of copyright, which was crucial to the use of microfilm, and he reprinted correspondence with W. W. Norton, president of the National Association of Book Publishers. These letters constituted a "gentlemen's agreement" that outlined the conditions under which microfilming of copyrighted material was permitted. Binkley also discussed the use of microfilming in making union catalogues [37] and in what he called an "assembled catalogue," that is, microfilm copies, in one location, of the cards of individual libraries. He envisioned that individual scholars could also assemble microfilm copies that would constitute complete coverage of a given topic, and he considered this a "new unit of intellectual activity" (159–60). [38] He believed that it would be beneficial to scholarship if the effort of some scholars were diverted to this activity, but he recognized that "one of the greatest obstacles to this diversion of effort lies in the aca-demic convention which honors any publication, but accords no recognition to the gathering of material if publication does not issue from it." [39]

In this merging of collecting and publishing, he expected the small librar-ies to become participants. Each unit in the "library system" would perform a task "proportionate to its resources." This idealist scholar believed that libraries would become not merely collectors of existing records, but that the "library of the future [would] . . . reduce to writing information that would otherwise go unrecorded." His faith in ordinary people throughout the coun-try, his desire to see a vast apparatus of contributors to historical learning, led

---

music in particular), he was also interested in radio and cinema as historical source materials of wide cultural significance. Chapter 13 of his 1936 *Manual* is "The Recording of Sound."

37. He was influential in furthering the Philadelphia-area union catalogue since he showed that technology could help in the process of copying cards.

38. These and the page numbers hereafter refer to the *Manual.*

39. Binkley considered this in an undated statement "An analysis of the resources available for the improvement of research materials with suggestions for their use," in Joint Committee Archive, box 1, folder Correspondence on Library Cooperation.

him to conclude the section on microfilm with a paean to the possibilities open to those in small towns: "There is no community so small that it does not offer to a sensitive mind aspects of human life that are worthy of record, and facts that should be entered in the dossiers of scholarship" (160). Indeed, he concluded his book (202) with the same vision: "The same technical innovations that promise to give aid to the research worker in his cubicle may also lead the whole population toward participation in a new cultural design."

Not that Binkley and the Joint Committee failed to devote attention to the scholarly world. To be sure, the technology could serve all, but technology alone, he came to recognize, would not change scholarly publishing. A failed attempt to change the structure of scholarly publication was instructive. At the January 29, 1932, meeting of the ACLS secretaries of constituent societies, the secretaries requested the Council "to investigate the subject of printing costs, with a view to effecting further economies in printing from type and to developing other methods, especially for small editions." [40] Subsequently, the Joint Committee devoted much of its energies to drawing up a project providing "for the establishment of a central agency, which would [18] receive the manuscripts of proposed publications, selected and sponsored by the various constituent societies of the two Councils, would determine the method of publication—by planograph or type-setting,—would estimate its cost, and would canvass the prospective purchasers, both libraries and individuals, in order to ascertain whether the demand for the work in question is sufficient to meet the expenses of publication. The agency would also be charged with procuring the publication and distribution of works that might finally be selected." [41] This idea of advance orders determining the method of reproduction fit perfectly with Binkley's analysis of the specialization of academic work, and it was a favorite of his.

No such project was ever established, but Binkley did not give up. His 1936 *Manual on Methods of Reproducing Research Materials* was a further stage in the battle, and it was having influence, to judge from a letter of Waldo G. Leland, permanent secretary of the ACLS, to Frederick P. Keppel, president of the Carnegie Corporation, dated June 9, 1937. Written with the aim of persuading Keppel to use his influence with the American Philosophical Society to organize a conference on the publishing problem, it stated: "Meanwhile, the idea of non-conventional publication is gaining ground rather rapidly and as the various methods of such publication are perfected, and especially as reading machines are made available at moderate prices [a reference to micro-

---

40. *Bulletin* no. 18 (October 1932), 138.
41. *Bulletin* no. 20 (December 1933).

film], I believe that in another year we shall be much nearer such solution of our problem as it may be possible to reach." That ungrammatical, albeit tactful phraseology, did indicate that opposition remained, as another letter of July 11, 1937, indicated: "I confess that the Executive Offices of the Council have a somewhat different view of the matter from that held by many members of the Council itself." [42] Besides that conservatism, familiar to advocates of electronic publishing in lieu of print, was the fact that it was difficult to obtain advance orders, and the effort, of course, entailed costs. Binkley also realized that demand for a book would continue, so he continued to hope for a method of publication on demand.[43]

More successful was the Joint Committee's role in the Historical Records Survey of the Works Progress Administration. It seems that Francis S. Philbrick of the University of Pennsylvania's Law School, who chaired the American Historical Association's Committee on Legal History, wrote to Binkley in January 1934 and proposed a national survey of state and local archives, to be conducted by unemployed white-collar labor. Binkley then got to work to try to solve the problem inherent in carrying out a project with thousands of individuals when the product that was wanted needed to be comparable across the country. At an early point he called a conference, and, then he and Schellenberg, executive secretary of the Joint Committee, drew up a plan.[44] In 1935, President Franklin Roosevelt established the Historical Records Survey under the WPA, with Luther H. Evans as National Director (he was later Librarian of Congress), and throughout the life of the WPA Evans and Binkley worked closely together to frame the rationale behind the Historical Records Survey and to obtain ongoing funding.[45]

---

42. These letters are in Carnegie Corporation Archive, III.A., Grant Files, American Council of Learned Societies folder, at Columbia University. Leland had brought the *Manual* to Keppel's attention on November 9, 1936.

43. The most important effort at publishing on demand was Robert J. Kerner's *Northeastern Asia: A Selected Bibliography* (Berkeley: University of California Press, 1939). For this 2-volume work of some 1350 pages, the Committee was able to cover by advance subscriptions almost all of the $1,700 cost of a master photo-offset copy, which permitted a considerable saving from the subsidy of $10,000 that would have been required for a printing from type. Of course, Binkley tried to further on-demand copying on microfilm. He supported the National Agricultural Library in its on-demand copying, and he advocated that other libraries, especially the Library of Congress, do likewise. The American Documentation Institute, Binkley hoped, would further on-demand filming and also push the issue of copyright, and for a time he was on its board, until he came to see the Institute as acting contrary to the interests of scholarship in general.

44. In a letter to Binkley of 31 August 1934, Philbrick referred to "our proposed state surveys," so he continued to be involved; see Joint Committee files, box 34.

45. For a brief account, see David L. Smiley, "The W.P.A. Historical Records Survey," in *In Support of Clio: Essays in Memory of Herbert A. Kellar,* ed. William B. Hesseltine and Donald R. McNeil

As part of his WPA work, Binkley was able to obtain funds to experiment with abstracting and indexing. In this, he followed his standard practice, which was to develop a methodology and determine costs, and he did so using Cleveland newspapers as a demonstration. Although he hoped that newspaper indexing would become a widespread part of a Depression-era relief program, followed by microfilming the newspapers, he anticipated that interested individuals would also do such work on their own. The model consisted of a forty-four-volume abstract/index of Cleveland newspapers from 1818 to 1935. (The project also compiled a list of the currently published foreign-language press, as well as the Jewish and African American press in Cleveland.)[46]

Binkley never urged that foundations make grants to libraries for the acquisition of materials; and although from 1930 to 1932 he had considerable correspondence on library cooperation, particularly in the collecting of government publications, he dropped that line of activity. Another early activity that he dropped was the effort to enumerate the categories of research materials needed by scholars in various fields, which was the work of a subcommittee chaired by N. S. B. Gras of the Harvard Business School. Although the constituent societies were asked to consider "how new materials for research in the humanities and the social sciences can be discovered and collected, and how all materials, both new and old, can be made available for research," the committee had to admit that "few research workers have given thought to the possible expansion of the resources of their fields in research material."[47] The meager responses, supplemented with statements by a few other individuals, did enable the committee to issue a 91-page mimeographed volume.[48] Its concrete result was to turn the subcommittee in the direction of education.[49]

That effort was based on the Joint Committee's awareness that research materials were to a considerable extent produced by various institutions, such as business and law firms as well as government bodies, as a more or less inci-

---

(Madison: State Historical Society of Wisconsin, 1958), 3–28. Smiley used Records Group 69 of the National Archives, which is the correspondence relating to the Historical Records Survey. Boxes 16–22 of the Joint Committee Records specifically concern the WPA—in general and also in Ohio.

46. A small portion of the multivolume published index to the general Cleveland newspapers has been digitized. http://web.ulib.csuohio.edu/SpecColl/annals/ The portion that has been digitized suggests that such abstracts and indexes would significantly increase the body of source materials on which students of the history of American culture draw.

47. *Bulletin* no. 15 (May 1931), 110 and 74.

48. *Committee Memorandum on Categories of Materials for Research in the Social Sciences and the Humanities. Prepared by the Sub-Committee on Categories of Materials* [n.p., 1933]. Later, Binkley confessed that he had never been able to find a methodology that would satisfactorily encompass the world of research materials.

49. ACLS *Bulletin* no. 22 (October 1934).

dental part of their activities. The goal, then, was to educate the creators of the records to preserve them. A pamphlet about business records was widely distributed; it went through three editions. One reason to urge the creators of the records to preserve them was that few university libraries had archival programs, and, in any case, Binkley calculated that libraries were already struggling to house a quantity of printed research materials that was doubling every twenty years (his figure).

Educational efforts were also directed at the public. Binkley wrote for various journals, but so did other committee members. The English professor Arthur H. Quinn published "New Frontiers of Research" in *Scribner's Magazine*.[50] Beneath the title was: "In an old trunk in your attic may be records, documents, or diaries which should be preserved. Libraries and research organizations are taking an added interest in anything which illumines the study of American institutions and American life." The article concludes in a Binkley-like manner: "To this enterprise the co-operation of every citizen of the United States is invited, and there are few indeed without the power to make their contribution." Lydenberg also produced a popular essay, "The Collector's Progress," published in the *Journal of Adult Education* (1940).[51]

Although it is possible to see much of the work of the Joint Committee through the framework of education (the *Manual*, of course, aimed to inform), Binkley had no single approach, certainly no plan of action. He would seize on whatever came along that offered possibilities. His support of union catalogues is another example. The paths gone down, the dead ends encountered, are more numerous and varied than can be described here. One explanation is that he saw himself in the role of advocate and intermediary, what is sometimes called today "the big-picture guy." He did not want to become tied down to operations. Perhaps he saw himself this way because it fit with his personality. Harry Miller Lydenberg recounted in a sketch published after Binkley's death a statement of a fellow worker, made when those in a room down the hall heard a door open, followed by footsteps: "Here comes Binkley, all five of him."[52]

Closest to his heart, though, was microfilming, especially on a large scale. It was how to get that accomplished on which he was flexible. Early on, in 1935, he seems to have had some hopes that the library community would, with some foundation support, be able to undertake large-scale microfilm-

50. Arthur H. Quinn, "New Frontiers of Research," *Scribner's Magazine* (1935): 95–97.

51. Harry Miller Lydenberg, "The Collector's Progress," *Journal of Adult Education* 12 (April 1940): 133–37.

52. Fisch, "Robert Cedric Binkley," 30n.

ing of early material. Keyes Metcalf, then director of the Reference Division of the New York Public Library, drew up such a plan on August 13, 1935, "Proposal for Reproduction of Research Material on Film."[53] It called for 100,000 exposures of various types of material: newspapers of both the United States and Europe, early American printing, English printing before 1640, incunabula, medieval manuscripts, manuscripts relating to American history from the Library of Congress, material listed in Henry Harrisse's bibliography of Americana. Metcalf's proposal, which called for initial financing by a foundation and ongoing support by subscribing libraries, did not get off the ground. Binkley's hopes for tying newspaper filming in with newspaper indexing, all with WPA funds, also did not work out. Later on, by 1938, Binkley had apparently given up on librarians as a group and on foundations and was supporting Eugene B. Power, who resigned from Edwards Brothers on July 1, 1938, in order to devote full time to his own company, University Microfilms.

Appointment of Archibald MacLeish as Librarian of Congress in 1939 enabled Binkley to dream even more boldly. He hoped that the Library of Congress would pursue massive copying of materials, printed and archival, in European institutions. He proposed beginning with copies of the printed catalogues of the great libraries of Britain and France, plus the German *Gesamtkatalog,* then getting copies of the Swiss, Dutch, and Danish union catalogues, combining them into one, and then using that catalogue to obtain microfilm copies of materials, selected by scholars, that were not in any American library.[54] MacLeish was cautious, one reason being that the plan called for American libraries to check their holdings against lists provided by the Library of Congress, then make purchases of the copies the Library had filmed. The caution was justified.

Microfilming on the scale envisaged by Binkley did not happen, but this memorandum, plus another one of November 27, 1939, "A National Acquisition Policy," fed into the discussions that ultimately led to the Farmington Plan, the postwar cooperative acquisition program that aimed at increasing American coverage of the publications of Europe. Also feeding into the Farmington Plan was the work of librarians, which Binkley kept MacLeish apprised of, when on December 11, 1939, he sent him a proposal from Metcalf, chairman of the ALA committee on photographic reproduction of library materi-

---

53. Keyes Metcalf, "Proposal for Reproduction of Research Material on Film," 13 August 1935, in Joint Committee papers, box 34.

54. Robert C. Binkley, "Memorandum," 30 October 1939, "Mr. MacLeish, Librarian of Congress," in Joint Committee papers, box 34.

als. It included a "proposal to request $100,000 from Rockefeller to microfilm on a large scale irreplaceable European materials, including any American archives not already covered by Project A of the Library of Congress, all English books printed before 1640, early printing from other European countries, classical and mediaeval manuscripts at least up to the year 1500, the 15,000 volume index of the Public Records [sic] Office, all material that has been moved from the British Museum and other London libraries into the country for safety, and the same for material from Paris and other cities." To this MacLeish replied on December 14, 1939, "Metcalf's proposal seems to me a sound one—at least it is a nibble at the cake."

The parties could not come to consensus on a plan of action, but the war in Europe had provided a new impetus to think boldly. "America must be in a position to keep western culture alive." So wrote Binkley in his memorandum of October 30, 1939. With that statement, the circle closed, and the United States had returned to seeing libraries and scholarship in the same way as in 1919, after the First World War.

Four months later, on April 11, 1940, Robert Binkley died; so he did not see the vast postwar growth of academia and libraries that was stimulated by the belief that they served a great national purpose—not merely keeping Western culture alive, but keeping civilization itself alive in the era of the Soviet threat.

Just before Binkley's death, in his early forties, he connected with a development that was to be even more portentous. Stuart Rice, the statistician, told him that Vannevar Bush, the MIT electrical engineer, was working on a machine to index microfilm. Binkley wrote to Bush on January 23, 1940, to ask for more information about the "micro-selector;" and Bush replied on February 14, 1940,[55] with an account of the "rapid selector" machine that

---

55. Binkley's letter to Vannevar Bush, 23 January 1940, reads:

> Stuart Rice has told me some fantastic things about a micro-selector or something of that kind that you have been contriving.
>
> I am interested in its possible application to fields in the orbit of interest to the Joint Committee on Materials for Research. Could you give me a little bit more of a clue as to what it is?

Bush's response, of 14 February 1940, is:

> Your letter of January twenty-third has been forwarded to me from the Massachusetts Institute of Technology. The rapid selector which is being built at MIT may indeed have applications in the field in which you are especially interested. I talked with Stuart Rice about the matter, for at the present time several of us are puzzling over the problem of introducing this equipment in some favorable way for the handling of scholarly material. If it has commercial usage, this aspect of the matter will be taken care of normally, but on the scholarly applications it may be possible to accomplish something quite unusual.

five years later he described in print in his pioneering essay, "As We May Think,"[56] which inspired many who subsequently developed hypertext.

It is clear that the world of microfilm, which, of course, continued on its own,[57] had stimulated development of the new technology that is now replacing microfilm for many uses. Bush may even have been influenced by Binkley to think about the new technology in broad terms. The essay "As We May Think" has no footnotes, but it is organized in a way that suggests Bush had been reading "New Tools for Men of Letters," which Binkley had published in the *Yale Review* in the spring of 1935. Bush began his essay as Binkley had, by emphasizing the specialization that had occurred. The second of his eight sections is about photography, and it emphasizes the possibilities of microphotography and then reading the text by projection. Bush notes especially that microphotography, through duplicating vast resources, creates a need for access, not just to extract but to select. To Bush, the ideal method of doing

---

Without going into detail, the device is a mechanism for rapidly running over a large number of items on microfilm and selecting out by code any desired items, which it then photographs on a separate small strip of film. The principal point is that it can survey these items at the rate of 1000 per second and it does not need to stop to make the photographic duplicate, so that it is very fast. The coding can be very detailed, and in fact on the present machine there is provision, I think, for ten alphabets.

I will be very happy indeed to tell you more about the matter if you wish. It may be that you will have some questions and, if so, I will be glad to reply to them as far as I can. If you should happen to be in the vicinity of Cambridge the most effective way of looking into the subject would be to visit the laboratory where the development is being carried on. This I think you will find it well worth while to do simply from the standpoint of the interest which the development has even although [*sic*] no specific applications were in mind.

I am grateful to the Manuscript Division of the Library of Congress for sending photocopies of the letters.

56. *Atlantic Monthly,* July 1945, available on the website of the *Atlantic Monthly.*

57. Microfilm and the learned societies were also linked by the Joint Committee on Microcopying Materials for Research, joint with the ACLS, the American Council of Education, and the National Research Council, this last meaning involvement of the scientific community. The consolidated list of SSRC committees, available on its website, indicates that it, too, was a sponsor of the committee. The NRC's representative on the committee was W. H. Kenerson. Although Kenerson is not recorded as being among Bush's correspondents, Archibald MacLeish and Bush were in touch over many years, as indicated by the Library of Congress finding aid. MacLeish and Binkley had had numerous contacts, and MacLeish was also a member of the Joint Committee on Microcopying Materials for Research. It had been appointed in 1940 to carry out the recommendations of the Conference on Microcopying Materials for Research in Foreign Depositories. Its report for 1941 in ACLS *Bulletin* no. 35 (October 1942) recorded that it endorsed a plan "submitted for advice by another agency, for a National Division of Library Cooperation" within the Library of Congress. That division was established, but it seems to have issued only one publication, Herbert A. Kellar, *Memoranda on Library Cooperation* (September 1941); the division is there called "Experimental Division of Library Cooperation."

so involved not indexes with their rules, but rather a system that worked by association. That will be done by a machine that he calls the memex. Thus, the scholar's workstation will consist of a screen that permits reading of microfilm, to which access is made available by the memex. Provision is also made for photographing notes, memoranda, photographs, and the like. The "associative indexing" is done by creating a code entered into a code book, with the code also appearing at the bottom of the microfilm image. Tapping on it will bring up other instances in which that code has been used. Then Bush writes, as Binkley would have, that in providing access to the past, his system would elevate the human spirit.

Binkley, the prophet, died before entering the promised land. He only saw from afar the possibilities of a new technology that made microfilm largely into an intermediate technology, save for its durability when produced under high standards. He was right about microfilm and preservation—technically—but nowhere in the files does he or anyone else indicate awareness that not all "copies" of a book are the same or that a given copy may not be complete. Similarly, nowhere in the files has there been found an indication of microfilm's limits, that not all texts will be readable, let alone convey what they do on paper—and that microfilm created for libraries the issue of preserving at least one copy on paper.[58]

Perhaps Binkley the scholar, the historian, would have come to see that microfilming actually entailed the possibility of loss, not preservation, when carried out in a culture dominated by the need—very real—for cost effectiveness, but where the guidelines developed to ensure that goal were created by managers distanced from the materials.[59] If Binkley did not see the dark side of microfilm—and it is the fate of advocates trying to change the world to be single-minded—we have him to thank for his help in bringing about the positive. Whoever consults a digital version of a book or newspaper that was earlier on microfilm is indebted to this pioneer.

Binkley's legacy is, however, broader than that. His example as a scholar thoroughly engaged in a disinterested way in libraries and the infrastructure of scholarship raises the question for us of how to further such involvement

---

58. Nicholson Baker, *Double Fold: Libraries and the Assault on Paper* (New York: Random House, 2001). Baker only mentions Binkley, no doubt because the widespread filming and discarding of newspapers occurred after Binkley's death.

59. The danger exists that large-scale digitization will be carried out under guidelines based on similar assumptions about the original and that holders of the originals, whether of the copy filmed or of other "copies," will discard the printed items, perhaps out of ignorance or space pressures. A digital copy is, however, by its nature more accessible than a microfilm copy, and that, combined with recognition of the dark side of microfilming, may limit destruction.

today. Binkley's ideas, put forth with clarity in a simpler age, bear ongoing examination. His recognition that libraries should be seen as a system can always be profitably considered. His insight into the specialization of scholarly interests as the fundamental cause of the publishing crisis leads to consideration of the factors inherently behind the problems of university presses today.

Binkley is relevant as well for reasons other than his example or his insights. His goal of a new cultural design brought about by technology continues to intrigue and challenge. Yes, we have a new cultural design brought about by technology. We even have the technology used to research and make available local histories, autobiographies, volumes of poetry, and the like. The fact that the technology is used this way does not mean that we have the new cultural design envisaged by Binkley. The question remains as to how our libraries, educational institutions, and scholarly societies can further a cultural design that is consonant with the most positive values of our history.

Chapter 12

Scarcity or Abundance?

Preserving the Past in a Digital Era

Roy Rosenzweig

On October 11, 2001, the satiric *Bert Is Evil* website, which displayed photographs of the furry Muppet in Zelig-like proximity to villains such as Adolf Hitler (see figure 12.1), disappeared from the web—a bit of collateral damage from the September 11 attacks. Following the strange career of *Bert Is Evil* shows us possible futures of the past in a digital era—futures that historians and other scholars need to contemplate more carefully than they have done so far.

In 1996, Dino Ignacio, a twenty-two-year-old Filipino web designer, created *Bert Is Evil* ("brought to you by the letter H and the CIA"), which became a cult favorite among early tourists on the World Wide Web. Two years later, *Bert Is Evil* won a "Webby" as the "best weird site." Fan and "mirror" sites appeared with some embellishing on the "Bert Is Evil" theme. After the bombing of the U.S. embassies in Kenya and Tanzania in 1998, sites in the Netherlands and Canada paired Bert with Osama bin Laden.[1]

This image made a further global leap after September 11. When Mostafa

---

This essay has been somewhat revised since its original appearance in the *American Historical Review* in June 2003, but no print publication, necessarily delayed by months, let alone years, can keep up with the ever-changing nature of the web. That serves to affirm the urgent need for scholars to be concerned with the future of the past. My thanks to a number of friends and colleagues for their generous and astute comments remain unchanged, and I continue as well to be grateful to Laurel Thatcher Ulrich and Pat Denault of the Charles Warren Center at Harvard University for providing the congenial setting in which most of this was written.

1. Greg Miller, "Cyberculture: The Scene/The Webby Awards," *Los Angeles Times,* 9 March 1998, D3. On Ignacio, see the interview "Dino Ignacio: Evil Incarnate," in Philippine Web Designers Network, *Philweavers,* www.philweavers.net/profiles/dinoginacio.html; Buck Wolf, "Osama bin Muppet," *ABC News,* www.abcnews.go.com/sections/us/WolfFiles/wolffiles190.html; "Media Killed Bert Is Evil," http://plaza.powersurfr.com/bert/, viewed online 15 April 2002, but unavailable as of 4 July 2002; Peter Hartlaub, "Bert and bin Laden Poster Tied to S.F. Student," *San Francisco Chronicle,* 12 October 2001, A12; Gina Davidson, "Bert and Bin: How the Joke Went Too Far," *The Scotsman,* 14 October 2001, 3.

Figure 12.1. Bert the Muppet at Hitler's side, from the now-defunct *Bert Is Evil* website.

Kamal, the production manager of a print shop in Dhaka, Bangladesh, needed some images of bin Laden for anti-American posters, he apparently entered the phrase "Osama bin Laden" in Google's image search engine. The Osama and Bert duo was among the top hits. *Sesame Street* being less popular in Bangladesh than in the Philippines, Kamal thought the picture a nice addition to an Osama collage. But when this transnational circuit of imagery made its way back to more *Sesame Street*–friendly parts of the world via a Reuters photo of anti-American demonstrators, a storm of indignation erupted. Children's Television Workshop, the show's producers, threatened legal action. On October 11, 2001, a nervous Ignacio pushed the delete key, imploring "all fans [*sic*] and mirror site hosts of 'Bert is Evil' to stop the spread of this site too."[2]

2. "Bert Is Evil!" in *Snopes.com,* www.snopes2.com/rumors/bert.htm; "Bert Is Evil—Proof in the Most Unlikely Places," in *HermAphroditeZine,* www.pinktink3.250x.com/hmm/bert.htm; Josh Grossberg, "The Bert-Bin Laden Connection?" in *E! Online News,* 10 October 2001, www.eonline.com/News/Items/0,1,8950,00.html; Joey G. Alarilla, "Infotech Pinoy Webmaster Closes Site after 'Bert-Bin Laden' Link," *Philippine Daily Inquirer,* 22 October 2001, 17; Dino Ignacio, "Good-bye Bert," in *Fractal Cow,* www.fractalcow.com/bert/bert.htm. See also Michael Y. Park, "Bin Laden's Felt-Skinned Henchman?" *Fox News,* 14 October 2001, www.foxnews.com/story/0,2933,36218,00

Ignacio's sudden deletion of Bert should capture our interest since it dramatically illustrates the fragility of evidence in the digital era. If Ignacio had published his satire in a book or magazine, it would sit on thousands of library shelves rather than having a more fugitive existence as magnetic impulses on a web server. Although some might object that the *Bert Is Evil* website is of little historical significance, even traditionalists should worry about what the digital era might mean for the historical record. U.S. government records, for example, are being lost on a daily basis. Although most government agencies started using e-mail and word processing in the mid-1980s, the National Archives still does not require that digital records be retained in that form, and governmental employees profess confusion over whether they should be preserving electronic files.[3] Future historians may be unable to ascertain not only whether Bert is evil, but also which undersecretaries of defense were evil, or at least favored the concepts of the "evil empire" or the "axis of evil." As yet, no one has figured out how to ensure that the digital present will be available to the future's scholars.

But, as we shall see, tentative efforts are afoot to preserve our digital cultural heritage. If they succeed, scholars will face a second, profound challenge—writing history when faced by an essentially complete historical record. In fact, the *Bert Is Evil* story could be used to tell a very different tale about the promiscuity and even persistence of digital materials. After all, despite Ignacio's pleas and Children's Television Workshop's threats, a number of Bert "mirror" sites persist. Even more remarkably, the Internet Archive—a private organization that began archiving the web in 1996—has copies of *Bert Is Evil* going back to March 30, 1997. To be sure, this extraordinary archive is considerably more fragile than one would like. The continued existence of the Internet Archive rests largely on the interest and energy of a single individual, and its collecting of copyrighted material is on even shakier legal ground. It has put the future of the past—traditionally seen as a public patrimony—in private hands.

Still, the astonishingly rapid accumulation of digital data—obvious to anyone who uses the Google search engine and gets 300,000 hits—should

---

.html; Declan McCullagh, "Osama Has a New Friend," *Wired News,* 10 October 2001, www.wired
.com/news/conflict/0,2100,47450,00.html; "Sesame Street Character Depicted with bin Laden on
Protest Poster," *AP Worldstream,* 11 October 2001. Nikke Lindqvist, *N!kke,* www.lindqvist.com/art
.php?incl=bert.php&lang=eng, provides an excellent chronicle of the unfolding story. Significantly,
many of the links on this site, which I first viewed in February 2002, were no longer working in
March 2003. In addition, as of July 2005 Ignacio's statement about taking down the Bert website was
no longer online, and *www.fractalcow.com* only says "this website is under deconstruction."

3. Jeffrey Benner, "Is U.S. History Becoming History?" *Wired News,* 9 April 2001, www.wired
.com/news/print/0,1294,42725,00.html.

make us consider that future scholars may face information overload. Thus scholars need to be thinking simultaneously about how to research, write, and teach in a world of unheard-of historical abundance *and* how to avoid a future of record scarcity. Although these prospects have occasioned enormous commentary among librarians, archivists, and computer scientists, historians and humanists have almost entirely ignored them. In part, that detachment stems from the assumption that these are "technical" problems, which are outside the purview of scholars in the humanities and social sciences. Yet the more important and difficult issues about digital preservation are social, cultural, economic, political, and legal—issues that humanists should excel at. The "system" for preserving the past that has evolved over centuries is in crisis, and scholars need to take a hand in building a new system for the coming century. Historians and similar scholars also tend to assume a professional division of responsibility, leaving these matters to archivists. But the split of archivists from historians is a relatively recent one. In the early twentieth century, historians saw themselves as having a responsibility for preserving as well as researching the past. At that time, both the vision and the membership of the American Historical Association—embracing archivists, local historians, and "amateurs" as well as university scholars—were considerably broader than they later became.[4]

Ironically, the disruption to historical practice (to what Thomas Kuhn called "normal science") brought by digital technology may lead "back to the future." The struggle to incorporate the possibilities of new technology into the ancient practice of history has led, most importantly, to questioning of basic goals and methods. For example, the Internet has dramatically expanded and, hence, blurred the audiences for history. A scholarly journal is suddenly much more accessible to high school students and history enthusiasts. And the work of history buffs is likewise more visible and accessible to scholars. Similarly, the capaciousness of digital media means that the page limits of journals are no longer fixed by paper and ink costs. As a result, the nature and purpose of the scholarly journals are questioned. Why do they publish articles with particular lengths and structures? Why do they publish particular types of articles? The simultaneous fragility and promiscuity of digital data requires yet more rethinking—about whether we should be trying to save everything,

---

4. John Higham, *History: Professional Scholarship in America* (1965; rpt., Baltimore: Johns Hopkins University Press, 1983), 16–20. See also Thomas Bender et al., *The Education of Historians for the Twenty-first Century* (Urbana: University of Illinois Press, 2004). To observe this broader vision is not to deny the very different historical circumstances (such as the disorganization of archives), the obvious blindness of the early professional historians on many matters (such as race and gender), and the early tensions between "amateurs" and professionals.

who is "responsible" for preserving the past, and how we find and define historical evidence.

A fundamental paradigm shift from a culture of scarcity to a culture of abundance may be taking place. Not so long ago, we worried about the small numbers of people we could reach, pages of scholarship we could publish, primary sources we could introduce to our students, and documents that had survived from the past. At least potentially, digital technology has removed many of these limits: over the Internet, it costs no more to deliver a scholarly journal to 15 million people than 15,000 people; it costs less for our students to have access to literally millions of primary sources than a handful in a published anthology. And we may be able to both save and quickly search through all of the products of our culture. But will abundance bring better or more thoughtful history?[5]

Scholars are not unaware of these challenges. Yet, paradoxically, these fundamental questions are often relegated to more marginal professional spaces—to casual lunchtime conversations or brief articles in association newsletters. But in this time of rapid and perplexing changes, scholars, in general, and historians, in particular, need to engage with issues about access to scholarship, the nature of scholarship, the audience for scholarship, the sources for scholarship, and the nature of scholarly training in the central places where we practice our craft—scholarly journals, scholarly meetings, and graduate classrooms. That scholarly engagement should also lead, I believe, to public action to advocate the preservation of the past as a *public* responsibility—one that historians share. But I hope to persuade even those who do not share my particular political stance that scholars need to shift at least some of their attention from the past to the present and future and reclaim, in the case of historians, the broad professional vision that was more prevalent a century ago. The stakes are too profound for historians and other scholars to ignore the futures of the past.

Archivists, librarians, public officials, and others have loudly warned about the threatened loss of digital records and publications for at least two decades. Words such as "disaster" and "crisis" echo through their reports and confer-

---

5. For interesting observations on "abundance" in two different realms of historical work, see James O'Toole, "Do Not Fold, Spindle, or Mutilate: Double Fold and the Assault on Libraries," *American Archivist* 64 (Fall/Winter 2001): 385–93; John McClymer, "Inquiry and Archive in a U.S. Women's History Course," *Works and Days* 16.1–2 (Spring/Fall 1998): 223. For a sweeping statement about political and cultural implications of "digital information that moves frictionlessly through the network and has zero marginal cost per copy," see Eben Moglen, "Anarchism Triumphant: Free Software and the Death of Copyright," *First Monday* 4.8 (August 1999), www.firstmonday.dk/issues/issue4_8/moglen/index.html.

ence proceedings. As early as 1985, the Committee on the Records of Government declared, "the United States is in danger of losing its memory."[6] More than a dozen years later, a project called "Time and Bits: Managing Digital Continuity" brought together archivists, librarians, and computer scientists to address the problem once again. Conferees watched the Terry Sanders film *Into the Future: On the Preservation of Knowledge in the Electronic Age,* and some likened it to Rachel Carson's *Silent Spring* and themselves to the environmentalists of the 1960s and 1970s. A *Time and Bits* website assembled conference materials and promoted "ongoing digital dialogue." But, as if to prove the conference's point, the site disappeared in less than a year. The computer scientist Jeff Rothenberg may have been over-optimistic when he quipped, "Digital documents last forever—or five years, whichever comes first."[7]

Those worried about a problem like digital preservation that lacks public attention are prone to exaggerate. Probably the greatest distortion has been the implicit suggestion that we have somehow fallen from a golden age of preservation in which everything of importance was saved. But much— really, most—of the record of previous historical eras has disappeared. And nondigital records that have survived into this century—from Greek and

---

6. Committee on the Records of Government, *Report* (Washington, DC, 1985), 9 (the committee was created by the American Council of Learned Societies, the Council on Library Resources, and the Social Science Research Council with funding from the Mellon, Rockefeller, and Sloan foundations); John Garrett and Donald Waters, *Preserving Digital Information: Report of the Task Force on Archiving of Digital Information* (Washington, DC, 1996); Paul Conway, *Preservation in the Digital World* (Washington, DC, 1996), www.clir.org/pubs/reports/conway2/index.html. For other reports with similar conclusions, see, for example, the 1989 report of the National Association of Government Archives and Records Administrators, cited in Margaret Hedstrom, "Understanding Electronic Incunabula: A Framework for Research on Electronic Records," *American Archivist* 54 (Summer 1991): 334–54; U.S. Congress, House Committee on Government Operations, *Taking a Byte out of History: The Archival Preservation of Federal Computer Records* (Washington, DC: Government Printing Office, 1990); Committee on an Information Technology Strategy for the Library of Congress, Computer Science and Telecommunications Board, Commission on Physical Sciences, Mathematics, and Applications, and the National Research Council, *LC21: A Digital Strategy for the Library of Congress* (Washington, DC, 2000), http://books.nap.edu/html/lc21/index.html; General Accounting Office, *Information Management: Challenges in Managing and Preserving Electronic Records* (Washington, DC: GPO, 2002); *NHPRC Electronic Records Agenda Final Report (Draft)* (St. Paul, MN, 2002).

7. Margaret MacLean and Ben H. Davis, eds., *Time and Bits: Managing Digital Continuity* (Los Angeles: Getty Conservation Institute, Getty Information Institute, and Long Now Foundation, 1998), 11, 6; Jeff Rothenberg, *Avoiding Technological Quicksand: Finding a Viable Technical Foundation for Digital Preservation* (Washington, DC, 1998), www.clir.org/pubs/reports/rothenberg/contents .html. The 1997 conference "Documenting the Digital Age" has also disappeared from the web, nor is it available in the Internet Archive. The Sanders film is available from the Council on Library and Information Resources, www.clir.org/pubs/film/future/order.html.

Chinese antiquities to New Guinean folk traditions to Hollywood films—are also seriously threatened.[8]

Another exaggeration involves stories about the grievous losses that never occurred. One widely repeated story is that computers can no longer read the data tapes from the 1960 U.S. Census. In truth, as Margaret Adams and Thomas Brown from the National Archives have shown, the Census Bureau had by 1979 successfully copied almost all the records to newer "industry-compatible tapes." Yet, even in debunking one of the persistent myths of the digital age, Adams and Brown reveal some of the key problems. In just a decade and a half, migrating the census tapes to a readable format "represented a major engineering challenge"—hardly something we expect to face with historical records originating from within our own lifetimes. And although "only 1,575 records . . . could not be copied because of deterioration," the absolute nature of digital corrosion is sobering.[9] Printed books and manuscript records decline slowly and unevenly—faded ink or a broken-off corner of a page. But digital records fail completely—a single damaged bit can render an entire document unreadable. Here is the key difference from the paper era: we need to take action now because digital items very quickly become unreadable, or recoverable only at great expense.[10]

Many believe—incorrectly—the central problem to be that we are storing information on media with surprisingly short life spans. But the medium is far from the weakest link in the digital preservation chain. Well before

---

8. Joel Achenbach, "The Too-Much-Information Age," *Washington Post,* March 1999, A1. See also Alexander Stille, *The Future of the Past* (New York: Farrar, Straus and Giroux, 2002); Council on Library and Information Resources (hereafter CLIR), *The Evidence in Hand: Report of the Task Force on the Artifact in Library Collections* (Washington, DC, 2001), www.clir.org/pubs/reports/pub103/contents.html.

9. Margaret O. Adams and Thomas E. Brown, "Myths and Realities about the 1960 Census," *Prologue: Quarterly of the National Archives and Records Administration* 32.4 (Winter 2000), www.archives.gov/publications/prologue/winter_2000_1960_census.html. See also letter of 15 August 1990, from Kenneth Thibodeau, which says that recovering the records took "substantial efforts" by the Bureau of the Census, quoted in House Committee on Government Operations, *Taking a Byte out of History,* 3. According to Timothy Lenoir, it is now too expensive to rescue the computer tapes that represent Douglas Englebart's pioneering hypermedia-groupware system called NLS (for oNLine System)—the basis of many of the features of personal computers. Timothy Lenoir, "Lost in the Digital Dark Ages" (paper delivered at "The New Web of History: Crafting History of Science Online," Cambridge, MA, 28 March 2003).

10. Marcia Stepanek, "From Digits to Dust," *Business Week,* 20 April 1998; House Committee on Government Operations, *Taking a Byte out of History,* 16; Jeff Rothenberg, "Ensuring the Longevity of Digital Documents," *Scientific American,* January 1995, 42–47. See also Garrett and Waters, *Preserving Digital Information.* Many Vietnam records are stored in a database system that is no longer supported and can be translated only with difficulty. As a result, the Agent Orange Task Force could not use important herbicide records. Stille, *Future of the Past,* 305.

most digital media degrade, they are likely to become unreadable because of changes in hardware (the disk or tape drives become obsolete) or software (the data are organized in a format destined for an application program that no longer works). The life expectancy of digital media may be as little as ten years, but very few hardware platforms or software programs last that long. Indeed, Microsoft supports its software for only about five years.[11]

The most vexing problems of digital media are the flipside of their greatest virtues. Because digital data are in the simple lingua franca of bits, of ones and zeros, they can be embodied in magnetic impulses that require almost no physical space, be transmitted over long distances, and represent very different objects (for instance, words, pictures, or sounds as well as text). But the ones and zeros lack intrinsic meaning without software and hardware, which constantly change because of technological innovation and competitive market forces. Thus this lingua franca requires translators in every computer application, which, in turn, operate only on specific hardware platforms. Compounding the difficulty is that the languages being translated keep changing every few years.

The problem is still worse because of the ability of digital media to create and represent complex, dynamic, and interactive objects—another of their great virtues. Even relatively simple documents that appear to have direct print analogs turn out to be more complex. Printing out e-mail messages makes rapid searches of them impossible and often jettisons crucial links to related messages and attachments. In addition, multimedia programs, which generally rely on complicated combinations of hardware and software, quickly become obsolete. Nor is there any good way to preserve interactive and experiential digital creations. That is most obviously true of computer games and digital art, but even a large number of ordinary web pages are generated out of databases, which means that the specific page you view is your own "creation"

---

11. Most Microsoft software moves into what the company calls the "non-supported phase" after just four or five years, although it offers a more limited "extended support phase" that lasts up to seven years. After that, you are out of luck. Microsoft, "Windows Desktop Product Life Cycle Support and Availability Policies for Businesses," 15 October 2002, www.microsoft.com/windows/lifecycle.mspx; Lori Moore, "Q&A: Microsoft Standardizes Support Lifecycle," *Press Pass: Information for Journalists* (15 October 2002), www.microsoft.com/presspass/features/2002/Oct02/10–15 support.asp. On media longevity, see Rothenberg, *Avoiding Technological Quicksand;* MacLean and Davis, *Time and Bits;* Margaret Hedstrom, "Digital Preservation: A Time Bomb for Digital Libraries" (paper delivered at the NSF Workshop on Data Archiving and Information Preservation, 26–27 March 1999), www.uky.edu/~kiernan/DL/hedstrom.html; Frederick J. Stielow, "Archival Theory and the Preservation of Electronic Media: Opportunities and Standards below the Cutting Edge," *American Archivist* 55 (Spring 1992): 332–43; Charles M. Dollar, *Archival Theory and Information Technology: The Impact of Information Technologies on Archival Principles and Methods* (Ancona, Italy, 1992), 27–32; GAO, *Information Management,* 50–52.

and the system can create an infinite number of pages. Preserving hypertextu-
ally linked web pages poses the further problem that to save a single page in
its full complexity could ultimately require you to preserve the entire web,
because virtually every web page is linked to every other. And the dynamic
nature of databases destabilizes mundane business and governmental records
since they are often embedded in systems that automatically replace old data
with new — a changeability that, notes the archival educator Richard Cox,
threatens "the records of any modern day politician, civic leader, businessper-
son, military officer, or leader." [12]

While these technical difficulties are immense, the social, economic,
legal, and organizational problems are worse. Digital documents — precisely
because they are in a new medium — have disrupted long-evolved systems
of trust and authenticity, ownership, and preservation. Reestablishing those
systems or inventing new ones is more difficult than coming up with a long-
lived storage mechanism.

How, for example, do we ensure the "authenticity" of preserved digital
information and "trust" in the repository? Paper documents and records also
face questions about authenticity, and forgeries are hardly unknown in traditional archives. The science of "diplomatics," in fact, emerged in the seventeenth century as a way to authenticate documents when scholars confronted
rampant forgeries in medieval documents. But digital information — because
it is so easily altered and copied, lacks physical marks of its origins, and,
indeed, even the clear notion of an "original" — cannot be authenticated as
physical documents and objects can. We have, for example, no way of knowing that forwarded e-mail messages we receive daily have not been altered.
In fact, the public archive of Usenet discussion groups contains hundreds
of deliberately and falsely attributed messages. "Fakery," write David Bearman and Jennifer Trant, "has not been a major issue for most researchers in
the past, both because of the technical barriers to making plausible forgeries,
and because of the difficulty with which such fakes entered an authoritative

---

12. Richard J. Cox, "Messrs. Washington, Jefferson, and Gates: Quarrelling about the Preservation of the Documentary Heritage of the United States," *First Monday* 2.8 (August 1997),
http://firstmonday.org/issues/issue2_8/cox/. See also Peter Lyman and Brewster Kahle, "Archiving
Digital Cultural Artifacts: Organizing an Agenda for Action," *D-Lib Magazine* 4.7–8 (July/August
1998), www.dlib.org/dlib/july98/07lyman.html. Voyager's CD-ROM explicating Beethoven's Ninth
Symphony — a landmark work in multimedia — no longer operates, in part, because Apple changed
a CD-ROM driver that the program relied on. Robert Winter, *Ludwig Van Beethoven Symphony No.
9* (Santa Monica, CA, 1991). Digital art presents particularly difficult problems; see, for example,
Scott Carlson, "Museums Seek New Methods for Preserving Digital Art," *Chronicle of Higher Education* (16 August 2002).

information stream."[13] Digital media, tools, and networks have altered the balance.

"It took centuries for users of print materials to develop the web of trust that now undergirds our current system of publication, dissemination, and preservation," notes Abby Smith of the Council on Library and Information Resources. Digital documents are disrupting that carefully wrought system by undercutting our expectations of what constitutes a trusted and authentic document and repository. But to make the transition to a new system requires not just technical measures (such as digital signatures and "watermarks") but, as Clifford Lynch, the executive director of the Coalition for Networked Information, observes, also figuring out responsibility for guaranteeing claims of authorship and financing for a system of "authentication and integrity management."[14]

Such questions are particularly hard to answer since digitization also undercuts our sense of who owns such materials and, thus, who has the right and responsibility to preserve them. Consumers (including libraries) have traditionally purchased books and magazines under the "first sale" doctrine, which gives those who buy something the right to make any use of it, including lending or selling it to others. But most digital goods are licensed rather than sold. Because contract law governs licenses, vendors of digital content can set any restrictions they choose—they can say that the contents may not be copied or cannot be viewed by more than one person at a time. Adobe's eBook reader even includes a warning that a book may not be read aloud.[15]

13. Margaret Hedstrom, "How Do We Make Electronic Archives Usable and Accessible?" (paper delivered at "Documenting the Digital Age," San Francisco, 10–12 February 1997); Luciana Duranti, "Diplomatics: New Uses for an Old Science," *Archivaria* 28 (Summer 1989): 7–27; Peter B. Hirtle, "Archival Authenticity in a Digital Age," in CLIR, *Authenticity in a Digital Environment* (Washington, DC, 2000), www.clir.org/pubs/reports/pub92/contents.html; CLIR, *Evidence in Hand;* Susan Stellin, "Google's Revival of a Usenet Archive Opens Up a Wealth of Possibilities but Also Raises Some Privacy Issues," *New York Times,* 7 May 2001, C4; David Bearman and Jennifer Trant, "Authenticity of Digital Resources: Towards a Statement of Requirements in the Research Process," *D-Lib Magazine* 4.6 (June 1998), www.dlib.org/dlib/june98/06bearman.html.

14. Abby Smith, "Authenticity in Perspective," in CLIR, *Authenticity in a Digital Environment;* Clifford Lynch, "Authenticity and Integrity in the Digital Environment: An Exploratory Analysis of the Central Role of Trust," in *Authenticity in a Digital Environment.* See also M. T. Clanchy, *From Memory to Written Record: England, 1066–1307,* 2d ed. (Oxford, 1993); and Research Libraries Group, *Attributes of a Trusted Digital Repository: Meeting the Needs of Research Resources; An RLC-OCLC Report* (Mountain View, CA, 2001), www.rlg.org/longterm/attributes01.pdf.

15. Brewster Kahle, Rick Prelinger, and Mary E. Jackson, "Public Access to Digital Materials" (white paper delivered at the Association of Research Libraries and Internet Archive Colloquium "Research in the 'Born-Digital' Domain," San Francisco, 4 March 2001), available at www.dlib.org/dlib/october01/kahle/10kahle.html.

But if libraries don't *own* digital content, how can they preserve it? The problem will become even worse if publishers widely adopt copy protection schemes, as they are seriously considering doing for electronic books. Even a library that had the legal right to preserve the content would have no reason to assume that it would be able to do so; meanwhile, the publisher would have little incentive to keep the protection system functioning in a new software environment. In general, digital rights management systems and other forms of "trusted computing" undercut preservation efforts by embedding centralized control in proprietary systems. "If Microsoft, or the U.S. government, does not like what you said in a document you wrote," speculates Free Software advocate Richard Stallman, "they could post new instructions telling all computers to refuse to let anyone read that document." [16]

Licensed and centrally controlled digital content not only erodes the ability of libraries to preserve the past, it also undercuts their responsibility. Why should a library worry about the long-term preservation of something it does not own? But then, who will? Publishers have not traditionally assumed preservation responsibility since there is no obvious profit to be made in ensuring that something will be available or readable in a hundred years when it is in the public domain and can't be sold or licensed. [17]

The digital era has not only unsettled questions of ownership and preservation for traditional copyrighted material, it has also introduced a new, vast category of what could be called semi-published works, which lack a clear preservation path. The free content available on the web is protected by copyright even though it has not been formally registered with the Library of Congress Copyright Office or sold by a publisher. That means that a library that decided to save a collection of web pages — say, those posted by abortion rights organizations — would technically be violating copyright. [18] The absence of this "process" is the most fundamental problem facing digital preservation. Over centuries, a complex (and imperfect) system for preserving the past has emerged. Digitization has unsettled that system of responsibility for

---

16. Committee on Intellectual Property Rights in the Emerging Information Infrastructure, National Research Council et al., *The Digital Dilemma: Intellectual Property in the Information Age* (Washington, DC, 1999), http://books.nap.edu/html/digital_dilemma/; Richard Stallman, "Can You Trust Your Computer?" *Newsforge,* 21 October 2002, http://newsforge.com/news forge/02/10/21/1449250.shtml?tid=19. The Digital Millennium Copyright Act makes it illegal to circumvent technical protection services. See Peter Lyman, "Archiving the World Wide Web," in CLIR, *Building a National Strategy for Digital Preservation: Issues in Digital Media Archiving* (Washington, DC, 2002), www.clir.org/pubs/reports/pub106/web.html.

17. CLIR, *Evidence in Hand.*

18. Committee on Intellectual Property Rights in the Emerging Information Infrastructure, National Research Council, *Digital Dilemma.*

preservation, and an alternative system has not yet emerged. In the meantime, cultural and historical objects are being permanently lost.

Four different systems generally preserve cultural and historical documents and objects. Research libraries take responsibility for books, magazines, and other published cultural works, including moving images and recorded sound. Government records fall under the jurisdiction of the National Archives and a network of state and local archives.[19] Systems for maintaining other cultural and historical materials are less formal or centralized. "Records" and "papers" from businesses, voluntary associations, and individuals have found their way into local historical societies, specialized archives, and university special collections. Finally, the semi-published body of material we have called "ephemera" has been most often saved by enthusiastic individuals—for example, postcard and comic book collectors—who might later deposit their hoard in a permanent repository.[20]

While research libraries have tried to save relatively complete sets of published works, other historical sources have generally been preserved only in a highly selective and sometimes capricious fashion—what archivists call "preservation through neglect." Materials that lasted fifty or one hundred years found their way into an archive, library, or museum. Although this inexact system has resulted in many grievous losses to the historical record, it has also given us many rich collections of personal and organizational papers and ephemera.[21]

But this "system" will not work in the digital era because preservation cannot begin twenty-five years after the fact. What might happen, for example, to the records of a writer active in the 1980s who dies in 2003 after a long illness? Her heirs will find a pile of unreadable 5¼" floppy disks with copies

19. As with our network of research libraries, this system is a modern invention. The first public governmental archive came with the French Revolution; the British Public Record Office opened in 1838, and the National Archives is of startlingly recent vintage: the legislation establishing it did not come until 1934. Donald R. McCoy, "The Struggle to Establish a National Archives in the United States," in *Guardian of Heritage: Essays on the History of the National Archives,* ed. Timothy Walch (Washington, DC, 1985), 1–15.

20. Don Waters, "Wrap Up" (paper delivered at the DAI Institute, "The State of Digital Preservation: An International Perspective," Washington, DC, 25 April 2002), available at www.clir .org/pubs/reports/pub107/contents.html; Dale Flecker, "Preserving Digital Periodicals," in CLIR, *Building a National Strategy for Digital Preservation.*

21. Michael L. Miller, "Assessing the Need: What Information and Activities Should We Preserve?" (paper delivered at "Documenting the Digital Age," San Francisco, 10–12 February 1997), copy in possession of author. To be sure, conventional archival practice has been biased toward the preservation of the records of the rich and powerful, although in more recent years energetic, "activist archivists" have sought out more diverse sets of materials. Ian Johnston, "Whose History Is It Anyway?" *Journal of the Society of Archivists* 22.2 (2001): 213–29.

of letters and poems written in WordStar for the CP/M operating system or one of the more than fifty now-forgotten word-processing programs used in the late 1980s.[22]

Government archives similarly continue to rely on the unwarranted assumption that records can be appraised and accessioned many years after their creation. A recent study, *Current Recordkeeping Practices within the Federal Government,* which surveyed more than forty federal agencies, found widespread confusion about "policies and procedures for managing, storing, and disposing of electronic records and systems." "Government employees," it concluded, "do not know how to solve the problem of electronic records—whether the electronic information they create constitutes records and, if so, what to do with the records. Electronic files that qualify as records—particularly in the form of e-mail, and also word processing and spreadsheet documents—are not being kept at all as records in many cases."[23]

This uncertainty and disarray would not be so serious if we could assume that it could be simply sorted out in another thirty years. But if we hope to preserve the present for the future, then the technical problems facing digital preservation as well as the social and political questions about authenticity, ownership, and preservation policy need to be confronted now.

At least initially, archivists and librarians tended to assume that a technical change—the rise of digital media—required a technical solution. The simplest technical solution has been to translate digital information into something more familiar and reassuring like paper or microfilm. But, as Rothenberg points out, this is a "rear-guard action" that destroys "unique functionality (such as dynamic interaction, nonlinearity, and integration)"

---

22. See Adrian Cunningham, "Waiting for the Ghost Train: Strategies for Managing Electronic Personal Records before It Is Too Late" (paper delivered at the Society of American Archivists Annual Meeting, Pittsburgh, 23–29 August 1999), available at www.rbarry.com/cunningham-waiting2.htm. For numbers of commercial word-processing programs, see House Committee on Government Operations, *Taking a Byte out of History,* 15.

23. SRA International, *Report on Current Recordkeeping Practices within the Federal Government* (Arlington, VA, 2001), www.archives.gov/records_management/pdf/report_on_recordkeeping_practices.pdf. This report responded to an earlier GAO report: U.S. Government Accounting Office, *National Archives: Preserving Electronic Records in an Era of Rapidly Changing Technology* (Washington, DC, 1999). Archival consultant Rick Barry reports that four-fifths of e-mail creators he surveyed "do not have a clue" whether their e-mail was an official record and that most are "largely unaware" of official e-mail policies. Quoted in David A. Wallace, "Recordkeeping and Electronic Mail Policy: The State of Thought and the State of the Practice" (paper delivered at the Annual Meeting of the Society of American Archivists, Orlando, FL, 3 September 1998), www.rbarry.com/wallace.html.

and "core digital attributes (perfect copying, access, distribution, and so forth)" and sacrifices the "original form, which may be of unique historical, contextual, or evidential interest."[24]

Another backward-looking solution is to preserve the original equipment. If you have files created on an Apple II, then why not keep one in case you need it? Well, sooner or later, a disk drive breaks or a chip fails, and unless you have a computer junkyard handy and a talent for computer repair, you are out of luck. "Technological preservation," moreover, requires intervention before it is too late to save not just the files but also the original equipment. The same can be said of what is probably the most widely accepted current method of digital preservation—"data migration," or moving the documents from a medium, format, or computer technology that is becoming obsolete to one that is becoming more common.[25] When the National Archives saved the 1960 U.S. Census tapes, they used migration, and large organizations use this strategy all the time—moving from one accounting system to another. Because we have lots of experience migrating data, we also know that it is time consuming and expensive. One estimate is that data migration is equivalent to photocopying all the books in a library every five years.[26]

Some like Rothenberg also worry, for example, about the loss of functionality in migrating digital files. Moreover, the process can't be automated because "migration requires a unique new solution for each new format or paradigm and each type of document that is to be converted into that new form." Rothenberg is also derisive about the practice of translating documents into standardized formats and then retranslating as new formats emerge, which he finds "analogous to translating Homer into modern English

---

24. Rothenberg, *Avoiding Technological Quicksand.* For the long controversy over NARA and the printing of e-mail, see Bill Miller, "Court Backs Archivist's Rule: U.S. Agencies May Be Allowed to Delete E-Mail," *Washington Post,* 7 August 1999, A02; Wallace, "Recordkeeping and Electronic Mail Policy"; GAO, *Information Management,* 57–65.

25. See Stewart Granger, "Emulation as a Digital Preservation Strategy," *D-Lib Magazine* 6.10 (October 2000), www.dlib.org/dlib/october00/granger/10granger.html, on this as the "dominant" approach. An even earlier intervention version of "migration" is to move digital objects to "standardized" formats immediately or as quickly as possible, to put them in non-proprietary, open-source, commonly accepted formats (for instance, ASCII for text, .tiff for images) that are likely to be around for a long time. Of course, popular standards are no guarantee of longevity; in 1990, NARA was arguing that spreadsheets formatted for Lotus 1–2–3 were not a preservation problem since the program was so "widespread." House Committee on Government Operations, *Taking a Byte out of History,* 12.

26. Warwick Cathro, Colin Webb, and Julie Whiting, "Archiving the Web: The PANDORA Archive at the National Library of Australia" (paper delivered at "Preserving the Present for the Future Web Archiving," Copenhagen, 18–19 June 2001). See also Diane Vogt-O'Connor, "Is the Record of the 20th Century at Risk?" *CRM: Cultural Resource Management* 22.2 (1999): 21–24.

by way of every intervening language that has existed during the past 2,500 years."[27]

Rothenberg's favored alternative is "emulation"—developing a system that works on later generations of hardware and software but mimics the original. In principle, a single emulation solution could preserve a vast store of digital documents. In addition, it holds the greatest promise for preserving interactive and multimedia digital creations. But critics of emulation tellingly note that it is only a theoretical solution. Probably the best strategy is to reject the all-or-nothing, magic-bullet approaches implicit in the proposals of the most passionate advocates of any particular strategy—whether creating hard copies, preserving old equipment, migrating formats, or emulating hardware and software. Margaret Hedstrom, one of the leading figures in digital preservation research, argues persuasively that "the search for the Holy Grail of digital archiving is premature, unrealistic, and possibly counter-productive." Instead, we need to develop "solutions that are appropriate, effective, affordable and acceptable to different classes of digital objects that live in different technological and organizational contexts."[28]

But even the most calibrated mix of technical solutions will not save the past for the future because, as we have seen, the problems are much more than technical and involve difficult social, political, and organizational questions of authenticity, ownership, and responsibility. Multiple experiments and practices are under way—more than can be discussed here. But I want to focus on some widely discussed approaches or experiments as illustrative of some of the possibilities and continuing problems.

One of the earliest and most influential approaches to digital preservation (and digital authenticity) was what archivists call the "Pitt Project," a three-year (1993–96) research effort funded by the National Historical Publications and Records Commission (NHPRC) and centered at the University

---

27. Rothenberg, *Avoiding Technological Quicksand.*

28. Margaret Hedstrom, "Digital Preservation: Matching Problems, Requirements and Solutions" (paper delivered at the NSF Workshop on Data Archiving and Information Preservation, 26–27 March 1999), http://cecssrv1.cecs.missouri.edu/NSFWorkshop/hedpp.html (accessed March 2002 but unavailable in May 2003). See also Margaret Hedstrom, "Research Issues in Digital Archiving" (paper delivered at the DAI Institute, "The State of Digital Preservation: An International Perspective," Washington, DC, 25 April 2002, available at www.clir.org/pubs/reports/pub107/contents.html). Rothenberg himself is currently undertaking research on emulation, and other emulation research is going on at the University of Michigan and Leeds University and at IBM's Almaden Research Center in San Jose, California. Daniel Greenstein and Abby Smith, "Digital Preservation in the United States: Survey of Current Research, Practice, and Common Understandings" (paper delivered at "Preserving History on the Web: Ensuring Long-Term Access to Web-Based Documents," Washington, DC, 23 April 2002), copy in possession of author. More recently, Rothenberg has apparently tempered his position on emulation versus migration.

of Pittsburgh School of Information and Library Studies. For historians, what is most interesting (and sometimes puzzling) about the Pitt Project approach is the way that it simultaneously narrows and broadens the role of archives and archivists through its focus on "records as evidence" rather than "information." "Records," David Bearman and Jennifer Trant explain, "are that which was created in the conduct of business" and provide "evidence of transactions." Data or information, by contrast, Bearman "dismisses as non-archival and unworthy of the archivist's attention."[29] From this point of view, the government's record of your Social Security account is vital but not the "information" contained in letters that you and others might have written complaining about the idea of privatizing Social Security.

The Pitt Project produced a pathbreaking set of "functional requirements for evidence in electronic record keeping"—in effect, strategies and tactics to ensure that electronic records produce legally or organizationally acceptable evidence of their transactions. Such a focus responds particularly well to worries about the "authenticity" of electronic records. But for historians (and for some archivists), the focus on records as evidence rather than records as sources of information, history, or memory seems disappointingly narrow. Moreover, as the Canadian archivist Terry Cook points out, the emphasis on "redesigning computer systems' functional requirements to preserve the integrity and reliability of records" and assigning "long-term custodial control . . . to the creator of archival records" privileges "the powerful, relatively stable, and continuing creators of records capable of such reengineering" and ignores artists, activists, and "marginalized and weaker members of society" who have neither the resources nor inclination to produce "business acceptable communications."[30]

29. David Bearman and Jennifer Trant, "Electronic Records Research Working Meeting, 28–30 May 1997: A Report from the Archives Community," *D-Lib Magazine* 3.7–8 (July/August 1997), www.dlib.org/dlib/july97/07bearman.html; Terry Cook, "The Impact of David Bearman on Modern Archival Thinking: An Essay of Personal Reflection and Critique," *Archives and Museum Informatics* 11 (1997): 23. See further Margaret Hedstrom, "Building Record-Keeping Systems: Archivists Are Not Alone on the Wild Frontier," *Archivaria* 44 (Fall 1997): 46–48. See also David Bearman and Ken Sochats, "Metadata Requirements for Evidence," in University of Pittsburgh, School of Information Sciences, the Pittsburgh Project, www.archimuse.com/papers/nhprc/. (Many parts of this site have disappeared, but this undated paper is available at www.archimuse.com/papers/nhprc/BACartic .html.) David Bearman, "An Indefensible Bastion: Archives as Repositories in the Electronic Age," in *Archival Management of Electronic Records,* ed. Bearman (Pittsburgh: Archives and Museum Informatics, 1991), 14–24; Margaret Hedstrom, "Archives as Repositories—A Commentary," in ibid.

30. Cook, "Impact of David Bearman on Modern Archival Thinking," 15–37. From another perspective, the Pitt Project broadened, rather than narrowed, the concerns of electronic archivists, since previously the focus had been on statistical databases. In one effort to join the emphasis on records as evidence with a broader social cultural focus, Margaret Hedstrom argues that "to benefit

Whereas the Pitt Project emphasizes archival professionalism, a narrowing of the definition of recordkeeping, a rejection of the custodial tradition in archives, and planning for more careful collecting in the future rather than action in the present, the Internet Archive has taken precisely the opposite approach. It represents a grassroots, immediate, enthusiast response to the crisis of digital preservation that both expands and further centralizes archival responsibility in ways that were previously unimaginable. Starting in September 1996, Brewster Kahle and a small staff sent "crawlers" out to capture the web by moving link-by-link and completing a full snapshot every two months. Although in part a philanthropic venture funded by Kahle, the Internet Archive also has a commercial side. Kahle's for-profit web navigation service, Alexa Internet (bought by Amazon in 1999 for $300 million), is what actually gathers the web snapshots, which it uses to analyze patterns of web use, and then donates them to the Internet Archive.[31]

---

fully from the synergy between business needs and preservation requirements, cultural heritage concerns should be linked to equally critical social goals, such as monitoring global environment change, locating nuclear waste sites, and establishing property rights, all of which also depend on long-term access to reliable, electronic evidence." Quoted in Richard J. Cox, "Searching for Authority: Archivists and Electronic Records in the New World at the Fin-de-Siècle," *First Monday* 5.1 (3 January 2000), http://firstmonday.org/issues/issue5_1/cox/index.html. The Pitt Project has been the subject of enormous discussion and significant debate among archivists; a full and nuanced treatment of the subject is beyond the scope of this article. Whereas Cook offers serious criticism of Bearman, the leader of the project along with Richard Cox, he also celebrates Bearman as "the leading archival thinker of the late twentieth century." Linda Henry offers a sweeping attack on Bearman and other advocates of a "new paradigm" in electronic records management in "Schellenberg in Cyberspace," *American Archivist* 61 (Fall 1998): 309–27. A more recent critique is Mark A. Greene, "The Power of Meaning: The Archival Mission in the Postmodern Age," *American Archivist* 65.1 (Spring/Summer 2002): 42–55. Terry Cook puts the story in historical perspective (but from his particular perspective) in "What Is Past Is Prologue: A History of Archival Ideas since 1898, and the Future Paradigm Shift," *Archivaria* 43 (Spring 1997), available at www.rbarry.com/cookt-pastprologue-ar43fnl.htm. The "Preservation of the Integrity of Electronic Records" project (called the UBC Project because it was carried out at the University of British Columbia) and the InterPARES project (International Research on Permanent Authentic Records in Electronic Systems), which built on the UBC Project, have taken a different approach, but they share the Pitt Project's emphasis on the problem of "authenticity" and on "records" rather than the broader array of sources that generally interest historians. Luciana Duranti, *The Long-Term Preservation of Authentic Electronic Records: Findings of the InterPARES Project* (Vancouver, 2002), www.interpares.org/book/index.htm. The December 2002 draft of the *NHPRC Electronic Records Agenda Final Report* suggests that the consensus among archivists is moving toward a broader definition of records. My understanding of these issues has been greatly aided by attending the December 8–9, 2002, meeting convened to discuss that agenda and by conversations with Robert Horton of the Minnesota Historical Society, who is the leader of that effort.

31. Carolyn Said, "Archiving the Internet: Brewster Kahle Makes Digital Snapshots of Web," *San Francisco Chronicle*, 7 May 1998, B3; Brewster Kahle, "Preserving the Internet," *Scientific American*, March 1997, www.sciamdigital.com; Kendra Mayfield, "Wayback Goes Way Back on Web," *Wired News*, 29 October 2001, www.wired.com/news/print/0,1294,47894,00.html; Mike Burner,

By February 2002, the Internet Archive (IA) had gathered a monumental collection of more than 100 terabytes of web data—about 10 billion web pages or five times all the books in the Library of Congress—and was gobbling up 12 terabytes more each month. That same fall, it began offering public access to most of the collection through what Kahle called the "Wayback Machine"—a wry reference to the device used by the time-traveling Mr. Peabody in the Rocky and Bullwinkle cartoons of the 1960s. Astonishingly, a single individual with a very small staff has created the world's largest database and library in just five years.[32]

In December 2001, shortly after the Wayback Machine became public, the search engine company Google unveiled "Google Groups," another massive digital archive—this one under purely commercial auspices. Google Groups provides access to more than 650 million messages posted over the past two decades to "Usenet," the online discussion forums that predate even the Internet. Although "ownership" seems like a dubious concept in relation to a public discussion forum, Google purchased the archive from Deja.com, which had brought the groups to the web but then collapsed in the Internet bust. Despite Deja.com's failure, Google sees the Usenet Archive as another attractive feature in its stable of online information resources and tools.[33]

"The Internet Archive Robot," e-mail to Robots Mailing List, 5 September 1996, www.robotstxt .org/wc/mailing-list/1258.html. On Alexa, see Rajiv Chandrasekaran, "Seeing the Sites on a Custom Tour: New Internet Search Tool Takes Selective Approach," *Washington Post,* 4 September 1997, E01; Tim Jackson, "Archive Holds Wealth of Data," *Financial Times* (London), 24 November 1997, 15; Laurie J. Flynn, "Alexa's Crusade Continues under Amazon.com's Flag," *New York Times,* 3 May 1999, C4. On other early efforts to "save the web," see Spencer Reiss, "Internet in a Box," *Wired,* October 1996, www.wired.com/wired/4.10/scans.html; Bruce Sterling, "The Life and Death of Media" (speech delivered at the Sixth International Symposium on Electronic Art, Montreal, 19 September 1995), available at www.chriswaltrip.com/sterling/dedmed.html; John Markoff, "When Big Brother Is a Librarian," *New York Times,* 9 March 1997, IV:3; James B. Gardner, comp., "Report on Documenting the Digital Age" (Washington, DC, 1997); Nathan Myhrvold, "Capturing History Digitally: Why Archive the Internet?" (paper delivered at "Documenting the Digital Age," San Francisco, 10–12 February 1997), copies of Gardner and Myhrvold in possession of author.

32. Hamish Mackintosh, Interview with Brewster Kahle, "Webarian," *Guardian,* 21 February 2002, 4, www.guardian.co.uk/online/story/0,3605,653286,00.html; Molly Wood, "CNET's Web Know-It-All Goes Where You Won't," *CNET,* 15 March 2002, www.cnet.com/software/0–8888–8– 9076625–1.html; "Seeing the Future in the Web's Past," *BBC News,* 12 November 2001, http://news.bbc .co.uk/hi/english/in_depth/sci_tech/2000/dot_life/newsid_1651000/1651557.stm. For a good explanation of the technical side of IA, see Richard Koman, "How the Wayback Machine Works," *O'Reilly Network,* 21 January 2002, www.oreillynet.com/pub/a/webservices/2002/01/18/brewster.html.

33. Google Employee, "Google Groups Archive Information Newsgroups," e-mail, 21 December 2001; Stellin, "Google's Revival of a Usenet Archive Opens Up a Wealth of Possibilities"; Danny Fortson, "Google Gobbles Up Deja.com's Babble," *Daily Deal* (12 February 2001); Michael Liedtke, "Web Search Engine Google Buys Deja.com's Usenet Discussion Archives," *Associated Press,* 12 February 2001.

Both IA and Google Groups are libraries organized on principles that are more familiar to computer scientists than to librarians, as Peter Lyman, who knows both worlds as one-time head of the University of California at Berkeley library and as a member of the IA board, points out. The library community has focused on developing "sophisticated cataloging strategies." But computer scientists, including Kahle, have been more interested in developing sophisticated search engines that operate directly on the data we see (the web pages) rather than on the metadata (the cataloguing information). Whereas archival and library projects focus on "high-quality collections built around select themes" and make the unit of cataloguing the web page, the computer science paradigm "allows for archiving the entire Web as it changes over time, then uses search engines to retrieve the necessary information."[34]

Projects designed by librarians and archivists generally have the advantages of precision and standardization. They favor careful protocols and standards such as the Dublin Core, the OAIS (Open Archival Information System), and the EAD (Encoded Archival Description). But the expense and difficulty of the protocols and procedures mean that less well funded and staffed archives and libraries often ignore them. Responding to presentations by advocates of standards at a conference, Jim Miller, a computer scientist, warned that if archivists push for too much cataloguing metadata "they might end up with none."[35]

The Internet Archive, which is the child of the search engines and the computer scientists, is an extraordinarily valuable resource. Most historians will not be interested now, but in twenty-five or fifty years they will delight in searching it. A typical college history assignment in 2050 might be to compare web depictions of Muslim Americans in 1998 and 2008. But any appreciation of the IA must acknowledge its limitations. For example, large numbers of web pages do not exist as "static" HTML pages; rather, they are stored in databases, and the pages are generated "on the fly" by search queries. As a result, the IA's crawlers do not capture much of the so-called deep web that is stored in databases. Multimedia files—streaming media and flash—also do not seem to be captured. In addition, the Internet Archive's crawls cannot go

---

34. Lyman, "Archiving the World Wide Web."

35. Miller quoted in Gardner, "Report on Documenting the Digital Age." For an overview of OAIS, see Brian Lavoie, "Meeting the Challenges of Digital Preservation: The OAIS Reference Model," 2000, www.oclc.org/research/publications/newsletter/repubs/lavoie243/; on EAD, see Daniel V. Pitti, "Encoded Archival Description: An Introduction and Overview," *D-Lib Magazine* 5.11 (November 1999), www.dlib.org/dlib/november99/11pitti.html. OAIS comes out of NASA and the space data community, not from the librarians. But they have embraced it.

on forever; at some point, they stop, since, as one of the computer scientists who manages them acknowledges, "the Web is essentially infinite in size."[36]

Anyone who browses the IA regularly encounters such messages as "Not in Archive" and "File Location Error" or even "closed for maintenance." Some pages are missing for legal and economic as well as technical reasons. Private, gated sites are off-limits to the Internet Archive's crawlers. And many ungated sites also discourage the crawlers. The *New York Times* allows free access to its current contents, but charges for articles more than one week old. If the IA gathered up and preserved the *Times's* content, there would be no reason for anyone to pay the *Times* for access to its proprietary archive. As a result, the *Times* includes a "robots exclusion" file on its site, which the IA respects. Even those sites without the robots exclusion file and without any formal copyright are still covered by copyright law and could challenge the IA's archiving of their content. To avoid trouble, the IA simply purges the pages of anyone who complains. It is as if Julie Nixon could write to the National Archives and tell them to delete her father's tapes or an author could withdraw an early novel from circulation.[37]

Thus the Internet Archive is very far from the complete solution to the problem of digital preservation. It does not deal with the digital records that vex the National Archives and other repositories because they lack the public accessibility and minimal standardization in HTML of web pages. Nor does it include much formally published literature — e-books and journals — which is sold and hence gated from view. And even for what it has gathered, it has not yet hatched a long-term preservation plan, which would have to incorporate a strategy for continuing access to digital data that are in particular (and

---

36. Raymie Stata, "The Internet Archive" (paper delivered at the conference "Preserving Web-Based Documents," Washington, DC, 23 April 2002). On deep versus surface web, see Lyman, "Archiving the World Wide Web"; and Roy Rosenzweig, "The Road to Xanadu: Public and Private Pathways on the History Web," *Journal of American History* 88.2 (September 2001): 548–79, also available at http://chnm.gmu.edu/resources/essays/d/9. Kahle himself indicates many of the problems and limitations of the Internet Archive in Brewster Kahle, "Archiving the Internet: Bold Efforts to Record the Entire Internet Are Expected to Lead to New Services" (paper presented at "Documenting the Digital Age," San Francisco, 10–12 February 1997), copy in possession of author.

37. On robots exclusion, see www.robotstxt.org/wc/exclusion-admin.html. Apparently, the IA will retroactively block a site without direct request, if it simply posts the robots.txt file. This would seem to mean that if someone took over an expired domain name, they could then block access to the prior content. There is some evidence, however, that the IA does not actually "purge" the content, it simply makes it inaccessible. For an intense discussion of these issues, see the hundreds of online postings in "The Wayback Machine, Friend or Foe?" *Slashdot,* 19–20 June 2002, http://ask.slashdot.org/askslashdot/02/06/19/1744209.shtml. For a pessimistic assessment of the legality of the IA's practices (though not explicitly directed at it), see I. Trotter Hardy, "Internet Archives and Copyright" (paper delivered at "Documenting the Digital Age," San Francisco, 10–12 February 1997), copy in possession of author.

time-bound) formats. Even more troubling, it has no plan for how it will sustain itself into the future. Will Kahle continue to fund it indefinitely?[38] What if Amazon and Alexa no longer find it worthwhile to gather the data, especially since acquisition costs are doubling every year?

Similar questions could be raised about "Google Groups." What if the company decides that there is no prospect of gaining adequate advertising revenue by making old newsgroup messages available (as, indeed, Deja.com previously determined)? While appreciating Google's entrepreneurial energy in preserving and making available an enormous body of historical documents, we should also look carefully at the way private corporations have suddenly entered into a realm—archives—that was previously part of the public sector—a reflection of the privatization sweeping across the global economy. At least so far, our most important, and most imaginatively constructed, digital collections are in private hands.[39]

Given that the preservation of cultural heritage and national history are arguably social goods, why shouldn't the government take the lead in such efforts? One reason is that at least some key aspects of the digital present—the *Bert* story, for example—do not follow national boundaries and, indeed, erode them. If national archives were part of the projects of state-building and nationalism, then why should states support post-national digital archives? The declining significance of state-based national archives may mirror the decline of the contemporary national state. So far, the Smithsonian Institution and the Library of Congress have worked with the Internet Archive only where they needed its help in documenting some particularly national stories—the elections of 1996 and 2000 and the September 11th attacks.

Another reason for the limited government role is that the digital preservation crisis emerged most dramatically during the anti-statist Reagan revolution of the 1980s. In the 1970s, for example, the electronic records program of the National Archives made a modest, promising start. But, as the archivist Thomas E. Brown writes, it went into "a near total collapse in the 1980s." The staff dropped to seven people by 1983, and, amazingly, this beleaguered group charged with guarding the nation's electronic records had no access to computer facilities. Things began to improve in the early 1990s, but, after 1993, the electronic records program suffered from further cutbacks in the federal work force. An underfunded and understaffed National Archives was hardly

---

38. Insiders have commented to me that the IA would disappear if Kahle left the project. But there are very recent signs (as of 2003) that the IA is broadening its base of financial support.

39. For a recent, brief overview of these trends, see Naomi Klein, "Don't Fence Us In," *Guardian,* 5 October 2002.

in a position to develop a solution to the daunting and mounting problem of electronic federal records.[40]

The Library of Congress also initially eschewed a leading role in preserving digital materials, as the National Research Council later complained. Here, too, one could detect the weakening influence of the state. The library's high-profile effort in the digital realm was "American Memory," which digitized millions of items from its collections and placed them online. Teachers, students, and researchers love American Memory, but it did nothing to preserve the growing number of "born digital" objects. Not coincidentally, American Memory was a project that could attract large numbers of private and corporate donors, who often saw sponsorship as good advertising and who paid for three-quarters of the project.[41]

Better-developed state-centered approaches to digital preservation have, not surprisingly, emerged outside the United States — in Australia and Scandinavia, for example. Norway requires that digital materials be legally deposited with the national library in return for copyright protection.[42] One of the key ways that the Library of Congress could help preserve the future of digital materials would be to aggressively assert its copyright deposit claims, which would finesse some of the legal and ownership issues troubling the Internet Archive.[43]

Nevertheless, the National Archives and the Library of Congress have very recently begun — prodded by outside critics and supported belatedly by Congress — to take a more aggressive approach on digital preservation. The archives is proposing a "Redesign of Federal Records Management" to respond to the reality that "a large majority of electronic record series of continuing value are not coming into archival custody." It is also working closely with

40. Thomas Brown, "What Is Past Is Analog: The National Archives Electronic Records Program since 1968" (paper delivered at the OAH Annual Meeting, Washington, DC, 2002), copy in possession of author. In 1997, Kenneth Thibodeau estimated that the NARA invested only token amounts (2 percent of its budget) in electronic records. Gardner, "Report on Documenting the Digital Age."

41. Committee on an Information Technology Strategy for the Library of Congress et al., *LC21*, http://books.nap.edu/html/lc21/index.html; Rosenzweig, "Road to Xanadu."

42. "Background Information about PANDORA: The National Collection of Australian Online Publications," *PANDORA*, http://pandora.nla.gov.au/background.html; Cathro, Webb, and Whiting, "Archiving the Web"; Colin Webb, "National Library of Australia" (paper delivered at the DAI Institute, "The State of Digital Preservation: An International Perspective," Washington, DC, 25 April 2002, available at www.clir.org/pubs/reports/pub107/contents.html). For British efforts to cope with digital materials, see Jim McCue, "Can You Archive the Net?" *Times* (London), 29 April 2002. On Sweden and Norway, see Warwick Cathro, "Archiving the Web," *National Library of Australia Gateways* 52 (August 2001), .www.nla.gov.au/ntwkpubs/gw/52/p11a01.html/.

43. There is anecdotal evidence that this is being seriously considered.

the San Diego Supercomputing Center on developing "persistent object preservation" (POP), which creates a description of a digital object (and groups of digital objects) in simple tags and schemas that will be understandable in the future; the records would be "self-describing" and, hence, independent of specific hardware and software. The computer scientists maintain that records in this format will last for three hundred to four hundred years.[44]

In December 2000, the Library of Congress launched the most important initiative, the National Digital Information Infrastructure Program (NDIIP). Even this massive and important federal initiative bore the marks of the anti-statist, privatization politics of the 1980s. Congress gave the library $5 million for planning and promised another $20 million when it approved the plan. But the final $75 million will be distributed only as a match against an equal amount in private funds.[45]

Although the future of the digital present remains perilous, these recent initiatives suggest some encouraging strategies for preserving the range of digital materials. A combination of technical and organizational approaches promises the greatest chance of success, but privatization poses grave dangers for the future of the past. Advocates of digital preservation need to mobilize

---

44. National Archives and Records Administration, *Proposal for a Redesign of Federal Records Management* (July 2002), 10, www.archives.gov/records_management/initiatives/rm_redesign.html; Richard W. Walker, "For the Record, NARA Techie Aims to Preserve," *Government Computer News* 20.21 (30 July 2001), www.gcn.com/vol20_no21/news/4752–1.html/; GAO, *Information Management*, 50. So far, POP remains, as a NARA staff member explained in April 2001, "beyond the state of the art of information technology." Adrienne M. Woods, "Toward Building the Archives of the Future" (paper delivered at the Society of California Archivists' Annual Meeting, 27 April 2001), accessed online 1 May 2002, but not available as of 20 June 2002. See also Kenneth Thibodeau, "Overview of Technological Approaches to Digital Preservation and Challenges in Coming Years" (presentation at the DAI Institute, "The State of Digital Preservation: An International Perspective," Washington, DC, 24–25 April 2002, available at www.clir.org/pubs/reports/pub107/contents.html). In June 2002, the GAO reported that, in general, NARA's electronic records project "faces substantial risks" and "is already behind schedule." GAO, *Information Management*, 3. But since this article was originally written in 2002, NARA's electronic records program has made considerable progress. See *NARA–Electronic Records Archive, http://www.archives.gov/era/*. Another important development not covered here is the rise of institutional repositories, often based on the DSpace platform. See Mackenzie Smith et al., "DSpace: An Open Source Dynamic Digital Repository," *D-Lib Magazine*, 9 January 2003; Clifford Lynch and Joan Lippincott, "Institutional Repository Deployment in the United States as of Early 2005," *D-Lib Magazine*, September 2005. For a more recent overview of preservation issues directed at a nonspecialist audience, see Daniel J. Cohen and Roy Rosenzweig, *Digital History: A Guide to Gathering, Preserving, and Presenting the Past on the Web* (Philadelphia: University of Pennsylvania Press, 2005), 220–46.

45. Amy Friedlander, "The National Digital Information Infrastructure Preservation Program: Expectations, Realities, Choices and Progress to Date," *D-Lib Magazine*, April 2002, www.dlib .org/dlib/april02/friedlander/04friedlander.html. For current status, see Library of Congress, *Digital Preservation,* http://www.digitalpreservation.gov/.

state funding and state power (such as the assertion of eminent domain over copyright materials) but infuse it with the experimental and ad hoc spirit of the Internet Archive. And we need to recognize that, for many digital materials (especially the web), the imperfect computer-science paradigm probably has more to recommend it than the more careful and systematic approach of the librarians and archivists. What is often said of military strategy seems to apply to digital preservation: "the greatest enemy of a good plan is the dream of a perfect plan."[46] We have never preserved everything; we need to start preserving something.

Given the enormous barriers to saving digital records and information, it comes as something of a surprise that many continue to insist that a perfect plan—or at least a pretty good plan—will eventually emerge. Techno-optimists such as Brewster Kahle dream most vividly of the perfect plan and its startling consequences. "For the second time in history," Kahle writes with two collaborators, "people are laying plans to collect all information—the first time involved the Greeks which culminated in the Library of Alexandria. . . . Now . . . many [are] once again to take steps in building libraries that hold complete collections." Digital technology, they explain, has "gotten to the point where scanning all books, digitizing all audio recordings, downloading all websites, and recording the output of all TV and radio stations is not only feasible but less costly than buying and storing the physical versions."[47] Librarians and archivists remain skeptical of such predictions, pointing out the enormous costs of cataloguing and making available what has been preserved, and that we have never saved more than a fraction of our cultural output. But, whatever our degree of skepticism, it is still worth thinking seriously about what a world in which everything was saved might look like.

Most obviously, archives, libraries, and other record repositories would suddenly be freed from the tyranny of shelf space that has always shadowed their work. Digitization also removes other long-term scourges of historical memory such as fire and war. The 1921 fire that destroyed the 1890 census records provided a crucial spark that finally led to the creation of the National Archives. But what if there had been multiple copies of the census? The

---

46. The quote is often incorrectly attributed to Carl von Clausewitz. It could be that it is simply a reworking of Voltaire's remark that "le mieux est l'enemi du bien" (the best is the enemy of the good) or of George S. Patton's dictum "A good plan violently executed now is better than a perfect plan executed next week."

47. Kahle, Prelinger, and Jackson, "Public Access to Digital Materials." See, similarly, Michael Lesk, "How Much Information Is There in the World?" an online paper at www.lesk.com/mlesk/ksg97/ksg.html.

ease—almost inevitability—of the copying of digital files means that it is considerably less likely today that things exist in only a single copy.[48]

What would a new, virtual, and universal Alexandria library look like? Kahle and his colleagues have forcefully articulated an expansive democratic vision of a past that includes all voices and is open to all. "There are about ten to fifteen million people's voices evident on the Web," he told a reporter. "The Net is a people's medium: the good, the bad and the ugly. The interesting, the picayune and the profane. It's all there." Advocates of the new universal library and archive wax even more eloquent about democratizing access to the historical record. "The opportunity of our time is to offer universal access to all of human knowledge," said Kahle.[49]

Kahle's vision of cultural and historical abundance merges the traditional democratic vision of the public library with the resources of the research library and the national archive. Previously, few had the opportunity to visit Washington to watch early Thomas Edison films at the Library of Congress. And the library could not have served them if they had. Democratized access is the real payoff in electronic records and materials. It may be harder to pre-

---

48. McCoy, "Struggle to Establish a National Archives in the United States," 1, 12. Indeed, one digital preservation program—LOCKSS (Lots of Copies Keep Stuff Safe)—relies on precisely this principle: http://lockss.stanford.edu/.

49. Lee Dembart, "Go Wayback," *International Herald Tribune,* 4 March 2002, www.iht.com/cgi-bin/generic.cgi?template=articleprint.tmplh&ArticleId=50002; "Seeing the Future in the Web's Past," *BBC News,* 12 November 2001. See also Joseph Menn, "Net Archive Turns Back 10 Billion Pages of Time," *Los Angeles Times,* 25 October 2001, A1; Heather Green, "A Library as Big as the World," *Business Week Online,* 28 February 2002, www.businessweek.com/technology/content/feb2002/tc20020228_1080.htm. The dream of a universal archive is also the nightmare of privacy advocates. In the paper era, the physical bulk of personnel files and bank, criminal, and medical records made them more likely to wind up in landfills than in archives. Even when they were preserved, the possibility of retrospective prying (was your neighbor's grandfather a deadbeat or a drunk?) was reduced by the sheer tedium of sorting through thousands of pages of records. But what if sophisticated data-mining tools ("tell me everything about my neighbors") made such searching easy? Even the "public" material on the web poses ethical challenges for historians. "The woman who is going to be elected president in 2024 is in high school now, and I bet she has a home page," exclaims Kahle. The Internet Archives has "the future president's home page!" Perhaps. But it also has the home pages of many other high school students, at least some of whom are going through serious emotional turmoil that they might later prefer to keep from public view. Kahle himself wrote a prescient 1992 article, the "Ethics of Digital Librarianship," which worries about "types of information that will be accessible" as "the system grows to include entertainment, employment, health and other servers." Menn, "Net Archive Turns Back 10 Billion Pages"; Wood, "CNET's Web Know-It-All"; Kahle quoted in John Markoff, "Bitter Debate on Privacy Divides Two Experts," *New York Times,* 30 December 1999, C1. See also Jean-François Blanchette and Deborah G. Johnson, "Data Retention and the Panoptic Society: The Social Benefits of Forgetfulness," *Information Society* 18 (2002): 33–45; Marc Rotenberg, "Privacy and the Digital Archive: Outlining Key Issues" (paper delivered at "Documenting the Digital Age," San Francisco, 10–12 February 1997), copy in possession of author; and "Wayback Machine, Friend or Foe?"

serve and organize digital materials than it is paper records, but, once that is accomplished, they can be made accessible to vastly greater numbers of people. To open up the archives and libraries in this way democratizes historical work. Already, people who had never had direct access to archives and libraries can now enter. High school students are suddenly doing primary source research; genealogy has exploded in popularity because you no longer have to travel to distant archives.

This vision of democratic access also promises direct and unmediated access to the past. Electronic commerce enthusiasts tout "disintermediation"— which is the elimination of the insurance and real estate broker and other intermediaries and the emergence of virtual spaces such as eBay made up of only buyers and sellers. In theory, the universal digital library might bring a similar cultural disintermediation in which people interested in history make direct contact with the documents and artifacts of the past without the mediation of cultural brokers like librarians, archivists, and historians. The sociologist Mike Featherstone speculates on the emergence of a "new culture of memory" in which the existing "hierarchical controls" over access would disappear. This "direct access to cultural records and resources from those outside cultural institutions" could "lead to a decline in intellectual and academic power" in which the historian, for example, no longer stands between people and their pasts.[50] The "Wayback Machine" encapsulates this vision of disintermediation by suggesting that everyone, like Mr. Peabody and his boy Sherman, can jump into a time machine and find out what Columbus or Edison was "really" like. Of course, most historians would argue that, while digital collections may put "the novice in the archive,"[51] he or she is not so likely to know what to do there. Still, the balance of power may shift.

Most historians have not embraced this vision in which everyone becomes his or her own historian. Nor have they enthusiastically endorsed the vision of a universal library that contains all voices and all records. In my informal polling, most historians recoil at the thought that they would need to write

50. Mike Featherstone, "Archiving Cultures," *British Journal of Sociology* 51.1 (January 2000): 178, 166. For examples of enthusiastic prophecy about such changes, see Francis Cairncross, *The Death of Distance: How the Communications Revolution Will Change Our Lives* (Boston: Harvard Business School Press, 1997); and Kevin Kelly, "New Rules for the New Economy," *Wired* 5.9 (September 1997), www.wired.com/wired/archive/5.09/newrules_pr.html. For a sober and sensible critique, see John Seely Brown and Paul Duguid, *The Social Life of Information* (Boston: Harvard Business School Press, 2000), 11–33.

51. The phrase comes from my colleague Randy Bass; see Bass and Roy Rosenzweig, "Rewiring the History and Social Studies Classroom: Needs, Frameworks, Dangers, and Proposals," *Journal of Education* (2000), available at http://chnm.gmu.edu/resources/essays/d/26.

history with even more sources.[52] Historians are not particularly hostile to new technology, but they are not ready to welcome fundamental changes to their cultural position or their modes of work. Having lived our professional careers in a culture of scarcity, historians find that a world of abundance can be unsettling.

Abundance, after all, can be overwhelming. How do we find the forest when there are so many damned trees? The psychologist Aleksandr Luria made this point in his famous study of a Russian journalist, "S" (S. V. Shereshevskii), who had an amazingly photographic memory; he could reproduce complex tables of numbers and long lists of words that had been shown to him years earlier. But this "gift" turned out to be a curse. He could not recognize people because he remembered their faces so precisely; a slightly different expression would register as a different person. Grasping the larger point of a passage or abstract idea "became a tortuous . . . struggle against images that kept rising to the surface in his mind." He lacked, as the psychologist Jerome Bruner notes, "the capacity to convert encounters with the particular into instances of the general."[53]

If historians are to set themselves "against forgetting" (in Milan Kundera's resonant phrase), then they may need to figure out new ways to sort their way through the potentially overwhelming digital record of the past. Contemporary historians are already groaning under the weight of their sources. Robert Caro has spent more than twenty-five years working his way through just the documents on Lyndon B. Johnson's pre-vice-presidential years—including 2,082 boxes of Senate papers. Surely, the injunction of traditional historians to look at "everything" cannot survive in a digital era in which "everything" has survived.[54]

---

52. See, for example, Geoffrey J. Giles, "Archives and Historians: An Introduction," in *Archives and Historians: The Crucial Partnership,* ed. Giles (Washington, DC: German Historical Institute, 1996), 5–13, who writes that "there is *too* much archival material for the archivists and for the historian to deal with" and notes feelings of "envy" of "ancient and medieval historians, who have so little material with which to work."

53. A. R. Luria, *The Mind of a Mnemonist: A Little Book about a Vast Memory,* trans. Lynn Solotaroff (New York: Basic Books, 1968), Jerome S. Bruner, foreword, viii. See the similar, but fictional, account in Jorge Luis Borges, "Funes the Memorious," in *Labyrinths: Selected Stories and Other Writings,* ed. Donald A. Yates and James E. Irby (New York: New Directions, 1964), 59–66.

54. Linton Weeks, "Power Biographer," *Washington Post,* 25 April 2002, C1. Carl Bridenbaugh's derisive view of sampling provides a good example of the traditional view that historians should look at everything: "The Great Mutation," *AHR* 68.2 (January 1963): 315–31, also available with other Presidential Addresses at www.theaha.org/info/AHA_History/cbridenbaugh.htm. Nevertheless, historians have always struggled with the problem of how to deal with large numbers of sources. Even medievalists worry about how to make sense of the huge numbers of documents that survive from twelfth-century Italy. Still, the digital era vastly increases the scale of the problem.

The historical narratives that future historians write may not actually look much different from those that are crafted today, but the methodologies they use may need to change radically. If we have, for example, a complete record of everything said in 2010, can we offer generalizations about the nature of discourse on a topic simply by "reading around"? Wouldn't we need to engage in some more methodical sampling in the manner of, say, sociology? Would this revive the social-scientific approaches with which historians flirted briefly in the 1970s? Wouldn't historians need to learn to write complex searches and algorithms that would allow them to sort through this overwhelming record in creative, but systematic, ways? The future gurus of historical research methodology may be the computer scientists at Google who have figured out how to search the equivalent of a 100-mile-high pile of paper in half a second. "To be able to find things with high accuracy and high reliability has an incredible impact on the world"—and, one might add, future historians. Future graduate programs will probably have to teach such social-scientific and quantitative methods as well as such other skills as "digital archaeology"(the ability to "read" arcane computer formats), "digital diplomatics" (the modern version of the old science of authenticating documents), and data mining (the ability to find the historical needle in the digital hay).[55] In the coming years, "contemporary historians" may need more specialized research and "language" skills than medievalists do.

Historians have time to think about changing their methods to meet the challenge of a cornucopia of historical sources. But they need to act more immediately on preserving the digital present or that reconsideration will be moot; they will be struggling with a scarcity, not an overabundance, of sources. Surprisingly, however, historians and other scholars have been scarce on this issue.[56] Archivists and librarians have intensely debated and discussed digitization and digital presentation for more than a decade. They have written hundreds of articles and reports, undertaken research projects, and organized conferences and workshops. Academic and teaching historians have taken almost no part in these conferences and have contributed almost

---

55. Stellin, "Google's Revival of a Usenet Archive Opens Up a Wealth of Possibilities"; Hedstrom, "How Do We Make Electronic Archives Usable and Accessible?"

56. To be sure, a number of key figures in digital archives and library circles (for example, Daniel Greenstein, Margaret Hedstrom, Abby Smith, Kenneth Thibodeau, Bruce Ambacher) have doctoral degrees in history, but they do not currently work as academic historians. Still, it would be logical for academic historians to build alliances with these scholars who have a foot in both camps. Thus far, academic historians have been much more likely to build ties to historians working in museums and historical societies than to those in archives and libraries.

nothing to this burgeoning literature. Historical journals have published nothing on the topic.[57]

Part of the reason is that preserving the born-digital materials for future historians seems like a theoretical and technical issue, tomorrow's problem or at least someone else's problem. Another reason for this disinterest is the divorce of archival concerns from the historical profession—a part of the general narrowing of the concerns of professional historians over the past century. In the late nineteenth and early twentieth centuries, historians and archivists were closely aligned. Perhaps the most important committee of the American Historical Association in the 1890s was the Historical Manuscripts Commission, which led to the AHA's influential Public Archives Commission. Archival concerns found a regular place in the AHA's Annual Meeting, the *American Historical Review,* and especially the voluminous AHA annual reports. Most important, the AHA led the fight to establish the National Archives. But in 1936 (in the midst of an earlier technological upheaval that came with the emergence of microfilm), the Conference of Archivists left the AHA to create the Society of American Archivists. The professions charged with writing about the past and preserving the records of the past have sharply diverged in the past seven decades. Today, only 82 of the 14,000 members of the AHA identify themselves as archivists.[58]

---

57. It is difficult to prove a negative, but one searches in vain through the participant lists at key digital archives conferences for the names of practicing historians. One exception was the Committee on the Records of Government, which had a historian, Ernest R. May, as its chair and another, Anna K. Nelson, as its project director. But perhaps significantly, that committee had a mandate that dealt as much with paper as electronic records: Committee on the Records of Government, *Report* (1985). Another partial exception was the February 1997 conference "Documenting the Digital Age" sponsored by NSF, MCI Communications Corporation, Microsoft Corporation, and History Associates Incorporated, which included a few public and museum-based historians but only one university-based historian. Similarly, history journals have provided almost no coverage of these issues. Archivists are not reading historians, either. Richard Cox analyzed the almost 1,200 citations in 61 articles on electronic records management published in the 1990s and found only a handful of references to work by historians. Cox, "Searching for Authority."

58. Cox, "Messrs. Washington, Jefferson, and Gates." Robert Townsend, Assistant Director of Research and Publications, AHA, kindly supplied membership information. One imperfect but telling indicator of the changing interests of professional historians: Between 1895 and 1999, the *American Historical Review* published thirty-one articles with one of the following words in the title: archive or archives, records, manuscripts, correspondence. Only four of those appeared after World War II, and they were in 1949, 1950, 1952, and 1965. Some representative titles include: Charles H. Haskins, "The Vatican Archives," *AHR* 2.1 (October 1896): 40–58; Waldo Gifford Leland, "The National Archives: A Programme," *AHR* 18.1 (October 1912): 1–28; Edward G. Campbell, "The National Archives Faces the Future," *AHR* 49.3 (April 1944): 441–45. For a good, brief overview of the AHA's active early archive and manuscript work, see Arthur S. Link, "The American Historical Association, 1884–1984: Retrospect and Prospect," *AHR* 90.1 (February 1985): 1–17. NARA's "Timeline for the National Archives and Records Administration and the Development of the U.S. Archival Pro-

But historians ignore the future of digital data at their own peril. What, for example, about the long-term preservation of scholarship that is — increasingly — originating in digital form? Not only do historians need to ensure the future of their own scholarship, but linking directly from footnotes to electronic texts — an exciting prospect for scholars — will be possible only if a stable archiving system emerges.[59] For the foreseeable future, librarians and archivists will be making decisions about priorities in digital preservation. Historians should be at the table when those decisions are made. Do they wish to endorse, for example, the Pitt Project's emphasis on preserving records of business transactions rather than "information" more broadly?

One of the most vexing and interesting features of the digital era is the way that it unsettles traditional arrangements and forces us to ask basic questions that have been there all along. Some are about the relationship between historians and archival work. Should the work of collecting, organizing, editing, and preserving of primary sources receive the same kind of recognition and respect that it did in earlier days of the profession? Others are about whose overall responsibility it is to preserve the past. For example, should the National Archives expand its role in preservation beyond official records? For many years, historians have taken a hands-off approach to archival questions. With the unsettling of the status quo, they should move back more actively into this realm. If the web page is the unit of analysis for the digital librarian and the link the unit of analysis for the computer scientists, what is the appropriate unit of analysis for historians? What would a digital archival system designed by historians look like? And how might we alter and enhance our methodologies in a digital realm? For example, in a world where all sources were digitized and universally accessible, arguments could be more rigorously tested. Currently, many arguments lack such scrutiny because so few scholars have access to the original sources — a problem that has arisen especially

fession," www.archives.gov/research_room/alic/reference_desk/nara_timeline.html, highlights the role of the AHA. It should be noted, however, that the AHA has made a notable contribution to archival issues through its central role in the National Coordinating Committee for the Promotion of History (NCC), which was crucial, for example, in winning the independence of the National Archives in 1984. The new National Coalition for History, which has replaced the NCC, has also made archival concerns central to its work. Access to archives and primary sources was, of course, a central preoccupation — indeed, an obsession — of early "scientific" and professional historians. See Bonnie G. Smith, "Gender and the Practices of Scientific History: The Seminar and Archival Research in the Nineteenth Century," *AHR* 100.4 (October 1995): 1150–76.

59. Deanna B. Marcum, "Scholars as Partners in Digital Preservation," *CLIR Issues,* no. 20 (March/April 2001), www.clir.org/pubs/issues/issues20.html. "Scholars," warns the CLIR Task Force on the Artifact in Library Collections, "may not see preservation of research collections as their responsibility, but until they do, there is a risk that many valuable research sources will not be preserved." CLIR, *Evidence in Hand.*

sharply in the controversies over Michael A. Belleisles's *Arming America: The Origins of a National Gun Culture* (2000). In a new digital world, would historians then be held to the same standard of "reproducible" results as scientists?[60]

Of course, when historians and other scholars get to the preservation table, they will discover a cultural and professional clash between their own impulses, which are to save everything, and those of librarians and archivists who believe that selection, whether passive or active, is inevitable. The National Archives, for example, permanently accessions only 2 percent of government records.[61] This conflict surfaced in the 1980s and 1990s, when librarians tried to bring in scholars to discuss priorities in preserving books that were deteriorating because of acidic paper. Librarians found the discussion "frustrating." "Many scholars," recalls Deanna Marcum, declared "that everything had to be saved and they could not make choices." Not surprisingly, scholars have responded very differently to Nicholson Baker's sharp attack on the microfilming and disposal of aging books and newspapers in *Double Fold* than have archivists and librarians. Whereas many scholars have shared Baker's outrage that books and newspapers have been destroyed, archivists and librarians have responded in outrage to what they see as his failure to understand the pressures that make it impossible to save everything. Whereas historians with their gaze fixed on the past worry about information scarcity (the missing letter or diary), archivists and librarians recognize that we now live in a world of overwhelming information abundance.[62] If historians are going to join in preservation discussions, they will have to make themselves better informed about the simultaneous abundance of historical sources and

---

60. I am indebted to Jim Sparrow for a number of the ideas in this paragraph. For detailed coverage of "How the Belleisles Story Developed," see *History News Network,* http://hnn.us/articles/691.html.

61. House Committee on Government Operations, *Taking a Byte out of History,* 4. For the assumption of selectivity among archivists, see, for instance, Richard J. Cox, "The Great Newspaper Caper: Backlash in the Digital Age," *First Monday* 5.12 (December 2000), http://firstmonday.org/issues/issue5_12/cox/index.html.

62. Abby Smith, *The Future of the Past: Preservation in American Research Libraries* (Washington, DC, 1999), www.clir.org/pubs/reports/pub82/pub82text.html; Marcum, "Scholars as Partners in Digital Preservation"; Nicholson Baker, *Double Fold: Libraries and the Assault on Paper* (New York: Random House, 2001). Compare, for example, Cox, "Great Newspaper Caper," and O'Toole, "Do Not Fold, Spindle, or Mutilate," with Robert Darnton, "The Great Book Massacre," *New York Review of Books,* 26 April 2001, www.nybooks.com/articles/14196. In 1996, the Modern Language Association issued a statement arguing "that for practical purposes, all historical publications, even those produced by mass-production techniques designed to minimize deviations from a norm, have unique physical qualities that may have value as a carrier of (physical) evidence in a given research project." CLIR, *Evidence in Hand.*

scarcity of financial resources that lead archivists and librarians to respond with exasperation to scholars' blithe insistence that everything must be saved.

Preservation of the past is, in the end, often a matter of allocating adequate resources. Perhaps the largest problem facing the preservation of electronic government records has nothing to do with technology; it is, as various reports have noted, "the low priority traditionally given to federal records management." In the absence of new resources, the costs of preservation will come from the money that our society, in the aggregate, allocates for history and culture. Richard Cox, for example, has argued that a greater portion of the budget of the National Historical Publications and Records Commission should go to electronic records preservation and management and correspondingly less money should go to the letterpress Documentary Editions that the commission also funds, since "most of the records represented by the documentary editions are not immediately threatened." This stance does not endear him to documentary editors, who are much better represented among professional historians than are archivists.[63]

The alternative to squabbling over inadequate resources that are appropriated for these purposes is joint action to secure further funds. When Shirley Baker, president of the Association of Research Libraries, challenged the historian Robert Darnton's favorable review of Baker's book and noted "choices have always had to be made" in the absence of "greater public commitment to the preservation of the historical record," Darnton responded by urging the establishment of "a new kind of national library dedicated to the preservation of cultural artifacts" (including disappearing digital records) and funded by income generated by the sale or rental of bandwidth.[64] Such state-based solutions return us to the kind of alliance between historians and archivists that led to building of the National Archives in the 1930s, an era of growing rather than waning confidence in the nation-state. Historians need to join in lobbying actively for adequate funding for both current historical work and preservation of future resources. They should also argue forcefully for the democratized access to the historical record that digital media make possible. And they must add their voices to those calling for expanding copyright deposit   and opposing copyright extension, for that matter—of digital

---

63. GAO, *Information Management,* 16; Cox, "Messrs. Washington, Jefferson, and Gates." Cox's article responded, in part, to an earlier article by Raymond W. Smock that argues, "historians should not rely on archivists alone to make decisions about what history to save or to publish." Smock, "The Nation's Patrimony Should Not Be Sacrificed to Electronic Records," *Chronicle of Higher Education,* 14 February 1997, B4–5.

64. Robert Darnton, Sarah A. Mikel, and Shirley K. Baker, "The Great Book Massacre: An Exchange," *New York Review of Books,* 14 March 2002, www.nybooks.com/articles/15195.

materials so as to remove some of the legal clouds hanging over efforts like the Internet Archive and to halt the ongoing privatization of historical resources. Even in the absence of state action, historians and other scholars should take steps individually and within their professional organizations to embrace the culture of abundance made possible by digital media and expand the public space of scholarship — for example, making their own work available free on the web, cross-referencing other digital scholarship, and perhaps depositing their sources online for other scholars to use. A vigorous public domain today is a prerequisite for a healthy historical record.[65] All of these actions need the support of historians and other scholars. If the past is to have an abundant future, if the story of *Bert Is Evil* and hundreds of other stories are to be fully told, then we need to act in the present.

---

65. See, for example, Vincent Kiernan, " 'Open Archives' Project Promises Alternative to Costly Journals," *Chronicle of Higher Education,* 3 December 1999; Budapest Open Access Initiative, www .soros.org/openaccess. On questions of public domain and privatization, see Lawrence Lessig, *The Future of Ideas: The Fate of the Commons in a Connected World* (New York: Random House, 2001).

Notes on Contributors

ELIZABETH AMANN is associate professor in the Department of Spanish and Portuguese at Columbia University and the author of *Importing Madame Bovary: The Politics of Adultery* (2006).

THOMAS AUGST is associate professor of English at New York University. He is the author of *The Clerk's Tale: Young Men and Moral Life in Nineteenth-Century America* (2003) and coeditor, with Wayne Wiegand, of *Libraries as Agencies of Culture* (2003).

MICHAEL A. BAENEN, special assistant to the president at the Massachusetts Institute of Technology, studied history at Columbia and Harvard universities. He is currently vice president of the board of the Portsmouth Athenæum.

KENNETH CARPENTER is retired from the Harvard University Library, where he served as editor of the *Harvard Library Bulletin*. He is the author of *Readers and Libraries: Toward a History of Libraries and Culture in America* (1996) and *The First 350 Years of the Harvard University Library* (1986), as well as editor of the microfiche collection *The Harvard University Library: A Documentary History* (1989) and *Books and Society in History* (1983).

JAMES GREEN is librarian of the Library Company of Philadelphia. His three essays on printing and book publishing in America from 1680 to 1840 appear in the first two volumes of the collaborative *History of the Book in America,* published by the American Antiquarian Society under the general editorship of David D. Hall. He is also coauthor, with Peter Stallybrass, of *Benjamin Franklin, Writer and Printer* (2006).

ELIZABETH MCHENRY is associate professor of English at New York University. She is the author of *Forgotten Readers: Recovering the Lost History of African American Literary Societies* (2002).

BARBARA A. MITCHELL, head of public services in the Frances Loeb Library, Graduate School of Design, Harvard University, has published in the *Harvard Library Bulletin* on the Harvard Library card catalogue.

CHRISTINE PAWLEY is associate professor in library and information studies at the University of Wisconsin–Madison. Her book *Reading on the Middle Border: The Culture of Print in Late Nineteenth-Century Osage, Iowa* was published by the University of Massachusetts Press in 2001.

JANICE RADWAY is professor and chair of the Literature Program at Duke University. She received her Ph.D. in English and American Studies from Michigan State University and is past president of the American Studies Association and former editor of *American Quarterly.* She is the author of *Reading the Romance: Women, Patriarchy, and Popular Literature* and *A Feeling for Books: The Book-of-the-Month Club, Literary Taste, and Middle Class Desire.* She is currently working on a book about girls' cultural production and subjectivity in the 1990s.

JAMES RAVEN is professor of modern British history at the University of Essex and director of the Cambridge Project for the Book Trust. His books include *British Fiction, 1750–1769* (1987), *Judging New Wealth* (1992), *The English Novel, 1770–1829* (coauthored, 2000), and *London Booksellers and American Customers* (2002). His *The Business of Books: Booksellers and the English Book Trade, 1450–1850* will be published in 2007.

KARIN ROFFMAN is assistant professor of English at the United States Military Academy at West Point. She has published in *Minnesota Review* and has forthcoming essays in *Modern Fiction Studies* and a collection on Edith Wharton and material culture. She is currently finishing a book on modernist women writers in libraries and museums.

ROY ROSENZWEIG is Mark and Barbara Fried Professor of History & New Media at George Mason University, where he also heads the Center on History and New Media (http://chnm.gmu.edu). He is the author, coauthor, and coeditor of numerous books including *The Park and the People: A History of Central Park* (1992), *The Presence of the Past: Popular Uses of History in American Life* (2000), *Eight Hours for What We Will: Workers and Leisure in an Industrial City, 1870–1920* (1985), and *Digital History: A Guide to Gathering, Preserving, and Presenting the Past on the Web* (2005).

Index

Note: Italicized page numbers refer to illustrations